Myths
of the
Tribe

Myths
of the
Tribe

When
**Religion, Ethics,
Government,
and Economics**
Converge

David Rich

PROMETHEUS BOOKS • Buffalo, N.Y.

Published 1993 by Prometheus Books

97 96 95 94 93   5 4 3 2 1

Library of Congress Cataloging-in-Publication Data

Rich, David.
    Myths of the tribe : when religion, ethics, government, and economics converge /
by David Rich.
    Includes bibliographical references.
    ISBN 0-87975-824-4
    1. Religions. I. Title.
BL85.R53   1993
291—dc20   93-17732
                                                                          CIP

Printed in the United States of America on acid-free paper.

Contents

Preface

This book is about the unifying relationships among religion, ethics, government, and economics, seeking to identify the threads connecting these institutions that govern our lives. What are the common elements among our organized religions, our ideas of ethics and morality, our economic systems, and our forms of government? The purpose of this book is to attempt an analysis of organized religion and its relationship to government, ethics, and economics, because organized religion seems to be one of the most important, yet least analyzed, subjects in the library. Religion is woven into the fabric of our daily lives and is integral to everything we do. Our belief in our religion determines whether we think we will survive this life.

An apparent difficulty in analyzing organized religion is its highly personal nature. Most discussion of religion is ripe with emotion, whether conscious or unconscious. The close scrutiny of religion, from the viewpoint of a religiously committed person, may create anxiety because such an examination may be perceived as a challenge to basic beliefs. The obvious solution is to approach the exploration of religion, and the related topics of cosmology, ethics, economics, and government, without emotion. Saying this, however, does not remove the difficulty, because religious faith answers the question of the meaning of life for many people. When the stakes are this high it's difficult to excise emotion. Still, I will try to be objective by employing a simple device—the use, insofar as possible, of universally accepted facts.

One pitfall to this examination may be language itself. The meaning we individually ascribe to a set of words may differ. An illustration of this was provided by Bertrand Russell when he said, "I am firm. You are stubborn. He is a pig-headed fool." Accordingly, I will use words carrying the least amount of emotional baggage whenever possible to avoid being characterized as a pig-headed fool when I intend only to be firm. I will not, however, shy away from asking questions that require blunt phrasing. Before beginning the substance of this book I invite you to consider an introduction by Robert Ingersoll to a speech he gave on May 8, 1888:

7

> I am here tonight for the purpose of defending your right to differ with me. I want to convince you that you are under no compulsion to accept my creed; that you are, so far as I am concerned, absolutely free to follow the torch of your reason according to your conscience; and I believe that you are civilized to the degree that you will extend to me the right that you claim for yourselves.

We used to debate our important national issues, and most of us, that is to say our parents and grandparents, participated in these debates. Now, instead of debating, we watch television and express our opinions by voting and in a few other ways. The purpose of this book is to spur debate. We should read other viewpoints and debate fairly. If we disagree, we should respond carefully, rationally, and logically to those whose views differ from our own. I hope that my readers are not only those who agree with me, but also those who disagree and who will instigate rational dialogue about institutions and ideas too long withdrawn from dialogue as sacrosanct.

Acknowledgments

Mary Alexon, June Behr, Ron Pelton, and Evan Sharf read the manuscript and kindly made comments, for which I am grateful. They are not personally responsible, however, for anything in this book and likely disagree with much of it.

Introduction

My kind have existed an instant in time, for a few thousand years, and are dwarfed in age by every other creature on the planet. The planet has been around ten thousand times longer than my kind. We're johnnies-come-lately.

The fish in the sea are my ancestors and have existed nine times longer than my kind. Our young still develop gills and a fish tail during the first quarter of their incubation. My fish ancestors enjoyed a lackadaisical existence, needing only to open their mouths for food and to swim moderately well. No other talents were necessary to life back then. When my ancestors were caught in twice daily tide pools and of necessity made to develop lungs, they were able to move onto solid ground and to encounter the traumas we've suffered ever since. It was no longer as simple as opening our mouths to obtain food. We had to hunt and scrounge for food and, on top of that, find shelter. Before our migration to land the surface of the ocean had protected us from all but the predators of the sea.

The dangers of the land consisted of far more than a hunt for food and shelter. Everywhere there were spirits to please, or the hunt would fail; predators, including others of our kind, would chase us from our shelter. To placate these spirits we developed elaborate rituals that remain a mainstay today. To control our fears we sought control over the uncontrollable.

Early on we worshiped the cave bear, burying our dead with food, tools, and weapons for the next life. We watched out for spirits in trees, rocks, rivers, and animals, and gradually began to worship mother goddesses and sun gods. These worshiping rituals would today be considered a combination of art, magic, and religion. Together they guaranteed eternal life so we would never die. This concept of eternal life made us superior to the other animals on the planet.

Every culture of my kind has thirteen ritualistic elements: song, exercise (standing, kneeling, bowing), exhortation, recitation of official texts, simulation (pretending), touching things, taboos, feasts, sacrifice, a congregation, inspiration, symbolism, and prayer. We call these rituals religion. Every group of my kind on the planet developed religions, all different and all infallible.

Our earliest recorded history began in 1500 B.C.E. with the Golden Age of Amenhotop III in Egypt, though human writing extends to 3000 B.C.E. Our history

9

for the 45,000+ years of prewritten existence is based on archeology and myths. These myths are the basis for the world's religions, all founded after 1500 B.C.E. Our entire recorded history is less than one-thirteenth of the time we have existed as a species.

During the first half of our 50,000 years of existence, three things occurred: (1) Cro-magnon man moved west into the area of Europe, presaging Horace Greeley by 41,800 years. The Cro-magnons founded the Cult of the Cave Bear, the world's oldest religion. (2) Neanderthal man succeeded Cro-magnon man, and then died out 10,000 years later, to be replaced by true homo sapiens: thinking man. The heroine of the book *Clan of the Cave Bear* was a Neanderthal who pioneered the replacement of the inferior Cro-magnons. The Neanderthals died out 22,000 years ago. (3) Man crossed the land bridge from Asia to North America. These were the accomplishments of the entire first half of our existence—our first 25,000 years.

The second half of our existence was frittered away with no major advancement, which is to say nothing improved the lot of the species until an additional 15,000 years had elapsed. Then a mere 10,000 years ago we racked up our next accomplishment and founded agriculture. Until this time thinking man had no time away from the daily hunt to think. Thus, after 80 percent of our existence had passed into history, agriculture began in the Middle East, in western Asia; now Israel, Turkey, Jordan, Iraq, Iran, the Saudi Peninsula, and Egypt. Agriculture began soon thereafter in China and the Indus Valley of India, becoming our fourth accomplishment. Jericho, one of our first cities, wasn't built until 7000 B.C.E., one thousand years after agriculture began. The first date in the Egyptian calendar is the equivalent of 4236 B.C.E. The traditional Christian date of creation is five hundred years later at 3760 B.C.E., or 4004 B.C.E., depending on who you ask. This was when things started popping, 5,700 years ago, after 90 percent of our existence was behind us. The Mayan calendar began the equivalent of 3372 B.C.E. The first Egyptian Dynasty was 3100 B.C.E. Knossos was founded by the Minoans on Crete in 2500 B.C.E. Stonehenge was begun in 1860 B.C.E. Knossos was destroyed by fire in 1400 B.C.E., making it the third longest civilization in our history. The longest)lived civilization was founded in the Indus Valley, lasting from 3500 to 1500 B.C.E. The next longest civilization was the Egyptian, lasting from 2800 to 1085 B.C.E.

The Greeks destroyed Troy in 1193 B.C.E. In 994 B.C.E. David captured Jerusalem, the little town where we consolidated the myths of our species and founded three of the major religions of the world, hundreds of years apart. These three religions claim two-thirds of the world's religious people, all offering a personal god, while no other major religions do. The first to be founded was Judaism about 600 B.C.E., with 18 million adherents estimated as of 1988 C.E. Six hundred years later came Christianity, with its current 1,700 million, and finally Islam, which can count 880 million followers, 10 million of whom attended Ayatollah Ruhollah Khomeini's funeral on June 6, 1989.

The oldest currently existing major religion is Hinduism with 660 million, founded on writings accumulated from 4000 to 1000 B.C.E., which spawned Buddhism (now 310 million) about the time Judaism was founded. Christianity was a similar offshoot from Judaism. These five religions total 3,568 million followers, leaving the remaining three major world religions, Taoist, Shinto, and Confucianism, with a total of 217 million followers. The followers of these eight religions constitute half the population of the world, though three of the eight have relatively few followers: Judaism, the smallest, with 18 million; Taoist with 21 million; and Shinto with 33 million. But for World War II, there would be more Jews than Taoists.

Rome was founded in 753 B.C.E. Buddha was born in 563 B.C.E., and Confucius in 551 B.C.E. Mohammed was not born until ten centuries later, in 570 C.E.

The belief in each religion's infallibility created major problems for humankind. If a set of beliefs are considered infallible, then every other different set of beliefs must be considered false and a blasphemy to the one true set of beliefs. The only solution is for the adherents of one set of beliefs to kill nonbelievers. From 1000 to 1808 C.E. it is estimated that up to 68 million people were murdered because of their religious beliefs; others assert that *only* a few million were murdered. No one knows the precise number because the Christian churches destroyed records detailing the various inquisitions, which were far from confined to the Roman Catholic Church. Sixty-eight million (or even half that) back then was a big chunk of the population. Throughout history, Christians have killed Muslims, and Muslims have killed Christians, and everyone has killed Jews. The killing was not of great concern to those who believed religious martyrs went directly to eternal life. Only fifty years ago another six million were killed in less than six years, because of their religious beliefs.

Humans have become highly efficient at religiously justified killing, but the connection of these killings with religion has never become an integral part of the knowledge of the general population because every country has a predominant religion which these facts would offend; accordingly, the facts are repressed from the history texts taught to our young. Religious killings continue unabated today in many parts of the planet including Northern Ireland, the Middle East, India, the former Yugoslavia, and other places where the religion of one country conflicts with the religion of a neighboring country or where there is religious conflict within the same country.

In an educated society it's the normal rule that value is determined by comparison shopping. Most people wouldn't shell out a hundred thousand dollars, pounds, marks, yen, or rubles for shelter without looking at several shelters and comparing their qualities. Most would not spend a few thousand dollars for a car or a hundred dollars for anything without comparison shopping, but when it comes to religion and the theoretical preservation of our souls, few shop. Over 90 percent of us are converted to the religion of our immediate ancestors between the ages of twelve and fifteen, which is not an age known for wisdom and judgment. Our image of "God," according to an Emory University study, is formed as children and remains at this sophistication level throughout our lives. Most never investigate the religion next door, much less any of the hundreds of religions that girdle the planet. Perhaps to do so would be blasphemy to our immediate ancestors, yet, by the basic definition common to all religions, we commit—without comparison shopping—to a set of beliefs that determines whether we will rise from the grave.

Not only do few shop, few know enough to shop. In the United States we abhor the illiteracy of our children and associates in the areas of geography and history, but as a people we know far less about religions or history than we do about the most popular television program or current movie. For example, in 1989, 63 percent of American children ages ten to thirteen recognized Freddie Krueger of *Nightmare on Elm Street* fame, while only 36 percent could identify Abraham Lincoln. Do 10 percent know the difference between Judiasm and Christianity, or Taoism and Buddhism? As a people, when it comes to both general knowledge and perhaps the most powerful force in the world, religion, we are collectively illiterate.

Some would argue that it is unrealistic to expect people to shop for values, that values are inherent in the culture and in our religions. But religion is not about values or ethics. It is about beliefs. If we are born in Iran, our only god is Allah; if in India, then our only god is Shiva and we long for Nirvana; and, if in the West, our only god is the Christian god, with some obvious exceptions. As memorialized in a well-known hymn, "That old time religion is good enough for me." George Santayana summed it up thusly, "To me, it seems a dreadful indignity to have a soul controlled by geography."

1

The Facts of the Universe

What sets humankind against itself? What is humankind's future in the universe? How do organized religions and national governments relate to that future? Can we avoid self-annihilation arising from the antagonisms generated by our national governments and organized religions or caused by environmental deterioration? To begin examining these questions requires that humankind be placed in its context in the universe.

The ability to analyze the role of humankind in the universe, or to judge anything accurately and intelligently, depends entirely on putting that thing into context. We cannot, for example, accurately and intelligently administer justice without considering all facts surrounding a crime and putting those facts into context. Merely to know that the defendant shot the victim is to know little of ultimate importance. All facts must be explored so the jury can determine whether the defendant shot the victim accidentally, in self-defense, or with other justification. Without putting the accusations against the defendant into context, which requires knowledge of all knowable and material facts, we cannot determine whether a crime has been committed.

Similar considerations must be observed when examining organized religion, forms of government, and economic systems. Religion in the abstract is incomprehensible; to understand religion, its historical role, and its relationship to ethics and government, requires us to look at ourselves in proper context, which is to say, our place in the universe.

We know that our physical role in the universe is relatively clear, based on elementary facts available in any grade-school science text. Specifically, the planet earth is so small and insignificant as to be meaningless. Write down the number of years you've been alive and under that write the number of years you haven't been alive, which beginning with the formation of earth totals 4,600,000,000 years. Play with the two numbers. Add them or subtract them and see how much the larger number changes. As stated by Ray Faraday Nelson, "It gives you a measure of how much your individual life matters when we look at it in perspective, when we take, as it were, the Long View. It gives you a measure of how much my life matters, how much anyone's life matters." It could lead to the conclusion that the human lifespan is less than a flicker of light against the fabric of time. Yet the foundation of all Western religions places the earth at the center of the universe and humans as the ultimate achievement of "God."*

Our sun is one of an estimated 400 billion stars in our local galaxy, the Milky Way. Thirty galaxies make up the neighborhood of our galaxy and are so distant that they are not fully visible through our most efficient telescopes. Without a telescope, away from city lights and pollution, we can see only a fraction of our own galaxy and spots of light from three other galaxies, Andromeda and the two Clouds of Magellan galaxies. Thus, out of over 200 billion galaxies in the universe, unaided by a telescope, we can see the lights of only four galaxies, including our own.

The primary difficulty in understanding the context of homo sapiens in the universe is to understand a number as large as a billion or even a mere million. We can easily comprehend numbers we use on a regular basis but these are small numbers. As children we needed no number over ten or so, and few adults, as a practical matter, use numbers over 100,000. The largest number in the Old Testament is 10,000. The concept of one million was not even invented until the thirteenth century and is taken from the Italian term for "a large thousand." A billion was not invented until the seventeenth century and even then was a curiosity without meaning. With the various national debts and inflation, a billion achieved practical meaning in this century but is not really comprehensible because no one can visualize a billion of anything.

Even if we could comprehend the number 400 billion, we would still not have begun to comprehend the universe because 400 billion is only the number of suns in our galaxy. There are about 200 billion galaxies in the known universe. Thus, to arrive at the number of suns in the known universe requires multiplying the number of suns in our galaxy times the number of galaxies in the known universe, 400 billion times 200 billion, which is 80,000,000,000,000,000,000,000, or eighty sextillion, which is so far beyond our possible comprehension as to be ludicrous. In addition to the eighty sextillion stars in the known universe, there are also other celestial bodies, such as planets and moons and comets and asteroids. Yet, according to the ancient myths of our religions, our little proton circling our remote sun is the center of "creation."

While exploring the sheer magnitude of many billion of anything, we should keep in mind that we haven't begun to define the extent of the universe, of which there may be an unseeable profusion. The meta-universe, or all there is, may be so much larger than the known universe as to be similarly uncomprehendible. The meta-universe may be so far beyond vast that comparing its size to the known universe may dwarf the size relationship between molecular and intergalactic structures, with the result that our little earth and solar system may be a part of a side universe off a side universe that stretches its reflection through giga-

---

*References to "God," "gods," or "god" are to concepts and do not constitute testimony or evidence proving the existence or nonexistence of a particular god, whether Christian, Muslim, Hindu, Greek, Roman, Egyptian, Sumerian, or other.

universes in a billion mirrors through infinity. We may never know its limits until we can travel faster than the speed of light forever.

Considering these facts in connection with the two largest Western religions (Islam and Christianity), it may become logically difficult to conclude that the creator of a universe with an immensity beyond our possible imagining sent his only son (do gods have sex or sons?) to die on earth, a tiny isolated orb, the third planet in a nine-planet solar system orbiting a star so minor that it is undetectable among the 400 billion suns of its own galaxy, a galaxy that is only one of hundreds of billions in the universe. The reason for sending the creator's son to earth was Eve's eating of an apple, which may be being eaten this very moment all over the universe. Does this mean that the Christian God's only son is traveling from insignificant planets in insignificant solar systems circling insignificant stars on the edge of billions of galaxies, to die and hurry on to the next planet?

Our sun is 33,000 light years from the center of the Milky Way galaxy. It takes the sun 225 million years (a cosmic year) to orbit the galaxy. The earth has made this orbit twenty-five times since it was formed 4.6 billion years ago, which was about 10 billion years after the universe began, according to the latest estimates, around 15 billion years ago. To translate this into more comprehensible terms, if you were the first modern homo sapiens (who appeared 50,000 years ago) and were still alive today, you would have existed only two minutes out of a comparative year since the galaxy and universe were formed. Therefore, if God created the earth he didn't rush into the creation of homo sapiens. The Christian God, who created the heavens and the earth on the first day as described in Genesis, used a day that was over 14 billion years in length.

Evolution takes time and it never stops. Try to imagine what kind of animal homo sapiens will be after another 50,000 years. The probability is high that we will have evolved into a related, but highly dissimilar (and hopefully improved) form. Kurt Vonnegut's *Galapagos* is a whimsical example of anticipating the immediate future of mankind. How much different will we be after ten million years, ten times our current length of time on earth? Can we even hope to accurately speculate on the conditions of our existence and form after another ten million years, which is only 1/1000 of the time the universe has been in existence and 300 times longer than mankind has yet existed? When God created humans in "his image," was that image reflected by homo erectus, Neanderthals, twentieth-century humans, seventieth-century humans, or some evolution of humans yet to come?

If we are made in the image of a god, do those made in his image include Hitler, Stalin, and the other villains of history? Are there cruel sadistic gods in whose image these men are cast? Which god is the image for racists, Ku Klux Klansmen, and shop-til-she-drops Imelda Marcos? Is God's image that of composite man? These questions should be contrasted with the fact that humankind did not practice agriculture until ten thousand years ago. How can we answer even hypothetically the question of human evolution and form a million years hence? Whose image will humans reflect then, or is God also evolving? Does the image concept have any substance at all?

Should we expect God to be the epitome of logic and indeed perfect, eschewing political alignments? To the contrary, no god of any major (or minor) religion is either logical or morally superior to the highest form of human such as Jesus Christ, Gandhi, Buddha, Mohammed, or Confucius, all of whom were nonviolent and nonjudgmental. None of the gods who head the religions inadvertently founded by these men (Gandhi founded no religion) are worthy of the ideals of these men. Their gods are routinely invoked by national leaders to justify mutual mass murder on both sides of any conflict.

Every species on earth is a result of a millennia of evolution, and man as a species illustrates this fact as well as any other species. The fetal human heart begins with one chamber then develops two like a fish, three like a frog, three and a half like a reptile, and, finally, four like other mammals. The same changes occur in our fetal blood, changing from fish blood to frog blood to reptile blood and finally to mammal blood. The salt in our blood and the amniotic fluid is proportionate to the salt in the sea from whence we came. Thus humans begin life as does all life, whether fish, frog, reptile, or dog. The facts of our embryology arguably illustrate our evolution and origins with more logic than a god theory derived from primitive humans.

Humans and apes represent a smooth, though not continuous, curve on the graph of evolution. Humans are not an out of character aberration but are similar to all animals.

Darwin described the relationship clearly:

> All have the same senses, intuition and sensations—similar passions, affections and emotions, even the more complex ones, such as jealousy, suspicion, emulation, gratitude and magnanimity; they practice deceit and are revengeful; they are sometimes susceptible to ridicule and even have a sense of humor; they feel wonder and curiosity; they possess the same faculties of imitation, attention, deliberation, choice, memory, imagination, the association of ideas, and reason, though in very different degrees.

Although fundamentalist Christian groups don't recognize evolution, the Roman Catholic Church does:*

> For some time, theologians regarded the theory [of evolution] with hostility, considering it to be in opposition to the account of creation in the early chapters of Genesis and subversive of belief in such doctrines as creation, the early state of man in grace, and the fall of man from grace. This state of affairs and the tension it generated led to considerable controversy regarding an alleged conflict between religion and science. Gradually, however, the tension was diminished

---

*Because Catholicism represents the largest portion of the largest world religion, its definitions, as contained in the *Catholic Word Book* (reprinted from the *Catholic Almanac*, Hungtington, Ind.: Our Sunday Visitor, Inc., 1973), will be used to *generally* illustrate Christian religious concepts.

with the development of biblical studies from the latter part of the 19th century onwards, with clarification of the distinctive features of religious truth and scientific truth, and with the refinement of evolutionary concepts. So far as the Genesis account of creation is concerned, the Catholic view is that the writer(s) did not write as a scientist but as the communicator of religious truth in a manner adapted to the understanding of the people of his time. He used anthropomorphic language, the figure of days and other literary devices to state the salvation truths of creation, the fall of man from grace, and the promise of redemption. It was beyond the competency and purpose of the writer(s) to describe creation and related events in a scientific manner.

It appears that the development of humans, though linked cousinlike to the primates, is of a qualitatively different species, which should relieve people who don't wish to be identified as having evolved from monkeys. We didn't evolve from monkeys; we evolved separately and in parallel with monkeys. If humans become extinct there is little chance we would redevelop on earth because our development was not directly related to the development of the one hundred other species of primates and appears to be a fluke of the first magnitude. Does this mean we were created by a god?

Evolution was taught by Aristotle and the ancient Greeks, such as Empedocles, in the fifth century B.C.E. Leonardo da Vinci wrote on evolution in code to avoid persecution by the Church. The ancient Greeks and Romans deduced that the earth was round, not flat, and that it revolves, hundreds of years before Christ. This knowledge, however, was suppressed by the Christian Church and survived only because the Muslim Arabs preserved it. The Church persecuted the astronomers of the day because the Bible implied that the sun revolved around the earth, which was deemed the center of the universe because God stopped the sun and moon in Joshua 10:12–14 and backed the sun up in Isaiah 38:2–8. The works of Kepler, Copernicus, and Galileo were banned for 150 years because they were considered atheistic and heretical.

This banning of established science continues as an active and effective force today in the United States. This force stems from fundamentalist religion and Creationists who believe that God made all life on earth during one six-day week 5,000 years ago, which tired God to the extent that he required a full day to rest. During the six days God worked, he spent five days creating the earth and everything on it and less than one full day creating the other billions of planets around billions of stars in billions of galaxies and the balance of the universe. The Creationists demand that this biblical "truth" be taught in our schools because they know that all sciences disagreeing with the 5,000-years-ago date, when the earth, planets, stars, and galaxies were created, are malarkey, including geology, astronomy, biology, physics, and other basic sciences. In November 1989, the California Board of Education voted to prohibit teaching the biblical story of creation in science classes and textbooks, but just barely, endorsing as a sop to the California Creationists:

Discussions of divine creation, ultimate purposes or ultimate causes are appropriate to the History/Social Sciences and English/Language Arts Curricula. . . . As a matter of principle, science teachers are professionals bound to limit their teaching to science and should resist pressure to do otherwise.

This original vote was superseded after an outcry by fundamentalists, to add the following: "Some people reject the theory of evolution purely on the basis of religious faith . . . [and such] personal beliefs should be respected and not demeaned." Should belief and superstition contrary to science and established fact be respected in our public schools? The California Board also struck the following language from its original resolution: "There is no scientific dispute that evolution has occurred and continues to occur; this is why evolution is regarded as a scientific fact."

According to the Rev. Louis Sheldon, director of the Traditional Values Coalition in Anaheim, California, the teaching of evolution is the teaching of religion: "If you talk about evolution, how can you talk about a personal God? If you came from a monkey, how can you have a God that answers prayers?" Concerning the amended resolution, Rev. Sheldon called it "crumbs from the table."*

Seventh and eighth graders at the Zion Lutheran School in Mayer, Minnesota, asked President Bush and the U.S. Postal Service to either recall stamps depicting dinosaurs, which give credence to the theory of evolution, or to give equal time by issuing a stamp that shows God created the world in six days.

The universal properties of the universe mean that life is probable and widely scattered all over the universe. The level of its intelligence, however, is a separate question. Because humans observe the universe and are part of it, the universe, through man, is observing itself. Because dominant species inexorably grow in size, any civilization must expand and dominate (not necessarily destructively) its own solar system, then galaxy, and finally the universe, in order to survive. The reasons for this are relatively simple. First, we have too few resources on earth to support our exploding population, which doubles every 35 years, for more than a few hundred years. Our population now is over five billion, expanding geometrically. In a hundred years our population will likely be 40 billion and in 200 years, 320 billion, which is 60 people for each one of us now existing. We literally must have *Lebensraum*. By definition if we do not have room to live, we cannot live. Second, our atmosphere will eventually deteriorate so that carbon-based life cannot be supported. How soon this will occur depends on our efforts to control the loss of ozone and the build-up of carbon dioxide. At this moment these efforts look less than promising. Even if we are completely successful in ending all human-caused deterioration of our atmosphere, however, it will deteriorate by itself in a million years or so. With earth having been in existence 4.6 billion years, a million more years of life on earth is less than a

---

*See Mark N. Trahaut, *Arizona Republic,* Sept. 4, 1989; Marc Hefsher, *Arizona Republic,* Sept. 30, 1989; Associated Press, *Arizona Republic,* Nov. 10, 1989.

hundredth of the time of earth's current existence. Relatively, humans have little time left on earth.

Will we explore the galaxy and universe or is this the stuff of speculative science fiction? It's almost incomprehensible that intelligent beings will not eventually explore their environment and routinely travel over interstellar distances once the technology is easily available at reasonable cost. If the eventual requirements of survival mandate abandonment of this solar system we will have no choice. Thus, the eventual destruction of the earth's atmosphere may not be fatal to our kind. The foregoing is remote for one reason only: we may not survive our national feuds and religious wars.

2

A Brief History of Our Major Religions

We are absolutely certain only about things we do not understand.

—Eric Hoffer

A basic problem in examining religion is to make certain we similarly understand the terms used. Religious terms have no meaning outside their social context. The ideas of Buddhism have little meaning for a Western-civilization Christian, and Christianity is incomprehensible to an adherent of an Eastern religion. (Scientific principles, on the other hand, are as clear in Russia or Antarctica as they are in any other location.) Comprehension of religious concepts is impossible without knowledge of the particular religion and extensive knowledge is usually required. In other words, there is nothing about any religion that is innate or logically necessary, though many religions have common threads.

Religion began in the caves of our ancestors.* The first religion was naturalistic, worshiping the sun, the source of all life on earth. The sun oversaw all and brought warmth. The absence of sun was cold, darkness, and death.

The sun-god is a principal deity in many ancient mythologies. In Greek mythology Apollo was originally a sun-god who fought to vanquish the serpent of night. In parallel Scandinavian mythology Balder was the personified sun who was in love with the maiden Dawn, yet he deserted her to travel through the heavens. They met at twilight and their tears of joy became morning dew. According to some Hindu legends, Krishna was the sun and at his birth the Ganges River erupted and life on earth began. Other sun-gods were the Persian Mithra, the Aztec Quetzalcoatl, and the Egyptian Horus. These gods were born on the day when the sun triumphs over winter, December 25.

Sun-gods often had divine fathers and human mothers who were virgins. The births of some were announced by the stars and attended by celestial music. Most were born in caves or other humble places, including Krishna, who was protected by shepherds.

---

*These common roots of religion were chronicled by a hero of the U.S. Civil War, Colonel Robert Ingersoll.

The tradition of tyrants trying to kill legendary divine figures is also common. All the babies in the neighborhood were killed when Krishna was born. The king sent his soldiers to kill Buddha but a miracle intervened making Buddha look twelve years old so the king's soldiers passed him by. King Typhon tried to kill baby Horus; the king pursued baby Zoroaster; King Cadmus went after baby Bacchus. Note the striking similarities between these ancient traditions and Christianity:

a. Sun-gods were born on December 25.
b. Most were worshiped by wise men.
c. Fasting for 40 days is a common mythical motif.
d. Many were violently killed.
e. Sun-gods rose from the dead.

Jesus Christ is a sun-god. The Lord God of the Old Testament is the sun (Ps. 84:11). When Christians pray they close their eyes as do all sun-worshipers. Even ancient man knew looking directly at the sun would harm the eyes; hence the closing of eyes in prayer to any god of the sun. There is nothing original in Christianity. The Bible draws heavily upon religions and myths far older than Christianity and Judaism.

A pagan myth held Ceres as the goddess of the fields and Bacchus as the god of the vine. At the harvest the pagans made cakes of wheat, which they ate saying, "This is the flesh of the goddess." They drank the wine and said, "This is the blood of our god." Similarly, baptism has not only been practiced by Christians, but by the Hindus, Egyptians, Greeks, and Romans.

The Brahman Adami and Heva were cast out of their Garden of Eden over four hundred years before the Christian Adam and Eve were thought of. The story of the great flood and resulting ark that saved the select Sumerians and two of each animal was written hundreds of years before Noah and his identical ark were penned for the Hebrew Bible.

The cross has been a central religious symbol since the ancient peoples of Italy, who before recorded time buried their dead under its symbol. The forests of Central America reveal ancient temples with carved crosses carrying bleeding figures. Babylonian carvings bear the symbol of the cross. The cross in ancient Egypt was a symbol of future life.

The Trinity originated in ancient Egypt, consisting of Osiris, Isis, and Horus, who were worshiped thousands of years before the Father, Son, and Holy Ghost were invented.

The Tree of Life was found among the Aztecs and the ancients in India and China before the Garden of Eden was thought of. Other ancient concepts antedating the Bible include the Fall of Man, the Atonement, and the Scheme of Redemption.

The earliest religions, after our Clan Bear days, focused on the mother goddess, a fertility and nurturing symbol. The worship of these goddesses died out when we began agriculture about 8000 B.C.E., but later reappeared about 4000 B.C.E. all over Europe and Asia. The mother goddess is denounced repeatedly in the

Old Testament as the sister of Baal, who in some early cultures was called Astarte or Ashtoroth and functioned as the center of legalized prostitution. Even though Christians are admonished in the New Testament to cast the first stone at a prostitute only if the individual executioner is without sin, for the last one thousand years prostitution has been persecuted as a sin by organized religion because prostitution is in direct competition with most religious beliefs.

A companion god to the mother goddess was the sun-god. An early major sun-god was Mithra, whose cult was founded in Persia about 1350 B.C.E. Mithra became a primary god of Rome and was worshiped throughout the ancient world. The Catholic bishop's hat is called a miter, copied from Mithra's headdress. Japan as the land of the rising sun is focused on a sun-god whose son was the emperor until deification was renounced by Hirohito after Japan's defeat in World War II. The prophesy in Malachi 4:2, promising a sun of righteousness, is interpreted as predicting the birth of Jesus, another sun-god. See also Revelation 21:23, which compares the light of the sun with God and his son. December 25 was the date of Mithra's birth; several Protestant hymns call Jesus the sun. Other sun-gods include Varuna, Krishna, and Vishnu. Christianity, therefore, fits into the mold of most older religions with a mother goddess and a sun-god begotten by a holy spirit. The story of the death of Jesus, his descent to hell (in the Apocrypha), resurrection, and ascent to heaven is identical to the story of Mithra. The common elements of Christianity and Mithraism include baptism, communion with consecrated wine, redemption, salvation, grace, rebirth, and eternal life. Other common elements are the wearing of fig leaves; the use of an ark to escape a world flood; a last supper by Mithra, which became a chief rite as the Eucharist; the presiding over a last judgment; and rebirth at the vernal equinox, otherwise known as Easter. Mithraism existed as a primary religion from 500 B.C.E. to 400 C.E. It continues today as part of most Western religions.

All human cultures contain parallels to the primary ancient gods. In the Bible Jehovah says, "Thou shalt not revile the gods" (Exodus 22:28, King James Version). Later versions of this verse were altered to reflect Christian monotheism: "You shall not revile God." Gods other than Yahweh (Jehovah) were spoken of positively in the Old Testament. By 100 B.C.E. these gods punished the wicked and rewarded the righteous with eternal life.

Except for the mention of "That one Thing" in Rig-veda (the basis for Hinduism, compiled from 3000 to 1000 B.C.E.), the first monotheistic religion was Egyptian, established in the 1370s B.C.E. with Aten, a sun-god. Egyptian religious literature is similar to Psalm 104, Job 38–41, and other Old Testament passages, all written well after this time period. There are similar parallels between Egyptian hymns and New Testament passages in Luke 17:21, Matthew 11:27, and other verses. The Christian concept of God in man is the same as the Brahman, the universal self through Atman, the Egyptian concept of Aten, and the Tao in Taoism.

Christianity arose from Judaism similarly to the evolution of Buddhism from Hinduism. By the time of Jesus most religions were monotheistic, though many retained remnants of animism. Islam was primarily monotheistic when founded by Mohammed but retains major animistic elements, such as worshiping spirits in rocks, trees, other relics or fetishes, and particularly the black stone at Mecca. Catholicism is a modified monotheistic system with its trinity and numerous saints to whom prayers are offered, plus the Virgin Mary; it, along with general Christianity, features numerous fetishes and other animistic items of worship such as the bread and wine of communion.

The oldest existing religion is Hinduism, founded in India between 3000 and 2500 B.C.E., though not organized and compiled into texts until 1500 B.C.E. Like all religions, its internal precepts are hopelessly contradictory. Human sacrifice is commanded, yet it is a sin to crush an ant or to eat meat. There are more Hindu priests, rites, and images than in ancient Egypt or Rome, yet Hinduism outdoes the Quakers in rejecting external trappings of religion. Central to Hinduism is the infamous system of four castes, the highest being the priests or Brahmans; then the warriors; then merchants, peasants, and artisans; and lastly, everyone else as untouchable. Whether a Hindu is reborn after death depends on Karma; poverty and wealth, health and disease depend on Karma or on how the person behaved in a previous life. Christianity has a related concept with sins of fathers visited on their children and their children's children. Because one receives his exact desserts as a Hindu, the poor must remain poor.

Life is evil and obscures one's unity with the infinite, which is neither God nor any sort of god. Hindus must reject worldly things until they can become one with the universal self and avoid a nearly never-ending cycle of rebirths. Unlike Western religions, Hindus seek an ultimate nothingness instead of an eternal afterlife and do not believe in "God." However, like all religions, there are sects and denominations that believe differently as to various details. Instead of allowing these differences to become divisive, most sects tolerate each other on the premise that no one has all the truth, and, thus, no one is wrong. Perhaps this concept is the most unique of any religion. Hinduism teaches: "Bow down and worship where others kneel, for where so many have been paying the tribute of adoration the kind Lord must manifest himself, for he is all mercy." Accordingly, Sri Ramakrishna became a Mohammedan and a Christian and concluded that all religions are equally true. Contrary to Christianity, Hindu Gods live in temples, which are not places of worship. While the purpose of most religions is to overcome death, Hindus seek to overcome life, 463 million strong and the third largest religion in the world.

Modern Hindu doctrines have introduced discontinuous reincarnation so that upon acceptance of Krishna as Lord, rebirths end. There are three Hindu Gods; Brahma the creator, Vishnu the preserver, and Shiva the destroyer; another trinity of sorts. All Hindus stress yoga to achieve unity with self and block out the material world. A state of trance means unity with the absolute, and for this a personal guru is necessary. Unity with Brahma may be obtained by earnestly seeking him for three consecutive days, or seventy-two hours. Probably anyone would see God after being in a trance for seventy-two hours. In psychology this is called a self-fulfilling prophesy.

Hindu parallels with Christianity include rituals, bathing or baptism, scripture reading, and recitation. The Hindu creation is described in a book written over four hundred years before Genesis was written. The Hindu Brahma decided to make a world with one man, Adami, and one woman, Heva, on the island of Ceylon. Adami and Heva were told not to leave the island, but a mirage created by the devil made the mainland look more enticing than the island. Adami and Heva, contrary to the instructions of their god, walked across a neck of land to the mainland whereupon the neck of land disappeared, leaving them on a mainland of sand and rocks. The Brahma cursed them to the lowest hell, but Adami defended Heva, saying it wasn't her fault, and Heva defended Adami, saying it wasn't his fault. For their selflessness, they were saved from expulsion to hell, but, as taught to all Hindus, humans thus fell from grace.

Another Hindu legend features a Hindu holy man named Menu who dipped water from the Ganges River and caught a little fish. The fish begged Menu to let it go. When Menu did so the fish warned him of a great flood and told him to build a huge ark to save his family and two of each animal on earth. Menu built the ark, and the flood came bringing Menu's old friend the fish, which had grown to the size of a whale and had a horn on its head. Menu tied the ark to the horn, and the whale towed the ark through the raging waves of the flood to a mountain top.

Through even a cursory study of other religions, we find there is nothing unique in the Christian religion or in any other religion; all religions originated with the superstitions and faint ancestral memories of primitive humans.

The great flood may have occurred twelve thousand years ago at the end of the last ice age. According to physical geographer John Shaw of Queen's University in Kingston, Ontario, the last glaciers may have acted as vast blankets, melting from underneath and within because of the earth's heat. When the glaciers began to recede, water trapped underneath may have been released, creating a massive worldwide flood. The flood is a folk myth in many societies, from Hindus and Christians to the Maori of New Zealand and the Indians of the Missouri Valley.

Buddhism is a modification of Hinduism and is the fourth largest religion, with 251 million adherents. It's the principal religion in Sri Lanka, Burma, Thailand, Tibet, half of Japan, and much of China. There are more Buddhists in the United States than in India, where Buddhism originated. As in Christianity and Hinduism, the central evil for Buddhists is the desire for material things. Unlike Hinduism, Buddhism has no priests, rites, or creeds. Each Buddhist walks alone and can salvage himself only through his own exertions. There are Buddhist monks, but they are not considered priests; their only possessions are a saffron robe, razor, begging bowl, water strainer, and needle. There is no Buddhist church and no leader. The basic teaching is to follow the middle way between the world and asceticism. Both pleasure and pain are to be avoided. "Those who say, do not know; while those who know, do not say."

There are no Buddhist deities. The sole goal of Buddhism is to abolish desire and thus to attain nirvana. The four noble truths are: life is suffering, desire leads to rebirth, desire should be renounced, and the path of morality is eightfold. This path of morality consists of the right view or knowledge, right thought, right speech, right conduct, right means of livelihood, right effort, right mind control, and right meditation.

Buddhists were the first ecologists, preaching selfless love for all living things, similar to Native American religions. Previous lives determine the present life's role; the key to life is self-responsibility. The three cardinal sins are sensuality/greed, anger/ill-will, and illusion/stupidity. Nirvana is not extinction but a oneness with perfection when the fires of passion die from want of fuel. The Buddhist "bible" consists of three books: *Jataka,* which chronicles Buddha's 550 previous lives, twice as long as the Christian Bible; *Sutra Pitaka,* the sermons of Buddha; and a description of how to escape from the wheel of life.

All religions change to survive, though the changes are usually so gradual as to be almost unnoticeable; Buddhism is no exception. Buddhism in China and Japan is called Shinto. This schism formed by the time of Christ and now has many versions with about thirty-three million followers. One major sect is rational and ascetic, denying the existence of the soul or of God and avoids the corruption of ideas by not describing or talking about them. Another sect, mystic, holds that nirvana is achieved by becoming and not by disappearing, that God exists but is beyond all human reason and that all is illusory. Accordingly, any general description of Buddhism is necessarily inaccurate because of its many varying sects. In China, for example, there are Buddhist priests who seek salvation for their followers but not for themselves. There is a Buddhist heaven that is achieved by faith and not by works; heaven is a paradise and not nothingness or the "incomparable misery" described by Hinduism.

Tibetan Buddhism has many monks, spirits, and demons; colorful pageantry and ritual; and a large dose of traditional Tibetan superstitions. The Japanese version is Zen Buddhism, which is closely related to Taoism (21 million members) and Confucianism (16 million members). Zen Buddhism believes in revelation by sudden jolt, similar to Christian conversion, renouncing ritual, scripture, and vows. Its code of chivalry is militaristic and the fountainhead of judo, jujitsu, and archery. The proper course is the middle way between extreme positions, though like Taoism, Zen Buddhism is anti-education, believing that study and reflection lead nowhere except to confusion, a reaction against Buddhism. Japan purged Buddhism in the eighteenth century, adopting State Shinto with acknowledged authority of the emperor/mikado. The fanatical loyalty of the Japanese in WWII came from the cult of the divine emperor. In November 1990 several thousand Japanese protested the enthronement ceremonies for Emperor Akihito on the ground that the state-funded ceremonies violated the constitutional mandate requiring separation of church and state. The many Shinto sects regard Mt. Fuji as sacred.

Confucius was born in 551 B.C.E., making him a contemporary of Buddha, Socrates, and Pythagoras. Neither Confucianism nor Taoism believe in a hereafter: "While you do not understand life, how can you understand death?" They believe that "absorption in the study of the supernatural is harmful" and, thus, adhere to a philosophy that is as pragmatic as American capitalism. Their goal is to enjoy the simple life, especially family and friends, as opposed to acquiring material objects. Confucius collected and rewrote many Chinese classical writings. His advice, as even Westerners know, is highly practical. For example, he said, "Do not think of all your anxieties; you will only make yourself ill." Confucius defined knowledge as knowing and admitting what we don't know. The yin and yang represent changing balances and circumstances in life. Five hundred years before Christ, Confucius posited the golden rule thusly: "What you do not want done to yourself, do not do to others." This earlier version of the golden rule is easier to follow and arguably superior as a practical matter, to the Christian version.

Confucianism recognizes an extended family with up to 250 living members, featuring tablets of ancestors. By remembering their ancestors, Confucianists believe they are remembering themselves. Their sole religious function is the worship or veneration of ancestors. China was ruled by Confucianists for two thousand years, except for a hundred-year interruption, through 1910. This interruption was imposed when the Taoists briefly came to power until 141 B.C.E. Taoism was founded by Lao-tse, who was born in 604 B.C.E., and is a pacifist doctrine teaching submission and humility, inaction and quietude induced by yoga breathing exercises to make the mind a blank. Taoism adopted the Buddhist gods, and there now exists a fusion of Buddhism, Confucianism, and Taoism, though their original doctrines contained basic conflicts. For example, Taoists are anti-education, believing that you should "do away with learning and grief will not be known," while Confucianism reveres learning. The resulting amalgam into Zen Buddhism is illustrated by two short poems: "Sitting quietly, doing nothing. Spring comes and the grass grows by itself." "We eat, sleep and get up; this is our world. All we have to do after that—Is to die."

Chronologically, the next great religions were those represented by the Greek and Roman gods. The Greek religion, like the Native American religions, was based on agricultural myths such as that of Demeter and Persephone with the planting and growing of corn. The Greeks adopted animistic entities, such as Eros, Fate, and Pan. The central gods were the Bright Gods: Zeus, Apollo, and Athena. The gods were indifferent to human quarrels and represented a combination of many local gods in order to unite diverse tribes into a single people. The existence of slaves required the solace of religion to allow the slaves to bear their tortured lives, similar to the solace of a future existence promised by the Roman Catholic Church to its poor masses. Then, as now, religion was associated with public functions, which were opened with sacrifices or prayers. Now, as then, there is peer pressure for all to participate in these public religious functions, though no conformity in belief is required. The use of gods in the Greek theater was not considered impious. The oracles of the gods were consulted before war was commenced or momentous decisions made, similar to today when national policy is formulated over prayer breakfasts and, in a recent administration, astrological forecasts.

Rome adopted a system parallel to the Greek gods, with minor exceptions involving later emphasis on animism and many more minor deities and spirits. The Roman system, like the Greek, was rooted in the family, with absolute authority of the father. Each occupation and each household object had an associated spirit or god. Janus was god of the door; Vesta, goddess of the hearth; the Penates, gods of the cupboard. All major events, as now, were marked by religious celebration: birth, death, puberty, and marriage. The entire ancient world believed in spirits lurking everywhere. The future was foretold by the entrails of beasts; by rain, thunder, and lightning; by magic, astrology, witchcraft, and miracles.

The Roman emperor was considered a deity, and there were several other underground religions, including the immediate predecessor to the Christian religion, the cult of Mithras. This cult was based on the Persian god of light, a sun-god, and was converted from being antagonistic to Christianity to becoming a part of Christian ritual and belief. The Mithras cult worshiped in underground temples that could hold fifty to one hundred people with a sacred communion of bread, water, wine, and ritual.

The five great religions founded between 600 B.C.E. and 600 C.E. that survive today are, in chronological order: Buddhism, Confucianism, Judaism, Christianity, and Islam. All are based on sacred scriptures. As previously noted, Buddhism, Hinduism, and Confucianism are not based on a personal god. Islam and Christianity feature a personal god, based on their antecedents from Judaism. The Jewish view is that God actively controls the destiny of a small nation, causing it to spread throughout the earth.

Judaism is based not on a single founder but on a series of prophets: Abraham, Moses, Elijah, Amos, Hosea, Isaiah, and Jeremiah. Both Jews and Christians claim all prophets are descended from Abraham's second-born son, Isaac, including Jacob, Joseph, Moses, David, Solomon, and, for Christians, Jesus. Muslims agree with this genealogy, adding that Islam and its prophet Mohammed come from Abraham's first son, Ishmael. Muslims don't accept the idea of Jesus' divinity, claiming Jesus instead to be a prophet on the same level as the other prophets and Mohammed.

The Hebrews were nomadic shepherd tribes that conquered agricultural Canaan as ordered by their god. Their first recorded appearance, before their religious ideas coalesced, was about 1400 B.C.E. In 1005 B.C.E. their power was consolidated for the first time, under David. Jehovah was a war god who defended his people in battle and against the Arab world. Judaism first combined ethics with religion to the everlasting detriment of ethics. Still, Judaism was a major intellectual development for that time, though arguably far more primitive than the Code of Hammurabi (1700 B.C.E.), which was a refinement of older codes.

The Hebrews were exiled from Jerusalem in 586 B.C.E. and then changed their name to Jews. For the first time Judaism became a personal religion. The return from exile, however, featured the exclusion of all foreigners and a strict prohibition against intermarriage so that the religion (it is a religion and not a race, according to rulings by the Israeli Supreme Court beginning in the 1960s) became exclusionary. As in all religions, there are major contending factions within Judaism. In July of 1989, after the Israeli Supreme Court ruled that people converted by conservative or reform rabbis must be accepted as Jews and admitted to Israel, the Interior Ministry, which is controlled by orthodox rabbis, ordered marriage bureaus and burial societies nationwide to obtain certificates of orthodox conversion before performing marriages or burials. Thus, reform or conservative converts are admitted to Israel but are considered second-class citizens. The dispute over who is a Jew has made Judaism an increasingly closed society. Of course, many groups constitute closed societies but probably none to the extent of the Jews, who have been forever persecuted as a result.

Rome's dispersal of the Jews helped spread monotheism throughout the world, also facilitating the spread of Christianity. Orthodox Judaism today sees itself as a divinely appointed promoter of righteousness, designated to lead the world to enlightenment, though it has no missionaries. Like many religions, the central theme is the family. To the orthodox, the law is complete and infallible, which is a tenet of all Western religions. The more liberal reform Jews believe the religion is evolving and that Jesus is an ethical figure. The specific tenets of Christianity are rejected, but the spiritual and ethical ideals, and the monotheism, are the same.

Every aspect of European and American civilization has been shaped by Christianity, which began as a popular social movement of Roman slaves and the poor. The New Testament, however, admonished slaves to obey their masters, to repudiate violence, and to seek no earthly kingdom. Christianity is a combination of Judaism and Greco-Roman religions, which teach fidelity to the law. For example, the Book of Daniel is believed to be an allegory of Greek domination and the terror of Nebuchadnezzar four hundred years earlier. The idea of an afterlife was introduced in Daniel 12:2–3. John the Baptist, and perhaps Jesus also, was from the Qumran sect of Hebrews, from which originated the Dead Sea Scrolls. The Qumran, which stood for sons of light, lived an isolated communal existence, shutting out the world and its evil, the sons of darkness. Like all inadvertent founders of the world's major religions, Jesus never saw himself as the messiah. (See Albert Schweitzer, *The Quest of the Historical Jesus,* 1913.) Jesus severely criticized ritual religion and would have disapproved of today's Roman Catholicism and all other Christian denominations, save perhaps such as the Quakers. He rejected rank, pride, wealth, exclusiveness, and even formal prayer. The Coptic Gospel of Thomas, discovered in the 1940s, is a collection of the sayings of Jesus written between 40 and 100 C.E., closer to the time of his existence than the other four Gospels. According to the Gospel of Thomas, Jesus not only objected to formalized prayer but said, "He who prays will be cursed." Jesus probably didn't author the Lord's Prayer.

Jesus' preferred form of an economic system would have been communistic, communalistic, or pure socialism. Jesus had great contempt for political leaders who ignore the suffering of their people, and announced his purpose to end conflict and establish a new kingdom of God, ending the quest for wealth and power. He said, "If thou wouldst be perfect, sell all that thou hast and give it to the poor and come follow me" (Acts 2:45). How many Christians have followed this central and explicit commandment? Jesus also said the rich, who in contrast to church members in developing countries of the world constitute a majority of church members in the United States, cannot enter his kingdom (Matt. 19:23 and Luke 6:24; see also, 1 Tim. 6:9 and Prov. 11:28). The religion closest to the teachings of Jesus is Buddhism.

Jesus would have disapproved of the current governments in the United States, Europe, and all capitalist countries. He would have been equally thrilled with the few remaining "communist" dictatorships and the other petty dictatorships around the world. There is probably not a government in existence today of which he would have approved. Western religion, with its formalistic inflexibility, would have been regarded by the historical Jesus as no better than totalitarianism.

Saul of Tarsus lifted Christianity out of its position as a Jewish sect and created a religion for the Greco-Roman world. Christianity became Greek in language and thought. As with all ancient religions it was founded on the idea of the seasons—rebirth after winter's death. Dionysus rose from the dead after three days, as did Attis, and became immortal. As with all religions of redemption Christianity features a god who dies and rises again; its followers obtain immortality by oneness with and obedience to the god. All such gods are born of a virgin made fruitful by divine touch or breath.

The Christian creed was influenced by Pythagoras, who characterized man as a fallen god in need of purification, and by Plato, who emphasized a reality beyond the visible world. Knowledge of the supernatural was needed to explain the universe, the unknown, and evil events. The new Christian church culled out fringe rituals and fanatic ideas to form a simplified religion with orthodox ideas and order. Early Christians were fiercely intolerant of other beliefs, as their successors have been throughout history and as many remain today. Their persecution bred discipline and loyalty, and they gained widening power as the Roman Empire declined. In 313 C.E. the Christian religion was established as the official church and organized as a monarchy. As Hobbes observed in *The Leviathan,* "The Papacy is no other than the ghost of the deceased Roman Empire, sitting crowned on the grave thereof." The decline of the Empire bred disorder, decay, and our modern religions.

The Roman Catholic Church has 850 million members, making up 60 percent of the Christian religion (Protestants number 450 million and Eastern Orthodox 66 million, all Christians totalling 1,666 million). The next two largest religions are Islam with 555 million and Hinduism with 463 million.

Catholicism is based on the historical certainty of Jesus' existence. Outside the New Testament Jesus is mentioned in the Jewish Talmud, Tacitus, Pliny, and Lucian, characterized as a crucified philosopher. Catholicism claims that the existence of God is provable by reason and that science supports Catholic theology and cannot be contrary to it: "Human reason, conscious of its own inferiority, dare not pretend to what is beyond it, nor deny those truths, nor measure them by its own standard, nor interpret them at will; but receive them with a full and humble faith" (Encyclical of Leo XIII, *Aeternia Patris,* 1879). This doctrine has created painful and reluctant change in Catholic theology. A hundred years later Pope John Paul II warned Stephen Hawking to stop searching behind the big bang, which was created by God according to Catholic theology. Physics and science need proceed no further. It will make no difference what science eventually establishes as the cause for the big bang. All religions will at that point synthesize their theology to fit the facts, as they've done throughout history, from Ptolemy and Copernicus to the present.

The early monastic orders vowed poverty, chastity, and obedience, and they founded colleges, hospitals, libraries, and music centers. As stated by Leo XIII, "the life which Christ dispenses must penetrate all the members and all parts of the body politic; law, institutions, schools, families, houses of the rich, workshops of the workers." The solution for social misery was "prayer and fasting." Papal infallibility was not adopted until 1870, making the pope the absolute authority on all questions of theology. The Vatican II Ecumenical Council held from 1962 to 1965 modernized Catholicism, dropping the requirement that all masses be in Latin and absolving the Jews of responsibility for the death of Christ, marking the end of the doctrinal basis for anti-Semitism.

The splintering of Protestantism from Catholicism was a gradual long-term revolt against the rigidity of Catholic theology, only to partially displace it with equally rigid Protestant theologies. The original impetus for Protestantism was the individual conscience, personal religious experience, and the right of private judgment with no priesthood through which the individual must be filtered to reach God. The Catholic Church exterminated those who wished to worship God directly. The next chapter will detail the excesses of Catholics and Protestants against each other and among themselves during the Reformation and the various Inquisitions; here we touch only briefly on the skeletal outlines of the Inquisitions.

In 1176, Peter Waldo of Lyons founded the Poor Men of Lyons, who were committed to giving their earthly goods to the poor, as expressly directed by Jesus. They were excommunicated in 1184 for arguing that all nonpoor priests (a majority of priests), bishops, and the pope were corrupt. The pope ordered the burning of hundreds of these men, and many were smoked to death in caves where they hid. The Inquisition began officially in 1232 to stamp out the Poor Men of Lyons, the Albigenses, and similar movements. Entire cities were exterminated in Italy, Spain, and France, such as Bezeirs and Carcassonne. The Albigenses ("The Pure"), rejected the sacraments and the pope, and they sought salvation through repentance, self-denial, renunciation of marriage, and celibacy. These forerunners of the Protestants, who were protesters in the truest sense, rejected the dual morality, wealth, and privilege accorded the priesthood, which was a corrupt lot. These reformers held that the Bible could be read by the laity and that war was immoral. This was considered blasphemy by Catholicism and was treated accordingly. The idea of war as immoral is considered the equivalent of blasphemy by all religions in existence today. Consider the Persian Gulf war, Panama, ad infinitum.

These early reformers included the Hus in Bohemia (Czechoslovakia), Wycliffe, and Martin Luther (1483–1546). The corruption of the Catholic priesthood was widespread. Many priests had concubines but absolved each other of that sin. They sold indulgences, forgiveness of sin, to the highest bidder and conducted pagan rites. The early Reformation was an attempt to clean up the Church and the priests' double standard, and to remove the Church from political affairs. Luther and many others felt that religion without direct personal involvement was illusory. Luther formed an alliance with the ruling class to win the Reformation against the peasant class, which he crushed, resulting in the slaughter of thousands.

The rigidity of the reformed Protestants was no better than the corruption of the Catholic Church. For example, John Calvin (1509–1569) was unbending in all his beliefs, including those mandating church attendance and forbidding adultery or blasphemy. Violators were punished with death. According to Max Weber, however, the Protestant theology with its work ethic, glorification of God, and frugality, became the linchpin for making capitalism work in the New World.

The Eastern Church split from Rome in the fifth century, but not until the watershed date of 1054 did the Eastern Bishops refuse submission to Rome. The result was persecution of the Eastern Church by both Rome and the Muslims. The laity is far more significant in the Eastern Church than in the Catholic or the Protestant, with Eastern services conducted primarily by the laity.

The Church of England and the Episcopal Church are an amalgam of Protestants and Catholics, with issues separating the two main sects such as whether bishops are the essence of the Church (High Church) or just good management (Low Church). The Presbyterian Church was established in Scotland with elected elders and was closely associated with the Congregationalists (now the United Church of Christ), who practiced pure democracy with no higher official than a local pastor. These separatists migrated from Holland to America, where they influenced the development of government and the democratic experiment here. Several state constitutions mirror the Congregationalist Constitution and the Mayflower Compact.

The Baptists took their name from the Anabaptists who, when founded in 1515, required adult baptism instead of infant baptism. In 1630, Baptist Roger Williams founded Rhode Island, which became the first state to grant complete tolerance in religious matters. The Baptists were divided by the Civil War and to this day the Northern Baptists are separate from the Southern variety. The many other Protestant sects are based on their own view of the Bible and forms of practice, such as the Moravians, a missionary-oriented church. The Methodist Church, with its circuit-riding preachers, is now the second largest Protestant church in the world (after Baptists), with over 15 million members. Other unique sects include the Quakers, Unitarians, and several hundred others. Much of Christianity is now closer to the pragmatic teachings of Confucianism, except for the Confucian worship of ancestors, than to the teachings of Christ.

The last great religion was founded by Mohammed (570–632), who united the philosophies of Judaism, Christianity, and Zoroastrianism, amalgamating these with the desert religion of the Arabs, based on the Koran (Quran). The new religion served to consolidate the Arab nations into an aggressive military force that conquered Syria, Egypt, and Persia in the seventh century, then India, China, and Spain, and was finally stopped by Martel at the French border. Muslims occupied North Africa, then Sicily in 827, threatening Italy. Constantinople fell to the Muslims in 1453, which was until then a Christian stronghold, and it has remained predominately Muslim ever since. The Crusades sought to rescue Palestine from the Muslims, defend the Byzantine Empire against the Turks, and restore

Christian unity. They failed miserably, primarily due to disorganization, lack of planning, and factionalism.

Mohammed married the wealthy widow Khadija and sired Fatima, who in turn married Mohammed's cousin, Ali; their descendants are the Shiah sect. At age forty Mohammed awakened to the God of the Christians and the Jews, attacking polytheism and animism, although to protect against evil, Muslims still worship spirits in trees, stones, and other relics or fetishes. Zoroastrian/Christian principles adopted by Islam include belief in the devil, angels, judgment day, hell, resurrection, the Old Testament (emphasizing Abraham and Moses), the New Testament, and the principles of early Christians. A principle charge of the Muslim religion is to expand by war and trickery based on their belief in "One prophet, one faith, for all the world." It is a Muslim holy war to kill unbelievers: ". . . kill them wherever ye shall find them." Christians, however, are not considered non-believers; the overwhelming majority of Muslims are not anti-Western and do not agree with Khomeini's bounty on Salman Rushdie. The Muslim concept of *jihad,* normally translated by Westerners to mean "holy war," actually means "struggle" in three separate contexts: ethics, justice and morality, and the fight against oppression of freedom and expression.

Other principle beliefs include the duty of submission to one absolute god and an afterlife featuring seven compartments of hell for nonbelievers. Christians have their own compartment, as do Muslim backsliders, Jews, Sabians, Magians, idolaters, and hypocrites, the last category creating some potential for overlap. The attributes of Islam heaven could tempt many to switch to Islam, with its promise of restored youth, joy, wine without harm, and an abundance of lovely women. It's unclear whether Muslim women will find fulfillment in such a heaven.

Islam permits no priests. Muslims regard the Christian Trinity as the worship of three gods, contrary to monotheistic principles. Islam means surrender to the will of God. The Muslim god hates oppression, injustice, usury, alcohol, and pork, but is kind to orphans and the poor; the giving of alms is a central tenet. The religion is a simple one, intended for the common person, and does not seek, like Christianity, to elevate humans above their means or abilities. A common person can easily observe the requirements of Islam. The five tenets are recognizing the one god Allah and Mohammed as his prophet; prayer; contributing alms for the poor, which constitutes a 2½ percent tithe (primarily performed for Christians by their government); at least one pilgrimage to Mecca; and observation of the Fast of Ramadan. Things in doubt may be safely ignored. Be not envious. Expect sickness and death; don't expect sunrise or sunset. A simple, practical religion. Similar to Christianity, however, Islamic sects and countries stray far from the teachings of their founding leaders, lapsing into harsh and unforgiving fundamentalism such as that in Iran and Iraq.

All law comes from the Koran, including that governing the military, social life, and commercial dealings. The Koran, like the Bible, is a divinely inspired work. It was written by the angel Gabriel next to the throne of Allah on a tablet with rays of light. It's difficult to read or understand, however, consisting of a collection of disjointed sayings, the bulk of which are either dull or pointless, though there are a few gems of wisdom. The Koran is similar to the Bible, though not as bloodthirsty as the Old Testament. The Koran is zealously consulted; children are required to memorize large portions, and this constitutes the bulk of their education. If there were no legal separation of church and state, Bible study would likely constitute education in the United States as it does in some poor Catholic countries. The good advice in the Koran includes giving alms to others without public credit, loving your neighbor, honoring your mother by digging a well for the thirsty, and similar injunctions suitable for a desert and other peoples.

Daily prayer is required, but the Muslim prayer is unlike Christian prayers, which primarily ask for things and interventions. The Muslim prayer is always the same: "God is great. I testify there is no God but Allah. I testify that Mohammed is the apostle of God." It's not a Christian begging prayer but praise to God with an unspoken request for guidance and forgiveness.

All Muslims are required at least once in their life, as ordered by Abraham on behalf of his son Ishmael, the ancestor of Mohammed, to go to Mecca and kiss the Käaba (animistic), a black meteorite about seven inches in diameter, displayed on the outside of the Kaaba, a stone building 12 yards by 10 yards by 15 yards high. The Kaaba was erected by Abraham on the site where God stayed his hand from sacrificing his son Ishmael (contended to be Isaac by Christians), signalling the birth of Islam. For more than thirteen centuries Muslims have been visiting Mecca at the rate of about two million each year during a one-week period, creating crowds that would be unimaginable in the West. This crowd is unique, indicia of class being prohibited because the religion relegates all to equality before Allah (compare Christianity). All wear the same attire whether ruler or peon, rich or poor, black or brown, man or woman. Christians have no such once-in-a-lifetime obligation; the closest comparable obligations for Christians are wedding and funeral ceremonies, which are not normally attended by two million people.

Muslims are regulated in all things such as inheritance, dowries, divorces, and the treatment of orphans. Divorce is accomplished by saying so. A man is allowed up to four wives, if he can support them, plus slaves and concubines. Christians are allowed a wife whether support is available or not. Unless all Muslim wives are treated equally, only one wife is allowed. Mohammed's special revelations allowed him more than four wives by taking on the divorced wife of his son, in return for which he was required to leave his concubine Mary alone.

The successors to Mohammed were the Caliphs, who spread the word by the sword, similar to the Christians of the time. Mohammed's descendants live in Iraq (Mesopotamia), Iran (Persia), and Pakistan, so it's easy to see why Mr. Rushdie was able to create such a ruckus there with *The Satanic Verses*. Most of the Muslims demonstrating against the book never read it, illustrating a common characteristic of most people, whether religious or not. We do as our leaders say, right or wrong, whether there's good reason for their position, as long as it fits our personal prejudices. Witness the furor over *The Last Temptation of Christ*. Although Westerners may consider the Shia fanatics in Iraq and Iran crazy, they're probably no more radical than members of any fundamentalist religion, Christian or Muslim. When right and wrong are black and white, arbitrary religious rules admit of no exception; our god is the only true god.

The two main Muslim sects are the Shiah (Mohammed's descendants) and the far larger Sunni, with four subsects. Westerners owe much to the Muslim religion, for without it we wouldn't have the writings of Plato and Aristotle, which were preserved by the Arab philosophers when considered heretical by the Catholic Church. From 600 C.E. to 1100, medieval Europe was backward while Muslims prospered, preserving scholarship and knowledge, flourishing in Cairo and Cordoba, teaching in the Greek tradition of logic and reason. Muslim scholars made all the advances in chemistry, physics, medicine, and algebra during this period.

Islam is making strides in Africa because of its comprehensible God, its simple clear rules, and its ease of obedience. Black Muslims are a lost tribe, representing the found nation of Islam, with notions of black superiority, similar to the notion of white superiority the West has held for centuries. Malcolm X's Black Muslims brought an international flavor to the civil rights movement in the United States. The twentieth century, however, is a major challenge to Islam because the religion's civil rules and the Koran are hopelessly out of date (witness its treatment of women). Muslims refuse to sign the United Nations declaration of civil rights because it guarantees the right to change religion. Conservative Islamic leaders, such as the late Ayatollah Ruhollah Khomeini, are paranoic on this point and others. The leader of the Iranian parliament, picked in August of 1989, Hojatoleslam Mehdi Karrubi, publicly stated that the 1987 riots at Mecca where over four hundred Muslims, mostly Iranians, were killed was "a calculated plot designed by American and Israeli advisers to prevent the spread of the Islamic revolution to other parts of the world." More candidly, Karrubi should have said that Christians and Jews oppose the spread of Islam. Much of Islam is anti-Western but then much of Christianity is anti-Eastern. There are substantial Muslim blocs that are more tolerant of the West and are even allied with the West, such as Turkey, which is becoming more secular with religion becoming less important.

Although Islam is a practical religion, it contains broad strains of mysticism drawn from Sufism. Christianity and all religions have this common core drawn from mysticism, requiring a genuine personal experience as the major turning point for the founder of the particular religion, whether that be Paul, Christ, Gautama Buddha, Mohammed, George Fox, or John Wesley. Each has exalted moments of intense emotional experience revealing that God exists and that God's existence need only be recognized to be felt. Devices ancillary to mysticism, depending on the tenets of the particular religion, include prayer, meditation, regulated and special forms of breathing, music, incense, dim or flickering lights, rituals, and prescribed posture. Some repeat sacred sentences or words and focus on sensuous imagery. Reasoning ceases and near catalepsy is reached, with or without visions, the hearing of voices, and the perception of light. Upon awakening there's a feeling of the knowledge of something special, though nothing of significance can be communicated. Sometimes the ritual creates erotic feelings, which may be one reason adolescence is the usual age for religious conversion in the West. Trances revealing God are contained in various biblical passages (see Num. 24:4,16; Acts 10:10; 11:5; 22:17).

Hindu mysticism emphasizes detachment from worldly things. Yoga is the means to obtain detachment from all, to reach complete isolation and achieve a soul devoid of desire. Sikhs also rely on yoga, chanting, stretching, and breathing deeply to reach the inner soul and "conscious rebirthing." Sikhs don't cut their hair, believing it releases positive electromagnetic energy. They instead cover their hair so the energy is harnessed and transmitted through the crown chantra, or head, considered one of the body's seven major energy centers, to create a personal harmonic balance.

The state achieved by yoga is not dissimilar to some forms of mental illness or the effects produced by the use of depressant drugs, such as alcohol or marijuana. An undeniable fact of all religions is their early and current reliance on hallucination producing mechanisms, such as a diet restricted to vegetables, breathing to the point of oxygen intoxication, dancing to exhaustion, flagellations, and the use of various drugs including alcohol (wine), peyote, cannabis, and mushrooms. Personal responsibility and judgment cease. The result is an awareness of supreme enlightenment, which cannot be articulated. According to briefs filed with the U.S. Supreme Court in Oregon's challenge to peyote use by Native Americans, it promotes a sense of reverie allowing the user to commune with tribal spirits, similar to the Catholic sacrament of transubstantiation in which the wine becomes the blood of Christ. The tribe in its brief argued that prohibiting the use of peyote would "in effect destroy the Native American Church." Oregon argued that if the tribe won, users of other drugs may establish a competing "church" based on sacraments of marijuana, cocaine, and crack. Oregon prevailed. Other drugs such as opium, hashish, and strong marijuana have effects similar to peyote and can easily be overdone, destroying the euphoria and creating terror or paranoia. Ask any survivor of the sixties culture.

Many religious experiences (if not all) result from such mechanisms, including speaking in tongues and lengthy sensory deprivation in the form of meditation and prayer.

The Pinal County chairman of the Arizona Republican Party during 1990 began GOP meetings by praying in tongues, which is a type of prayer in which participants utter unintelligible sounds they believe originate with God. According to chairman David J. Hinchcliffe, "We just get right down to it. In fact, we start praying in tongues. And its unreal. There are some people very nervous with that, as you can well expect."

Divine rapture originated from intoxication, with drugs and the like, creating experiences indistinguishable from those labeled religious. Between a fourth and a third of people who take psilocybin (a hallucinogenic mushroom) have a religious experience. Do such mechanisms lead to an experience that proves the existence of God?

These descriptions of major religions and their key common elements apply similarly to the by-ways of religion, such as the Druses of Lebanon, the Assassins, the Fifth Monarchy Men, the Ghost Dance Religion of poor Nevada Indians in the 1880s, or the Cargo Cults of Melanesia who built runways in the belief that a plane would come if they prayed diligently, bringing all their material wants. A *People* magazine survey found that a fourth of all Americans have received personal messages from God. In a similar vein, a 1991 Gallup poll found that a fourth of Americans believe in ghosts, a tenth have seen or spent time with ghosts, a sixth have conversed with a dead person, over half believe in the devil, a tenth have had a conversation with the devil, a seventh have seen UFOs.

There are many other cults and sects that qualify as religions, such as Jim Jones's followers and the Moonies. Many attract older women with money who apparently feel more camaraderie with these sects than with their children and grandchildren. In the northwestern United States three sects lured thousands of followers, such as in Yelm, Washington, where a 35,000-year-old guru Ramtha is channeled by a forty-three-year-old housewife. In Paradise Valley, Montana, a forty-nine-year-old mother of four claims to be the true vicar of Christ. In Medford, Oregon, a twenty-nine-year-old channels 2,000-year-old Mafu. Many elderly women have sold their property and given the proceeds to these cults. Exit counselling to wean their mothers away from the cults has resulted in lawsuits by mothers against their children.

Other well-known sects include Jehovah's Witnesses, who believe in the immediate coming of Christ based on a vision in Daniel; scholars believe this passage actually is a disguised report by Daniel of current events in Rome and Israel. The Jehovah's Witnesses have 370,000 members.

A fundamentalist Protestant preacher, William Miller, gathered hundreds of his followers in 1843 to await the end of the world; Miller relied on Daniel 8:13, which predicted the world would end 2,300 mornings and evenings after the fall of Jerusalem. "Twenty-three hundred mornings and evenings" was interpreted to mean 2,300 years after 457 B.C.E., the year 1843. When the world failed to end as predicted by Miller, his followers gave him the consolation of becoming the Seventh-day Adventists.

The Hasidic Jews, a sect established in the eighteenth century, look for the Messiah and refuse to recognize the existence of Israel. The center for Hasidic Judaism is Brooklyn, N.Y.

The Navajo religion is concerned with harmony in the community, the environment, and living one's life in contentment. Tony Hillerman described it as a concern with holistic health: "If you are not content then you are probably sick or you are going to be sick. Their notion is to restore the ailing person back to a state of harmony and beauty."

The Church of Jesus Christ of Latter-Day Saints, whose followers are known as Mormons, was founded in 1830 by Joseph Smith. It is Christian but not Protestant, and it holds many of the Christian tenets such as the virgin birth, immortality, the Trinity as distinct "persons," communion, eternal marriage, and baptism; other tenets are unlike mainstream Christianity, such as the baptism of ancestors who missed their chance and abstinence from tea, coffee, alcohol, and tobacco. Mormons also believe that God was a human who evolved into godhood and that those who obey the Bible and its equal counterpart, the Book of Mormon, will also become gods and goddesses, ruling their own world as

God rules the earth. The second coming will occur in Jackson County, Missouri, where Christ will establish a New Jerusalem and rule for a thousand years. Polygamy was adopted by Mormon founder Joseph Smith, but rescinded by God in 1890 so Utah could become a state. It is Mormon tradition that their prophet Levi sailed from the Holy Land to the New World in 600 B.C.E. The Golden Plates of the Book of Mormon came from Moroni, whose father buried them in New York in 421 C.E. Joseph Smith was murdered by a mob in Carthage, Illinois, in 1844. Brigham Young moved the group to Utah where they reign at this writing. They have nine thousand full-time lay missionaries and two million members. If you live in Utah and are not a Mormon, you have little possibility of political advancement or commercial success.

New Age religious groups include those that venerate crystals, those who believe cats meditate, those believing themselves aliens who've met Jesus, and those who believe the Star of Bethlehem was a UFO and Jesus was beamed up. Saul Bellow remarked, "A great deal of intelligence can be invested in ignorance when the need for illusion is deep."

3

The Basics of Religion

One man's religion is another man's poison.

—Anonymous

Religion is nigh impossible to define. This chapter will instead trace its origins and purpose; examine religious experience and miracles; compare its basic tenets to those of education; survey its impact on our attitude toward sexuality, homosexuality, and women; enumerate the positives of religion, explore the relationship between religion and money; and summarize what the separation of church and state means in theory and in practice.

The Origins of Religion

The history of our religions is rooted in the fears and insecurities of primitive humans. The central appeal of all religion is the same: to fulfill the basic human yearning for security and personal control over our lives, which is obtained by ritual and other trappings of religion. Dr. Andrew Baum, a professor of medical psychology at the University of Maryland and an authority on survivors of disasters, states:

> People have a need to explain misfortune. It seems too unacceptable to our species to believe that things happen randomly. . . . [When it comes to the how and the why] it's almost better for you to delude yourself. [Without concepts such as fate and destiny to lean on] we begin to lose our confidence in our ability to control the world.

Bertrand Russell in his book *Why I am not a Christian* argues that there are three impulses for organized religion: (1) the fear of death, (2) conceit that the members are a chosen people, and (3) hatred of those others who fail to recognize the one true religion. Fear of death is a natural human condition; it would be unnatural not to prefer life. Conceit and competitiveness are also natural human characteristics as evidenced by intense nationalism and religiosity, our capitalistic economic system and survival of the fittest resulting in evolution of the species. The resulting hatred of the "other" endangers the species.

The Purposes of Religion

The primary purpose of most Western religions is to escape death, the same hope that has driven man since ancient times, as evidenced by the form of Neanderthal burials 50,000 years ago with accompanying tools and food for the afterlife. At all times and in all places humans have yearned for immortality, thus our early belief in animism and the powers of the dead, which has shifted to a belief in a power beyond death. This belief was central to the Egyptians. Their Book of the Dead promises that "Thou shalt exist for millions of millions of years."

Hindus believe they are reborn after death but rebirth is a punishment, which living in starvation conditions in India has meant since time immemorial. At the end of a good life the deceased moves up the food chain to a higher caste, eventually up to the level of Brahman. If the life was led badly, the deceased must start again at the bottom of the chain while awaiting rebirth on 9,000 miles of burning coals in hell and successive hells. Nirvana is not the achievement of nothingness but of a true bliss, similar to the Christian heaven.

It's unclear whether there's an afterlife available in Confucianism or Taoism, except for the emperor and other nobles, though there does appear to be survival after death for some period of time as embodied in ancestor worship rituals. On the other hand, neither have a conception of "God" but instead are oriented to almost pure pragmatism, which would admit of little afterlife speculation. The emperor was considered immortal until immortality was renounced by Hirohito. His successor, Emperor Akihito, was installed on the Chrysanthemum Throne in November 1990, after spending time cloistered with the spirit of the sun goddess Amaterasu, legendary founder of the Japanese nation. The government stated it was "not in a position to make any comment as to whether the emperor does or does not acquire such a divine nature."

Judaism could lay substantial claim to life after death, witness Ezekiel 37, which is interpreted by Jewish scholars as portending the resurrection of Israel as a unified state, and the references in Isaiah 26:19, Daniel 12:2, and Ecclesiastes 12, the last mirroring the Egyptian concept of the soul's return to God. There is much in the Apocryphal Books on life after death; ancient Jews believed in immortality. The Pharisees believed the body was resurrected while the Sadducees believed only the soul was resurrected. The Babylonian Talmud, circa 600 C.E., listed three hundred arguments for the resurrection of the dead. Orthodox and conservative Jews still believe in an afterlife, but without hell, for they also believe that death atones for earthly sins. Most Jews, however, believe this life is all there is.

The mystery religions of Greece taught that the pure in heart would receive eternal life, a concept adopted by Christianity in Matthew 5:8. These religions used baptism to symbolically cleanse converts. Paul expounded Christian immortality in Acts 9:1 and 1 Corinthians 15:51–52. Mormons believe that most are destined to heaven with the better Mormons becoming gods and goddesses who associate directly with God, lesser Mormons and regular Christians fraternizing with Jesus, and others mingling only with angels.

The ideas of Karl Radner, a leading Catholic theologian, have been summarized by Gerald McCool in two essays, titled "The Life of the Dead" and "The Resurrection of the Body," to describe the reasoning by which Christians believe humans possess a soul and are thus immortal:

> Since man is an incarnate spirit, the human soul, even after death, retains its relation to the material world. Thus the dead are still concerned with the evolution of the world's history. Man's ultimate future, his unity with the Trinity at the Parousia [the Second Coming], is a *human* future. Therefore it requires the resurrection of the body and a glorified life in a new heaven and a new earth. So Christ's Second Coming will be truly the glorification of his material creation. . . . As we have seen, man is an incarnate historical spirit. Therefore a purely spiritual union with God, a *Visio Beatica* in which man's glorified body would have no part, cannot be the final perfection of man. Christ's victory, the triumphant result of his work in creation history, cannot have as its goal the disappearance of his material creation. Thus those blessed men and women who share in Christ's triumph at the Second Coming will be fully human members of the perfect society which will live with the Incarnate Christ on His glorified earth.

Such reasoning requires the making of many assumptions.

The idea of eternal life is inculcated into our minds as children, primarily to influence our good behavior, and becomes an unshakable belief based on sheer hope. The desire for eternal life is the same as the desire to continue living, which we all experience.

Without the promise of immortality and heaven, which is offered in return for belief, religion would have little purpose, at least to the Western mind. The promise of immortality is central to the Christian religion as illustrated by the most translated verse from the Bible. "For God so loved the world, that he gave his only begotten Son, that whosoever believeth in him should not perish, but have everlasting life" (John 3:16). Without this concept the Christian religion would likely not exist. When the stakes are as high as immortality and the opportunity to sit with the gods forever, extensive self-delusionary and visionary experience is to be expected. Most of mankind has a profound hope for eternal life, to avoid death, and to elevate man above the animals. Why should we believe in survival after death when there is no evidence of its truth and all evidence points in the opposite direction?

Religion is a necessity for many, for without it there would be no hope for the future. Religion is a security blanket without which life may seem silly and insignificant.

Today's zoologists and biologists recognize that humans are in a real sense immortal: "Humans are nothing but temporary survival machines, robot vehicles blindly programmed for someone else's benefit," according to Oxford zoologist Richard Dawkins, discussing his influential book, *The Selfish Gene* (1976). The reality of our immortality is the genes that replicate their exact copies through millions of years. We are here to replicate our genes; there may be no other purpose in life, biological or otherwise.

Religion acts as a cultural unit of reproduction, which Dawkins calls a "meme." Most religions are unconsciously controlled by the genes of their members with the result that birth control is prohibited by most denominations within the world's four largest religions: Christians (overwhelmingly Catholic in numbers), Muslims, Hindus, and Buddhists. Similarly, there are no contraceptives in nature; the genes program the sexual urge and we blindly follow, except insofar as we exercise birth control. Birth control is a primary individual means of control over personal destiny, which is one reason it is prohibited by the major religions.

There are also many good and practical reasons for religious affiliation. We conform to get ahead and make business contacts. Most of us fit on a continuum between church attendance to get ahead in business and true believers, with relatively few at either extreme of the spectrum; we're a classic bell-shaped curve when graphed according to our religious sincerity.

Catholicism explicitly recognizes the insincerity of some parishioners based on the definition of contrition in *The Catholic Word Book* as "Sorrow for sin coupled with a purpose of amendment." Contrition for the purpose of hedging bets is called "imperfect contrition or attrition," which arises "from a quasi-selfish supernatural motive; e.g., the fear of losing heaven, [and] suffering the pangs of hell." Even bet-hedging contrition, however, is "sufficient for the forgiveness of serious sin when joined with absolution in confession." How many of us pay organized religion lip service because we would otherwise be shunned, fail in business, or become ineligible for politics?

The Evidence of Religious Truth

Religious experience cannot be denied so the question arises—what is its meaning? Basic human psychology tells us that we experience mentally whatever is necessary for us to cope with our fears and anxieties. The only consistent factor in all religious experience is that people see only symbols or beings from their own religious teachings. A Christian never sees Buddha in a vision and a Buddhist never sees Christ. Only Catholics see the Virgin Mary and only Muslims see the archangel Gabriel; only Taoists have religious revelations that all government is bad. This consistency leads to the conclusion that religious experience comes solely from the mind.

Since religious experiences arise from the mind, the question becomes how these experiences differ from seeing Casper the Friendly Ghost or pink elephants and whether such experiences more likely prove the existence of God than the existence of Casper or pink elephants. Is it relevant that the Bible repeatedly recognizes the existence of unicorns (Num. 23:22; Job 39:9, 10; Pss. 29:6, 92:10—though biblical scholars now argue that the term was mistranslated for animals similar to large oxen)? Does the existence of a headache prove the existence of Satan based on the religious explanation from the Middle Ages that a headache is caused by devils banging around inside the head? From a scientific point of view there is no difference between a man who eats too little and sees heaven and a man who drinks too much and sees snakes. Both result from abnormal physiological conditions.

Miracles are at least a cousin to religious experience and faith healing. When no natural explanation exists for events it would appear no more logical to say they are caused by God as to conclude they are caused by the human mind. The miraculousness of human potential and strength in crisis is well known, so why do we assume that God causes whatever we can't readily explain? If an explanation is acceptable without proof then any explanation is equally valid. Asserting that an invisible God produced an unrepeatable miracle is the same as saying that the cause is unknown or the conditions cannot be reconstructed easily.

The forms of miracles reveal their origins. In Colfax, California, a colorful apparition of the Virgin Mary appeared on the wall at St. Dominic's Catholic Church every morning from Thanksgiving until a rainy morning when the image failed to appear. A physics professor concluded that the image was a reflection caused by sunlight through a stained-glass window reflecting from one of six hanging light fixtures, which had been repaired the day before Thanksgiving. On that cloudy morning believers took pictures claiming that "they saw angels . . . taking Mary away." To the delight of local entrepreneurs selling videos, key chains, refrigerator magnets, and T-shirts with the legend, "I saw the light," the image reappeared with the sunshine.

Every Tuesday and Saturday evening beginning in 1989, Estela Ruiz, the mother of a state legislator from Phoenix, Arizona, hosted five hundred people who gathered in her back yard to say the rosary, celebrate mass, and listen to messages from apparitions of the Virgin Mary. In the house hangs a picture of the Virgin Mary painted by Mr. Ruiz, whose hand, according to a message from the Virgin, was guided by her to complete the painting. Apparitions of the Virgin, which no one has seen except Mrs. Ruiz, look like the painting. The Virgin's messages parallel those imparted by the Virgin at what is now a world-famous apparition site, Medjugorje, Yugoslavia, and began three months after Mr. Ruiz returned from a pilgrimage to Medjugorje. According to the pastor of a Catholic Church in Scottsdale, Arizona, "This is the second time she's [the Virgin] come to the Americas. The first was when she came as Lady of Guadalupe [1531]." The Catholic Church was urged to designate the apparition as Our Lady of the Americas.

A three-member diocesan commission investigated the Ruiz claims and concluded that it and similar claims by other members of the St. Maria Goretti Catholic Church in Scottsdale "are explainable within the range of ordinary human experience." Nine youths and the pastor of the church, the Rev. Jack Spaulding, claimed to be receiving messages directly from the Virgin Mary and Jesus Christ. The bishop for the Phoenix Diocese, Thomas J. O'Brien, ruled that "there may not be . . . any unequivocal claim of miraculous interventions," but that the prayer meetings could continue as long as no one claimed miracles were occurring. The Rev. Spaulding said he would be obedient to the bishop, though "It doesn't change what's happening. It continues to happen." Rev. Spaulding claimed that the investigation was done poorly. Thursday-evening services at the church continued to attract about five hundred people a week, who attended to share the messages received by Spaulding and the nine youths. Spaulding noted that more came every week. These Thursday-night prayer meetings also grew out of pilgrimages to Medjugorje led by Rev. Spaulding, which included the Ruiz family. Arizonans are among the most frequent vistors to the Yugoslavian shrine.

The diocesan chancellor, Rev. Timothy Dowern, who is also the canon lawyer, concluded those involved with Rev. Spaulding need an emotional side to their faith: "People need to be in touch with that part of their faith," noting that apparitions and locutions are common in Catholicism, particularly when the Church is perceived as cold.

The Roman Catholic Bishop for Yugoslavia, Pavao Zanic, called the apparitions of the Virgin Mary at Medjugorje a "fraud" surrounded by "religious blindness and fanaticism." Of the fifteen bishops on a commission led by Zanic, eleven concluded there was nothing supernatural in the events; two Franciscan members claimed them authentic, one said there was a kernel of validity, and one abstained. Zanic stated that none of his hundred diocesan priests believed in the apparitions.

Pope Urban VIII (1623–1644) said, "In roses like this [apparitions], it is better to believe than not to believe, for, if you believe, and it is proven true, you will be happy that you believed, because Our Holy Mother asked it. If you believe, and it should be proven false, you will receive all blessings as if it had been true because you believed it to be true." According to the *Book of Lists 3* the Virgin Mary made 232 "confirmed" appearances in thirty-two countries (all to Roman Catholics) between 1928 and 1975. A miracle cured thousands of crippled and diseased peasants in Guatemala in 1987 after they viewed an image of Christ that appeared on the side of a church. The faithful continued to believe even after a rainstorm revealed the image to be a Willie Nelson poster that had been covered by a recent whitewash of the church.*

All religions have their miracle cures and apparitions. A stray cat in Kuala Lumpur, Malaysia, appeared in 1988 on its hind legs with its paws held forward and was regarded as a reincarnation of Buddha. The cat appeared regularly in a local prayer hall, apparently to meditate.

Muslims in England flocked to the house of a man who cut an eggplant open and found the seeds formed the name of Allah in Arabic. In the first month, forty-five hundred pilgrims journeyed to the man's house to observe the seeds, and the town's mosque designated the eggplant a holy object.

New Times (Phoenix, Ariz.), Feb. 1, 1989, p. 27.

Why do all religions look for historic verification of their truth and never find it? Consider the Shroud of Turin and the search for the Ark on Mt. Ararat. There is no evidence that anything described in the Bible ever occurred. It would be remarkable if the Bible were accurate because it's admittedly made up of oral traditions recorded hundreds of years after the occurrences purported to be described. The Old Testament is a Hebrew folk myth, similar to the Christian folk myth of the New Testament.

Education, Science, and Religion

The Christian religion purports that the truth is fully known, thus limiting inquiry and fostering superstition; anyone disagreeing with religiously ordained truth historically was considered a heretic; human sexuality without the sanction of the church or the state and outside of narrowly accepted practices guaranteed eternal damnation; social injustice was to be remedied in the next life only; tolerance was for nonbelievers. The pope in 1981 personally instructed the world's leading physicists not to further investigate the big bang because he said it was created by God, according to Stephen Hawking's nonfiction bestseller, *A Brief History of Time,* but Mr. Hawking ignored the pope's directive and concluded that the universe likely had no creator, which means there is no spirit in the sky that religion calls God. Religion responded swiftly. At a "Heavenly News" gathering in Washington, D.C.'s National Cathedral, an astronomer noted the similarities between the Big-Bang theory and Genesis 1:3, which says, "And God said, let there be light." At the same conference a theologian said the creation depicted in Genesis was never intended as a statement of scientific fact, but was an act of worship demonstrating the exiled Jewish community's belief in order amid the chaos of exile. Christian leaders, as reported by the Associated Press, announced that the "Big Bang supports science and religion." However, a 1991 Gallup Poll found that 47 percent of Americans thought God created humans in their present form within the past ten thousand years, 40 percent said we developed under God's plan over millions of years, and 9 percent said we developed without a god; 4 percent were undecided. The Associated Press conclusion was that facts change no one's mind.*

The Catholic Word Book (a pamphlet containing excerpts from the *Catholic Almanac;* see note on p. 16) defines faith as "the assent of the mind to truths revealed by God, the assent being made with the help of grace and by command of the will on account of the authority and trustworthiness of God revealing." The rule of faith is similarly defined as belief that "must be professed in the divinely revealed truths in the Bible and tradition as interpreted and proposed by the infallible teaching authority of the Church." Those who do not believe based on faith or revealed truth are pagans.

Arizona Republic, April 25, 1992.

Faith is a tribute to stubbornness in the face of facts. We are noted for our inability to accept facts that run counter to our beliefs, and this is unlikely to change.

When scientific facts fail to conform to the Bible, the Christian churches claim the facts are false. Some of us pity Muslims who believe the Koran is divinely inspired, and we defend Salman Rushdie. If Rushdie skewered the Bible similarly, however, many Christians would demand censorship and some would call for death to the heretic.

Throughout history, where the Bible has ruled, the populace has been uneducated. In 1570, for instance, Philip II forbade Spanish citizens to study outside of Spain, fearing Protestant influence; Spanish universities became no more than facades. All writings were censored. Shakespeare was scissored apart; adverse references to the Church and its heroes were deleted. As late as 1800 there were few elementary schools in Spain. In 1896, only 30 percent of Spanish adults could read, and as late as 1927 a woman was sentenced to two and a half years in prison for saying "The Virgin Mary had other children after the birth of Jesus."* She had impiously relied upon Luke 2:7 and Galatians 1:19. In 1910 the Church still prohibited education for women on the grounds that education would harm them. Only by legally separating church and state has any form of government contained the excesses of the Christian churches.

Comparing religion to science, religion attempts to control without understanding, while science advances solely through understanding. A theologian gains "knowledge" through divine revelation, which constitutes absolute truth and, because everything is known, justifies a closed mind. *The Catholic Word Book* defines theology as "knowledge of God and religion, deriving from and based on the data of divine Revelation, organized and systematized according to some kind of scientific method." Theology, though, constitutes the opposite of a scientific method; a true scientist is required always to be open-minded and accepts only truths that are proven.

Knowledge is normally defined as being based on evidence that establishes fact, not on belief without evidence. If religion had not controlled human society for the last five thousand years, the human race would be advanced far beyond its present state of knowledge and science. Because the Bible teaches that the end is near, religion has never thought it appropriate to find out about the natural world. As stated by Caliph Omar when offered the remnants of the great Greek library at Alexandria, "If the books agree with the Koran, the Word of God, they are useless and need not be preserved; if they disagree with it, they are pernicious. Let them be destroyed." Fortunately, other Muslim leaders preserved Greek literature.

When the movable printing press was invented in the 1500s the Church required permits to print books for several centuries thereafter. The Index Expurgatorius banned all books not acceptable to the Church. Of course, censorship has never been confined to the Catholic Church but has been practiced equally by all religions.

*G. G. Colton, *Inquisition and Liberty* (1938).

Luther called Aristotle, "a devil . . . a wicked sycophant, a prince of darkness . . . a beast, a most horrid imposter on mankind . . . this twice execrable Aristotle," all because of Aristotle's scientific method.

When the Church suppressed the scientific method, Islam exercised scientific leadership. Nobel Peace Prize winner Naguib Mahfouz, points out:

> In our victorious battle against Byzantium, [Islam] gave back its prisoners of war in return for a number of books of the ancient Greek heritage in philosophy, medicine, and mathematics. This is a testimony to the human spirit's demand for knowledge, even though the demander was a believer in God and what was demanded was the fruit of a pagan civilization.

The Christian churches still hold that truth is available only through divine revelation.

The steam engine was originally invented by Hero, a mathematician in 100 B.C.E., but all scientific progress was halted with the advent of Christianity and for centuries after; the steam engine was finally reinvented in the 1750s by James Watt. Alexandrian mathematicians proved that all objects fall toward the center of the earth; this was not rediscovered until Newton in the seventeenth century. The study of physics was outlawed by Pope Alexander in 1163. Francis Bacon was excommunicated and imprisoned for discovering that many things attributed to demons were naturally caused. His discovery of the telescope and microscope was suppressed for centuries.

Galileo escaped burning at the stake, his sentence being commuted to life in prison, because he stated under threat of the stake:

> I, Galileo, being in my 70th year, being a prisoner and on my knees, and before your Eminences, having before my eyes the Holy Gospel, which I touch with my hands, adjure, curse and detest the error and the heresy of the movement of the earth [that it revolved around the sun instead of being the center of the universe as taught by the infallible Catholic Church].

Galileo was tried twice during the Roman Inquisition, and his investigation was reopened by the Church in 1980. His innocence was announced by Pope John Paul II at a meeting of the Pontifical Academy of Sciences on Halloween 1992.

The Catholic Church began its index of banned books in 1538 by order of Pope Paul IV. The ban carried the death penalty for any bookseller violating it and was enforced in Spain until 1804. Many books had been banned before the Index was begun. By 1534 no book could be printed without Church permission. Licenses were prohibited for printing translations of the Bible. All libraries were expurgated. In addition to Spain, the Index was enforced in Belgium, Bavaria, Portugal, Italy, France, and Germany. Italian science was the world leader before the adoption of the Index; it never recovered its preeminence. In 1619 Kepler was banned. Dante and Galileo were censored; many authors were hanged or burned. The Index also banned all works by Dumas, Hobbes, Hume, More,

Proudhon, and Voltaire, as well as selected works by Descartes, Kant, Locke, Mill, Rousseau, Spinoza, Darwin, Defoe, Gibbon, Flaubert, Montaigne, Montesquieu, Diderot, Zola, and Stendahl.

Religiously inspired censorship continues today. On June 26, 1990, the Vatican issued *Instruction on the Ecclesial Vocation of the Theologian,* concluding that the church has suffered "serious harm" from criticism, the Congregation for the Doctrine of the Faith ordering Catholic theologians to uphold its teachings or keep quiet: "To succumb to the temptation of dissent . . . is to allow the leaven of infidelity to the Holy Spirit to start to work." On December 13, 1990, over four hundred Catholic theologians charged the Vatican with denigrating women's rights ("feminism is consistently viewed with suspicion"), slowing the ecumenical drive for Christian unity, and undermining the college of bishops. This response came partially as a result of the Vatican requiring a loyalty oath, treating dissent as defiance, and requiring candidates for bishop to be "screened to insure their unqualified opposition to the ordination of women." The Catholic Theological Society of America reacted by accusing the Vatican of unfairly restricting the free speech rights of women and the American Church. The San Francisco archbishop responded by suggesting that free speech is far less important then the impact on the faithful of criticism directed at the Vatican.

In Dayton, Ohio, the founder of the Victory Bible Church in 1990 announced plans to hold an annual celebration by burning books authored by Muslims and Jehovah's Witnesses, along with pornography and "satanic paraphenalia." The church distributed flyers urging residents to collect such books, including those on New Age religions, witchcraft, yoga, transcendental meditation, Christian Science, horoscopes, playing cards, secular albums, tapes, and bumper stickers. The pastor said he didn't care whether his bonfire offended everyone in the city: "What God says is what's important to me."

My Friend Flicka was excised from fifth- and sixth-grade reading lists after parents in Green Cove Springs, Florida, complained it contained vulgar language, specifically referring to a female dog as a "bitch" and using the word "damn." Another children's book, *Abel's Island,* was removed from the list because it referred to drinking wine. The books most often removed from library and school bookshelves in the United States are, in order of frequency, *Catcher in the Rye,* by J. D. Salinger; *The Grapes of Wrath* and *Of Mice and Men,* by John Steinbeck; *Go Ask Alice,* an anonymous work; *Forever,* by Judy Blume; *Our Bodies, Ourselves,* by the Boston Women's Healthbook Collective; *The Adventures of Huckleberry Finn,* by Mark Twain; *The Learning Tree,* by Gordon Parks; *My Darling, My Hamburger,* by Paul Zindel; and *1984,* by George Orwell.

The United Methodist Church in April 1992, through its Board of Pensions, approved action to pressure Kmart Corp. to remove "adult" books and magazines from its subsidiary corporation, Waldenbooks. The Board also filed a resolution that officials of ITT Sheraton and the Marriot Corp. were inappropriately allowing "risque" movies to be shown on in-room channels in the firms' hotels and motels, as was Time Warner on Cinemax cable-TV.

*   *   *

The field of medicine has also suffered because of religious censorship. Medicine in the eyes of the Catholic Church consisted of holy relics, which were (and are) used to generate revenues. The Church resented any scientific advance that would depreciate its income from these bits of bone and hair. Relics are described in *The Catholic Word Book:*

> The physical remains and effects of saints, which are considered worthy of veneration inasmuch as they are representative of persons in glory with God. First class relics are parts of the bodies of saints, and instruments of their penance and death; second class relics are objects which had some contact with their persons.

In the fourteenth century, Pope Pius V ordered doctors excommunicated if a priest was not associated with their medical treatments. Upon excommunication the practice of medicine was forbidden because the Church controlled the state. Surgery was opposed because it interfered with the pureness of the body on resurrection day.

Jews and Muslims developed medicine during the Middle Ages. The plague was blamed on the Jews because their doctors taught sanitation and fewer Jews died. Accordingly, the Jews were executed for hexing Christians and causing the plague. Luther declared, "Satan produces all the maladies which inflict mankind." It was considered heretical to use quinine to treat malaria or to inoculate for the prevention of smallpox. Muslims had discovered inoculations but they were condemned by the Catholic Church.

Religion hasn't changed. Children of Christian Scientists die yearly because their parents believe in miracles and prayer and refuse to allow medical doctors to attend their illnesses and diseases. During 1989 and 1990 Christian Scientists were convicted of involuntary manslaughter, felony child abuse, or child endangerment in Arizona, California, Florida, and Massachusetts for withholding medical treatment from their children. An international spokesman for the sect claimed these criminal cases interfered with the First Amendment guarantee of religious liberty. Defense co-counsel in the Massachusetts case said, "We're literally talking about the extinction of a religion through this prosecution." The Church ran a two-page ad in a Boston newspaper headlined, "WHY IS PRAYER BEING PROSECUTED IN BOSTON?" A 1989 *Journal of the American Medical Association* article concluded that Christian Scientists die younger than the rest of the population, based on a study tracing the medical records of 30,000 plus members over a period of fifty years.

An unemployed couple in Wilkes-Barre, Pennsylvania, was convicted of third-degree murder in 1989 for starving their fourteen-year-old son to death during a six-week fast while they set aside four thousand dollars for God. The family stopped eating on November 22, 1988, and their son died on January 3, 1989. Their twelve-year-old daughter recovered and was placed in foster care. They received probation, as do most parents who refuse medical treatment to their dying children or who starve them to death. Such is the reverence with which organized religion is regarded in this country.

Jehovah's Witnesses refuse blood transfusions, according to one elder, because they are "a preview of the sacrifice Jesus would make, shedding his blood. . . . The sanctity of blood transcends our view of life itself. We feel it's that important not to compromise."* A Witness willingly accepting a blood transfusion is excommunicated.

Because we will never be in complete control of our environment, religion will always have its place. We all have a craving to understand, to trust our secular and religious leaders, and to believe they know what is good for us better than we do. Religion is an explanation to adults such as adults give to children. Religion achieves security by promising infallibility and demanding belief in it. All religions cannot have the mysteries of existence perfectly deciphered, but each and every one of them assures us with perfect seriousness that it knows all there is to know about the origins of the universe, the meaning of life, and the purpose of humans on earth. With the hundreds of religious denominations, minor religions, and sects in the world, the chances of picking the one true religion are hundreds against us. The pope in March of 1989, at a meeting with American Bishops, described the Catholic attitude in terms that would apply to any religion: "We are the guardians of something given, and given to the Church Universal; something which is not the result of reflection, however competent, on cultural and social questions of the day, and is not merely the best path among many, but the one and only path to salvation."

Not only is the infallible single road to salvation the foundation of almost all organized religions, it is the basis for religious wars since time immemorial. Ecumenical leaders urged efforts to end the "cold war" among religions, as did Protestant, Jewish, and Catholic representatives at a Los Angeles conference in February of 1990. A Methodist theologian at the conference said ending the "war" could be accomplished by bringing out "new overlaps among our faiths." A Jewish leader said, "The creation of a world at peace was one of the foundation stones of both Judaism and Christianity," which is being undermined by the "cold war." Because all religions are infallible by definition, the ending of this "cold war" continues to be infinitely more difficult than ending the simple one between the West and the Communist bloc.

As summarized by Ingersoll:

> Every church pretends to have found the exact truth. This is the end of progress. Why pursue that which you have? Why investigate when you know? Every creed is a rock in running water: humanity sweeps by it. Every creed cries to the universe, "Halt!" A creed is the ignorant Past bullying the enlightened Present.

---

*Cox News Service, *Arizona Republic,* June 30, 1990.

Except for purposes of entertainment, only truth has value. There's no subject too sacred to investigate or understand. The inhibition of the search for truth in any area of life is an inhibition to the progress of the species. We shouldn't reject fact on the orders of any person, whether king, president, or pope. No ideas are sacred but should all be subject to investigation and debate. The truth should not require us to cringe or bow in fear, to pray or to praise. Truth is. It can extinguish the flames of hell, the hypocrisy of fear, and the repetition of sacred shibboleths.

Sex, Women, Homosexuality, and Religion

There's no clear relationship between religious affiliation and sexual preferences or practices; for religion and the religious, most aspects of sex are considered the equivalent of sin. Most conservative or fundamental religions are against sex education, masturbation, coitus outside of marriage, coitus within marriage unless for procreation, prostitution, birth control, homosexuality, and divorce. Many religions instead favor celibacy, frigidity, and impotence.

The American adult population has an average of seven sex partners after age 18, while divorced adults have an average of 13 sex partners, according to a University of Chicago survey conducted in 1988 and 1989. Boys age 15 to 19 have already had an average of six sex partners. An eighteen-year study by the Centers for Disease Control found that girls ages 15 to 19 increased their premarital sexual activity between 1970 and 1988 from 28.6 percent to 51.5 percent; 25.6 percent of 15-year-old girls have sex, increasing to 75.3 percent for 19-year-olds. The religious crusade against sex education isn't working and can never work. Humans are sexual animals as illustrated by the fact that 47 percent of men and 26 percent of women enjoy sex more than money. The gulf between religion and reality is enormous though religion always tries to make us less sexual.

The Catholic Word Book defines "chastity" as "properly ordered behavior with respect to sex," and "virginity" as "embraced for the love of God by religious with a public vow or by others with a private vow, [and] singled out for high praise by Christ (Mt. 19:10–12) and has always been so regarded by the Church." The practical impact of the religious attitude toward sex was illustrated by a letter to Ann Landers in August 1989 where the writer complained that her husband liked sex just prior to leaving for mass and she couldn't do that because it had connotations of sin, even within marriage.

The historical role of women in all churches has been subserviency. Men rule women as chattels in the Bible. "Unto woman he said, I will greatly multiply thy sorrow and thy conception; in sorrow thou shalt bring forth children, and thy desire shall be to thy husband, and he shall rule over thee" (Genesis 3:16). Lest we believe this attitude is restricted to the Old Testament, see also 1 Peter 3:1–7, Ephesians 5:22–24, and 1 Timothy 2:8–14.

As summarized by the Women's Caucus of the Harvard Divinity School, "Since very early in the Christian era the churches have clearly been among the most powerful of the societal forces for subduing women and keeping them in their place."* The New Testament bears testimony: "Let a woman learn in silence, with all submissiveness. I permit no woman to teach or to have authority over men; she is to keep silent" (1 Timothy 2:11–12). Women are explicitly forbidden to preach or to speak in church:

> Let your women keep their silence in the churches; for it is not permitted unto them to speak; but they are commanded to be under obedience, as also saith the Law. And if they will learn any thing, let them ask their husbands at home: for it is a shame for women to speak in the church.
>
> 1 Corinthians 14:34–35

Many churches counsel battered women to remain with their abusive husbands. A San Clemente, California, woman said, "They asked, 'Has your husband committed adultery?' I said, 'No.' They said, 'Then God will not release you.' " Women considering leaving husbands who beat them are quoted scripture from Ephesians and 1 Peter instructing them to submit to their husbands.†

What is the biblically mandated purpose of women? "Neither was the man created for the woman; but the woman for the man." This is similar to women's place in Islam and in Islam heaven, to serve at the pleasure of man. Anwar Sadat (assassinated in 1981) earmarked thirty seats in the Egyptian Parliament for women, but the reservation was rescinded under pressure from Muslim fundamentalists, who labeled his widow, Jehan Sadat, an "atheist" and "enemy of the family." Only fourteen women served in the Egyptian Parliament in 1989, compared to thirty-four when Sadat was president. Other reforms protecting women in matters of marriage and divorce were struck down by the Egyptian Supreme Court in 1985 as contrary to the Koran, though they were reinstated after extensive protest. Saudia Arabia issues no driver's licenses to women, because car-driving by women "contradicts the Islamic traditions followed by Saudi citizens," according to its Interior Ministry. After the United States relocated 400,000 Gulf War troops in Saudi Arabia, many of whom were women who drove, forty-nine defiant Saudi women drove cars in Riyadh, resulting in threats of serious punishment. Six were suspended from their teaching positions at King Saud University. Jehan Sadat points out that Islamic restrictions on women are based on Arab traditions and not on the Koran, which "gave women rights 1400 years ago that many Western women acquired only in the past 100 years, such as the right to be educated, to own and sell property, or to keep their own names after they marry." But Arab traditions continue, such as reflected in Col. Moammar Gadhafi's statement to Jehan Sadat that woman's societal role is "no different than that of cows who are destined to become pregnant, give birth and suckle their young."

All religions codified societal attitudes toward women when their holy books

---

*Gail B. Shulman, ed., *View from the Back of the Synagogue: Sexist Religion and Women in the Church* (1977).

†Tracy Weber, *Arizona Republic,* March 1993.

were written between 1,300 and 5,000 years ago; it's difficult to update the word of God.

Woman has been treated as the scapegoat for the troubles of the secular and religious worlds since the "beginning":

> For Adam was first formed, then Eve. And Adam was not deceived, but the woman being deceived was in the transgression. Notwithstanding she shall be saved in childbearing, if they continue in faith and charity and holiness with sobriety.
>
> 1 Timothy 2:13–15

Because woman originated the sin of the world by taking the apple from the serpent, she's responsible for the world's woes.

Consider the impact of God saying to young girls through the holiest of holy books that they are fit only for bearing children and keeping their mouths closed, always subservient to the male. These teachings are reinforced by parents, Sunday school teachers, and the minister; they govern behavior related to sex, including marriage, divorce, contraception, and sexual relations. Why have women taken several thousand years to progress toward equality with men? Equality is far from realized, even in Christian countries such as the United States.

Historians trace a direct relationship among the Judaic patriarchal family structure, the concept of women as chattels (Exodus 22:16), and the double standard giving men sexual freedom and none to women. The characterization of women in the Bible is black and white, good woman and bad woman, temptress and virgin; the distinction is sexual activity.

The role of Jewish women in a patriarchal society and in the synagogue is subjection; their place is in the home. The status of women in Judaism is that of "other," unclean or sinful. Judaism is dominated by men and admits of no unflawed heroic women; as hard as God tried he couldn't create an obedient woman. Women in the Bible are greedy, slothful, envious, frivolous, coquettish, gossipy, jealous, light-fingered gadabouts. (See Isaiah 3:16 and Genesis 18:10, 30:1, 31:19, 34:1.) The near-heroic women featured in these texts are belittled. Jewish women are raised to be wives and mothers; not adult human beings.

The Jewish male's morning prayer is "Blessed art thou, O Lord our God, King of the Universe who has not made me a woman." The corresponding female prayer ends in, "who has made me according to Thy will." The prayer for a newborn male is for "Torah, marriage and good works"; the female prayer is for "reverence, marriage and good works." Women cannot lead Orthodox services or read from the Torah. In many synagogues men and women sit separately. Women are body and men are spirit. Some of this inequality arose from the difference in marriageable ages—twelve and a half for women but late teens or twenties for men. In Talmudic times women referred to their husbands as "Rabbi," a term used by a slave or student to refer to the master; men referred to their wives as "my daughter."

A preoccupation with menstruation permeates Judaism. An Orthodox Jewish woman may have no contact with her husband during her menstruation, and he is forbidden on pain of sin to look on her face or form and must daily thank God he was not born a woman. These aren't relics of a barbaric past but the facts of everyday Orthodox Jewish life. Vivian Gornick describes what must be the thoughts of a Jewish woman in the study of an Orthodox rabbi:

> Why, in this room I am a pariah, a Yahoo. If the rabbi should but look upon my face, vile hot desire would enter his being and endanger the salvation of his sacred soul; when my body discharges its monthly portion of blood and waste, he dare not even pass over to me an object that will touch my hand, much less sleep with me if I am his wife, for that monthly waste in me is disgusting, and it makes me disgusting. It is offal, dung, filth. It reminds him of what no holy man ever wishes to be reminded; that he is matter as well as spirit. So he has made a bargain with God and constructed a religion in which I am all matter and he is all spirit; I am . . . the human sacrifice offered up for his salvation . . . so that the strength of concentrated spirituality will course through his veins.*

Most primitive societies regard a menstruating woman as possessed by evil spirits; her power to attract men is thought to increase supernaturally. Women since pre-cave days were segregated during menstruation. The religious ideas conceived in these early times reflect our primitive beliefs, such as in Bali today where menstruating women are forbidden to enter places of worship.

Our earliest recorded creation myth is from Babylon; the goddess Nammu (the "sea") created the universe by giving birth to the earth and the heavens. Nammu later evolved to Tiamat (the "salt-water ocean"), who was aided by Apsu (the "sweet-water ocean") to birth all there was, which included demons, scorpion men, and centaurs. Tiamat, possibly because of her irregular birthing habits, was slain by Marduk, the god of Babylon when ruled by Hammurabi. When the male was discovered as necessary to procreation, the dominant goddesses were overthrown by male gods. By the Roman period religion was a branch of government, where as a practical matter it remains today.

Woman evolved from the tiller of the soil (man was the hunter) and the earth mother to become a chattel of the male. Women were first chattels of their fathers, then of their husbands, and finally of their sons. The oldest profession was not prostitution but priesthood. Priests eventually became the procurers of prostitutes operating from the temples.

No stigma was attached to prostitution in Sumerian times. Prostitutes provided much of the temple income and were required to advertise: "A common harlot shall not veil herself [as other women]; her head shall be uncovered. Anyone who sees a common harlot veiled shall arrest her. They shall beat her fifty strokes with rods, and they shall pour pitch on her head."†

---

*Gail B. Shulman, *View from the Back of the Synagogue* (1974).
†Reah Tannahill, *Sex in History* (1980).

The Egyptians finally banned prostitutes from their temples; meanwhile Solomon had seven hundred marriages and wives. Augustine said prostitution was shameful and immodest but necessary: "Yet remove prostitutes from human affairs, and you will pollute all things with lust; set them among honest matrons, and you will dishonor all things with disgrace and turpitude." Thomas Aquinas opined, "Take away prostitutes from the world, and you will fill it with sodomy." Thus continued temple prostitution in Europe, limited to servicing Christians.

The Greeks invented lusty gods. Aphrodite was born from the foam on a wave of semen and bore Hermaphrodite, who sported both male and female sex organs, and Priapus, who was always erect. Heracles bedded fifty virgins in one night, including his nephew Jolaus and "Hylas, he of curling locks." Pederasty was preferred with sixteen-year-old boys but banned with boys under age twelve. The older male mentor teaching young lads was the basis for higher Greek education from 600 to 400 B.C.E., as it also was in Buddhist Japan in the tenth century C.E. Plato's ideal of love was based on pederasty. Women in Greece were second-class/slaves, permitted neither political nor legal rights. The Greek female gods were all flawed, similar to the women in the Old Testament. However, the Greeks invented dildos for female pleasure and began formal acceptance of lesbians.

Rome recognized three types of marriage, with the lowest level being valid or dissolved at the male's option after a year's trial; this is the foundation for our Valentine's Day. After three days' abstinence, the trial marriage could begin anew without further commitment. Vestal virgins were required to remain chaste to insure military victories. When Rome was defeated at Cannae in 216 B.C.E., six vestal virgins were sacrificed. By 200 B.C.E. divorce was easily obtained by ordinary men and women, women having attained emancipation. Divorce was impractical for men because they would be required to repay the woman's dowry to her father. Then came Christianity.

Constantine's declaration of Christianity as the official religion in 316 C.E. was a political move to unite the decaying Empire, and it worked, though not to the benefit of Rome. Less than one hundred years later in 410, Rome was sacked by Alaric the Great, imposing the Dark Ages until the Renaissance. The Church became the Empire and confirmed itself as the true successor to imperialistic Rome when it began the Crusades. The historic threads of Christianity were Babylonian realism, Hebrew absolutism, Greek Platonism, and Roman material-ism, resulting in Christian realistic forgiveness, an absolute single god, platonic dualism, and money-seeking materialism. During the Dark Ages only the Church was able to enforce law and order, through threats of hellfire. Only Church leaders could read or write, which resulted in censorship, then called revealed truth. Sin was based not on New Testament concepts but on the writings of Jerome and Augustine, who reacted to the excesses of the Roman Empire. Jerome urged celibacy for all, which was considered ascetic compared to Roman sexual perfidy and materialism. He wrote in the fourth century, "I should like every man to take a wife who cannot manage to sleep alone because he gets frightened at night." People responded by embracing celibacy. Origen of Alexandria castrated himself in response to Matthew 19:12, which instructs men to "make themselves eunuchs for the kingdom of heaven's sake."

The best-selling nonfiction book in 1990 Germany and Italy was *Eunuchs for the Kingdom of Heaven* by Uta Ranke-Heinemann. The title paraphrases the passage in Matthew quoted above, which is the Catholic basis for requiring celibate priests but which Ranke-Heinemann says refers to adultery and has nothing to do with priests. The author concludes that church leaders from Augustine to Pope John Paul II are "bachelors and celibates who have twisted the original meaning of the Catholic faith. Today there are many people who laugh at them, who no longer believe what they say. And I ask you, whose fault is that?" Ranke-Heinemann bases her book on research showing that the Church degrades women, glorifies a twisted celibacy cult, and interferes in the sexual relationships of married couples. Cardinal John O'Connor of New York, though admitting he'd not read the book, called it "dirty" and "preposterous," saying, "it's time we stopped buying the line of purveyors of hatred and scandal and malice and libel and calumny" and that he was "sick of their perversions," likening the book to "scrawling dirty words about the church on bathroom walls."

St. Paul called celibacy superior to marriage and denounced prostitution because in sex "the two shall become one flesh" (1 Corinthians 6:15–16). Paul concluded it was better to marry than to burn with desire but advised married couples to abstain from sex for one season a year in order to better enjoy prayer. The Church held that men from the waist down and all of women were the product of Satan. Christian folk legends called sex "an experiment of the serpent" and marriage "a foul and polluted way of life." (Both Jerome and Augustine were former sinners who had lusted after women. Augustine had prayed, "Give me chastity—but not yet.") The Church fathers called intercourse fundamentally disgusting: "filthy and degrading" (Arnobus), "unseemly" (Methodius), "unclean" (Jerome), "shameful" (Tertullian) and "a defilement" (Ambrose). The Church regarded sex as acceptable only before the fall; pre-fall sex in the Garden of Eden was considered cool and mechanical for the dual purposes of procreating and showing appreciation for the act of creation. The sin of eating the apple from the tree of knowledge caused selfish impulses in humankind, which, as a result, seeks filthy sexual pleasure and lust without control. Upon expulsion from the Garden we became aware of our nakedness and covered it to avoid willful activities by our genitals, requiring fig leaves to cover the pudenda, which derived from the Latin *pudere,* "to be ashamed." Every act of coitus was sinful, and resulting children were born into sin. Accordingly, Jesus was required to be born free of sin, without there being an act of sex, *ergo* the virgin birth and the Virgin Mary.

In 386 C.E. Pope Siricius decreed no intercourse between priests and their wives, to no avail. Abstinence orders by the Church were lost in Church corruption; but by the eleventh century Gregory VII was able to prohibit clerical marriage. The German priests declared they'd rather give up their lives than their wives, and they did. Still, the unenforceable Church rules on celibacy were ignored by most. The Church blamed families on Satan, calling children a bitter pleasure and denigrating wives as weak, slow, unstable, deceitful, and untrustworthy. A virtuous husband rejected his wife's advances, and vice versa. The Church decreed that sex was unnecessary to marriage, though it allowed for procreation if not practiced frequently. The devout were required to abstain on Thursdays in memory of Jesus' arrest, on Fridays in memory of Jesus' death, on Saturdays in memory of the Virgin Mary, on Sundays in memory of the resurrection, and on Mondays in commemoration of the dead. Tuesdays and Wednesdays were largely wiped out with the ban on intercourse during feasts, festivals, the forty days before Easter, Pentecost, and Christmas, and the seven, five, or three days before Communion, ad celibacious. The admonition in the Old Testament to "be fruitful and multiply" was interpreted to help hurry along the Messiah. Since he had already arrived, there was no more need for sex. Also, with the Christian era, women found themselves with the added burden that divorce had been prohibited.

Required celibacy of priests has been reaffirmed by the 1990s Church as a "countercultural force," showing there's more to life than the pursuit of pleasure. Pope John Paul II instructed priests in October 1991 to "follow the path that Jesus Christ opened, embracing voluntarily and joyfully the gift of priestly celibacy."*

A twenty-five-year study released in August of 1990 based on interviews with 1500 people, however, revealed that about 40 percent of U.S. priests ignore their vows of celibacy.† According to the study, done by R. W. Richard Sipes, a former priest, 20 percent pursue heterosexual behavior, 10 to 13 percent are homosexually active, and 6 percent are involved with minors. One-third of those interviewed were priests undergoing psychotherapy, one-third were priests sharing their stories in workshops or informally, and one-third were lovers of priests. The study also found that only half of priests generally support the idea of celibacy, and only 2 percent fully achieve it because of required abstinence from masturbation. Secular psychology deems sex as normal, healthy, and necessary to well-being.‡ The International Synod of Bishops stated in response that celibacy shows there is "more to life than the pursuit of personal satisfaction." Up to 23 percent of priests are homosexually oriented, though only half those are active sexually.

Celibacy and loneliness cause many priests to abandon their parishes. Chicago is the largest archdioscese in the United States and loses one priest every eighteen days; it lost twenty-five in the first six months of 1990. In thirty years the number of priests in training has dropped by 89 percent. Prof. Richard McBrien of Notre Dame University notes the celibacy rule, which is man-made, has become more important than the Eucharist. Celibacy, however, has been required of priests since the Second Lateran Council of 1139, the same Council that began the Roman Inquisition. As a result of the exit of priests, by 1990 there were three hundred U.S. parishes under lay pastors, most of whom were nuns or married women.

In 1991 the Archbishop of Milwaukee picked a married layman to head a parish and asked the pope's permission to ordain the layman. Although Pope John Paul II has repeatedly declared that only celibate men may become priests, the Archbishop said he saw "no other way out of this very difficult situation"

---

*Los Angeles Times, Arizona Republic, October 16, 1991.
†Associated Press, Arizona Republic, August 12, 1990.
‡See Richard Sipes, A Secret World: Sexuality and the Search for Celibacy (1990).

than the ordination of married men, which is preferable to closing or merging parishes to form megaparishes or to assigning priests as circuit riders. The archdiocese's projected 26 percent decline in the number of priests by the year 2000 is less drastic than that faced in many other dioceses, and far better than the situation in some traditionally Catholic countries such as Brazil.

On October 15, 1991, while visiting Brazil, Pope John Paul II reaffirmed priestly celibacy, though of 4,000 priests ordained in Brazil in the 1980s, only 1,500 remain. The main reason given for leaving the priesthood was to marry. The United States has one priest for every 1,500 Catholics while the ratio in Brazil is one for every 8,000. The rapid growth of Protestant sects in Brazil was blamed by the pope for the priest shortage. Brazilian archbishop Cardinal Aloinsio Lorscheider called priestly celibacy an "anacronism" while Pope John Paul II told Brazilian seminarians to "follow the path that Jesus Christ opened, embracing voluntarily and joyfully the gift of priestly celibacy."

Catholics under Communist rule in Czechoslovakia were served by "secret priests," many of whom were married to help conceal their double existence. Under former Czechoslovakian law, holding religious instruction was deemed "a hindrance to state control of the church" and carried a two-year jail sentence. The married "secret priests" are now rejected by the Vatican while it supports their pro-Communist colleagues. Prague's Bishop Miloslav Vlk calls the "secret priests" "somewhat exalted people who overestimated the tragedy of the situation [under Communist rule] and overreacted to it." These priests, former bulwarks of the Church, remain abandoned though hundreds of parishes are vacant because of a shortage of un- married priests. The only hope for the "secret priests" is to convert to the Greek Orthodox Church, which permits priests to marry. In March 1992, the ordination of married Czech priests was revoked by the Vatican via pastoral letter.

May 1992 surveys in the United States and Ireland found that 75 percent of U.S. Catholics favored expanding the priesthood "to include married priests" (up from 58 percent in 1983 and 49 percent in 1971) while 79 percent of Irish Catholics said priests should be allowed to marry. Only 17 percent of Irish Catholics opined that priests should remain single and chaste with half those questioned saying they'd lost some confidence in the church when it was revealed that a popular bishop had fathered a child in the United States.

The ancient Christian prohibition against women teachers was reiterated by the Vatican in 1977, which stated it didn't "consider herself [sic] authorized to admit women to priestly ordination," refusing to consider the Virgin Mary as the equivalent of an Apostle, stating that only priests have a "natural resemblance" to Jesus Christ and that for a female priest "it would be difficult to be seen in the minister the image of Christ." St. Paul stated that because Eve had beguiled Adam to sin, her wages were silence forever.

The ordination of women is a controversial subject in most religions. Although the Catholic Church prohibits female priests, the monthly magazine *U.S. Catholic* found that 76 percent of its readers would welcome female priests, a third felt perpetuating an all-male priesthood was sinful, and 69 percent felt Jesus would have ordained women. A majority of the respondents were women. A priest who invited three women to celebrate mass with him in a Minneapolis Catholic Church because he felt women were treated unfairly by the Church was barred from further priestly duties and threatened with excommunication for himself and the three women.

Seventh-day Adventist women leaders in Denver urged members to stop tithing to the church until it agreed to ordain women, offering to hold tithes in an escrow account until ordination of women was approved. The women concluded that the "bottom line is green." Many Adventist women in Denver started attending other churches or stopped tithing.

The first woman ordained in the United States was a Congregational Church minister in 1853. Women in 1990 made up 8 percent of the clergy, almost doubling the figure from a decade ago. Women make up 40 percent of seminary enrollments. The highest numbers of women have been ordained, in numerical order, by Assemblies of God, Salvation Army, United Church of Christ, and the United Methodists. Questions still arise, however, over whether a female pastor can conduct funerals without crying (would a few tears from the minister hurt?), preach every week, and manage a family. Few women have risen to levels of preeminence, instead being accepted primarily in associate roles, as pastors in smaller churches or as ministers of music. Female pastors also report the expectation that a good pastor must be neglecting her family. Congregants often expect the clergywoman to bake cookies for church events and participate in women's circles.

The first Lutheran female bishop was ordained in Hamburg, Germany, in April 1992, which critics say could lead to schism. Bishop Maria Jesper was consecrated in the summer of 1992 as the leader of the 950,000 Lutherans, constituting 95 percent of Hamburg Protestants. The Rev. Edgar Spir quoted St. Paul's injunction against women speaking in church and vowed his own early retirement.

The ordination of female priests by the Australian Church by April 1992, threatened a schism in that church. The General Synod of the 3.7 million member Church considered in the summer of 1992 whether to allow any of the Church's twenty-four dioceses to secede if they object to female priests. The Perth diocese had ordained ten female priests earlier in 1992, though the Sydney Diocese's evangelicals had argued that it was wrong for women to have authority over men in the family or in church.

The Church of England voted in mid-November 1992 to allow female priests, though the measure must still be passed by the British Parliament, which is expected in early 1994. A thousand priests responded by threatening resignation. The Vatican called the action "a new and grave obstacle to the entire process of reconciliation with the [Roman] Catholic Church."*

The Catholic Church historically recognized a single allowable position for intercourse, male dominant. Other positions were deemed too animalistic, failing to confirm male dominance or suspected of retarding conception. Pleasurable intercourse was sinful, as stated by Benedicti, echoing St. Jerome, in his *La Somme des Pechez* (1601): "The husband who, transported by immoderate love, has inter-

---

*Jill Serjeant, Reuters, *Arizona Republic,* Nov. 12, 1992.

course with his wife so ardently in order to satisfy his passion that even had she not been his wife, he would have wished to have commerce with her, is committing a sin."

Contraception was also considered a major sin, equivalent to murder and requiring penances ranging in length from three to twelve years. Oral and anal intercourse were considered contraception methods. Coitus interruptus required two to ten years penance. Penances required fasting (bread and water only) and abstinence from sex and other pleasures. Abortion was considered slightly less sinful if accomplished within forty days of conception, after which the fetus acquired a human soul. Because abortion was highly dangerous it was considered to carry its own penalty; still, St. Jerome called women procuring abortions "threefold murderesses: as suicides, as adulteresses to their holy bridegroom Christ, and as murderesses of their still unborn child."

Men raping or seducing other than a virgin or married woman were counselled to use contraception and keep quiet, thus avoiding confession. Male homosexuals were condemned by Pope Gregory III as harboring "a vice so abominable in the sight of God that the cities in which its practitioners dwelt were appointed for destruction by fire and brimstone," which is a creative interpretation of Genesis 19:4–11. Christianity was combatting the favorable attitude toward homosexuality held by its predecessor, Mithraism, which had prevented its ban for hundreds of years after Christianity became the state religion.

The favored Church punishment for homosexuality was castration and display of the offender with mutilated genitals. St. Thomas Aquinas later "proved" that homosexuality was unnatural, thus lustful and heretical. His analysis was confirmed by the 1976 Vatican *Declaration on Certain Questions Concerning Sexual Ethics,* which is also followed by the United Presbyterian Church of the United States, Episcopals, and Methodists. Thus, from the fourteenth century, homosexuals have been condemned in the West. Homosexuals were banned in France longer than witches; the last homosexual bonfire in France occurred in 1725. Homosexuality carried the death penalty in Great Britian until 1861 (seldom enforced) when the penalty was reduced to ten years to life in prison, and legalized in 1967 for consenting adults, unless in the army, navy, or police.

The Christian repression of medicine has also colored Christian attitudes toward male homosexuals. The Church insisted on trust in prayer and miracles as the only legitimate means to overcome disability and disease, because disease was caused by evil spirits as a punishment from God for sin. That conclusion continues with religious support today; witness fundamentalist religious pronouncements on AIDS.

Many religious people today regard homosexuality as the gravest of sins and are homophobic, particularly in connection with AIDS. Religious leaders and other public figures justify homophobia by AIDS; AIDS allows those with an anti-gay prejudice to express it openly. The death toll from AIDS in the United States passed 100,000 in December 1990. U.S. health officials estimate that one million have been infected and from 1991 through 1993, that 200,000 will die. Twenty percent of those dying through 1990 were not gay, 14 percent were heterosexual, and 6 percent were intravenous drug users. This 14 percent figure was ignored by the American public until Magic Johnson announced his retirement from professional basketball on November 7, 1991, because he tested positive for the human immunodeficiency virus, which causes AIDS. A *Los Angeles Times* poll in November 1991 found that 99 percent of those surveyed had read or heard of Johnson's announcement. Forty-nine percent (56 percent men) felt the AIDS message should encourage safe sex for young people, while 45 percent (53 percent women) said the message should be abstinence from sex. Also in November 1991 the United States Catholic bishops rejected safe sex as a means to combat AIDS or to curb overpopulation.

By April 1992, the Centers for Disease Control found that most American high-school students have unprotected sex, though 95 percent know that unprotected sex risks AIDS. AIDS is the second leading killer of men and the fifth leading killer of women ages twenty-five to forty-four, and it is growing most rapidly among teenagers.

The pope actively condemns homosexual acts. Because the pope is infallible and in direct communication with God, his condemnation causes guilt in gays and hatred of gays. Homosexuals are held by many to be a proxy for evil and are faced with an open and intractable hatred associated with no other minority. AIDS has given bigots an excuse to express their homophobia. Psychologists believe that the largest basis for homosexual bias is a combination of fear and self-rightousness, wherein homosexuals are considered a threat to basic morality. A survey of 2,823 eighth to twelfth graders found that three-fourths of the boys and half the girls felt it would be bad to have a homosexual neighbor. Most people biased against gays rely on religious orthodoxy, which holds homosexuality to be a sin.

The Catholic Bishop for Brooklyn named in February 1990 called a gay Catholic group not morally equal to heterosexuals and barred them from using diocesan facilities. These condemnations are rooted in the Judeo-Christian heritage, driving gays from religion. Although two tenets of Western religion are unconditional goodness and love of God for all, this doesn't apply to gays. Instead, the Catholic Church has described gays as "objectively disordered" and "inclined toward evil."*

In mid-1992 the Vatican formally declared its support for discrimination against homosexuals in public housing, health-care benefits, and employment as teachers, coaches, and military personnel. The Vatican pronouncement stated that "sexual orientation does not constitute a quality comparable to race, ethnic background, etc., in respect to discrimination," even though 78 percent of U.S. Catholics in 1992 favored equal job opportunities for homosexuals, up from 58 percent in 1978, according to a Spring 1992 Gallup Poll.

In May 1990, Episcopalians became embroiled in their own gay-related controversy when a California priest attempted to bar an African bishop from speaking

---

*See Bishop Thomas Daily, *Arizona Republic,* Feb. 23, 1990; Alissa Rubin, *Arizona Republic,* Nov. 15, 1990.

when it became known that the bishop intended to condemn homosexual activity. Some argued the confrontation reflected cultural differences between third-world churches, which emphasize evangelism, morals, and fighting poverty, and American-European churches, which emphasize justice issues such as women's rights and homosexual fairness. Conservatives pointed to the incident as "a further demonstration of the rejection of the Bible as the word of God." The African bishop discussed rapid church growth in his native Kenya versus the decline in church attendance in the United States, concluding, "homosexuals and lesbians have taken over the church leadership in the U.S.A. and there is no way God is going to bless this church with growth."

In late 1992 the General Board of the National Council of Churches voted 90–81 to deny membership to the Metropolitan Community Churches, composed of 30,000, primarily gays and lesbians. The only three choices offered to gays by Western religion are to change their orientation, celibacy, and spurious heterosexual marriage. Never is a gay relationship used in religion as an example of perfect or divine love, though homosexuality is as physically natural as heterosexual relations. Instead, religion pictures gays as depraved, sinful, and shamed, as in the biblical term "sodomite," and seeks to sever gay relationships, which for gays is identical to requiring divorce. Paradoxically, gays were the spiritual leaders and shamans of civilization since ancient times, until abhorred by the Catholic Church, actively beginning in the twelfth century. They are welcomed in the West by less than 1 percent of all denominations, such as Quakers and Unitarians. Other religions and society in general treat gays in a fashion that makes them outsiders, not belonging to church, family, society, or the work place.

The Catholic church has debated long and hard whether God is punishing AIDS sufferers. The conclusion reached by bishops in Baltimore in November 1989 gave no answer, instead urging compassion for AIDS sufferers and rejecting the use of condoms or needle-exchange programs to control the spread of AIDS among intravenous drug users. The bishops concluded that chastity before marriage and fidelity within marriage are the only "morally correct and medically secure" means of preventing AIDS. Cardinal O'Connor stated, "The truth is not in condoms or clean needles. These are lies, lies perpetrated often for political reasons on the part of public health officials . . . by some health-care professionals who believe they have nothing else to offer persons with AIDS or [those] at risk . . . lies told by well-meaning counselors."*

At Pope John Paul II's AIDS conference in Vatican City, however, also in November 1989, the Rev. Rocco Buttiglione concluded that AIDS was divine punishment for immoral behavior. The pope said, "We are not far from the truth if we say that parallel to the spread of AIDS, there has been a sort of 'immunodeficiency' on the level of existential values that cannot but be identified as a real disease of the spirit." Several theologians in attendance said that if either or both parties to a marriage test positive for AIDS, the only proper course is abstinence, not condoms. In his opening address Cardinal O'Connor said,

---

*Associated Press, *Arizona Republic*, Nov. 14, 1989.

"Throughout its history, the church has always distinguished between sin and the sinner, condemning the sin and embracing the sinner."

While religion distinguishes between sin and the sinner, science has concluded that homosexuality is natural, occurring in all species. The American Psychiatric Association declassified homosexuality as a mental illness in 1973, and in 1975 the American Psychological Association resolved that "homosexuality per se implies no impairment in judgment, stability, reliability, or general social or vocational capabilities." There appears to be little difference between the psychosocial development of children raised by heterosexuals or by lesbians, according to University of Virginia psychologist and researcher Charlotte J. Patterson in the spring 1993 first issue of the American Psychological Association's *Contemporary Perspectives on Gay and Lesbian Psychology*. A 1950s study by Evelyn Hooker found that homosexuals can't be distinguished from heterosexuals on psychological tests. Research by Frederick Whitam of such diverse cultures as the United States, Central America, and the Philippines found that "homosexuality occurs at the same rates with the same kinds of behavior," concluding the source is biological. The Kinsey studies found that people fall into seven general categories of sexual orientation, ranging from exclusive preference for the same sex to exclusive preference for the opposite sex, with many in between.

Newsweek magazine asked about "The Future of Gay America" in its March 12, 1990, cover story. Sixty percent of the letters received in response were critical of gays, and 40 percent were sympathetic. A letter from Marjorie M. Otte of Altadena, California, described the rationale for the 60 percent who were anti-gay:

> You devote seven pages to homosexuality, but nowhere is it reported that the reason so many of us oppose it is that God says it is wrong and repugnant. Both the Old and New Testaments condemn homosexual activity and Christians and Jews alike have an obligation to resist its acceptance. Surely, people commit other hideous sins, but they do not take to the streets to brag about it or expect to be patted on the back or given special privileges because of it. I certainly do not think that we "straight" people should be expected to accommodate the perverted desires of homosexuals under any circumstances.

Two mainstream Protestant denominations, however, recently ordained gay ministers, Lutherans in San Francisco and Episcopalians in New Jersey. Formal disciplinary charges were filed by Bishop Lyle Miller against the Lutheran congregations for ordaining two lesbians and a gay man on January 20, 1990. A bishop speaking for the church's national offices in Chicago said such ordinations "undermine the unity" of the church, forcing it to "initiate disciplinary procedures against these congregations." The Associated Press story said the ordinations "represent a historic foothold in mainstream Christianity by homosexuals, whose sexual orientation generally has been tolerated only if it was not consummated." The gay man ordained said that as a result of the ordinations, "our lives and intimate relationships are to be honored, blessed, supported and respected." The two dissident congregations were suspended for five years from the Evangelical

Lutheran Church of America based on a report that makes the suspensions permanent on December 31, 1995, if they fail to lift their ban on "practicing homosexuals" in the clergy or the unauthorized ordinations are not rescinded.

The National Association of Evangelicals accused President Bush of "courting" the homosexual lobby when he invited gay-rights leaders to attend a White House signing of the Hate Crimes Statistics bill and the Americans with Disabilities Act. Evangelical leaders said Bush had "sacrificed" his role as upholder of traditional values and warned that if gay-rights activists succeed in making "this decade the Gay '90s in a sense totally unthinkable a century ago" that "Almighty God is either going to have to judge the United States or apologize to Sodom and Gomorrah."

President-elect Clinton announced that he would lift the military ban on gays. By mid-December 1992 the American public was equally split while the military opposed the idea by 74 percent in a *Los Angeles Times* poll released in late February 1993.*

The Episcopal ordination of a gay man on December 16, 1989, stirred great controversy. The newly reverend J. Robert Williams stated before the ceremony: "Opening the church closet is a major part of what the ministry is about. Everybody knows there are a lot of gay clergy. What's different here is telling the truth about it." The Episcopal Church had ordained a lesbian woman in 1977, but the ordination of Williams was criticized by the Episcopal Synod of America, which was founded in the summer of 1989 with six active bishops as members. Rev. Titus Cates of Fort Worth said the ordination of a practicing homosexual would represent "a rejection of the Bible as the word of God."† The Louisville-based Prayer Book Society of the Episcopal Church passed an emergency resolution on December 20, 1989, calling the ordination "specifically and directly" in conflict with a resolution adopted at the Church's 1979 General Convention, which called the ordination of gays "not appropriate." The day before the ordination, however, the presiding bishop said the referenced resolution lacked canonical force, noting the General Convention had been unable to either strengthen the resolution or reverse it. Two weeks after the ordination, the ordaining bishop expressed his "profound regret" and "deep anger" at having performed the ordination, admitting it had "caused harm to the church." Less than a month after his ordination, Williams challenged church concepts of monogamy and chastity at a Detroit symposium, causing the angry regretful remarks by Williams's former champion, the ordaining bishop, who immediately called for Williams's resignation from his position as director of a diocesan ministry to gays and lesbians and suspended Williams from all priestly activity. The bishop called Williams's remarks "intemperate and tasteless." This same week, the presiding bishop and his prelates said they "believe it is not appropriate for this church to ordain a practising homosexual or any other [sic] person who is engaged in heterosexual relations outside of

*Associated Press, *Arizona Republic*, Dec. 18, 1992; *Los Angeles Times*, *Arizona Republic*, Feb. 28, 1993.

†George W. Cornell, Associated Press, *Arizona Republic*, May 26, 1990.

marriage."

A 1991 poll of U.S. Presbyterians found that 90 percent oppose the ordination of "self-affirming, practicing homosexual persons." Two-thirds also oppose ordination of celibate homosexuals; thus, 23 percent shift to support ordination of a homosexual who doesn't have sex. The general assembly of the Presbyterian Church voted 534 to 31 in 1991 to affirm past statements declaring homosexuality wrong. The Presbyterian Church in America voted almost unanimously in 1991 that "all sexual intercourse outside of marriage, including homosexuality and lesbianism, is contrary to God's word, and is sin."

In May 1992 the Methodist Church's governing body voted 710 to 238 that homosexuality is "incompatible" with Christian teaching and the North Carolina Baptist Convention voted 59 to 28 to expel two churches that supported homosexuals. Also in May 1992, the National Council of Churches cancelled plans for meeting with a primarily homosexual denomination, the Universal Fellowship of Metropolitan Community Churches, citing the "divisiveness" of homosexuality in church and society.

After four years of debate, the largest branch of Judaism, with 1,560 rabbis and 1.5 million members, voted in June 1990 to welcome sexually active gays and lesbians as rabbis. The Reform rabbis concluded that "for many people, sexual orientation is not a matter of choice . . . and therefore not subject to change. . . . Sexual orientation is irrelevant to the human worth of a person." Opposition to the move was based on Leviticus 18:22, which says, "Thou shalt not lie with mankind, as with womankind. It is abomination." The primary opposition was based on the scriptural admonition to be fruitful and multiply. Others countered that the scriptures cannot be taken literally; otherwise prostitutes must be stoned to death.

The celibacy required of Catholic priests has also shoe-horned the Catholic Church into condoning pedophilia by refusing to investigate allegations or to condemn priests convicted of child molestation. Between 1985 and 1990, dozens of priests were charged with pedophilia-related offenses, costing the Church at least $90 million in legal claims, according to St. Paul, Minnesota, lawyer, Jeffrey Anderson. He has thirty-eight lawsuits pending against twenty-four priests in eight states. From 1982 to 1992, over 400 U.S. Catholic priests and brothers were reported to civil authorities as molesting children, resulting in over $400 million in settlements, legal fees, and therapy costs for victims and clerics.

Christians are more concerned with sexual issues other than priestly pedophilia, such as prayer and sex education in public school, birth control, nude sculpture, divorces, and television programs such as "Dallas." In March 1989 a Vatican theologian, Cardinal Eduard Gagnon, told U.S. Catholic bishops that it's crucial that Americans follow Church teaching on sexuality instead of allowing Planned Parenthood, feminism, divorce courts, and "Dallas" to dictate American tastes in sex. The meeting participants criticized divorce courts as "not fully in conformity with church law," criticized feminism as having "a deleterious effect on the family," and said theologians are recognizing "the social and moral disaster a contraceptive mentality can lead to." Planned Parenthood was accused of "encouraging promiscuity" and undermining Catholic teaching, although an estimated 80 percent of

American Catholics use birth control. Nothing was said about priestly pedophilia, though "Dallas" was accused of promoting subtle pornography.

Although same-sex marriages are not religiously sanctioned, individual churches within particular denominations consecrate the relationships of same-sex couples, including the United Methodists, the Unitarian Universalists, and the mainly homosexual metropolitan Community Church. The primary objection by some religious leaders is that certain phrases in the traditional wedding vows may be seen as equating the ceremony with "holy matrimony." The public relations officer for the United Methodist Church commented on a particular ceremony, saying, "You can always find a Methodist preacher [who] had done everything irregular there is to do."

A 1987 Gallup survey found that 64 percent of Episcopalians oppose the Church blessing same-sex relationships, while a December 1989 survey by Episcopalians United found that 88 percent oppose blessing homosexual unions. The Episcopalian Church is considered one of the more liberal Protestant denominations.

Fundamentalist religions excommunicate gays. Antonio Feliz converted from Catholicism to Mormonism when his parents told him to, and thus grew up Mormon, becoming a bishop to a Utah ward and writing speeches for then-President and Prophet Spencer Kimball. Mormons, however, consider homosexuality a chosen lifestyle and upon discovering Feliz was homosexual, excommunicated him. A spokesman for the Mormon Church commented, "Chastity before marriage and fidelity to your marriage partner during marriage—that's the Lord's standard and that's the Church's standard." Feliz points out that the Book of Mormon doesn't mention homosexuality, though it does teach tolerance and love, and that the founder of the Mormon Church, Joseph Smith, "was sealing [marrying] men to men."

The Mormon Church issued a statement in 1991 that all sexual contact outside of marriage, including "homosexual and lesbian behavior, is sinful. Those sins, though portrayed as acceptable and even normal by many in the world, are grievous in the sight of God."

The Evergreen Foundation, whose members are primarily Mormon, sponsored a 1990 two-day conference in Salt Lake City titled, "You Don't Have to be Gay." The president of the Utah AIDS Coalition responded that "Reorientation therapy is to psychiatry what bloodletting is to the healing arts." In September 1990 the Gay and Lesbian Mormons General Conference was keynoted in Phoenix by a minister who pointed out that "The Lord said my house is for all—*all*—not just for people who have sex in the missionary position. . . . God doesn't create garbage. Your sexuality is part of creation that God has given you. If 10 percent of you are gays and lesbians then God has given a tithe to the Mormon Church." (Similar to Islam, Mormons believe in sex after death and that God has a goddess with whom he is sexually active.)

After the 1989 San Francisco earthquake, fundamentalists concluded that God was punishing homosexuals. One Pentecostal preacher in the city said, "The homosexual relationship is totally against God's plan—God made Adam and Eve, not Adam and Steve." Who does religion believe made Steve?

Great Britain doesn't criminalize homosexual activity, except that involving minors. The Labor Party voted in 1989 to lower the age of homosexual consent from twenty-one to sixteen, the legal age for heterosexual consent. In May 1989 Denmark, by a lopsided parliamentary majority, allowed homosexuals to marry. Among the first eleven male couples to marry were Eigil Axgil, age 74, and Alex Axgil, 67, who had lived together for forty years. They adopted a new last name as a combination of their first names. Christian fundamentalists demonstrated across the street from their ceremony, calling it "Sodom's Day." The Danish law gives homosexuals the same rights as heterosexuals in marriage, except it prohibits the adoption of children. Many states in the United States, however, now allow female homosexuals to adopt children, and San Francisco and Boston allow homosexuals to enter into a registered partnership.

The Dutch government introduced legislation in 1991 to legalize homosexual marriages. Although stopping short of providing a religious sanction, the proposal would affect property ownership, joint pension rights, social benefits, taxation, inheritance, and divorce.

Other religions and cultures treat sex far differently than Christians. The Tao of China held "The more women with whom a man has intercourse, the greater will be the benefit from the act; If in one night he can have intercourse with more than ten women it is best." This philosophy permeated Chinese thought for two thousand years through the "Supreme Path, the Way, Tao." One yin plus one yang equals Tao, which equals change. The prime goal was to live in harmony with nature, similar to American Indians. Sexual intercourse was the meshing of yin and yang. The Chinese published many books on sexual matters, which were fully accepted by society, though they'd be considered pornographic by many Westerners. The Eastern openness to sex stifled the spread of Christianity and Hiniajana Buddhism, both repressive of sexual knowledge. Except for sadomasochism all sexual practices were acceptable, though excessive use of dildos was discouraged. This sexual openness was repressed beginning in the second century B.C.E. when Confucianism began its ascendance. Still, Tao sexuality and Confucianist sexual repression were considered yin and yang until the twelfth century. Most Chinese were polygamous, especially in the middle classes, being allowed as many concubines and wives as could be afforded. Ten women in one night was practically achievable, in theory. Chinese women were treated as Western women were treated, however, as chattels, not allowed to participate in politics or business.

For Hindus, as for Taoists, sex was considered a religious obligation. The combining of pleasure and love was considered one of the four main goals of life. The Kama Sutra emphasized explicit sex and romantic strategies. Hindus also had temple prostitutes to help support the temple financially at their height in the eleventh century.

Muslims, like Christians, blame the ills of the world on women because of Eve's role in causing the ouster of Adam from the Garden of Eden. Women are punished by Islam in eighteen ways, paralleling those traditional in Christianity, ranging from segregation during menstruation to delaying remarriage upon widowhood. Outside the harem, women were required to be veiled; inside the harem, they were virtual prisoners. The Ottoman Turks, upon conquering Constantinople in 1453, embraced the harem, the secrets of which were kept until the death of the last Sultan in 1909. Westerners always thought the harem was filled with hundreds of semi-naked women, heavy perfume, cool fountains, soft music, and all possible physical pleasures. Instead the harem consisted of between three and twelve hundred women learning housekeeping and coffee-making. One woman would become the mother of the next sultan and, if sufficiently strong, the ruler of the empire. During the early medieval period, thirty-five of the thirty-eight Caliphs were sons of foreign slave girls. The ascendance to power guaranteed cut-throat competition among harem women with sons, as each mother vied to gain the favor of the sultan for her son. The alternative to the son's succession to the throne was death; a fifteenth-century law of Muhammed II required fratricide so that all brothers were killed when the next sultan was chosen.

The status of women in Europe changed drastically between 1100 and 1550 from a sex despised by men and themselves to that of respect and veneration as the mother figure. The Crusades brought fresh ideas to Europe and decimated the supply of men. With the men off crusading, women controlled and ran the great estates, surprising themselves and the remaining men by doing very well. The Byzantine idealization of the Virgin Mary was adopted, replacing the concept of all women being Eve. Courtly love began and women became ladies. This new culture was derived from the Arab Muslims and resulted in romance poetry and troubadours singing of romance and beauty. Chivalry was born.

The hunt for evil women began at the same time—the hunt for witches. In the fifteenth and sixteenth centuries thousands of women were destroyed. In the small Swiss Canton of Vaud, 3,371 witches were executed between 1591 and 1680. Wiesensteig, Germany, a small town, burned sixty-three women in the single year of 1562; Obermarchtal burned 7 percent of its population as witches in two years.

Pope John XXII emphasized the hunting of witches, followed by papal decrees in 1374, 1409, 1418, 1437, 1445, and 1451. St. Augustine and St. Thomas Aquinas believed miracles were caused by high magic and that witches wielded low magic. Heresy and sorcery were linked in the 1300s. By the sixteenth century, witches were burned by the hundreds. Women were accused of making a pact with the devil, which allowed them to fly up chimneys after having been greased with the fat of slaughtered infants, whose blood they drank. They flew on broomsticks, spindles, or goats to meetings of witches at midnight on Thursdays, worshiping the devil in the form of a large black bearded man, or a goat, or a toad. They ritually kissed the goat under its tail or the mouth of the toad, had sex orgies, and ate human organs. The details varied by locale. Witch hunts centered in Germany, Switzerland, and France, later spreading to the fledgling United States.

A witch's existence was proved by torture, growing out of the Inquisitions, self-fulfilling the prophesy of the Bible that witches are to be killed. Certain women were automatically considered witches; wise women, midwives, and folk doctors; poor women, spinsters, and widows not subject to male control. Whole families of women were burned—mother, daughter, cousin, aunt, and grandmother. About 80 percent were women; the male witches were cripples or the handicapped, criminals, and relatives of female witches. The new Protestants were worse than the Catholics in hunting and exterminating witches, particularly in England. Witches were believed in by Luther, Calvin, and Zwingli. The craze died with the Inquisitions, but the Inquisitions didn't die until the 1800s.

The Bible is the basis for painting women as witches. See Deuteronomy 18:11–12 and Exodus 22:18, the latter of which says, "Thou shalt not suffer a witch to live." Pope Innocent VIII in the fifteenth century endorsed *The Witches Hammer,* coauthored by Inquisitor Springer, which provided:

> The very word *femina* (woman) means one wanting in faith; for *fe* means "faith" and *minus* "less." Since she was formed of a crooked rib, her entire spiritual nature has been distorted and more inclined toward sin than virtue. . . . It is thus clear why women especially are addicted to the practice of sorcery. The crime of witches exceeds all others. They are worse than the devil. . . .

John Wesley said, "Giving up belief in witchcraft is in effect giving up belief in the Bible."

The Church opposed anesthetic for women during childbirth because Genesis 3:16 says, "I will greatly multiply thy pain and thy conception; in pain thou shalt bring forth children." Women were burned alive for seeking anesthetic. As stated by Elizabeth Cady Stanton, "The Bible and the church have been the greatest stumbling blocks in the way of women's emancipation. . . . The whole tone of church teaching in regard to women is, to the last degree, contemptuous and degrading."*

We've come a long way from the days in New England when the accusation of witchcraft would likely result in death of the accused. One witches' coven was formally recognized as a religion by the state of Rhode Island, established with the help of the Witches Anti-Defamation League. In October 1988, the Rosegate Coven of witches applied for non-profit religious status and received it in early 1989. The coven is known as Our Lady of the Roses Wiccan Church. The primary motive in seeking religious status was to combat the public confusion of witches with satanists.

The comparative labelling of sexually active men and women illustrates the double standard at its most obvious—a promiscuous woman is a harlot; a promiscuous man is a stud. There is no female equivalent in the English language for stud (compare slut). There is no comparable male sexual prohibition in the Bible to that against harlotry, though men are cautioned against masturbation because that would result in a wasting of semen. The prohibition against adultery was against relations with a married woman because that would undermine the clean patriarchal lineage and constitute conversion of the husband's property.

According to Kinsey, the most important impact on a woman's sexuality is her degree of religiosity, no matter the religion. A third of unmarried devout Catholic women experience orgasm, while almost three-fourths of nondevout unmarried Catholic women do so; the same ratio holds true after marriage.

---

*Gail B. Shulman, *View from the Back of the Synagogue* (1974).

Devoutness appears to promote masturbation and homosexual activity among women as safe alternatives to conventional sex outside marriage. According to Masters and Johnson, religious orthodoxy is the prime indicator of sexual inadequacy. For many religious women, sexual dysfunction becomes a way of life. Many develop "pelvic anesthesia" after marriage, or vaginismus, a psychosomatic condition where the pelvic muscles become so constricted that coitus is impossible. Most (if not all) such women are the products of a strict religious upbringing. Sexual problems related to religious instruction lead to strained marriages and result in extramarital affairs and divorce. Kinsey concluded that 75 percent of all divorces include sexual problems. The religiously devout are taught to avoid sex, except for procreation, which results in divorce and no procreation. A 1989 study at the University of Montevallo in Alabama reported that a woman's more conservative overall attitude toward sex is tied directly to her religiosity, compared to less religious men, concluding that these differences are learned in connection with religion. The most comprehensive study of divorce was conducted by William J. Goode; religious devoutness was found to be the prime factor statistically correlatable with divorce rates. Those religions prohibiting divorce are less likely to divorce than the more liberal Protestant and Jewish religions, probably from fear of excommunication. Should a person be forced to remain in a personally abusive or emotionally destructive relationship because a religion threatens excommunication as the alternative? Religiously oriented people suffer greater trauma and guilt from divorce. The double standard is evident in the fact that men are twice as likely to divorce their wives for infidelity as their wives are to divorce them for playing around.

Sexual repression affects mothering roles, particularly in pregnancy, childbirth, and nursing. Amenorrhea, the psychological suppression of menstruation, avoids adult sexuality and conception, lessening sexual anxiety. Many physical disorders associated with pregnancy are related to sexual anxiety, such as excessive vomiting and weight gain. Aversion to breast-feeding is related to a dislike of sex and nudity. Nakedness is equated with shame (Exodus 32:25; Revelations 3:18, 16:15). Many women who don't nurse are too embarrassed or too modest. The inability to nurse appears to be related to an intolerance to masturbation. The earliest formative periods of a child's life may be molded by the mother's aversion to sex, much of which is religiously related.

The double standard, abetted by religious teachings, encourages prostitution, according to Kinsey and Ira Reiss. Prostitution is a recognized, though illegal, sexual outlet for men. The illegality is almost exclusively visited on the prostitute, not the men who frequent her. Before about 1920, unmarried women had no societally accepted sexual outlet. Since 1920, the number of women who dabble in premarital sex has grown so that the sexes are almost in parity. The demand for prostitutes has lessened. This "sexual revolution," slowed perceptibly by AIDS, has caused some religious women to develop a split personality, allowing heavy petting stopping short of coitus. A Christian who "goes all the way" is treated differently, depending on whether the person is male or female. As previously noted, our language preserves this distinction. A sexually fallen woman may be excluded from her church community, especially upon pregnancy.

A 1969 study by Lynn and James Smith found that the majority of "swingers," or wife-swappers, were religious; 50 percent Protestant, 20 percent Catholic, 7 percent Jewish, and a smattering of other religions. Many explained their participation by a desire to overcome religiously engendered inhibitions; many women reported a decrease in guilt and an increase in self-esteem, a connection confirmed by other studies of sexual fulfillment and self-esteem.

Some Protestant churches are changing their attitudes toward sex. A 1970 Presbyterian Task Force suggested removing the stigma traditionally attached to masturbation, particularly for divorced, widowed, or intentionally single parishioners. The study also encouraged caring relationships "not confined to the married and about-to-be-married." Although the Presbyterian Church refused to endorse the study, it voted to release it as a discussion document.

Only when it comes to sex and sensuality do most churches preach absolute literalism of Bible scriptures. Churches are torn between considering their flock as innocent babes to be kept in their pristine state forever or as the innately sinful who will eventually scandalize the church with sexual excesses: oppressive rules guarantee rebellion. The familial relations of a primitive tribe of Hebrews thousands of years ago, now carved into the Bible, have little connection to much of anything, much less modern standards of love and sex.

Illustrating one Catholic priest's attitude toward female sexuality is the statement by the Reverend Roger E. Griese, former pastor of the Sacred Heart Church in Dayton, Ohio: "Let's face it; miniskirts are the uniform of hookers. See any movie or TV show with street women? They all make a sexual display of themselves, 'showing their wares' and stimulating men to sexual immorality. Shorts worn in public, except at a tennis court or picnic, are the same. . . . No lady would appear in public, much less in church, dressed like this." This statement is another illustration of the double standard. Women cause men to be immoral. Why do men have no responsibility of their own? Does the celibacy of Catholic priests have any bearing on the Rev. Griese's position? In September 1989, Archbishop Pilarczyk instructed Rev. Griese to ease enforcement of his dress code; Rev. Griese refused and was removed by the archbishop from his pastorate in January 1990, based on acts by Griese that "often led to embarrassment for the Church."

In April 1990 a panel of U.S. Catholic bishops denounced sexism as a sin but continued to defend the Church's refusal to ordain women as priests. The panel praised the work of Christian feminists but warned against "radical feminist groups," which advocate "such aberrations as goddess worship, witchcraft, liberation from conformity to the sexual morality taught by the Church or the acceptance of abortion as a legitimate choice for women under pressure." The statement admits some Church practices have "depersonalized and depreciated women," leaving them as "objects of suspicion, condemnation, condescension or simply ignored." In April 1992, U.S. bishops called sexism a moral and social evil that the Catholic Church should oppose in its youth education programs and battles for equal pay. The bishops supported female deacons and altar servers but upheld the male priesthood and bans on artificial contraception.

Notwithstanding the discrimination against women in religious seminaries, the only reason enrollments haven't dropped precipitously is the influx of women beginning in the 1970s. By 1985, a third of those seeking ordination in mainline Protestant seminaries were women. Those religions that prohibit the ordination of women are experiencing a crisis in the decline of their clergy. The population of Catholics in the U.S. grew by 15 percent in the last twenty years, while the number of graduate level seminarians fell by half. In 1970 there were 37,000 active priests serving 50 million Catholics. Now fewer than 25,000 priests serve 55 million Catholics. The Church projects by the year 2000 that the number of Catholics will reach 65 million while the number of active priests will decline to 18,000. The shortage of priests has forced some Catholic churches to merge and others to close. U.S. Catholics are importing priests from the Philippines, Haiti, Korea, and India. Some Catholic leaders believe this influx stalls long-term solutions to the shortage problem, such as opening the priesthood to married men and to women.

Protestants and Jews are experiencing a similar crisis, though at a lesser level because of women enrollees in their seminaries. More liberal Protestant sects, such as Episcopalians, generally support the ordination of women ministers. Although more women are being ordained by more denominations, in proportion to men they receive fewer jobs and lower level jobs upon ordination. The real problem isn't getting the first job, which is usually available as a college chaplain or assistant, but by the third job change women fall significantly behind male clergy in size of church and salary. More churches are open to women pastors, but many balk at accepting a second woman pastor for fear of becoming known as a woman's church. The nature of religion is such that if it changes at all, it changes slowly. The problem is how to change infallible doctrine without it being revealed as fallible.

The greatest burden imposed on women by many religions is the prohibition of birth control (and abortion, dealt with separately in the ethics section of this book). Sex is officially prohibited, except for purposes of procreation. The impact of this doctrine, which is central to Catholicism, Mormonism, many Protestant denominations, and Islam, on women and the world at large is enormous. *The Catholic Word Book* calls contraception an unnatural act, as "against the order of nature." Donor artificial insemination is prohibited, as described in *The Catholic Word Book:* "In view of the principle that procreation should result only from marital intercourse, donor insemination is not permissible. The use of legitimate artificial means to further the fruitfulness of marital intercourse is permissible." The pope reaffirmed in May 1990, while on a tour of Mexico, that couples using contraception have "closed themselves to God and opposed his will."

World population increases ninety million a year and continues to spiral upward. The United Nations and private demographers predict geometric population increases reaching a catastrophic level within thirty years, unless worldwide family planning is strengthened. These enormous increases are in third world countries where religion dominates, usually Catholic, Muslim, or Hindu.

The prohibition against birth control has made Islam the world's fastest growing religion with almost a billion members in 1989. The average Islamic woman bears six children, and, if the rate continues, Muslims will constitute almost a fourth of the world's population in thirty years. Bangladesh is losing its battle to fight the population explosion, which lengthens its lead as the most densely populated country in the world. K. T. Hosain, a Dhaka University social scientist says, "There is not a ghost of a chance that this [population reduction] target can be achieved in a poor, largely rural and traditional society bound by Islamic mores against artificial birth control measures." Females are ostracized if they practice birth control.*

The prohibition against birth control is self-serving for any religion. The best way for a religion to grow is to enjoin birth control, baptize infants, and perpetuate the passage of the family religion from generation to generation, in perpetuity. Any violation by a woman requires excommunication from the male-dominated religion she was raised to serve. This situation also serves to keep women in poverty. The number of babies born to single mothers in the United States rose from 3.8 percent in 1951 to 25 percent in 1989; most will be raised in poverty. Over one million unmarried teenage girls become pregnant in the United States each year while many conservative religions oppose sex education in public schools. The reason our public policy continues to avoid talking about the problem is that the problem is mandated by organized religion. Pat Robertson illustrated the fundamentalist attitude toward sexual equality for women in a fund-raising letter opposing the Iowa equal rights amendment in September 1992, citing a "secret feminist agenda" that is "not about equal rights for women. It is about a socialist, anti-family political movement that encourages women to leave their husbands, kill their children, practice witchcraft, destroy capitalism and become lesbians."†

Hindu women are also subservient to men and religious tradition. When two Hindu women married the wrong men in 1990 because their vision was obstructed by long veils, the village elders refused to exchange the spouses because the ceremony was religious and thus final. Females in India are subjugated to the point that a fourth of the 12 million girls born each year die before the age of fifteen, victims of neglect and infanticide because of their gender. Many female fetuses are aborted because of the high expense of raising and marrying off a daughter. UNICEF found that many girl babies are poisoned or choked to death. A girl is expected to do twice as much work as a boy. The ratio of women in some Indian states has fallen to 800 per 1000 men.

The Positives of Religion

There are positive aspects of religion. The average regular churchgoer is better off psychologically then a nonattender, perhaps because the traumas of everyday life fall away when compared to the prospect of a carefree afterlife.

---

*Deutsche Presse Agentur, *Arizona Republic,* March 13, 1993.

†Michael Isikoff, *Washington Post, Arizona Republic,* Oct. 1992.

Similarly, strong commitment to a religious faith improves chances of good health. The religious generally suffer less heart disease and cancer. According to Dr. David Larson, research psychiatrist at the federal government's National Institute of Mental Health, "The more conservative they are, the higher the level of intensity of their religiosity, the more the health benefits." The primary benefit is in reduced stress and depression. Seventy-five percent of widows are aided by their faith in religion and an afterlife. Religiously induced guilt (such as that experienced by the 6 percent to 17 percent of Americans who believe in the real possibility that they will go to hell) may outweigh for some the psychological and health benefits. However, for the terminally ill and disabled, religion is a great solace.

We know that hope, no matter its source, reduces stress and anxiety, lengthening life. A thirteen-year study by a Stanford University psychiatrist of the effects of psychotherapy on eighty-six women with advanced breast cancer, concluded that talk therapy helped reduce their depression and anxiety, helping them to come to terms with death.* Women in psychotherapy lived an average of thirty-seven months while those outside the group with similar diagnoses lived nineteen months on average. Hope by itself is real; the source of the hope and its efficacy are irrelevant.

Religious people who are unsure of their ultimate destination suffer increased stress and depression. Reality (particularly of certain death) for anyone, religious or not, can be depressing. As an antidote to general depression, religion ranks fifth and ninth out of the top thirteen choices, according to George Gallup's book, *The People's Religion,* which catalogs years of Gallup polls. First in popularity for relieving depression is spending more time with television, reading, music, or a hobby; second is seeking out friends to talk to; third is talking to family members; fourth is eating more or eating less; and fifth is prayer, meditation, or reading the Bible. Ninth on the list is seeking out a pastor or religious leader, which ranks behind shopping or spending more, exercising more, and spending more time at work. It's the specter of death that attracts most of us to religion; for the otherwise depressed, the remedies are more secular.

Another possible benefit of religion is its increasing involvement in social issues. The National Association of Evangelicals opened its forty-eighth annual conference in Phoenix in March 1990 with the environment and worldwide human-rights violations on its agenda, in addition to more traditional issues of euthanasia, the domestic political agenda, and evangelization in Eastern Europe. The theme of the conference was stewardship, a biblical term associated with care for the earth, which covers everything from raising money to involvement with people and governments. Other Christian sects and denominations are pursuing similar interests, including the rapidly developing "Liberation Theology" in many Third World countries, particularly in Central and South America. For almost the first time religion is braving opposition to established government.

Some of this new social awareness arose from Vatican II, where the conferring

---

Lancet, October 14, 1989.

bishops recognized that the Church historically has been allied with the government in power, the middle classes, and the wealthy, though most of its members are the poor. However, the primary social result of Vatican II was a declaration that priests and nuns should avoid the appearance of wealth and wear simple costumes.

A major benefit of religion is the sense of fellowship engendered by common beliefs, the formation of the "us." The Rev. Andrew Greeley is "Catholic despite the Vatican and despite my cardinal." He concludes that Catholics don't base their decisions on whether to remain Catholic on pronouncements by the Vatican on such matters as sexual morality, particularly since 80 percent use birth control contrary to Church directions, but on whether they have become a part of the Catholic community, which nurtures them and gives them a sense of belonging. These 80 percent naysayers receive Communion yet reject the teaching in a "sense that God understands the importance of sex in marriage, even if the pope doesn't." Greeley believes that religion, like myth, symbolizes reality with poetry at its heart.

This sense of community and oneness was illustrated by the reaction of thousands who were baptized simultaneously in Corona Del Mar, California, in August 1990. A twenty-seven-year-old man said, "I feel loved. It's just a feeling in your heart. I can't explain it but you know it." A thirty-one-year-old woman said, "Now I won't feel empty anymore. Now I feel like I have a personal relationship with Jesus. It's wonderful." The sense of community was summed up by a thirty-two-year-old woman who said, "I can walk up to any one of these people and they are my brother and sister."

Religion for many is their primary positive connection with their fellow human beings in a stress-producing, highly competitive, and cold-appearing world. However, this sense of community has evolved worldwide into a syndrome of "us versus them"; those outside the particular religion are considered inferior, resulting in war.

Some Phoenix baby boomers are rediscovering religion.* A wife raised Catholic and a husband raised Lutheran attended several churches after deciding "something was missing" in their lives. They gauged sermons, music, congregation size, and friendliness before choosing a Lutheran Church that the wife described as nuturing "unbelievable friendships—spiritual friendships. We didn't really have any family in the area and I feel like these people are my surrogate family."

A 1991 Gallup Poll found that half of all boomers expected "to spend more time seeking the basic meaning and value of life in the next five years." In response, many churches with boomer-dominated populations cater to a list of nontraditional needs such as the $2 million gymnasium built by the First Assembly of God Church in Phoenix, which features aerobics classes and a weight room, and the Community Church of Joy in Glendale, Arizona, which offers a counseling center with support groups for alcoholism, abuse, divorce, sexual addiction, and multiple-personality disorders. A new member of the First United Methodist Church of Glendale said, "When I went back, I found what it was. I found the contact

---

Phoenix Gazette, May 1992.

I needed. It brings peace of mind more than anything, because I've always sort of had a fear of death. This gives me the feeling of something beyond death." The pastor of a Greek Orthodox Church with a 90 percent boomer membership said, "They seek honesty and integrity. It's a real community, not like a business or institution, which is something we're trying desperately to avoid."

The Separation of Church and State

Although the United States Constitution pays it lip service, there's no real separation of church and state in the United States or in any country where religion is legal. One reason is because the majority of Americans see no practical need to separate church and state. A 1987 opinion poll by the Williamsburg Charter Foundation on religion and public life revealed that we're consistently inconsistent. Over half of us pay lip service to the notion that church and state should be separated, thus preferring the idea of "a high wall of separation between church and state" to the proposition supported by a third of us that "the government should take special steps to protect the Judeo-Christian heritage." However, 80 percent said it was acceptable for cities to erect a manger scene or menorah on government property.

When the 11th Circuit Court of Appeals in Atlanta declared prayers before school-sponsored events to be unconstitutional on January 3, 1989, it was uniformly ignored in those states within the 11th Circuit, Georgia, Florida, and Alabama. When the United States let the decision stand by refusing on May 30, 1989, to review it, prayer continued before high-school football games in this Bible-belt region. The mayor of Childsburg, Alabama, led those attending the season opener in prayer: "We thank you Lord that we do live in a free land, a free land where we can pray. Bless us now, keep our players safe." Police confiscated a banner stating that church and state don't mix, saying it was prohibited by city ordinance.

The front page of the *Arizona Republic* on January 30, 1989, carried an article titled "GOP leaders assail Christian-nation call." The first paragraph stated: "Republican party leaders Monday criticized a resolution proclaiming the United States a Christian nation, two days after the statement won easy approval at the party's state convention." The article described the resolution as saying that "Christian principles 'have been eroded by certain human forces' and the Arizona Republican Party embraces those principles." The resolution declared the United States a "Christian Nation," a republic constitutionally established "upon the 'absolute laws' of the Bible, not a democracy based on the changing whims of the people." It concluded that these " 'absolute laws' have been eroded by certain human forces not abiding by these Christian principles, and freedom, as has been enjoyed, is rapidly being taken away." The Republican Party's executive director and the state GOP chairman, the latter of whom is Jewish, "would have preferred that it said Judeo-Christian nation."

The "Christian nation" idea began in Arizona with Governor Evan Mecham, who in a December 1987 speech to an Arizona Jewish group said the United States is "a Christian nation where Jews and Moslems can live in peace and religious freedom, and where Jesus Christ is the Lord of the Land." Supporters of the resolution hoped to include it in the Republican Party's national platform in 1992. The author of the resolution described opponents as "evil forces," elaborating: "Communists have infiltrated this country and then purportedly prepared themselves for strategic positions in government, education and in the churches."

One example of religion dominating political issues is found in Utah, where a 1989 statewide poll found that legalized gambling was favored by 60 percent to 37 percent. Every Utah poll since 1985 has favored a lottery. Franklin, Idaho, on the Utah border, is the gaming capitol of Idaho because of betting by Utah residents. The mom-and-pop grocery store in town has sold over 1.3 million lottery tickets, averaging 6,000 sales every Saturday, and is called the home of the Utah lottery. The reason Utah has no lottery and will never have a lottery notwithstanding the preferences of its residents is that its legislators are Mormons and their religion forbids gambling, alcohol, smoking, and caffeine. Thus, Utah residents are among the healthiest in the nation, though perhaps also among the most bored.

When the Islamic Society of North America met in Phoenix in July 1989, it concluded that until the United States becomes an Islamic nation, justice, morality, and economic stability cannot be achieved. Siraj Wahaj, leader of New York's Muslim population said, "The only way this country can have human rights is to establish Islam. What America and the Western world needs is guidance, and the only way to get guidance is from the Koran and Sunnah." Economic changes mandated by Islam would require a no-interest banking system, because charging interest is prohibited by the Koran. Moral changes would require outlawing alcohol and placing veils on women.

The United States Constitution is contrary to the Bible. The Constitution states that all political power is inherent in the people, who retain the inalienable right to alter the government as they deem expedient. Romans 8:1–2 states there is no power except for God; such power is ordained by God, and resisters to this power are damned. The impetus for exclusion of God from the U.S. Constitution came from George Washington, Ben Franklin, James Madison, Ethan Allen, Thomas Jefferson, and the Adamses. George Washington wrote into a treaty with Tripoli, "The government of the United States of America is not, in any sense, founded upon the Christian religion."

The President of the United States regularly hosts a National Prayer Breakfast, which began in the Eisenhower years, consisting of "a 90-minute round of prayer and testimonials at a Washington [D.C.] hotel" (*Time*, 6 February 1989). The United States Senate declared 1990 as the "International Year of Bible Reading," which was endorsed by President Bush and eighteen state governors. The aim was to have one billion people read the Bible in 1990, nonstop from Genesis to Revelation. President Reagan had declared 1983 as "The Year of the Bible," which critics say was used by fundamentalists to promote prayer in public schools. President Bush was more receptive to meeting with U.S. religious leaders than even President Reagan. On January 19, 1990, U.S. Secretary of State James Baker voiced strong support for church work in El Salvador, rejecting a Salvadoran government claim that the churches were fronts for the rebels.

President Bush proclaimed a "National Day of Prayer" on February 3, 1991, asking 250 million Americans to pray for divine aid in the Persian Gulf War, which he called a "just war." Meanwhile Saddam Hussein declared God to be on Iraq's side in a "holy war" against the Western invaders. The United States is the most religious nation among major industrial democracies, giving Bush an approval rating of over 80 percent during his "just war."

The day after the Republican National Convention renominated him for president in August 1992, George Bush called the Democratic Party godless: "If I could make one political comment, I was struck by the fact that the other party took words to put together their platform but left out three simple letters: G-o-d."

Public schools teach "creation science," proscribe "voluntary prayer," include a prayer ceremony with every graduation ceremony, release children from regular school time for religious instruction, and fail to include a mention in history courses of the atrocities of the currently predominant U.S. religions that tortured and executed millions of people (heretics) for eighteen hundred years.

Until February 21, 1989, when the United States Supreme Court decided the *Texas Monthly* case, all religious property was exempt from taxation by local governments in forty-five states and by the federal government. In addition to broad exemption from property taxes, California and Idaho exempt meals from sales tax when served by a religious organization; Georgia, South Dakota, and Washington exempt tax on sacramental wine; Virginia and Missouri charge no tax on church owned automobiles; and Mississippi exempts from its amusement tax those programs "consisting entirely of gospel singing and not generally mixed with hillbilly or popular singing." The cost to government from revenues lost by these exemptions is enormous. The revenues must be made up by other tax-payers. Each of us are required by law to subsidize religion. In its *Texas Monthly* plurality opinion the Supreme Court held that a state may not constitutionally exempt church books and publications from a sales tax. Three justices opposed any special privileges for religion; three tolerated a nodding acquaintance, without explaining how big a nod is allowable; and the other three varied according to the circumstances. The *Texas Monthly* case may foretell a gradual severing of the two-hundred-year special symbiotic relationship between our governments and organized religions.

On January 17, 1990, the United States Supreme Court ruled that items sold by television evangelists may be taxed by states like any other items. The Court held its previous concern that a license tax might "act as a precondition to the free exercise of religious beliefs is simply not present where a tax applies to all sales and uses of tangible personal property in the state."

There's a direct correlation between religious affiliation and socio-political views. Most Catholics (59 percent) and Protestants (80 percent) are politically liberal, while few (13 percent) fundamentalists are liberal, according to a study by the Center for Media and Public Affairs at Smith College in 1989. About half of

Catholics, two-thirds of Protestants, and 91 percent of fundamentalists believe private enterprise is fair to workers. Eighty percent of Protestants and Catholics believe government should help reduce the disparity between rich and poor, while only 43 percent of fundamentalists would support such a policy. On family and sexual issues alliances shift: two-thirds of Protestants support abortion while about a fifth of Catholics and fundamentalists do so. Eighty-three percent of fundamentalists oppose women working who have small children, versus 28 percent of Protestants. Over 90 percent of fundamentalists believe the focus of the church should be to convert people to Christianity at home and abroad; about half of Protestants and Catholics agree. Thus politics and religion go hand in hand, though views may be highly divergent on core social issues among the major faiths.

Religion has always (until very recently) been careful to be facially subservient to the state; many legal holidays in most countries are religious holidays, including the two most important holidays in this country—Christmas and Thanksgiving. Even secular holidays, such as the Fourth of July, Memorial Day, and Labor Day, feature religious representatives on the reviewing stands with celebrations opened by a blessing and prayer. Most U.S. Presidents invoke God regularly, especially President Reagan, who closed his last address to the American people by saying, "God bless you. And God bless the United States."

Arnold Toynbee, in *An Historian's Approach to Religion,* described the failure to separate church and state:

> The effect of this capture of higher religions for alien mundane purposes has been doubly disastrous. On the one hand the captured higher religions have been diverted from their true mission of preaching a new gospel in which God is revealed as being Love. . . . Whole-heartedness can rise to sainthood when it is directed to the religious purpose that is its true end, but it is apt to descend to demonic savagery when it is prostituted to the service of mundane causes.

Religion and Money

Although the Bible describes the love of money as the root of all evil (not an unreasonable conclusion), religion and money, tithes and offerings, are inseparable. Tithes and tithing are mentioned thirty-seven times in the Bible. Over eighty billion dollars was contributed to religions in 1980. These billions were not used to feed and clothe the poor because suffering in this life is not only considered unimportant, but it is encouraged. Religion is in the business of saving souls, not mere physical bodies. These billions instead went to support religious leaders and to buy buildings, which do as much to glorify the particular religion and its corporeal leaders as to glorify its God. One of every five human beings in the world, or one billion people, suffer from malnutrition, poor health, or disease. In Arizona alone 50,000 people go to bed hungry every night; 30,000 of these are children. Still, most of the hungry live in Catholic and other fundamentalist countries: Central America, South America, Asia, and Africa.

In his 1988 book, *Prosperity and Poverty: The Compassionate Use of Resources in a World of Scarcity,* Calvin Beisner concludes that real Christian concern about poverty could solve the problem easily. Using a rough estimate of the income of U.S. church members, one percent of their income, which is only one-tenth of the expected tithe, would be sufficient to eliminate poverty. In Phoenix, when the homeless seek places to sleep, accommodations are provided by state and city tax money. The churches contribute little, though church buildings are used only a fraction of the time and few are used at night.

The average church member's tithe is 1.9 percent, or less than a fifth of the amount mandated by the Bible. Protestants give the bulk of this percentage while Catholics average .9 percent as a tithe. Jews give an average of 1.5 percent. Islam requires a 2.5 percent tithe as alms for the poor. The reasons for giving vary widely. One parishioner was told by his priest that "God will be better to you if you give more." The Rev. Andrew Greeley estimates that U.S. Catholics withhold seven billion dollars in donations yearly because of their attitudes toward papal authority, birth control, and church corruption.

Professor of theology James Cone, of the Union Theological Seminary in New York, was interviewed by *USA Today* upon his honoring in November 1989 at the Howard University divinity school's conference on black theology. Professor Cone was asked, "Why are churches so silent in the face of social chaos?" He answered, "With few exceptions, churches are primarily focusing on their own survival, building bigger churches and holding fund-raisers for their pastors."

Catholic schools are no longer able to subsidize their poorer students because, according to the president of the Arizona Council for Academic Education, "We don't have the resources to help the poor."

The Yoga Bhajan, leader to three million of the world's fifteen million Sikhs, described the relationship between money and religion: "Religious men became very corrupt because we religious men have to go and get money from you. We compromise for a better congregation, to attract rich people."

Recent examples include Jim and Tammy Bakker. The supporters of the PTL were undeterred by the facts surrounding the Bakkers. Contributions continued until Jim Bakker was convicted of twenty-four counts of fraud and conspiracy. He was sentenced to forty-five years in prison and fined $500,000 for swindling $3.7 million from his followers. To his followers, the facts were irrelevant and still are. Jim Bakker began serving his term in the Federal Medical Center in Rochester, Minnesota, a facility where the guards don't carry weapons and the windows have no bars. In December 1992, U.S. District Judge Graham Mullen decided Bakker's sentence was too harsh, reducing it to eight years.

After the PTL scandal, television evangelists shifted their focus from national to local politics. At a 1990 convention, one leader said televangelists are urging their followers to continue the Christian battle before school boards and city councils instead of in Congress, to prevent the further spread of "secular humanism," modern sexual mores, and the "breakdown in traditional Judeo-Christian values."

They have been remarkably successful. Two-thirds of the eighty-eight fundamentalist candidates for lower level office won 1990 elections in Southern

California.*

Religious institutions rival governments in their inefficiency when spending income; taxes and tithes similarly get lost in the bureaucratic shuffle. The difference is that it's impossible to obtain even a general accounting of how religious contributions are spent. The percentage of church income that reaches the poor and needy is minute. Still, religious leaders oppose recent proposals to cut tax deductions for "charitable" contributions to churches, according to the general secretary of the National Conference of Catholic Bishops, on the basis that "weakening the incentives for contributions would not only be counterproductive but contradict the repeated calls by President Bush for increased involvement by the non-profit, private sector in addressing needs of the less fortunate in our society." Is it unfair to point out that little or nothing goes from churches to the "less fortunate" and that church buildings, such as the Vatican, are expensive to keep up? Vatican II recognized that Vatican finances are a public relations disaster and acknowledged the following facts: Vatican assets in 1965 equalled the wealth of the French government and were five times the British reserve, excluding Vatican wealth represented by its works of art and real estate. Vatican funds were deposited in the Bank of the Holy Spirit, which is fully invested. Cardinals are chauffered around Rome where most Italian citizens must ride scooters or walk. The Catholic palace in Karachi is a particular affront to the local poor. The Church destroys agriculture and institutionalizes poverty by distributing U.S. farm commodities.

The leaders of all major organized religions are used to wealthy living. Protecting church property and Christian missionaries has justified Western imperialism, making Easterners suspicious of Western missionaries and their wealth. Vatican II's primary recommendation was that priests and nuns wear simple costumes to avoid the appearance of wealth.

Two reasons the Vatican is strapped for cash are its incompetence and dishonesty in handling its billions. Its 1989 budget had a projected shortfall of $78.2 million (up from $65 million in 1988) with the result that its bank, renamed the Institute for Religious Works, was restructured. The restructuring was overseen by Archbishop Paul C. Marcinkus, who headed the bank for twenty years and was charged by the Italian government with being an accessory to the fraudulent bankruptcy of Banco Ambrosiano in 1982, caused by the disappearance of $1.3 billion. The missing money was transferred by loans made to ten fake companies in Latin America controlled by the Vatican Bank. An Italian Court in 1988 saved Archbishop Marcinkus by annulling his arrest warrant on the grounds that Italy has no jurisdiction over Vatican affairs. Although the Vatican denied wrongdoing, it paid $250 million to the creditors of Banco Ambrosiano in recognition of its "moral" responsibility in the collapse.†

In November 1989, the second largest Catholic archdiocese, that in Chicago, announced it could be broke by 1993 when its chief financial officer said it will

---

*The Economist, Arizona Republic, Dec. 6, 1992.

†Los Angeles Times, Arizona Republic, March 11, 1989; Associated Press, Arizona Republic, Oct. 31, 1990.

exhaust all its savings.

Other churches do better with their money and resources and are growing vigorously. A prime example is the Church of Jesus Christ of Latter-day Saints, which is a diversified corporation engaged in such businesses as insurance, broadcasting, publishing, satellite communications, schools, property development, department stores, and hotels. Mormons contribute (as of 1991) about $4.3 billion yearly in tithes to the church while church-owned business generated about $100 million, which would place the church about 110th on the *Fortune 500* list. It is one of the largest landowners in the country with holdings in all fifty states, all tax exempt. Its stock and bond portfolio exceeds one billion dollars, and it has television and radio stations in many major cities. Its worldwide missionary program is second only to the Roman Catholic Church, which has about 150,000 missionaries to the Mormon's 44,000, which cost Mormons $550 million a year. The church regards accounting for its expenditures as do all churches, succinctly described in advice given to the church's first counselor, President Ezra Taft Benson, by his father, Gordon B. Hinckley:

> He reminded me that mine is the God-given obligation to pay my tithes and offerings. When I do so, that which I give is no longer mine. It belongs to the Lord to whom I consecrate it. What the authorities of the church do with it need not concern me. They are answerable to the Lord, who will require an accounting at their hands.

All churches say, "Trust us with your money. We're infallible." The Mormon Church goes the extra mile to obtain new members by offering interest-free loans to Tongan converts.

A Jesuit scholar at St. Louis University, Rev. John Kavanaugh, warns that advertising is evangelism for the worship of money. Kavanaugh describes the American mania with shopping: "This is not just a psychological system. It is a *theological* system. . . . This is our culture's ultimate system of values. Most advertising—I'm talking about the good ads, not just really bad ones—associates all positive values with the act of purchasing." Kavanaugh cites examples of "eternity perfume," "I shop, therefore I am" bumper stickers, and a girl holding a *Seventeen* magazine with the caption "Her Bible." He suggests that advertisements may be designed to make people depressed so they shop more to escape the depression: "Perhaps someone has realized happy people do not need to buy as much. I believe we are taught to turn away from intimacy, from relationships, from family, from solitude, in order to focus our desires on wanting more and more things." Thus, the average American will watch four years of TV commercials by age seventy-five, and it works. Kavanaugh found a seventh-grade class could identify over fifty brands of designer jeans, over forty brands of beer, but only twelve political leaders. The churches' greatest concern is money, but this also reflects society as a whole.

The sources of Vatican wealth include the Inquisition and the Crusades, which for hundreds of years drained the resources of poor church members. In all wars until the 1800s, the booty of the losers was split between the Church and the state. Charlemagne required all conquered peoples to join the Church or die. Tithes were compulsory. Upon the death of Charlemagne in 814, the Pope inherited the wealth of the Empire. After Pope John XXII was elected in 1316, he confiscated a fortune valued at forty times the wealth of France. The French government was unable to raise 400,000 florins to ransom King John; Pope John XXII died worth twenty-five million florins. During the Middle Ages, in addition to penances, indulgences, and confiscations, the Church levied taxes heavier than those imposed by kings. Franciscans were burned during the Inquisitions for wearing their frock, which symbolized their vows of poverty.

Catholics in Arizona made headlines in 1989 by praying for a man who pledged to give them $100,000 a year for ten years beginning in 1983 and who in 1976 gave one million dollars to Mother Teresa. That man was Charles Keating, later convicted by the federal government of manipulating Lincoln Thrift into bankruptcy and defrauding thousands of depositors. Keating was helped in his dealings with government regulators by the recipients of his other contributions, the two United States senators from Arizona and three senators from other states. The vicar of the diocesan Office for Worship and pastor of St. Timothy Catholic Church in Mesa, Arizona, said, "Prayers have a power, and I know Charlie will land on his feet." On April 10, 1992, Keating was sentenced to ten years in prison and fined $250,000, after being found guilty of seventeen security fraud counts. He awaited trial in five other cases, including a $1.2 billion class action, a $130.5 million suit by the federal Office of Thrift Supervision, and a $2.5 billion fraud and racketeering trial. Lincoln Thrift was the most expensive bankruptcy in the national savings and loan scandal, totalling over two billion dollars.

The North American Securities Administrators Association and the Council of Better Business Bureaus released a report in 1989 titled, "Preying on the Faithful: The False Prophets of the Investment World." Since 1985, securities agencies alone (as opposed to general law enforcement) took action against the bilking of 15,000 Americans by "religiously oriented investment schemes" totalling $450 million. Examples included an Arkansas case where believers invested $10 million with a man who claimed he was "blessed by God with extraordinary business abilities" and an $18 million scheme that attracted investors by printing Bible verses at the end of their monthly statements. Arizona scams included a coin promoter who cited revelations by St. John as proof that investors needed to buy gold and silver in preparation for the final days. Securities officials believe the fraud is far greater than the cases reported, as many people would rather take their losses then admit gullibility. Officials suggest wariness of "Christian financial planners," the use of religion to obtain business, new church members who spring from nowhere with sure-fire investments, and claims that "religiously based investments are not regulated by state laws."

4

Does God Exist?

To many Americans . . . a drought . . . is the will of God, and they flock to
the churches to pray for rain under the impression that the plans God has made
are so trivial and unimportant that He will change them if asked to do so.
　　　　　　　　—Isaac Asimov, *Extraterrestrial Civilization*

A person asserting the existence of a fact normally has the burden of proving
the asserted fact. If a plaintiff sues on a contract, it's up to the plaintiff to prove
the existence of the contract and not up to the defendant to prove its nonexistence.
One reason the law operates in this fashion is that a negative, or the nonexistence
of a fact, cannot be proved. Therefore, the burden of proof lies where it belongs—
on the person asserting the existence of a fact or a particular god. Unfortunately
for theists, no argument for the existence of God has met any measure of proof.
The four primary arguments for the existence of God are internally illogical.

Notwithstanding acknowledged deficiencies, organized religions cling to the
arguments for the existence of God treated below. *The Catholic Word Book*
notes that "the First Vatican Council declared that the existence of God and
some of his attributes can be known with certainty by human reason, even without
divine revelation."

The first argument is the "first cause" principle, based on the seemingly logical
argument that everything is caused by something, and, therefore, the universe
must have been caused by God. The illogic of the argument is evident upon
its statement. Even if everything does have a cause (unprovable), that doesn't
mean the universe was created by God. It could have been created by Mortimer
or fatcat or little fairies or aliens or microbes. The Christian version of God
is an omnipotent, omnipresent, perfectly good, all-knowing, and disembodied spirit.
There is no logical necessity that the creator of the universe, whether that be
Mortimer, fatcat, God, or an infinite list of possibilities, is omnipotent, omnipresent,
good (or even nice), all-knowing, or a disembodied spirit.

The "first cause" argument contains the insupportable assumption that the
creator of the universe (if there were one) must come from outside the universe,
which is part of the Christian definition of God. Still, the first cause argument

is demonstrably illogical and has been conceded to be such for hundreds of years. One main difficulty with the "first cause" argument is that if we concede everything must have a first cause, then God must have a cause, and there appears to be no answer to the question of who created God. No matter what, something was created out of nothing, unless the universe has always existed.

The second argument for the existence of God is the "design" argument. Because nature is ordered and rational, with strict operating rules, the argument is that someone must have designed it and that someone must be God. The chief illustration used to support this argument is that of a watch with its exact machining and internal intricacies, which leads to the inescapable conclusion that it had a maker. The maker is so wonderful that he must also have a maker and that maker must be God. The argument stops short without revealing its implicit conclusion that man's wonderful maker, God, could have no maker.

The design argument assumes that an inanimate complex object proves the existence of God, instead of proving the existence of an animate object, such as a cat or a tree, or even man. What is necessary to prove or disprove the existence of God? Does the fact that all human and other animals have legs exactly long enough to reach the ground prove the existence of God? A chair may be used to barricade a door, or a tree branch as a walking stick, or a dead cat as a boomerang. Does a particular use prove the existence of a particular creator or any creator at all? The design argument provides as much support against the existence of God as for it, which is to say, no support one way or the other.

A more logical (scientifically supportable) argument is that evolution is the sole creator of the design, so that, given enough time, life itself evolves and continually refines itself within the design of nature. Does this exclude the possibility that God programmed evolution into nature to do God's work in the creation of life and the human species? Of course not, but it remains both remote and speculative without discernible logical support. It would seem absurd to conclude that humans are the culmination of God's handiwork, for if that be true, then we have a defective God who has created a far from perfect piece of handiwork. He created Hitler, Stalin, and the Indians who slaughtered Custer, all of whom may be considered good or bad, depending on our individual perspectives.

Kant logically solved the complaint that God could not have created himself with the hypothesis that God is outside the universe and thus not subject to the rules of causality. Kant's hypothesis begs the question, though, because there is no reason not to as easily accept the hypothesis that the universe just happened. There is no support for either theory, and the short answer is that we simply don't know. Man, however, has evolved the faculty of logical deduction and the talent for judging statistical probability, and when we come right down to it, after examining all the evidence, the existence of God appears beyond remote.

The third argument is that God must exist simply because we have the concept of God. Just because we have a concept, however, does not mean the thing exists—witness unicorns (maybe they did exist and maybe God is dead), werewolves (ditto), Elvis rising from the dead (or any other entity rising from the dead), and multiple other examples.

The fourth argument for the existence of God is that there must be a basic lawgiver because humans are cognizant of certain basic moral concepts. Absolute moral law requires an absolutely moral mind, or God. The logical difficulties with this argument are numerous. Probably no two people in the world could agree on ten basic moral concepts. The simplest and clearest moral concept, that we shouldn't kill other human beings, is riddled with the exceptions recognized by most religions: war, execution of criminals, self-defense, mercy killing, and the withdrawal of life support from the hopelessly ill. Thou shalt not kill, except in lots of circumstances. The conclusion is that there may be no such thing as absolute morality, or at least none on which anyone can absolutely agree.

The laws of nature cannot imply a lawgiver because natural laws are descriptive, not prescriptive, such as would be made by a lawgiver or legislature. Prescriptive laws are those of ethics and religion—do this and do not do that—quite different in kind from the laws of nature. Simply because God might be a possible cause of the laws of nature doesn't mean that God probably or certainly is. The existence of natural laws also doesn't mean that they are the only possible laws. There could easily be infinite variations so that gravity would cause objects to fall a foot per second faster or slower, ad infinitum. All variations, from the point of chance, are equal and are as probable as there being no laws at all, i.e., chaos. If God exists he would do so whether the universe is orderly or chaotic; the ordered state of the universe adds no support to an argument for the existence of God.

Notwithstanding the uniform rejection of these arguments by logicians, *The Catholic Word Book* definition of God uses these arguments as the basis for the proved existence of God:

> The existence of God is an article of faith, clearly communicated in divine Revelation. Even without this Revelation, however, the Church teaches, in a declaration by the First Vatican Council, that men can acquire certain knowledge of the existence of God and some of his attributes. This can be done on the basis of principles of reason and reflection on human experience.
>
> Non-revealed arguments or demonstrations for the existence of God have been developed from the principle of causality; the contingency of man and the universe; the existence of design, change and movement in the universe; human awareness of moral responsibility; widespread human testimony to the existence of God.

Contemporary Catholic theologians, such as Karl Rahner, characterize God as unknowable even in heaven:

> Even when the human spirit has been elevated to the supernatural order [goes to heaven], God remains its mysterious Horizon, whose unobjective presence is necessary for every act of knowledge, but who is never understood himself. God remains the Free Creator who can be known only through the dynamism of the human spirit's loving self-surrender to him. Because God can be known only through an act of loving obedience, the Christian Mystery is essentially religious.

What Rahner appears to be saying is that the only way to understand God is through pure belief, "loving self-surrender" or "loving obedience," but God even then and in heaven remains an undecipherable cipher. George Zebrowski in an article titled "Life in Godel's Universe: Maps All the Way," which appeared in the April 1992 *Omni* magazine, compared similar closed and ultimately unknowable systems:

> Nothing can ever count against it. A trivial example: Little green men live in all refrigerators, but they disappear when the door is opened. Another example is a religious dogma of any kind, held on faith. Both of these are what [Karl] Popper calls "reinforced dogmas," because they have a built-in resistance to any kind of test; they contain as part of the idea an injunction against questioning them. . . . Dogmas are the enemies of Godel's universe because they attempt to *end* all discussions and tests of truth; they are totalitarian viruses for the mind, preventing the creative growth that Godel's proof implies is possible. . . . Completeness is a form of death; wildness is a form of fertility, growth.

No proof for the existence of God has ever been offered that would be admissible in any court of law in any country in the world. Only faith is available to support a belief in God. Religious faith and superstition are two areas of human life insupportable by rationality or fact. If God existed, shouldn't there be some shred of evidence somewhere of a force defined as all-pervasive and powerful? It's insufficient to argue that the existence of God explains everything for which we have no other ready explanation. It is far more honest to say, "I don't know," than to say, "God did it," particularly since no one "knows" whether God exists.

The existence of miracles is based on identical logic, according to their definition in *The Catholic Word Book* as events that "cannot be explained by the ordinary operation of laws of nature and which, therefore, are attributed to the direct action of God." The ignorance of natural causes is not the equivalent of the nonexistence of natural causes. An explanation given without supporting proof is the same as any explanation, or no explanation, and is equally valid.

There are cogent arguments against the existence of God that arise directly from the Christian definition of God. A main one has to do with the existence of evil. If God is omnipotent, if he can do anything and win any battle or contest, then why does evil exist? Is God willing to prevent evil but unable to do so, and thus, not omnipotent? Or is God able to prevent evil but unwilling to do so, and thus, indistinguishable from evil? The Christian answer is that God is so far above us as not to be understandable in these terms, which is no answer at all. If we stray from the path of logic, there is no hope for our kind, for in an illogical world good is equal to evil and nothing makes sense.

It appears impossible that a good God would permit evil. For example, why would God will the death of an infant in a burning house? If such is God's will, then why should society punish the arsonist who set the fire and was merely doing God's will? Can we defend God by saying he is good, and therefore the evidence against him is misleading because in the long run the baby's death was all for the good? If a bystander could have saved the baby from the burning house without harm to himself but did not, would we call the bystander good? What kind of God is it who clearly could have saved the baby from the burning house but did not?

The religious answer is that babies trapped in burning houses are necessary to create moral urgency in mankind. Should we then abolish firefighters so God won't have to personally set more fires when moral urgency falls below a certain level? Is the arsonist a hero in creating moral urgency? Moral urgency could be further maximized by abolishing the medical profession and hospitals, and then we could all become Christian Scientists. There would be no reason to promote peace, prevent famine, and wipe out disease; we could return to the Middle Ages when religion ruled all. If there is an excuse for God to allow disasters and deaths of infants, what is it? Picture the infant in the burning house and God observing from afar as the flames lick the crib, and then the sheets. It would still not be too late for God to wave an incorporeal finger and save the baby. What reason could God have for sitting on his incorporeal behind as the flames explode and envelop the screaming child? Does it matter whether such a God exists?

A fundamentalist answer to the existence of evil is Satan. Unfortunately, no religion specifically describes the origins of this prince of darkness and Satan's inherent inconsistency with the tenets of the Christian religion. If God created everything, why did he create Satan? Was God a young god at the time, not realizing the havoc he was releasing in the world? The devil is not mentioned in the Old Testament, though devils are mentioned numerous times; Satan is mentioned three times with no reference to his origins (masculinity of Satan is assumed). There are thirty mentions of the devil or devils in the New Testament, including Christ giving authority to his disciples over devils (Luke 9:1), making devils subject to Christ (Luke 10:17), and stating devils believe in God and tremble (James 2:19). If these passages are correct, why is God or Christ tolerating such devilish evil? The New Testament states that Satan is to be transformed into an angel of light (2 Cor. 11:14) and that one thousand years after the Second Coming he is to be let out of prison (Rev. 20:7). Why does the devil receive only a one-thousand-year sentence while human sinners are relegated to hell forever?

If God is all-powerful, why doesn't he kick the devil's butt and be done with the scamp? Who created the devil, apparently as the equal of God? Surely God didn't create the devil. If so, God must be somewhat less than infallible, since he picked Satan as one of his angels, arguably one of the monumental God-blunders of all time. If God had the devil in a pit, why did he let him out again? Inattentiveness? How did Satan "force" God to send his son to earth? The logical answer to any of these questions appears to destroy the credibility of the Christian religion. If the answer given is not logical, then it is neither creditable nor worthy of belief.

Another alternative answer to the God/evil question is that evil is only the absence of good and God is not responsible for the absence of good. If so, then for what is God responsible and what kind of God is that? Another answer is that evil brings man to spiritual health and maturity. It appears more logical to conclude that evil (and life) brings death and that the proponents of the argument should re-read George Orwell's *1984,* particularly those portions on "doublespeak."

Another argument is that there's no accounting for good if there's no God. Would it be equally logical to conclude that there's no accounting for evil if there's no Satan? Does the existence of beauty, fidelity, or friendship mandate the existence of a particular supernatural being? What does one concept necessarily have to do with the other?

The probability that the Christian God exists is equal to the probability of the existence of the gods of ancient Rome, Greece, and Egypt or the gods of Jonestown, Babylon, and the Clan of the Cave Bear. Logic can neither prove nor disprove the existence of the Christian God or any other "God."

What if, as logic may dictate, there is likely no God? If there is no God, we need not bow and scrape and crawl before the images of a nonexistent God; we need not follow the arbitrary rules of organized religion that make life on earth miserable and foment endless wars; we could discard our primitive superstitions.

5

Religious Tolerance and Censorship

When only the Roman Catholic Church had copies of the Bible, interpretation and belief were easily kept uniform. When the printing press was invented and Bibles became available to the masses, they read the Bible instead of relying on the interpretation of priests. The populace began to think for themselves, and no one since has been able to agree on the meaning of biblical words, phrases, and ideas. To belong to a particular religion requires absolute belief without deviation from the religion's interpretation of its official text. The invention of the printing press in the early 1400s continued the bloodshed of the various inquisitions and the wars of religion, which have not yet ceased.

No organization can survive if its basic tenets are successfully challenged. Any religion would collapse if its followers refused to observe its official tenets. Disagreement with basic tenets presents a challenge to the entire structure of the religion. If one tenet were to change, that necessarily implies that any or all others may similarly be subject to change, which means the tenets are not infallible, possibly signalling the end to the religion. Disagreement with a religious tenet is a challenge to the religion's infallibility and very existence, which cannot be tolerated.

As a result of the impossibility of religious toleration there have been no greater atrocities in the history of the world than those committed in the name of religion, and no religion is exempt from this truth. Catholics burned Lutherans, and Lutherans burned Episcopalians, who burned Presbyterians, and vice versa, over generations. To this day no heretic has been forgiven by any church (with the exception of Joan of Arc). Tolerance is mentioned nowhere in the Bible.

The concept of heretic was invented by those who said to love your neighbors and turn the other cheek. The foundation for the concept of heresy is a belief in intellectual slavery—if someone believes differently, ostracize or kill him. Based on this concept, Christians killed Christians by the millions for eight hundred years. (It's always been o.k. for Christians to kill Muslims, and vice versa.) The idea of heresy is now de-emphasized and is only incidentally contained in such as *The Catholic Word Book*. The partial excising of heresy as a concept, however, has not been replaced by the concept of tolerance.

According to Monsignor John Essef, who lived for years in the Levant, writing in *Our Sunday Visitor,*

> In every place where Islam has become a majority—without exception—it has imposed Shari'a Law and subjects non-believers to live in that Muslim state as second-class citizens. . . . To the fundamentalist Muslim, ecumenism is anathema and dialogue is weakness, indifference and a betrayal of Allah. For Islam, there is only one revelation: the final word has been spoken in the Qur'an, and Mohammed is the final prophet.

Monsignor Essef failed to mention that the fundamentalists of any religion feel ecumenism is weakness and a betrayal of their particular god and that Christian fundamentalists act the same as Muslim fundamentalists. Would it be inaccurate to say that for fundamentalist Christians there is only one revelation: the final word has been spoken in the Bible and Jesus Christ is the final prophet? In countries or states where Catholicism or another Christian sect is in the majority, members of other religions are second-class citizens and have little chance at political office. In most religions the final word is that of their god. All other gods of all other religions are heretical, whether the word "heresy" is de-emphasized or expressly used.

The Christian God of the Bible avenges the blood of his servants and renders vengeance to his adversaries (Deut. 32:43). God avenges the enemies of his children (Isa. 1:24). God avenges his own elect (Luke 18:7), and he does it speedily (Luke 18:8). The enemies of the Lord will perish (Ps. 92:9).* This is the morality of the Christian religion in relation to other religions and peoples.

Christians, Muslims, and Jews

The history of anti-Semitism is a history of Christianity.† Christians celebrated the destruction of the Jewish Temple in Jerusalem in 70 C.E. as punishment by the Christian God for Jewish rejection of Jesus Christ. Even before the advent of Christianity, however, Romans and Greeks spread stories that Jews were lepers driven from Egypt and that they practiced ritual murder of Greeks. Because the Jews held to only one god, rejecting the multiple Greek and Roman gods, and

---

*"Appoint a wicked man against him; let an accuser bring him to trial. When he is tried, let him come forth guilty; let his prayer be counted as sin! May his days be few; may another seize his goods! May his children be fatherless, and his wife a widow! May his children wander about and beg; May they be driven out of the ruins they inhabit! May the creditor seize all that he has; may strangers plunder the fruits of his toil! Let there be none to extend kindness to him, nor any to pity his fatherless children! May his posterity be cut off; may his name be blotted out in the second generation! May the iniquity of his fathers be remembered before the LORD, and let not the sin of his mother be blotted out! Let them be before the LORD continually; and may his memory be cut off from the earth." 109th Psalm

†Most of the following history of anti-Semitism is taken from *Antisemitism: A History Portrayed,* published by the Anne Frank Foundation in Amsterdam, 1989.

stayed by themselves in close-knit communities, they were held in suspicion and ostracized. Evolutionary psychologist John Pearce identifies a logical and natural reason for anti-Semitism:

> In the hunting-and-gathering stage of human development, for which we are all still wired biologically, other people, strangers, were the most dangerous creatures one was likely to encounter. You were far more likely to get yourself killed by an outsider to your clan than by a natural disaster or an animal. To fear strangers is just as natural, just as fundamentally human, as to love your own family.

Our continuing psychological division into groups, whether religious, political, economic, racial, sexual, or any other, serves to further solidify the us-against-them syndrome, encouraging strife.

The first wholesale slaughter of Jews occurred in Alexandria in 38 C.E. Men, women, and children were dragged through the streets, beaten to death, and burned on bonfires after they were declared intruders for ridiculing Herod Agrippa, a representative of the Roman Emperor.

In the second century, the Christian Bishop of Sardis accused the Jews of murdering God:

> Even Pilate washed his hands, you killed him on the great Holy Day (Jewish Passover). You killed the Lord in the middle of Jerusalem. . . . He who created the universe was himself nailed to the wood. The Lord was killed. God was murdered. The King of Israel was eliminated by Jewish hands. Oh, this unheard of murder! Oh, this unheard of injustice!

Matthew 27:25 says, "Then answered all the people and said, His blood be on us, and on our children." By the third century this was interpreted to mean, "Therefore they let Christ's blood flow not only over the Jews who were contemporaries of Jesus, but also over all the generations of Jews to come until the end of time."

Relative tolerance ended in 313 C.E. when Christianity became the official religion of the Roman Empire. The Jews were excluded from entering Jerusalem except one day a year; violation resulted in death.

Augustine called Jews degraded and fit only to be slaves to the Church. The laws formulated between 213 and 437 C.E. were codified into the Theodosian Code in 438 and contained two chapters of anti-Jewish laws, Jews being described as a depraved sect, a criminal religion, and an infectious disease. The Justinian Code of 534, which is the basis for European and American law, relegated Jews to second-class citizenship, provided death for anyone tempting a Christian to convert to Judaism, forbade sex between Jews and Christians, prescribed banishment and loss of all possessions for circumcising a Christian, excluded Jews from all public offices, and required death and confiscation of all possessions for anyone building a new synagogue.

Mohammed saw Islam as perfecting Christianity and Judaism, but declared holy war on all nonbelievers, particularly Jews. The male Jews in Medina were slaughtered, the women and children deported. The Koran provides: "Thou wilt surely find that the strongest in enmity against those who believe are the Jews and the idolaters" (Sura V:85). Beginning in 807, Jews in Muslim countries were required to wear yellow badges and to live separately. In some locales they were required to shave their heads and to wear lead or iron seals around their necks. According to Islamic tradition, "A Jew will not be found alone with a Moslem without planning to kill him."

Pope Stephen III objected to Charlemagne and his successors, the Carolingians, giving equal rights to Jews. He wrote to the Bishop at Narbonne:

> Overwhelmed by concern and alarm, we received your message that the Jewish people, who remained unruly towards God and averse to our customs, have been given the same status as Christians on Christian ground. . . . Christians work the Jewish vineyards and fields. Christian men and women live with these traitors under one roof and defile their souls with blasphemous words day and night; these unfortunate wretches must humble themselves to those dogs every day, every hour, and accede to their every whim. Justice alone demands that the promises made to these traitors be declared invalid, so that the death of the crucified savior will finally be avenged.

The First Crusade began with the slaughter of thousands of Jews along the Rhine. The property of dead Jews was used to support the Crusades. The Crusader army commander Godfrey of Bouillon was reported to say that he would "avenge the blood of his Savior by spilling the blood of the Jewish people . . . and [he] also wanted to prevent Jews from fleeing to escape the bloodbath."

Muslims murdered six thousand Jews in the Moroccan city of Fez in 1037 and in 1066 killed over five thousand in Granada, Spain. The Muslims gave the Jews the choice of death or conversion, the same choice Christians later offered to Jews in Spain. Beginning in 1215 with the Fourth Lateran Council, which declared the communion wafer to be the actual body of Christ, Jews were required by the pope and his bishops to wear round yellow badges in France and pointed hats in Germany. The stated purpose was to prevent Christians, out of ignorance of identity, from having sex with Jews.

On June 19, 1239, Pope Gregory IX ordered confiscation of all copies of the Talmud. French Dominicans carried out this order on the first sabbath in Lent by raiding the synagogues and removing all Hebrew literature. All the Jewish literature in Paris was burned on a central bonfire in 1242. Pope John XXII reiterated the order that all copies of the Talmud be burned in 1322, on the eve of the Jewish Passover.

Legends began in the Middle Ages that the Jews ritually murdered Christian children to obtain blood for mixing with their unleavened bread during Passover, to add potency to their wine or to remove the "stink of Jews." When a child was not easily available, the Jews were reputed to steal a host (the communion wafer representing the body of Christ) and to burn or puncture it to obtain fresh blood of Christ, thus again ritually crucifying him. The Catholic Church certified many miracles where the host was rescued from Jews who were later burned at the stake.

Jews were accused of poisoning well waters and causing the plague. These accusations in Switzerland and Germany resulted in Jews being tortured on the rack, beheaded, and burned at the stake. Sixty large Jewish communities and 150 smaller ones were razed and all occupants slaughtered. After all Jews were killed in Zwolle, Switzerland, in 1349, the burgomaster stated, "They have been killed for the love of God with fire and the sword." A German newspaper, however, wrote that the Jews were killed to obtain their possessions: "Their jingling coins formed the poison that killed the Jews."

During the Middle Ages, Jews and their possessions were considered the property of the sovereign.

In 1412, the Laws of Valladolid required Jews to live in enclosed areas, to continue wearing badges, and to grow beards. Jewish doctors were prohibited from treating Christians. Pope Sixtus IV issued a papal bull in 1478 allowing Ferdinand and Isabella to establish a special inquisition against baptized Jews, which had been sought by Spanish Bishops for decades. This inquisition was compared to the Last Judgment; the Church was only doing what awaited Jews in hell. Jews had previously been required to be either baptized or burned at the stake. Most continued to follow Jewish doctrine in private, hence the Christian solution to purify the blood by burning or banishing all Jews. Popes Alexander VI, Leo X, Clement VII, and Paul III approved of the "purity of the blood" statutes, the infamous Limpieza de sangre. Baptized Jews were called *marranos* (swine) and thousands were burned at the stake until 1492, when Ferdinand and Isabella banished all Jews on a few days notice, requiring 150,000 to flee the country with few possessions, leaving most of their wealth for Ferdinand, Isabella, and the Church. By the 1600s the Jews were depicted as eternally wandering the earth without a country. Banishments were justified by Jesus' example in the Bible of driving the Jewish moneychangers from the Temple.

Martin Luther originally sided with Jews in their opposition to forced membership in the Catholic Church, but, when the Jews also refused to convert to Protestantism in 1543, he published a violently anti-Semitic tract titled *On Jews and Their Lies:*

> What must we do with this cursed and vile race of Jews? . . . In the first place, their synagogues should be burned down and what does not burn must be covered with mud. This must be done for the honor of God and Christianity so God may see that we are Christians and we have not simply tolerated or approved that His Son and His Christians have been subjected to lies, curses and slander. In the second place, their houses should be pulled down and destroyed. They must be housed in stables like gypsics. . . . Third, their books should be taken from them. Fourth, rabbis should be forbidden to give any more lessons on pain of death. Fifth, they should not be allowed to move around freely. Let them stay home. Sixth, they should no longer be allowed to charge interest.

The money that is taken from them should be spent to help Jews who agree to be baptized.

Pope Julius III celebrated the Jewish New Year in Rome on September 9, 1553, by publicly burning all books owned or written by Jews. He also ordered all Jewish books burned throughout the empire. The order was reissued by Pope Paul IV in 1559, who had on July 12, 1555, begun confining Jews in Rome within their ghetto from sunset to sunrise where they lived until 1848 on 2 two-and-a-half acres of unsanitary and cramped housing. The purpose of the ghettos, besides quarantining Jews from associating with Christians, was to show the world that God was continuing their punishment for murdering his son. Pope Pius V banished all Jews from Italy, except the punishment ghettos in Rome and Ancona. Jews previously were banished from Venice (1497), Genoa (1516 and 1550), and Naples (1540).

The eighteenth-century enlightenment and the French Revolution continued the traditional treatment of the Jews. Voltaire regarded Jews as "an ignorant, barbarian people, who combine the foulest greed with a terrible superstition and an uncompromising hatred of all the peoples who tolerate them and at whose cost they enrich themselves." The French, however, gave equal rights to Jews after the revolution on the theory that if persecution of Jews ceased, they would give up their odious customs and religion; they would become emancipated by no longer being Jews.

Between 1848 and 1879, anti-Semitism became the basis for political parties and the election of national candidates in Germany and Austria. Because the Jews had no country, they were suspected of being traitors by their countries of residence, the most famous example being the Dreyfus affair in 1894 France.

Army Captain Alfred Dreyfus was accused of passing military secrets to the Germans. He was convicted on forged evidence; his main sin was being a Jew. Dreyfus was rehabilitated only after ten years in prison and a scathing expose and challenge to the French government by Emile Zola. During this period Jewish shops were plundered and Jews assaulted. One columnist described the Dreyfus sentencing: "Death to the Jews, cried the mob when the stripes were torn from his captain's uniform . . . when a progressive and doubtlessly highly civilized people can come to this, what can be expected of other people?"

Anti-Semitism in Russia was preserved by the Russian Orthodox Church, arguing that the Jewish presence polluted Holy Russia. Jews were segregated, taxed into poverty, granted citizenship privileges only upon conversion to Christianity, and required to give twenty-five years of military service. The crackdown on Russian Jews began in March, 1881, when Alexander II was assassinated. Alexander III (1881–1894) believed the Jews were an especially accursed people because they had "crucified the savior," responding to his father's assassination by oppressing the languages, cultures, and religions of non-Russians. By 1891, all Jews were expelled from Moscow. A 1990 poll in the *Moscow News* found that 8.8 percent of all respondents agreed that "the Jews deserve to be punished because they crucified Christ." In Moscow alone, with a population of nine million, this means 800,000 Muscovites believe today's Jews killed Christ and should be punished.

In *Mein Kampf* (1924) Hitler described his assessment of the Jews:

And when such a tumor was carefully cut open, a little Jew was found like a maggot in rotting wood, who often blinked with eyes blinded by the sudden light. . . . what was used here to destroy all human values was a pestilence with more fatal results than those the Black Death had. Now the Jews serve as carriers of bacilli of the worst kind, and they infect souls everywhere. As is typical of all parasites, the Jew keeps enlarging his territory; he lives at the cost of his host and spreads like a dangerous bacillus.

According to his close personal friend, Dietrich Eckart, Hitler was greatly influenced by Luther's later writings and attitude toward Jews. Hitler appreciated the Catholic Church's similar attitude, saying in 1938, "In the Gospels, the Jews cried out to Pilate, when he refused to have Jesus crucified: 'His blood be on us and our children.' Maybe I have to fulfill this curse."

Beginning April 1, 1933, all Jewish shops and businesses were boycotted in Germany, and on April 7, all Jewish officials were fired. Hitler told two visiting Catholic bishops on April 26, 1933, "I am being attacked for the way I treat the Jews. The Church has regarded the Jews as parasites for fifteen hundred years and has banished them to the ghetto. They knew what the Jews were worth. I am only continuing what has been happening the last fifteen hundred years. I may be doing Christianity the greatest of favors."

The official terror began on November 9, 1938, when hundreds of synagogues were burned, Jewish houses and shops were looted and thirty thousand Jews were deported to camps. The ancient religious discrimination against Jews was officially reimplemented in Germany. They were required to wear a yellow star; the identification of a person as Jewish was supplied through the records of the Christian churches in Germany and occupied territories. The only complaint made by the churches was that they should be reimbursed for the onerous administrative burden of checking their records to trace Jewish genealogy.

In December 1941, the month the first permanent extermination camp was established in Chelmno, Poland, six Evangelical Church bishops and the head of the Lubeck Lutheran Church issued the following declaration:

The regulations of the "Reichspolizei" have July 7 [1941] branded the Jews as the born enemies of the people and of the Third Reich. From bitter experience centuries ago, Martin Luther advised governments to take strict measures against Jews and to banish them from German society. The Jews have opposed, misused or tampered with Christianity from the Crucifixion to the present day for their own profit. Christian baptism brings no change in the nature of a Jew, which is determined by race. Because the Evangelical Church in Germany has been ordered to give pastoral guidance to members in their religious life, it demands that Christians of the Jewish race be removed from the Evangelical Church.

Although the world did not find out for years, on January 20, 1942, a short meeting by top Nazis, in the villa Wannsee in Berlin, officially adopted the final solution. On January 31 German execution squads reported having murdered 229,052 Jews in the Baltic countries. In that same year, Rabbi Nietra of Czechoslovakia asked Catholic Archbishop Kametko to help prevent the deportation of the Jews. The Archbishop replied:

> It is not a question of deportation. There [in Germany] you will not die of hunger and misery. They will murder all of you, old and young, women and children at once—it is the punishment you deserve because you murdered our Lord and Savior, Jesus Christ. There is just one possibility of escaping this fate; convert to our religion and then I shall do my best to have the order revoked.

The first selections for the gas chambers in Auschwitz-Birkenau occurred on June 23, 1942. The last gassing occurred there at the end of October 1944. Nobel Peace Prize winner Elie Wiesel has asked pertinent questions:

> In all the turmoil, this relationship [between Christians and Jews] must be reconsidered. Because a new truth struck us: when the victims were all Jews, the murderers were all Christians. What explanation is there that a Hitler or a Himmler was never excommunicated by the Pope? That Pope Pius XII never considered it urgent, or even necessary, to condemn Auschwitz? That in the SS there was a high percentage of Christians who remained devoted to their Christian tradition until the end? That certain murderers went to confession between murders? And that all of them came from Christian families and had enjoyed a Christian upbringing? How can it be explained that being a Christian did not make their hands tremble when they shot down children, nor their consciences rebel when they drove naked and battered victims into the factories of death?

Knowing the history of religions, including Judaism, the explanation is simple. Religion has been the basis for most wars in the history of man and the height of unimagined cruelties. The number of religions without the taint of human blood prominent in their history can be counted one hand and would include the Quakers and a few others. Israel treats non-Jews as second-class citizens, at best, and justifies the killing of Palestinian Muslims as self-defense.

During WWII all countries barred Jewish immigration. Franklin Delano Roosevelt was indifferent to the problem of Jews under German rule, as were the American people and the Pope. The Jewish problem under German rule was way down the priority list, especially compared to winning the war. The Jewish uprising in Palestine in 1936 had made Britons and Americans wary of Jewish claims. Because the outcome of the war was unclear until mid-1943, it wasn't until early 1944 that FDR established the War Refugee Board, probably saving about 200,000 lives; too little, too late. There is always the question of how much more could have been done, however, when the war effort was top priority. Even Jewish communities did little, primarily because until four people escaped from Auschwitz in 1944 no one knew or believed the full extent of the horror. Palestinian

Jews were divided on whether to concentrate resources on rescuing Jews or building the new state. The official U.S. policy was to put all its energies into winning the war as the best way to help. The Allies bombed within four kilometers of Auschwitz but never bombed the railway leading there, which would have stopped the deportations to the biggest death camp of all.

The confrontation between Christians and Jews was rekindled at Auschwitz in the 1980s. In 1987, the archbishops of Paris, Krakow, Lyons, and Brussels, including a total of eighteen Catholic and Jewish leaders, signed an agreement to move a Catholic Carmelite convent from a site next to the fence around the Auschwitz death camp by February 1989. In August of 1989, the Krakow Archbishop repudiated the agreement because Jewish leaders had protested the Catholic Church's failure to meet the deadline and were fomenting anti-Polish feelings. During a Jewish protest at the site, workers at the convent allegedly kicked, punched, and ejected a rabbi and six students who had occupied the grounds to protest the broken agreement. The Jewish group called the convent a desecration of the Jews' memory because of its twenty-three-foot high cross on the lawn where Auschwitz prisoners had been gunned down. (Executed prisoners included both Christians and Jews.)

William F. Buckley pointed out that Jewish anger over the convent was aroused by a fund-raising letter from Brussels urging Catholics to contribute money to the convent where prayers would be said for conversion of the Jews. The agreement to move the convent was negotiated in response to Jewish protests about the fund-raising letter. After the February 1989 deadline expired, several Jewish protesters were expelled and claimed to have been beaten. The Cardinal primate of Poland then asked "Dear Jews" not to go around pretending to be members of a chosen race and to spare the convent from politicization by non-believers. Buckley argued that it would be subtle anti-Semitism "to act as though it were not worth it to pray for the conversion of Jews to Christianity," pointing out that in Israel it's illegal to carry on Christian missionary work. He said:

> Christians are enjoined to spread what they believe to be the special joys of their faith worldwide, and a mark of disrespect for other religions is any failure to try to expose them to what one is committed to believing to be the word of the Lord. . . . Elie Wiesel said, "Tell the nuns to go and pray, but to pray elsewhere." He is right. Who knows, he may yet be converted.

Ground was broken in February 1990 for a new convent. Cardinal Macharski announced the abandonment of plans to also build a center for a Christian-Jewish dialogue near the site, however, because of what he called an "atmosphere of aggression and disquiet sown among us" by the Jewish protests. The cornerstone for the new Carmelite convent was laid in November 1991 by the Archbishop of Krakow. No Jews attended the laying of the cornerstone.

The spokesman for the Vatican observatory, which is developing with the University of Arizona a telescope complex on top of an Arizona mountain allegedly considered sacred by the San Carlos Apache Indian Tribe and opposed for development by environmentalists, said on April 8, 1992, that opposition to the complex was "part of the Jewish conspiracy . . . [coming] out of the Jewish lawyers of the ACLU to undermine and destroy the Catholic Church." The associate director of the Anti-defamation League of B'nai B'rith's Los Angeles office said the remarks were "disturbing, but all too common." The director of the ACLU in Phoenix defended the Vatican spokesman's right to make the remark: "It's a free speech right to say what he believes, no matter how truthful or fair or narrow-minded or bigoted or racist it might be."

Mainline Protestant denominations, such as the Episcopalians, the Presbyterians, and the United Church of Christ, accept a "two-covenant" theology, which maintains that God's covenant with the Jewish people was never abrogated and that Jews do not need to become Christians to attain salvation. Kenneth A. Myers, writing in the October 8, 1990, issue of *Christianity Today,* an evangelical publication, calls the two-covenant theology essentially heretical because "there is no other name [than Jesus] by which we are saved." The founder and executive director of Jews for Jesus explicity calls the two-covenant theology heresy, stating that "from the time of the early church, the Jews have been the most Gospel-resistant people" and concluding that "persecutions of the Jews, instead of becoming a reason to cease telling Jews the gospel of God's love in Christ, should have become an impetus to do that."

Death-dealing conflicts among organized religions will continue inexorably, as long as organized religion exists.

The Crusades

The two primary atrocities of the Christian Churches spanned hundreds of years and are known generically as the Crusades and the Inquisitions. These two innocent-sounding and even patriotic terms hide a history of horror. Were we ever told in school how many millions perished in the Crusades and for what purpose other than glory for Western civilization and the Christian religion? There were seven principle Crusades and many expeditions to drive the Muslims from the Holy Land, to free it from the "infidels" and capture Jerusalem.

The First Crusade was ordered by Pope Urban II on November 28, 1095, drawing six million people over several years, or about 10 percent of the population of Europe. The drawing card to drop everything and go fight the infidels was the forgiveness of all sins and guaranteed entry into heaven—the archetypal Holy War. Out of six million people, who participated in several waves, twenty thousand reached Jerusalem, massacring the inhabitants, young and old, women and children. An eyewitness description stated, "In Solomon's Porch and in his Temple, our men rode in the blood of the Saracens up to the knees of their horses."

The seed for the Crusades was planted when the Persians seized the True Cross in their 614 C.E. capture of Jerusalem, massacring 65,000 Christians and selling the 35,000 survivors into slavery. Jerusalem was retaken by Emperor Heraclius in 630 C.E., but resurrendered to Caliph Omar in 638. By 717 the Muslim empire had spread to North Africa, Spain, Persia, and India. The Muslims tolerated those who worshiped one God, such as the Christians and Jews (though Christians and Jews were second-class citizens in Muslim countries); others were killed or converted to Islam. Christian pilgrimages to Jerusalem were allowed by Muslim authorities, as required by the Catholic Church for penance.

The first crusade officially began on August 15, 1096, but peasants led by Peter the Hermit were anxious to begin and left nine months earlier, soon after the Pope's November order, arriving in Constantinople in July 1096. Of Peter the Hermit's fifteen thousand followers, three thousand survived their crossing into Asia Minor, escaping back to Europe by ship.

The second wave of peasants left Europe in mid-1096, slaughtering Jews found on the way and confiscating their possessions. The second wave was turned back at the Hungarian border and, by autumn, had been defeated. The third wave consisted of the great lords and noblemen who set out in late 1096, well armed and with about one hundred thousand men, prepared to live off the land, which meant living off the people whose land they passed through en route. Most had sold their possessions, intending to settle in the newly conquered Holy Land. The booty of battle became so lucrative, however, that only four hundred miles from Jerusalem, after taking Antioch, the nobles began to settle in. Their men threatened mutiny and insisted on continuing. After three years of battle, starvation, and disease, the first and only successful Crusade reached Jerusalem and conquered it on July 14, 1099, with only twenty-three hundred men surviving. All Jews were slaughtered and infidels expelled. The Muslims immediately reconquered the lands between Jerusalem and Constantinople, however, closing the previously protected route to Jerusalem.

The second crusade was organized by Pope Eugenius III in 1146, led in one part by King Louis VII, the other part by the German emperor. The Germans got as far as Hungary in 1147; the balance as far as Asia Minor; the survivors were back in Europe by 1149.

The third crusade was organized with English sailors and fisherman, sailing in the spring of 1147. They conquered Lisbon, Portugal, and went no further.

By 1149 the Muslims had retaken Antioch. In 1187 Saladin destroyed all the remaining Christian forces in the Holy Land except in Jerusalem and a few isolated cities. By October 2, 1187, Jerusalem surrendered to Saladin. Pope Urban III died of grief on hearing the news of the Christian defeats. Saladin personally slaughtered those knights he disliked, but spared 95 percent of them, including the kings of France and England and the German emperor. Before they could retreat by sea, European re-enforcements began arriving and Saladin was cut off at Acre. The Christian and Muslim armies began alternately starving each other, depending on who had control of the sea. The German Emperor Barbarossa drowned, so his army left. The French King Philip was young and ineffective; the only true leader was English King Richard the Lion-Hearted who was a brilliant acid-tongued homosexual. Acre was under siege from August 1189 until its surrender on July 12, 1191. Saladin violated the negotiated peace so Richard slaughtered his 2,700 best soldiers. Thereafter, Saladin killed all captured

Christians. The war was finally settled by declaring Jerusalem a neutral city, allowing Christians to visit freely, and awarding Saladin a port city.

The fourth crusade was ordered by Pope Innocent III. The Crusaders sailed from Venice in November 1202, capturing Constantinople from the Greek Emperor Alexius III and installing Alexius IV in his place. Alexius IV reneged on his agreement to allow the Crusaders free access to Constantinople and was murdered. Constantinople was ruled by the Franks until 1261. The Fourth Crusade then dissolved, the Pope being sufficiently grateful for the recapture of Constantinople, ousting the Greeks who had created the great schism in 1054.

The Children's Crusade began and ended in 1212, most dying or straggling home after the promised miracle, that the sea would part to allow their passage, failed to occur. This Crusade gave the term a bad name; besides, the infidels were allowing Christians to visit Jerusalem and not interfering with the Christian ports of Tyre and Acre, which prospered by trade with the Muslims.

The fifth crusade was a small one organized by Pope Honorius in 1217. Few left Europe and far fewer arrived in Acre. After the King of Hungary returned home, the balance went from Acre to invade Egypt in 1218, following a strategy suggested by Richard the Lion-Hearted twenty-five years earlier. After three years of siege the Crusaders captured Damietta in Egypt and started toward Cairo. The summer flood of the Nile trapped them and they were all captured. The Sultan let them go on their promise not to return for at least eight years. This Crusade failed because Emperor Frederick II did not arrive (or even leave Europe) as promised, and he was twice excommunicated as a result. After his excommunications, Frederick tried to get back in the good graces of the Pope by sailing to Acre in 1228, but the knights refused to follow Frederick because of his excommunications. Still, by February 1229, Frederick was able to enter into a treaty with the Sultan (who had no desire to fight) and to obtain control of Jerusalem, Bethlehem, Nazareth, most of Galilee, and the two seaports of Jaffa and Lyda. Neither the Sultan nor Frederick (an atheist) were interested in religious disputes and, though the treaty pleased them, it greatly displeased their followers. By his death in 1250, Frederick was reputed to be the Anti-Christ.

With the Frederick/Sultan treaty due to expire in 1239, the pope tried to organize another crusade, but few responded. The Egyptian Sultan died in 1238, so the area was in disorder. When the few French troops landed in Egypt, half were destroyed and the rest ran. The infidels retook Jerusalem but abandoned it without occupation. The new Sultan retook Jerusalem on June 11, 1244, letting all six thousand inhabitants leave unharmed. Unfortunately, Bedouins slaughtered most of them and only six hundred arrived on the coast. On October 17, 1244, Acre was pillaged in the bloodiest battle since the First Crusade, leaving only thirty-three Knights Templar surviving. By this time the Mongols had conquered Russia, Poland, and Hungary and threatened to take all of Europe, having reached the Adriatic. We'd probably all be Muslims if their leader, Genghis Khan, hadn't died; the Mongols retreated to elect another Khan.

With the Mongol threat removed, the next crusade was led by St. Louis in August of 1248, who arrived at Damietta in June 1249 and easily took the city because of his bravery and the unorganized Muslim defenders. The victory was short-lived; because of annual Nile flooding they couldn't proceed and all became ill. They surrendered Damietta to save lives. The Muslims killed all the sick and captured St. Louis. The surviving knights were back in Acre by 1250. St. Louis was ransomed back to France in 1254. The Muslims leveled Antioch in 1268 and it never rose again.

St. Louis began his second, and the last, crusade in July 1270 but only freed Carthage. The Muslims retreated to Tunis where they were besieged, but both St. Louis and his son died there of disease. Tripoli was destroyed in 1289, and Acre was destroyed on May 18, 1291, with Tyre abandoned the next day. No Christians were left in the Holy Land. In 1295 Islam was adopted as the official religion of Persia and the Mongol empire.

The Crusades lasted two hundred years, killing millions of Jews, Christians, Muslims, and the unaffiliated. There has been bad blood between Christians and Muslims ever since—witness Iran, Iraq and the rest of the Western world. The heroes and leaders of the Crusades, the Templar Knights, upon their return to Europe were suppressed by the Catholic Church in 1309 after being tortured to confess heresy. Because the knights were populist figures, they represented a rival to the power of the Church. Accordingly, their goods were confiscated, and they were left paupers. Philip the Fair burned fifty-four Knights Templar in Paris on May 12, 1310.

The Inquisitions

There was no single inquisition with one centralized all-powerful tribunal wreaking havoc on nondevout Catholics. Instead, there were various Inquisitions established with various motives in different time periods and in various countries. With no legitimate society in Europe outside the Catholic Church, dissent threatened the fabric of society. By the eleventh century dissent began to be treated as a combination of heresy and treason. The Inquisitions evolved from that time in Italy, France, and Germany, spreading to Spain in a far different form in the late fifteenth century, and then to possessions of Spain in the New World.

To understand the various Inquisitions requires substantial background in the history of the Roman Catholic Church: absolute power corrupting absolutely. By the 1100s, the Church controlled all of Europe. Kings, princes, and armies were subservient to the priest, and far below bishops and the Pope. The lowest priest was believed to have supernatural powers; his person and possessions were inviolate. Because the priest was above the law, his crimes were not subject to secular authority, which was in all events subservient to the Church. The only discipline against a priest came directly from Rome, and there was no discipline in Rome. The means to political power was through the priesthood, which, with few exceptions, attracted the unscrupulous. Religious affiliation remains a *sine qua non* of political power in most countries of the world, including the United States.

The traditional Christian values of humility, charity, and self-abnegation disappeared in the Middle Ages. The Christian flock was viewed as sheep to be shorn (compare Protestant televangelicals today), and the priests were expert shearers. Bribery ruled. For example, the Archbishop of Tours lifted excommunication from King Philip I in exchange for Philip appointing the Archbishop's male courtesan, Flora, to head the See of Orleans. Popes lived with concubines, female "relatives," nuns, and the daughters of priests. Priests bled the people dry in order to raise the exactions required by the pope. The pope sold letters allowing any bearer to excommunicate whomever the bearer pleased. Excommunication meant banishment from Europe. Pay or leave. These letters were often forged, as was the Papal seal; bishops sold their own letters, and many priests kept concubines. By 1397, during the age of Chaucer, eighty priests in the Hereford Diocese were accused of keeping one or more concubines. Divorces were sold; marriages required large bribes to absolve the parties from violating taboos against possible consanguinity in remote past generations. Priests made regular gifts to boys aged seven to fourteen and awarded churches to some youngsters. Tithes were enforced against the poorest of the poor, who received nothing in return, except their immortal souls. Competing jurisdictions within the Church collected tithes many times over from the same parishioners. There were fines for every conceivable sin, and confession was required of all. Communion was not available until all fines and exactions had been paid. The Church diplomatically suggested to the dying and their families that only if the estate were willed to the Church could the Church be expected to pray for the soul in Purgatory so it could get to heaven. The Church settled for a law passing a third of all estates to it. Many nunneries were houses of prostitution. Criminals joined abbeys to escape prosecution. Many churches became wine bars featuring jugglers, actors, gamblers, and whores. The Church owned Europe and was absolutely corrupt.

Some Church leaders tried to stem the tide of corruption, but with little effect. Scattered abbeys fed the poor during famines, especially the famine of 1197. Several bishops tried over and over for reform. Pope Alexander III denounced the sale of dispensations, limiting their effectiveness to one year. Much of the dispensation system was implemented to compete with the Muslims, who promised eternal bliss and free concubines to all who died as martyrs. The Church promised the same to participants in the Crusades, without the concubines. Before the end of the Crusades in 1291, far greater dispensations were required to obtain participants. Dispensations from all sin (guaranteed entry to heaven without passing Purgatory) were granted to those who would pay for others to go in their place. Dispensations were also given for sins of fathers and mothers. The priests liberally applied their levers: the Eucharist (the communion wafer), holy relics, holy water, exorcism, and prayer. Anything could be had for a price.

Even uneducated peasants began to suspect that something was wrong. The most difficult heresy for the Church was the accusation that the sacraments were polluted by sinful priests. Gregory VII in 1074 confirmed that no one should attend the mass of a priest who had a concubine, but this was neither enforced nor enforceable. Instead of purifying the churches, this order emptied them. The Church thereafter could not admit the sacrament was invalid if the priest had sinned.

The first heretics were burned at Orleans in 1017. The rebellion grew and other leaders arose: Henry, Monk of Lausanne; Arnold of Brescia (burned in 1155); and Peter Waldo of Lyons. These heretics relied on biblical texts and were far more learned in the Bible than most priests, bishops, or even the pope. They gave away their earthly goods, seeking to contrast their own behavior with that of the priests, who sold penances and dispensations. They had many followers who were disgusted with the corruption of the Church and, accordingly, constituted a real threat to the Church.

The Catholic Church considered the Bible too profound for common people, only modifying this position in 1965 with the Second Vatican Council. The Council of Beziers in 1233–34 forbade possession of the Bible in Latin. Any person failing to turn in his Bible for burning was deemed a heretic. The authority of priests now is based on the ability to interpret the "seemingly" contradictory provisions of the Bible. Yet priests in the Middle Ages were ignorant of the Bible, while heretics knew it forwards and backwards. Because the heretics were more skillful with the Bible than the Inquisitors, they were not allowed to argue theology with them, upon pain of death.

Heretics, such as the Waldesians, reproached the Church for its wealth, feudal privilege, sinful priests, sex without reproduction, and any portion of the Catholic dogma not supported directly by the Bible, which left little. They heretically held that it was better to feed the poor than to adorn church walls, arguing that Christ had no mitre, sable, or bejeweled chalice. They said the inquisitorial courts were not for justice but for the monetary gain of the Church.

Alonso II of Aragon decreed in 1194 that heresies and heretics were public enemies, and listening to them was treason to the Church, requiring confiscation of the listeners' goods. Any injury inflicted on a heretic brought the favor of royalty. Alonso's son, Pedro II, added burning at the stake as the appropriate penalty for listening to heresy. In these early days foretelling the formal Inquisitions, the populace would drag heretics out of prison to burn them, in Soissons in 1141, Leige in 1144, and Cologne in 1051. The Church initially protested that vigilante justice was too harsh. Still, the rebellion spread and the Church began to see the wisdom of its followers. The rebels were simple men, detesting the corrupt priesthood. Their main offense was their zeal in making converts and their great success. Many memorized the whole Bible, or at least the New Testament. Those persecuted felt themselves to be the only true Catholics. By 1167, the Cathari ("pure"—no sex or possessions) set up a parallel church in southern France. Death for heresy was officially proclaimed in 1209.

In July 1209, the Cathari headquarters at Breziers, France, was stormed by recently returned Crusaders, on orders of the Church, who slaughtered twenty thousand men, women, and children in three hours. The preferred method of killing heretics, other than by fire, was to first mutilate them by cutting off the nose, then tearing out the eyes and tongue.

The Bishop of Toulouse killed over 500,000 heretics during the early 1200s, resulting in the establishment of the Kingdom of France for the kings of France. Innocent III at the 1215 Lateran Council ordered the faithful to report all heretics for extermination. He believed that the fall of Jerusalem in 1187 signaled the 666 years of the beast of the Apocalypse, evidenced by the swarming spread of Islam. The purpose of the council, attended by bishops, abbots, and representatives of most secular rulers, was to reform the Church, reconquer Jerusalem, and suppress heresy. The Council ordained the fifth crusade for June 1, 1217, and prescribed various penalties for heresy, including the usual ones of confiscation, removal from public office, and excommunication plus punishment by the secular arm, which meant death. Also required were expulsion from lands, the reporting of other heretics and the removal of any bishop failing to follow these rules. By 1325 the Cathars were completely exterminated.

The Catholic Word Book justifies the Inquisition[s] by saying, "The Inquisition was a creature of its time when crimes against the faith, which threatened the good of the Christian community, were regarded also as crimes against the state, and when heretical doctrines of such extremists as the Cathari and Albigensians threatened the very fabric of society."

Gregory IX entrusted the Inquisition to the Dominicans in 1233, and this began its organized phase. Gregory set the stage in 1231, requiring excommunication of all Cathars, Waldensians, heretics, their followers and friends, and those failing to denounce known heretics. The document also prohibited representation by an attorney, excluded the children of heretics from the Church, and required the demolition of the home of any heretic. Acquittals were almost unknown. The Inquisition would excommunicate or declare heretical any civil magistrate who refused to burn a heretic. Perjurers and heretics were allowed to testify against any accused. The testimony of two people was required for a conviction of heresy, but the testimony of only one was sufficient to justify torture, and torture usually resulted in a confession so that a second witness was unnecessary. Favorable witnesses were not available because they would be labeled as heretics for testifying in support of an accused heretic.

Heresy was treason because there was no separation of church and state, and an accusation of treason allowed the confiscation of the accused's property. There was no need to wait until conviction to confiscate the accused's property because the verdict was known in advance in practically all cases, similar to drug-case confiscations today.

Since an accusation of heresy, even against the dead, resulted in confiscation of all property, trials of the dead became very lucrative and resulted in complete estates passing to the Church and the impoverishment of the accused's heirs. A popular proverb in the 1200s was "Justice is a very profitable job." The Church sold offices allowing their purchasers to try people for heresy. The only means to escape an accusation of heresy was by bribery, which was difficult since upon accusation all goods available for bribery were confiscated. Often the accused would face preliminary questioning. At this stage fines, mitigations, and dispensations were both available and rampant. The combination of the Crusades and the Inquisition impoverished the entire population of Europe, except those connected with the Church and its subordinate secular authorities.

The various Inquisitions (Roman Catholic, Protestant, and Spanish) lasted over eight hundred years, from 1017 to the 1800s.

The best-known Inquisitor before the Spanish Inquisition was Bernard Gui. The following is an account of his trial of the Waldesian heretic Hugh of Vienne, in 1321:

> He refused to swear, pretending the feigned reason that he dared not, because, having sworn on another occasion, he had incurred the falling sickness. . . . Therefore, we, Bishop of Pamiers, intimated and explained to him the written law, that any man suspected in matters of faith, and brought before the judge, and required to swear as to the truth, must be judged a heretic if he refuse to swear; yet he would on no account swear; nay, he said that it repented him to have sworn elsewhere before the said bishop and the Inquisitor of Carcassonne, saying that he had thus sinned grievously and believed that it would be a sin to swear again; nor, though oftentimes required, would he thenceforth swear to tell the truth in a case of faith. . . . Item, he said that man sinneth who compelled another to swear, for the Lord hath commanded us not to swear. Item, that he believed his soul would be saved if he were judged to death for the said cause [of refusing to swear]. Item, asked whether the secular powers can without sin condemn to death men guilty of mortal crimes, as homicides and other felons, he answered that he knew not what to believe in this matter, for the Lord commanded Thou shalt not kill. Item, he said and affirmed that he would persist and live and die in the aforesaid faith, though often questioned [on that point]; nor would he swear in any manner. Item, he said and affirmed that he would not believe or obey the Lord Pope, if he told him it is lawful to swear to the truth, and that Purgatory existed, and that the prayers of the Church availed dead men. Item, that he did not believe himself subject to the Lord Pope, but to God alone. Afterwards it was said and expounded to him that, unless he revoked and abandoned these errors, he would be proceeded against as an impenitent and obstinate heretic; yet he answered that he would stand by them in life and death; nor would he in any way abandon them; to wit, that swearing is sinful, for the truth or for other causes; that there is no Purgatory after this life; that prayers for the dead avail them not; that excommunication, however rightly and canonically pronounced, did not shut him out from the Kingdom of God or from spiritual benefits; and that the secular powers which possess jurisdiction sin when they slay malefactors: also, that he held himself not subject to the Pontiff of Rome except when he commandeth the same as God doth.*

Waldesians persisted for centuries in out-of-the-way places and exist today, though their principles have been absorbed by mainstream Protestants or now are considered trivial. In 1393 the Inquisition burned 150 Waldesians in one day at Grenoble; Waldesians were slaughtered en masse by the Church in 1488 and 1686.

An inquisition was commenced by either a special individual summons or a general summons to the populace in the area. When an individual was accused, he was first told by his priest, who announced the name from the pulpit for

---

*G. G. Colton, *Inquisition and Liberty* (1938), p. 1945.

three consecutive Sundays, after which the accused was expected to, and usually did, turn himself in to the nearest secular prison to await trial. Those failing to turn themselves in were automatically excommunicated, becoming outcasts. A general inquisition began with a sermon, after which heretics who confessed were absolved from excommunication and sentences were passed. Confession by itself was insufficient to obtain absolution. The accused was also required to implicate at least one other person as a heretic, otherwise he was sentenced to life in prison or burned at the stake. Because accuseds were required to implicate others, the number of accuseds would snowball, and much of the community would become accused of heresy. One woman in 1254 implicated 169 other heretics.

The Inquisition honed barbarity to its finest point once torture was officially authorized in 1256. The tools of the Inquisition were ingenious devices. The six most used kinds of torture were: (1) Ordeal of water. The accused was forced to swallow between five and ten liters of water until confession was obtained. We know today that ingesting water in such an amount causes the brain to swell and results in death. (2) Ordeal of fire. The accused's feet were caked with animal fat and placed into a roaring fire until confession; the feet were literally fried. (3) The pulley (also known as the Strappado). The arms were tied behind the back, and the accused was hoisted by his wrists to the ceiling and then dropped, pulling the arms from their sockets. This was repeated as necessary until confession. (4) The wheel. The accused was strapped to a large wheel and his body beaten with hammers, bars, and clubs until confession or death. (5) Stivaletto or brodequins. The accused's legs were strapped to boards, and wedges were driven between the board and legs until the pressure crushed or splintered the leg or confession was obtained. (6) The rack. The body was stretched until pulled apart or until confession.

Because of the religiosity of the Catholic and reformed Protestant creeds and sects, people were slaughtered for thinking the following: that there was one God or there was a Trinity of Gods/God; that the Holy Ghost was younger than God or God was older than Christ; that good works saved a man without faith or faith was sufficient without good works; that a baby was not burned eternally for failing to have his head sprinkled by a priest; or that three entities added together made more than one. People could also be killed for speaking of God as having a nose, saying God is an essence, or denying God used his finger as a pen; for denying that Christ was his own father; for believing in Purgatory or not believing in Purgatory; for pretending priests can forgive sins or denying such power; for denying witches ride through the air on sticks; for saying the Virgin Mary was born like other people; for saying a man's rib is not large enough to make a regular-sized woman; for saying all prayers are answered,or that none are; for denying diseases are sent to punish unbelief or sin (such as AIDS today); for denying the absolute authority of the Bible; for possessing a Bible; for attending mass or refusing to attend mass; for carrying a cross or refusing to carry a cross; or for being a Catholic, a Protestant, an Episcopalian, a Presbyterian, a Baptist, or a Quaker. Every virtue has been a crime, and every crime a virtue.

A curious chapter in the Inquisitions involved the rivalry between two Franciscan sects, resulting in the excommunication on December 30, 1317, by John XXII of the splinter Fraticelli sect, which followed vows of poverty in imitation of St. Francis of Assisi. Because of the fear of extremist movements, poverty was condemned in 1323 and, according to the 1638 Vatican manuscript *Codice Urbinate,* over fifteen thousand Fraticelli were executed. The distinctions between saint and heretic were faint.

The intensity of the Inquisitions varied by time and locale. Venice was independent so its inquisitors grew rich, not having to share confiscations with the Church or the state. Few punishments other than confiscation were imposed. The Inquisition was so corrupt (meaning the Church failed to receive its share) in Venice that Boniface VIII suspended it in 1302.

The Aztecs of Mexico were conquered in 1521, and the Inquisition of Mexico began in 1522. The beginnings of the Mexican Inquisition were largely political, directed against Cortes and his followers. When Cortes went to Honduras in 1524 he left his cousin Rodrigo de Paz in charge. The Inquisition imprisoned de Paz and tortured him, roasting his feet until his toes fell off, and then burning his feet to the ankles in an attempt to find out where Cortes hid his gold.

In Mexico's first ten years of the Inquisition only one person was exonerated. Doctors were targeted because the Church resented their interference with the Churches' role in healing. Many were accused of being Lutheran. Indians were persecuted for venerating their original gods after conversion. Dominicans and Franciscans tried each other for heresy over differences in scriptural interpretation, such as whether a Church member receives grace from the sacraments or is already in a state of grace upon conversion. A formal edict against the Jews was issued in 1523. The first burnings for heresy in Mexico occurred on October 17, 1528. From 1572 through 1601 over a thousand trials were held with accusations against Jews and Protestants, and especially Lutherans and Germans suspected of being Lutheran. Some heretics were sold as slaves. Hundreds of volumes of sixteenth-century manuscripts detail the Mexican Inquisition.

The Inquisition also proceeded in other Catholic countries during the same period, such as Peru, Guatemala, and the Philippines. The Inquisition lasted in Sicily from 1487 to 1782. It was also waged in Sardinia, the Canary Islands, Portugal, and all of South America.

The Inquisition in Spain was a marginal improvement over the wholesale slaughter of the Jews. In Spain, as in France and Italy centuries earlier, the Catholic Church was corrupt. Most priests kept concubines, and the courts were run by bribery. Ferdinand and Isabella united Spain, driving out the Moors and destroying the castles of forty-two robber barons, making Spain the most modern country in Europe and its most efficient totalitarian state. Ferdinand considered the conversos, "converted" Jews, to be his biggest problem. They filled his court and ran much of the country. (Lest Anglo-Saxons become smug, Edward I expelled all Jews from England.)

The Spanish Inquisition was established in 1478 by order of Sixtus IV, though controlled by the crown, which appointed the Inquisitors and kept confiscations.

The Inquisitors kept concubines and took bribes, which horrified Sixtus IV, who ordered fair trials henceforth and stated that the Inquisition in Spain was motivated by confiscations. His order had been issued in response to a bribe by conversos and was never enforced after Ferdinand refused to alter Inquisition methods.

By 1560 a witness could be bought to testify to anything. Inquisitor Lucero kept a permanent witness handy for use against anyone he wished to destroy, and witnesses were even allowed to appear as different persons during the same trial. Jews offered ransoms to Ferdinand, but Isabella refused their acceptance. On March 20, 1492, all Jews were ordered expelled by July 31 under pain of death. The order was not published in Barcelona until May 1, however, so Jews residing there had three months to settle their affairs, sell their nonportable possessions, and leave. Those who failed to meet the deadline had all their goods confiscated and were killed. Those fleeing were able to keep few possessions, and many were robbed and murdered in Spanish seaports and in other countries upon their arrival. About fifty thousand Jews converted to Christianity, in theory, and stayed in Spain.

The Spanish fetish for a pure Spain and pure blood resulted in a similar order against the Moors in 1609. The Moors were given three days to leave the country. Their goods were forfeited, they were robbed of what they still had on the way out of the country, and women and children were sold as slaves. The engineer of the expulsion of the Moors, Archbishop Ribera, was beatified by the Church. Catholics may now pray to God in his name.

In December 1990, the Vatican proposed beatifying Queen Isabella I of Spain as the first step in her elevation to sainthood, in time for the five hundredth anniversary of Columbus's discovery of America, which brought Christianity to the New World. The move outraged Jews and Muslims. The head of the Federation of Spanish Jewish Communities called Isabella "a symbol of intolerance," pointing out that her canonization "would reopen old wounds that we thought were closed forever."* Jewish representatives in Spain, Italy, and Britain asked the Vatican to shelve the petition. The chairman of the Islamic Society for the Promotion of Religious Tolerance was quoted in the *London Times* as saying, "Muslims and Jews were forced at the point of a sword to convert to Christianity or die. She is more a demon than a saint." The postulator arguing Isabella's case before the Vatican called her "one of the great women of history" and "one of the great Christians of history," though he admits to be hard-pressed to find one miracle attributable to Isabella. (Two miracles are needed for beatification.)†

By 1786 the Spanish Inquisition was comparatively dormant, though it still pulled people from their beds in the middle of the night and employed torture, and priests uniformly lived with women. The last Inquisitorial execution in Spain was in 1834, and the Inquisition officially ended in Spain in 1869. Thus, the Inquisition lasted over eight hundred years from the first execution in 1017 to the last execution in 1834. No one knows how many were killed in the various

---

*Associated Press, *Arizona Republic,* Dec. 28, 1990.

†William Scobie, *London Observer* Service, *Arizona Republic,* Dec. 30, 1990.

Inquisitions, though estimates range into the tens of millions over its eight-hundred-year reign of terror. Even a relatively conservative number such as twenty million (some estimate sixty million), because of the low population of the world during this time period, would be a percentage equivalent today of hundreds of millions slaughtered.

Today the archives of the Catholic Church remain sealed in Rome, but over the eight centuries of the various Inquisitions millions of people were murdered by the Christian Churches. We will never know how many were slaughtered in the name of religion. *The Catholic Word Book* explains the Catholic Archives: "The strictest secrecy is always in effect for confidential records concerning matters of conscience, and documents of this kind are destroyed as soon as circumstances permit." The Church responded to the cruelty of the Inquisition by canonizing the worst of its Inquisitors in 1712.

The term "Inquisition" was dropped from the official title of the Inquisition in 1908 by Pius X and was henceforth known as "The Holy Office." In 1965 Pope Paul VI renamed it "The Sacred Congregation for the Doctrine of the Faith," which it remains today.

The Nature of Religious Toleration

Religious toleration is a recent concept. The toleration by any religion of other religions and the nonreligious increases in direct proportion to that religion's loss of power and inability to do anything concrete about heresy. When the Catholic Church exercised absolute power, heresy meant confiscation of all property, exile, imprisonment, torture, and death.

When Henry VIII established the Episcopal Church, he instructed Parliament to pass "An Act for abolishing of diversity of opinion":

> First, that in the sacrament was the real body and blood of Jesus Christ. Second, that the body and blood of Jesus Christ was in the bread, and the blood and body of Jesus Christ was in the wine. Third, that priests should not marry. Fourth, that vows of chastity are of perpetual obligation. Fifth, that private masses are to be continued; and, Sixth, that auricular confessions to a priest must be maintained.*

The punishment for denying the first article was death, denial of the others required imprisonment, and two denials also resulted in death. (None of these articles is part of the Episcopal dogma today.) The American colonies enacted laws similar to the following:

> That is any person shall hereafter, within this province, wittingly, maliciously, and advisedly, by writing or speaking, blaspheme or curse God, or deny our

---

*Robert Ingersoll, *Ingersoll's Greatest Lectures* (1944).

savior, Jesus Christ, to be the Son of God, or shall deny the Holy Trinity, the Father, Son, and Holy Ghost, or the Godhead of any of the three persons [sic], or the unity of the Godhead, or shall utter any profane words concerning the Holy Trinity, or any of the persons [sic] thereof, and shall be convicted by verdict, shall, for the first offence, be bored through the tongue, and fined twenty pounds to be levied of his body. And for the second offence, the offender shall be stigmatized by burning in the forehead with the letter B, and fined forty pounds. And that for the third offence the offender shall suffer death without the benefit of the clergy.*

Gore Vidal puts the American founding in perspective:

Actually, the Puritans had been driven out of England because no one could stand them. They went to Holland where they proceeded to persecute the Dutch, who eventually drove them out. Our history books say they were driven out because of persecution—yet they were persecuting the Dutch who put them on boats and headed them west.†

Every Christian has a duty to kill the enemies of God, and if anyone hints there's another God, Christians are duty bound to kill the bearer of the suggestion, whether the suggester is father, mother, relative, friend, or wife (Deut. 13:6–11). God's children read the Bible and understood the words differently, and, therefore, slaughter resulted. Millions of good people are Christians. They are hard-working and self-sacrificing. Many believe, however, that disagreement with the Bible is a mortal crime and that disbelievers are eternally damned. The Bible orders unbelievers slain.

The plain fact is that tolerating the believers of another god is treason to any religion's one true god. How can a believer be true to his god if he tolerates other gods, when by the infallible principles of his religion there's only one god, which is the god of his religion?

The primary reason for religious toleration, such as through the Council of Churches, is to end religious wars. It isn't working and logically, because of the central concept of all religions, can never work. All religions differ and, no matter how slight the differences, to fundamentalists the dogma of all others is heresy, blasphemy, and possible cause for damnation. The following is a summary of the state of recent religious tolerance.

Not only Catholics but also Protestants continued to disfellowship or excommunicate members. The 3.8 million member Jehovah's Witnesses disfellowshipped forty thousand members in 1989, the most publicized case being a man who was cast out because he allowed his infant daughter to undergo a blood transfusion. When his daughter died four years later, those family members who remained Jehovah's Witnesses were forbidden, by their church, to attend the funeral. Members remaining in the church are ordered to avoid contact with disfellow-

---

*Ibid.

†David Reiff, interview with Gore Vidal, *Elle,* April 1990.

shipped members. The result is often referred to as "spiritual death." According to one former member, "many face the breakup of their family and are turned off to God and organized religion. Many end up suicidal."

Salman Rushdie made additional headlines in 1990 for other than his literary output. In December 1990, Rushdie announced that he had embraced Islam, would decline to allow the issuance of *The Satanic Verses* in paperback, and would allow no further translations of the book, which sold over a million copies in English, was translated into fifteen languages, and was banned in over twenty countries. One writer reacted by stating that "to allow any group to exercise suppression is to suppress every subject, since there is a group waiting to be offended by every interesting subject." Militant Muslims reacted to the Rushdie statement by demanding that the British government end its protection of Rushdie so Muslims could kill him, saying, "God Almighty's edict cannot be revoked and must be carried out under all circumstances." (A British Muslim group concurred, though its Netherlands counterpart stated that the death order should be lifted, saying, "Ninety percent of Muslims think Rushdie should be allowed to live freely.") The Ayatollah Ali Khamenei (successor to Ayatollah Khomeini, who pronounced the death sentence on Rushdie) said that the death sentence is irreversible even if Rushdie "becomes the most pious Muslim of his time."

A holiday for Martin Luther King was voted down by the residents of Arizona in 1990, culminating an eighteen-year civil rights struggle, which created deep divisions in the state that may long endure. The fight against the holiday was led by fundamentalist religious leaders, including former governor and devout Mormon, Evan Mecham. The King holiday was finally adopted in 1992 in Arizona, after the impeachment and removal from office of Governor Mecham for alleged campaign law violations.

In October 1990, Israeli soldiers fired on Palestinian demonstators, killing nineteen outside the Al Aqsa mosque on Temple Mount, one of three pilgrimage destinations specified for Muslims by Mohammed. This mosque sits next to the Dome of the Rock, both built thirteen hundred years ago. Israeli extremists have threatened to dismantle and ship the mosque to Mecca. The Israelis claim the Islamic temples must be removed to make way for a third Jewish temple on the site, saying, "We are ordered by God, the Bible and history to do it." Muslims, however, believe Mohammed ascended to heaven from the site, leaving his footprint behind in stone. As a result of the tension, the Israeli defense minister called the area a "ravine of hate," bringing fears that Jerusalem was sliding into chaos reminiscent of Beirut and Belfast. The city is split into two separate districts of 350,000 Jews and 150,000 Arabs. Jerusalem streets were quiet on Christmas 1990 with one German tourist calling the situation "very, very fearful. . . . here you cannot feel peace." Curfews restricted Arabs to refugee camps and Arab districts. Visitors to Manger Square in Bethlehem were required to pass through a metal detector with armed soldiers watching from atop the Church of the Nativity. It's been this way, off and on, for two thousand years.

Also in 1990, India featured war between Hindus and Muslims resulting in hundreds of deaths when Hindu fundamentalists tried to seize a Muslim mosque three hundred miles southeast of New Delhi. Violence erupted in twenty-two of the state's sixty-three districts and also in Bangladesh and Pakistan where Muslim mobs attacked Hindu shops on hearing of the clashes in India. The World Hindu Council says the 430-year-old mosque is built over the birthplace of the Lord Rama, one of the most revered Hindu gods. Muslims naturally dispute Hindu claims, saying that relinquishing the mosque would jeopardize hundreds of other Muslim sites. The violence toppled the government of Indian Premier V. P. Singh, who had opposed construction of a Hindu temple on the site. Religious riots left hundreds dead in India after Hindu fundamentalists demolished this 430-year-old Muslim mosque in December 1992. Hindus believe that sixteenth-century Muslim invaders destroyed the Hindu temple. Hundreds of thousands of Hindus and Muslims were killed when India was partitioned to form Muslim Pakistan in 1947.*

In his book, *East to West: A Journey Around the World* (1958), Arnold Toynbee describes a similar situation resulting from the 1947 partition of the twin cities of Amritsar and Lahore in the Panjab region of northwest India and Pakistan. Amritsar was a Sikh creation and Lahore primarily Muslim, but because of the partition the inhabitants of neither were allowed to cross into the territory of the other. Toynbee sums up the inability of governments and religions to live at peace:

> In one respect the "higher" religions have brought calamity on the World and discredit on themselves: they have seldom been content to live and let live, side by side; and their attempts to eliminate one another have been responsible for some of the bitterest conflicts and cruellest atrocities that have ever disgraced man's history. In this, the two world religions of Jewish origin, Christianity and Islam, have been the worst offenders; but Hinduism, and even Buddhism, have not been guiltless.

By August 1992 the slaughter of Slavic Muslims in former Yugoslavia by Christian Serbians in Bosnia-Herzegovina was recognized by the United Nations as genocide, similar to the *Kristalnacht* and holocaust of the Nazis against the Jews; again Christians are fighting Muslims as they have in the past and appear likely to continue doing so indefinitely. The Serbians were alleged to maintain ninety-four concentration camps of Muslims, continuing their policy of "ethnic cleansing," more accurately described as slaughter in the name of religion.

In *An Historian's Approach to Religion,* Toynbee further analyzes the inherent difficulties of religious tolerance:

> The fruit of Pharisaism is intolerance; the fruit of intolerance is violence; and the wages of sin is death. The Mahometans [Islam], according to the principles of their faith, are under an obligation to use violence for the purpose of bringing other religions to ruin; yet, in spite of that, they have been tolerating other religions for some centuries past. The Christians have not been given orders to do anything

*Associated Press, *Arizona Republic,* Dec. 8, 9, 19, 1992.

but preach and instruct; yet, in spite of this, from time immemorial they have been exterminating by fire and sword all those who are not of their religion . . . if the infidels [non-Christians] were to agree to submit to a competitive examination in which the marks were to be awarded for intelligence, for learning, and for the military virtues [sic], we ought to take them at their word; for, on these terms, they would inevitably be beaten at the present day. On all these three points they are far inferior to us Christians. We enjoy the fine advantage of being far better versed than they are in the art of killing, bombarding, and exterminating the human race.

A true brotherhood of man can succeed only when organized religion disappears, but its disappearance should neither be expected nor its prohibition advocated, because outlawing religion would be as effective as outlawing any superstition.

6

Superstition and Religion

The first superstition originated with our Neanderthal ancestors' belief in an after-life. We sensed spirits all around us, in rocks and rivers, in bears and beasts, in the wind and the sun. We reasoned that if spirits inhabited inanimate objects, lower animals, and the forces of weather, we must individually have a spirit within us that lives on after our death. So we buried cooking and hunting utensils with our Neanderthal dead, and our first superstition became the basis for Western religion.

Because there were spirits everywhere and life was unpredictable, we devised rituals and other means of placating the unseen, to conjure favorable destinies and survival beyond the grave. These spirits explained lightning and thunder, eclipses and seasons, birth and death. Spirits gave warnings to animals, which eluded our hunt. It was "other worldly" for a tree to grow from an acorn, so we explained it by reference to the spirits. Hardships and disease were caused by evil spirits that we learned to soothe through sacrifices and rituals. We elaborated our superstitions into set rules to reduce anxiety and make the universe seem predictable—we established organized religion.

Astrology and voodoo, Catholicism and Judaism, lucky charms and rituals give us a sense of peace and control. Believers in religion profess to turn their lives over to God. Turning control over to another being, whether existent or nonexistent, relieves the individual of personal responsibility as long as the person follows the tenets of the particular religion, lucky charm, or ritual (such as in Alcoholics Anonymous). If these tenets are not followed, then anxiety is created, not relieved. The religious solution is a rededication of lives to God. If religious people were truly dedicated to God, the religious tenets would not have been violated and bad luck would not have befallen the faithful.

One primary difference between religion and superstition is that most of us are religious but most deny being superstitious. Instead of calling ourselves superstitious, we say we "have beliefs" or "take precautions." The attitude of most is that "I have beliefs" and "you are superstitious." Both religion and superstition, however, are belief in spite of or without evidence.

It is instructive to compare the practices of most, if not all, organized religions, including modern Catholicism, with the definition of "Occultism" in *The Catholic Word Book:* "Practices involving ceremonies, rituals, chants, incantations, other cult-related activities intended to affect the course of nature, the lives of practitioners and others, through esoteric powers of magic, diabolical or other forces; one of many forms of superstition."

Our current superstitions, sayings, religious ideas, and holidays are inextricably linked to our ancient religions and superstitions. Horseshoes are considered lucky because the Archbishop of Canterbury in 959 published a story of a blacksmith who shoed the devil with horseshoes, so a horseshoe above the door is supposed to keep the devil away. Horseshoes also keep away witches, which is why witches ride broomsticks instead of horses.

Crossing our fingers mimics the ancient symbol of the cross; good luck supposedly follows. The pre-Christian version was a greeting by linking fingers, symbolizing intersecting spirits, a forerunner to the handshake. Crossing fingers into King's X was supposed to give immunity from a lie. Saying "God bless you" in response to a sneeze was originally ordered by Pope Gregory the Great in the sixth century when a sneeze during the plague foretold an early meeting with one's "maker." The number thirteen is considered unlucky because the Ides (usually the thirteenth day of the month) was viewed by the Romans as an ominous day.

The halo was originally a crown symbol. It was discouraged by early Christians as pagan, but finally integrated into Christianity. The word "amen" originated in Egypt about 2500 B.C.E. as "amun," meaning hidden one, the name of the highest Egyptian deity. The Hebrews adopted it to mean "so it is," or "trustworthy." These concepts originated in our oldest religions and continue today as integral parts of our modern religions.

Many of the ancient rules of etiquette originated in *The Instructions of Ptahhotep,* the Miss Manners of Egypt circa 2500 B.C.E., and ended up as Proverbs and Ecclesiastes in the Bible. When the writing of the Old Testament began in about 700 B.C.E., these customs of etiquette had been around for at least eighteen hundred years.

Our spirits and gods today are those invented by our ancestors, based on traditions and superstitions dating before we measured time. These were natural mistakes and honest exaggerations made up by a species with a love for the marvelous.

Superstition is not only a bad joke but a broadly common human weakness. Superstition treats "make believe" the same as reality, a children's game. Where religion dominates a people or nation, humans become puppets of the unseen and unknowable, remaining children and never becoming adults. Human dignity is replaced by ritual and astrology, sacrifice and voodoo. Progress ceases and liberty ends. Superstition artificially sets one human above another—popes, priests, and preachers are holier and better than anyone else. Superstition imprisons the virtuous, tortures thinkers, chains the body, and orders cessation of freedom of speech. A difference in opinion about the substance of substanceless superstitions is heresy and blasphemy. Superstition counts human love as degrading; elevates monks above fathers, nuns above mothers, and faith above fact. Superstition creates an elitist heaven, a hell of eternal revenge, a world of unceasing religious wars and hatreds and an enemy of rationality, medicine, and science. The poverty of every country in the world is roughly proportionate to the sincere belief of its citizens in orthodox religion.

Superstitions plagued our ancestors in the Middle Ages and made their lives a miserable sham. There was no universal education; perhaps one in twenty thousand could read and write. There was no progress or invention, only religion and prayer. Priests were the shepherds of the people, against knowledge, thought, and doubt. Human toil was used to support the pious and the useless and to build magnificent churches while church members lived in hovels and slums. For hundreds of years Christianity concentrated on wresting the empty sepulcher of Christ from the Muslims, killing millions, while the Christian God lost battle after battle.

Our products of value have come from science and the unreligious who freed the slaves, clothed the poor, fed the hungry, lengthened our lives, secured our homes, and provided us with the richness of art, music, books, and travel. None of the advances of mankind have been derived from religion or superstition of any flavor.

We're all part of large segments of society known for their superstitions. Gamblers are superstitious and resort to random numerology, such as betting odometer readings, license plate numbers and the dates of birthdays and anniversaries. Stockbrokers are highly superstitious, which is logical considering the control they exert over the stock market, which is nothing more than socially acceptable gambling.

Like any superstition or religion, astrology is the way millions cope with fear of the unknown. Nancy Reagan felt about astrology the same as most of us feel about religion; the purpose is to hedge our bets:

> I knew, of course, that if this ever came out, it could prove embarrassing to Ronnie—although I never imagined just how embarrassing. But as long as I worked with Mike Deaver, I knew my secret was safe. . . . Mike believed it was a good idea to get Joan's input. . . . You learn something from living in the White House, and I didn't think an astrologer should be sent checks signed by the First Lady. And so I asked a friend back in California to pay Joan and I reimbursed her each month. . . . [Concerning the President's reaction, he asked], "Honey, what was that about?" . . . When I told him, he said, "If it makes you feel better, go ahead and do it. But be careful. It might look a little odd if it ever came out." . . . I had always considered it as a private project, something I did to hedge our bets, to try to keep Ronnie from getting shot again—and to keep me from going mad with worry. If I hadn't taken every step I could think of to protect my husband, and Ronnie had been shot again, I would never have been able to forgive myself.

A 1984 Gallup poll found that 55 percent of American teenagers believed in astrology. Eighty percent of those reading the daily newspaper read their horoscopes; a fourth of women believe there's something in it, as do a sixth of men. The three Magi/wisemen were astrologers, according to astrologer Laurie

Brady, who styles herself as Chicago's "Astrologer to the Stars," and who responded to the McGervey and Silverman studies:

> You know, I have been on radio shows, television shows. I was once on David Susskind's show with all these scientists, and none of them knew how to make [an astrological] chart. I said, "You know nothing about astrology; how can you argue with me? I'm a professional."

Sports figures are famous for their clothing fetishes during a hot (or cold) streak. During the regular 1988–89 season, the Chicago Bulls were swept by the Cleveland Cavaliers 6–0. For the playoffs the Bulls changed hotels in Cleveland to the one where they'd stayed when beating the Cavs in the 1988 playoffs, and switched from white shoes to black shoes; size 18s for John Paxson, Scott Pippen, and Will Perdue couldn't be found so they dyed theirs black.

London license plate officials dropped the number 666 after motorists complained that this biblical number of "the beast" caused serious bedevilment in their lives. Revelation 13:18 refers to "the number of the beast; for it is the number of a man; and his number is six hundred threescore and six." Besides a motorist who claimed her car took control of her, and one whose son had been "a quiet, home-loving boy" until required to drive a van with a 666 license, Ronald Reagan on retirement had his California address changed from 666 to 668 St. Cloud Drive. Tennessee in 1988 was forced by complaints to remove 666 from its license plates after motorists refused to accept them, claiming they bore the mark of the devil.

The connection between organized religion and our superstitions is illustrated by the study of any primitive people. An American anthropologist, Alma Graham, and her writer husband, Philip Graham, studied the Beng ethnic group in the Ivory Coast, Africa, for fourteen months beginning in the fall of 1979. The villagers dressed similarly to you and me, lived in adobe houses, and entertained themselves with late-night storytelling instead of watching television. When the husband found himself with writer's block he did what any Beng villager would have done; he consulted a noted female diviner in a distant village. The diviner placed his previous writings on an animal skin, then held a brass pan with several black pebbles and water made milky by a white powder designed to draw spirits. She watched the pebbles and announced that the writer should sacrifice a white hen on the next sacred day, and then a goat. They then toasted with palm wine.

The writer followed the diviner's directions. An animist priest poured the chicken blood over the previously sticky roots of a sacred tree and then the blood of a goat. The writer again started writing, of course, about the ceremony. This world of spirits was used to explain every occurrence in the village, whether disease, insanity, or misfortune.*

---

*Philip Graham, "A Writer in a World of Spirits," *Writer's Digest* (Dec. 1989).

We were told of the spirits who lived in the tall iroko tree dominating the nearby coffee fields and who sometimes could be heard singing at night, a whistling wind. A hundred yards farther away in the rain forest was another spirit village, the home of a polygamous spirit man who flew at night from one invisible village to another, visiting each of his two wives, and whose path was through our court-yard. The sound of the wind on those nights was the sound of his flight. Indeed, we discovered that the wind itself was the very movement and sound of all spirits, and in the forest encircling the village each swaying tree and shaking branch was their transfigured presence. Soon Alma and I grew attuned to the order of invisible things, as Kouassi [a friend in the village] carefully recounted to us the cosmology that was carried inside every person we passed on a village path or bargained with in the market; another universe in familiar bodies, and the multiplication, in a crowd, of strange, shared secrets. The spirits lived within the Beng and therefore around them as well, for those anterior presences also filled up their outer world.

The Beng experience is parallel to the voodoo experience in the making of Haitian zombies, related by James Michener in his book *Caribbean.* Four certifiable zombies are under protection by the Haitian government, and they were all zombified in the same manner. The zombie in *Caribbean,* Lalique Hebert, was seventeen years old when a jealous sister paid a voodoo *bucor* to "kill" her. The medical doctor rescuing zombies for the Haitian government described the zombie maker:

> Like a bishop in the Catholic church, who can claim a straight-line inheritance from Jesus Christ, he's a straight-line descendant of some notable native doctor in Africa. But he has to be extremely skilled in making nice distinctions. Too much of his magic powder, the target dies. Too little, the target does not pass into perfect suspension, comes awake too soon, suffocates in his grave.

The voodoo *bucor* has the knowledge of secret and powerful poisons and drugs that can induce the suspension of life functions. The clinical death of the target is accurately certified by a medical doctor. The target is buried in a sixteen-inch-deep grave, dug up the second day, and resuscitated by the *bucor,* who keeps the resurrectee in a suspended state (by depriving the target of salt) and later sells the target as a slave in another region. Lalique Hebert had been a zombie slave for eleven years when she was discovered and slowly weaned away from her voodoo religious and drug-induced conversion. Her fellow villagers shunned her, letting her sleep on the streets. The investigator asked the villagers where Lalique had been sleeping: "Maybe sleep here. Maybe against that wall. . . . Not good have zombie in village. She come for revenge, maybe. Someone here in bad trouble, maybe. . . . She try to stay, people drive her out. . . . Zombies go many places. They not need eat . . . sleep . . . think. Missy, they not like you and me."

The spirits around us have been harnessed by our religions with gods indistinguishable from the Beng spirits and the voodoo spirits, residing within us and constituting the soul. How does any religion differ from that of primitive peoples? Both describe the unknowable in terms of speculation and superstition. How is one preferable over or distinguishable from the other? How can anyone intelligently decide the truth among Beng spirits, Catholicism, Judaism, Buddhism, voodoo, Taoism, or any of the hundreds of religions, sects, and cults of the spirit, except to admit a preference for the traditional religious flavor of our immediate ancestors? Our sole advancement in fifty thousand years has been our consolidation of various spirits into one spirit called God. Even this refinement, however, is illusory, because Western Christians still believe in billions of spirits—Father, Son, and Holy Ghost make three (or one) plus angels, saints (for some), devils, and souls numbering in the umpteen billions.

Why do we believe undocumented and undocumentable things? Do we care about facts? Perhaps we don't want to know, hoping what we don't know won't hurt us. A currently popular example of this can be seen in books by Robert Fulghum, such as *All I Really Need to Know I Learned in Kindergarten,* and *It Was on Fire When I Lay Down on It,* the latter of which contains the following epigraph: "I believe that imagination is stronger than knowledge—that myth is more potent than history. I believe that dreams are more powerful than facts—that hope always triumphs over experience—that laughter is the only cure for grief. And I believe that love is stronger than death." Fulghum is unfortunately correct. We're more comfortable with our beliefs than with having to reconcile our beliefs with contrary facts, which might start our belief systems crumbling from within. Then we would have to think for ourselves, and there is nothing more strenuous and disconcerting. For these reasons neither superstition nor religion will likely recede in popularity.

Many believe the universe operates on the principles of science as embodied in the forces of nature without the intervention of an unseen god or other superstition. If there's no God, Christian or otherwise, that doesn't mean life is meaningless. Life is full of meaning, and so is death. Without death there'd be no evolution, no progress, and no change. Is the life of any animal meaningless because it dies? If faithful Fido dies, has his life been without meaning? Is the significance of giving gifts diminished by the discovery that Santa Claus doesn't exist, or is the significance of gift-giving enhanced? What is required for meaning in life? Would there be more meaning to life if there were life after death, or would that simply constitute a longer life? Is there less meaning to a short and quality life than to a long and unhappy life? Without death we'd be forever suspended without the mechanism of natural selection and evolution to claw us upward. Our species would be frozen in space and time. Life and death force evolution to create a higher order. The meaning of life is to create this higher order, to bring improvement to the species and to the quality and quantity of life. We can perhaps evolve to a higher intelligence and ability to cope with one another, individually and as nations. Our increased ability to communicate across cultures and miles and to store information may speed our development geometrically.

There are many positive aspects to rejecting superstition. Everyone in the universe becomes equal. There are no lost souls or heretics to kill or convert.

The only guidepost would be sensory perception. Whether God or gods exist becomes meaningless. Morality would be determined by human needs existing in this world without guessing what a remotely possible other world might hold in store. There would be no personal immortality, no eternal hobnobbing with the gods, no guilt based on religious shibboleths, and no threat of divine anger. Human potential would be the touchstone of life. There would be no delusions.

7

Religion, Ethics, and Morality

Moral indignation is jealousy with a halo.

—H. G. Wells

A primary reason for the severe reaction against any critical examination of religion is the assumption that without religion there'd be no morality or ethics. This assumption is without substance. More atrocities have been committed in the name of religion than in the name of Lucifer or any secular leader. Without organized religion the human condition would drastically improve, together with the state of human morality and ethics.

If we threw out organized religion, what would happen to the substance of the Ten Commandments? Nothing. Every civilized (and not so civilized) country in the world has codified the only ethical Commandments, four of the last five of the Ten Commandments, into its laws, and this has been true for centuries: "You shall not commit murder. You shall not commit adultery. You shall not steal. You shall not give false evidence against your neighbor."

Where in the world is it, or has it ever been, legal to murder, commit adultery, steal, or give false evidence, whether the local government is Christian, Jewish, Muslim, Taoist, Buddhist, Hindu, Moonie, or Subrodominaciac?

The lower animals act ethically toward the members of their own species— certainly more ethically than humans. Horses don't organize armies to slaughter other horses, nor do any of the lower species. Is that because these species are not sufficiently intelligent? Birds feed blind birds, and biologists find that the fittest for evolution are not necessarily the strongest, but those that combine for mutual support. Creatures highly organized to this end include ants, bees, termites, beavers, muskrats, apes, parrots, and most lower animals.

Social opinion is the greatest molder of our conduct, for good and for bad. Humans have always been social, living in groups. A high level of cooperation historically was required for survival, requiring the development of ethics long before the codification of organized religion.

Many older societies have long traditions of hospitality—Bedouins, Arabs, Turks, and Afghans. There are some differences in our moral codes, but most of our kind are highly ethical, except in their general attitude toward outsiders or noncitizens who are not political allies. Most older societies are democracies, with the entire community or tribe participating in decision-making. Most are scrupulously honest, at least those that have had little contact with Western man. It is primarily civilized people who steal from and defraud others. Most tribes have little or no property ownership, except for small items of personal possession, so there is little concept of stealing. The Carib Indians have a saying if something is missing, "there has been a Christian here." Truthfulness is practiced more often in these "backward" societies than in our own.

The Golden Rule was in existence for hundreds of years before the Bible was thought of: "Treat others as thou wouldst thyself be treated"—India, 1000 B.C.E.; "Do not that to thy neighbor that thou would not suffer from him"—Greece, 600 B.C.E.; "Do to every man as thou wouldst have him do to thee; and do not to another what thou wouldst not have him do to thee. This preceptively dost thou need"—Confucius, 500 B.C.E. Aristotle said the same. Socrates drank hemlock because he thought ethics was independent of religion. Thus was ethics the core of human society long before Christianity was thought of.

Although Muslim countries are far more harsh on property crimes than western countries, the ethical four of the Judeo-Christian-Islam Ten Commandments are the core of the criminal law in all countries, including what little is left of the communist bloc. The only Commandments that have made no inroad into the criminal law of any country are the six nonethical Commandments (I label the last two Commandments nonethical because they implicate thought "crimes," the failure to venerate father and mother or the coveting of the neighbor's wife):

> You shall have no other god to set against me. You shall not make a carved image for yourself nor the likeness of anything in the heavens above, or on the earth below, or in the waters under the earth. You shall not bow down to them or worship them; for I, the LORD your God, am a jealous god. I punish the children for the sins of their fathers to the third and fourth generations of those that hate me. But I keep faith with thousands, with those who love me and keep my commandments. You shall not make wrong use of the name of the LORD your God; the LORD will not leave unpunished the man who misuses his name. Remember to keep the sabbath day holy. . . . Honour your father and your mother. . . . You shall not covet your neighbor's house.

Without exaggeration the first commandment, prohibiting the tolerance of other gods, by itself has caused the deaths of millions.

Clearly and without question there is nothing generally wrong with the Christian (and other religions') system of ethics, though specifics may be the other side of barbaric. The Bible as a moral guide is full of good and wise sayings and precepts mingled with foolish and horrific concepts, similar to the Koran and other holy books.

Slavery was upheld by all churches and their orthodoxy until a hundred years ago. Slavery is commanded by the Christian and Jewish God. Is slavery ethical, or is it moral only when it coincides with national policy, such as until recently in South Africa or in the United States a 150 years ago? Segregation was still the law in parts of the United States less than fifty years ago.

Out of 53,000 Catholic priests in the United States, three hundred are black, which is slightly over half of 1 percent. The Church blames the deficit on the lack of black seminarians and declining seminary enrollment by all races. Before Vatican II in 1965, however, blacks were barred from the priesthood and full participation in the Church. Blacks couldn't receive communion until after all whites had received it. The record of the Protestant churches is no better. The logical conclusion is that Christianity is racist, either de facto or intentionally. Since organized religion reflects society, however, it would be no less accurate to conclude that Western society* is racist (as is Eastern society and all society, the reasons for which are explored in chapter 10).

Rev. George Stallings was excommunicated in 1989 and removed from the Catholic priesthood for forming the African-American Catholic Congregation in Washington, D.C. Stallings described the Catholic Church as "primarily a white, racist institution in the United States." The Catholic Church said Stallings excommunicated himself by setting up the Church in defiance of Cardinal James Hickey and by publicly disagreeing with Catholic teaching. Rev. Stallings opened the Kuumba (Swahili for creativity) Temple in Philadelphia in April 1990, with 1,100 attending, and planned a seminary and elementary school in Washington, D.C. He was consecrated as a bishop in May 1990 by a prelate of the "Old Catholic" order, which traces its roots to Utrecht, Holland, in the 1870s. The "Old Catholics" were formed in reaction to the declaration of papal infallibility by the First Vatican Council. Stallings contends that Black Catholics want to "see their God with black eyes and think about their God with a black mind, to no longer worship a white God."

Islam welcomes blacks, but is no less racist than Christianity. The son of Elijah Mohammed, W. Deen Mohammed, is the leader of mainstream black Muslims in the United States. His father was blatantly racist, calling the white man a devil and seeking a separate state for black Americans. W. Deen Mohammed calls his father's ideas "retarded"; he dissolved the Nation of Islam established by his father, encouraging his followers to join the mainstream of Islam, which two million black Americans have done. He does say, however, blacks should marry only within their own race, because it's more natural and helps strengthen the race: "We shouldn't even be bringing up mixing with other people." Many Christians would agree.

Interracial couples seeking to marry are discouraged by many (if not all) religions. The racism is subtle, focusing on the difficulties biracial children suffer in adjusting to our less than subtly racist society and failing to fit into either racial world. This is the stance of the Focus on the Family ministry headed by the Rev. James Dobson in Pomona, California. A spokesman for the ministry, Vice President Paul Hetrick, says, "Focus takes the position that marriage is a

---

*"Racism is American as Apple Pie." Associated Press, *Arizona Republic,* Jan. 9, 1991.

risky business. Not just interracial marriage, but any marriage." The Bible has not one word for equality or human rights.

Louis Farrakhan is the leader of what's left of the Nation of Islam, which has a reputation for being racist and anti-Semitic. Mainstream Islam accepts Christians and Jews. Malcolm X was assassinated in 1965 for arguing that the Nation of Islam was wrong to use Islam as a vehicle for prejudice. A publication of the Nation of Islam, *What Muslims Believe*, says:

> We believe the offer of integration is hypocritical and is made by those who are trying to deceive the black peoples into believing that their 400-year-old open enemies of freedom, justice and equality are, all of a sudden, their friends. Furthermore, we believe that such deception is intended to prevent black people from realizing that the time in history has arrived for the separation from the whites of this nation.

The Nation of Islam believes the white man is the devil, with no little support. According to Dr. Abdul Alim Muhammad, a surgeon who works full-time for Farrakhan, it can't be denied that whites have made life hell for blacks, forcing blacks from their African homelands, dragging them across the ocean to become slaves, and treating them no better than dogs if they survived the voyage. Calling white men devils is based on two alternative translations of a specific passage in the Koran. The Nation of Islam translates the passage, "On the final day of judgment, the guilty one will be the blue-eyed devil." The translation accepted by mainstream Islam is, "On the final day of judgment, the guilty ones will be the ones who are spiritually blind."

It's perhaps difficult for Anglos to understand the psychological state of blacks and other minorities in the United States. When a white man commits a crime, whites don't consider it a reflection on whites; when a black or other minority commits a crime, it's considered a racial crime, reflecting on the minority race. In February 1990, a report in the *New England Journal of Medicine* found that men in Bangladesh, one of the poorest countries in the world, have a better chance to live to age forty than men in Harlem, a community in New York City where 41 percent of the people are below the poverty line and 96 percent are black. The death rate for blacks in Harlem is twice that of U.S. whites.

The racism of society, every society, is indisputable. Would we stand in amazement, however, if a zoological study found that white cattle believe black, brown, and yellow cattle to be biologically inferior; that black cattle believe white cattle are blue-eyed devils; and that yellow cattle believe the economic problems of white cattle are caused by the mixing of white cattle with brown and black cattle? Is racism excused by religiosity or nationalism?

It appears on balance, considering its racism and inherent violence, that religion has been a negative thing for mankind. Religious wars have killed more people than all natural catastrophes combined. Unless we believe human slaughter and violence improve the state of humankind, organized religion has been a negative factor in the world since its invention by primitive humans.

For example, nowhere does the Bible condemn war. Instead, the Bible glorifies war, which has been a mainstay of most religions since time began and continues in the Middle East, Ireland, Israel, India, and all over the globe. The God of the Old Testament makes it clear what desserts are just for the other side in war:

> Every one that is found shall be thrust through, and every one that is joined unto them shall fall by the sword. Their children shall be dashed to pieces before their eyes; their houses shall be spoiled and their wives ravished. . . . Their bows also shall dash the young men to pieces; and they shall have no pity on the fruit of the womb; their eye shall not spare children.
>
> (Isa. 13:15–18)

> Slay utterly old and young, both maids and little children, and women.
>
> (Ezek. 9:6)

> Happy shall he be, that taketh and dasheth thy little ones against the stones.
>
> (Ps. 137:9)

Lest we think this is Old Testament nonsense repudiated by more enlightened Christians, we need only think of the numerous atrocities committed in the name of Christ throughout the last two millennia.

It's easy to understand why Muslims, Jews, and Christians have been at odds for hundreds of years, focused in the Middle East, where they began on the same small parcel of land. In Jerusalem stands the Dome of the Rock, a seventh-century mosque, from which Muslims believe Mohammed sprang to heaven on his horse. On the same spot Jesus taught in the great temple originally built by Solomon, which was razed long before the Dome of the Rock Mosque was built. The Western Wall in Jerusalem is Judaism's holiest shrine. It's reasonable that any of these religions would wish to have control. Until organized religion disappears, there can be no peace in the Middle East.

When Israeli soldiers killed Palestinian protesters in May 1989, Iranian Parliament Speaker Hashemi Rafsanjani suggested that:

> Palestinians retaliate [against] Zionist brutality with attacks against Americans and other Westerners and their interests around the world. If, in retaliation for every Palestinian martyred in Palestine, they kill and execute, not inside Palestine, five Americans or Britons or Frenchmen, [the Israelis] would not continue these wrongs. [Palestinians should] hijack planes . . . blow up factories in Western countries. [Otherwise, Jerusalem] would not be liberated.

The previous month the Israeli army and police kept Arabs from attending Friday prayer services in Jerusalem, a day after Israel was condemned by the U.N. General Assembly for alleged human rights violations. The purpose for blocking Muslims from attending their services was to show Israel's control of its land.

Religion is the pivotal issue in the Middle East, as illustrated by a ruling of leading Orthodox rabbis in September 1989 that Jewish law forbids Israel from withdrawing one inch from the occupied West Bank. The rabbis, in a one-page statement, said that "Pikuach Nefesh," a central idea in Judaism that saving lives overshadows other commandments, "obliges us not to retreat from the borders we hold today. Withdrawal of the Israeli army may increase the danger of fatal attacks from the abandoned territory." The result is a religious commandment forbidding withdrawal from the Palestinian territories. An Israeli Labor Party legislator charged the rabbinate had "become a part of the political establishment and somehow lost its spiritual authority, becoming a pawn in the political game."

Modern Christians can't live in peace among themselves either, as evidenced in Northern Ireland and its centuries of Catholics killing Protestants and Protestants killing Catholics. How did it begin and why is it continuing? A visitor to Belfast or Derry could ask any two local residents and receive two diametrically opposed answers. The battle line pits Gaelic Catholic Ireland against Protestant England and loyalist Irish who are primarily Ulster Protestants. When the Republic of Ireland voted to join the European Economic Community in 1972, England suspended its government in Northern Ireland, recognizing that it existed only to serve Ulster Protestants. Much of the enmity between the two religious factions derives from the Great Famine of 1845–49 when hundreds of thousands of poor Irish starved, and the Irish people blamed England for genocide. Sir Charles Edward Trevelyan, who ran England's famine relief policy, felt Irish starvation was deserved as "the design of a benign Malthusian God who sought to relieve overpopulation by natural disaster." The Catholic survivors (whose population had been swollen because of the prohibition against birth control) became dedicated enemies of their Protestant Anglo-Irish rulers, seeking to glorify their peasant Gaelic Catholic culture. The tradition continues: Protestants are loyalists to England and Catholics are nationalists. When the 1937 Constitution of the Free Irish State was adopted, it provided the Catholic Church "a special position . . . as the guardian of the faith professed by the great majority of the citizens." The clause was repealed by referendum in 1972 but no means were provided for taking Protestant Ulster into the Irish political mainstream. As succinctly described by Thackeray in his *Irish Sketch Book* of 1842: "To have an opinion about Ireland, one must begin by getting at the truth; and where is it to be had in the country? Or rather, there are two truths, the Catholic truth and the Protestant truth. . . . Belief is made party business."

When pure belief, the touchstone of organized religion, is the basis for anything, human life suffers and society is diminished. Meanwhile, the killing continues. Since the outbreak of violence between Catholics and Protestants in 1969, 2,922 murdered through the second week of November 1991 when seven people were killed. The Ulster Volunteer Force, an outlawed Protestant loyalist group, claimed responsibility for three deaths (two Catholics and one Protestant), saying that two Catholics were targeted and expressing deep regret at the Protestant's death. The Irish Republican Army retaliated the next day, killing four Belfast Protestants.

War has been waged in another part of the world for over seven years, but few Westerners have heard of it. At stake is the possession of the Siachen, a glaciated wasteland in the Himalayas between Pakistan-occupied Kashmir and

Chinese territory. The combatants are Indian Hindus against Pakistani Muslims. Conditions are so harsh that only a third of the casualties are due to combat. The fighting occurs at altitudes above 19,000 feet in knee-deep snow, over two-hundred-foot crevasses, and on walls of ice where temperatures frequently drop below minus fifty degrees. Soldiers carry sixty-five-pound packs, ice picks, skis, shovels, and ropes, and before leaving for combat both sides visit their respective enclaves where either images of the Hindu gods Rama, Shiva, and Ganesha have been hung by the Indian troops or the holy symbols of the Muslim god have been hung by the Pakistani troops.

Religious war continues in Catholic East Timor, a former Portuguese colony on an island off the north coast of Australia that Indonesian Muslims invaded in 1975. After fifteen years of fighting, war and famine have killed a third of the population. Few have heard of the war because Indonesia sealed its borders, allowing no admittance to foreigners or reporters. Life is so closely controlled that villagers must answer to twice daily roll calls. Pope Paul II visited there in October 1989, and only then did Indonesian officials allow admission to the foreign press in an attempt to convince the world that the fighting had ceased. Unbelievably, the pope's greatest concern during his visit was the government's birth control program, which distributes contraceptives to the populace. The local bishop stated that no birth control is needed since so many have died.

India has also been the location of religious wars for hundreds of years, resulting in millions of deaths in the last fifty years alone! About one million people were killed in 1947 during the conflict between Hindus and Muslims that ended in the formation of the state of Bangladesh; three million more were slaughtered in 1971 when Bangladesh became independent.

Violence always results when religious people attempt to force their beliefs on nonbelievers. In Flagstaff, Arizona, for example, in May 1989, three men and a women were indicted for beating a blind woman named Virginia Hayes in an attempt to force her to accept their religious beliefs. (Authorities declined comment when asked to identify their particular religion.) The beatings continued for several months, involving, according to the indictment, "physical restraint, malnutrition, sleep deprivation and exposure to the cold." Hayes was forced to perform physical labor and was beaten with "sticks, clubs and various pieces of wood." The four accused were charged with kidnaping, aggravated assault, endangerment, and fraudulent schemes. The last charge was the result of their allegedly rigging an automobile accident to mask the injuries suffered from the beatings. In February 1991 the four defendants were convicted of conspiracy, endangerment, and attempted fraudulent scheme (the last for staging the auto accident), all nonfelony "dangerous" offenses, and acquitted of felony charges of kidnaping and aggravated assault. The defendants were sentenced to one year probation, but in 1991 the conspiracy to commit endangerment was reversed because the defendants, though causing the injuries to the blind woman, were not under any legal obligation to obtain medical treatment for her.*

---

*Mark Shaffer, *Arizona Republic,* Feb. 21, 1991.

People have even starved their children to death or deprived them of medical care, resulting in death, with the excuse that religion made them do it. In Pace, Florida, on February 8, 1988, a mother (with a college degree in community mental health) succeeded, after five months of effort, in starving her four-year-old daughter to death. The mother had four other healthy kids and a refrigerator full of food. According to the mother, the Christian God had found her daughter to be possessed by the demonic spirits of disobedience, gluttony, lust, and lying, for which the prescribed punishment was fasting and beatings. The mother's diary kept track of the remedies:

> Sept., 1987: It [the demon] did not eat Saturday . . . didn't feed it because of her behavior. Sunday, it had nothing to eat. Monday and Tuesday the same. Nov. 9: Feed her not, for I have no more mercy for this one . . . she attempts to hurt thyself . . . she is a crazed animal. Why do you doubt me? Know that I am the Lord thy God. Obey, obey, I say. Dec. 9: Hit her in the mouth, in the mouth, I say. Keep to the diet . . . spare not the rod of correction . . . speak less and whip more . . .

The mother's attorney argued that she had been in a "religious hypnotic trance." She pled guilty to murder in the third degree, meaning there was no intent to kill, and was sentenced to seven years in prison. (In 1990 the Arizona Supreme Court affirmed the ten-year sentence of a black man for selling a single marijuana cigarette.) Kimberly's mother will be eligible for parole in three years. If a person believes in a god who instructs the person to exorcise a demon by whatever means, every religion requires obedience to that commandment. How does one distinguish between true gods and untrue gods, true commandments and untrue commandments, true religions and untrue religions?

John List was tried in 1990 in Elizabeth, New Jersey, for murdering his eighty-four-year-old mother, his wife, and three children in 1971. He left a letter for his pastor, listing the reasons for the murders, which included:

> With Pat [daughter age 16] being so determined to get into acting I was also fearful as to what that might do to her continuing to be a Christian . . . Also, with Helen [wife] not going to church I knew that this would harm the children eventually . . . At least I'm certain that all have gone to heaven now. If things had gone on who knows if this would be the case. . . . I'm only concerned with making my peace with God and of this I am assured because of Christ dying for me.

John List was sentenced to life imprisonment.

The books of the Old Testament are not books of morality and ethics but books of crimes. They teach revenge, eternal pain and damnation, human sacrifice, and poverty to prepare for a paradise no one is likely to experience. Is this morality and ethics? The Bible excludes any mention of education. Education is anathema to religion, since the root of all sin is Adam and Eve eating from the Tree of Knowledge. Is it moral for religion to denigrate education? The only issues publicly and repeatedly raised by religions in connection with education are whether to allow prayer in public school, release-time for religious studies, sex education studies, and similar noneducational issues. Is there a connection with the fact that 700,000 children drop out of United States schools every year and another 700,000 receive diplomas without knowing how to read or write? Sixty percent of those graduating don't even know enough to fill an average entry-level job. The percentage of students graduating from school has dropped every year since 1984.* One problem is forty thousand separate school districts that are governed by local boards catering to the religious, so that religious issues predominate. School districts generally don't concentrate on teaching students to think; instead, public and private schools seek to indoctrinate the party line of the locally dominant religions, usually Christianity and Judaism. Philosophers Will and Ariel Durant, authors of *The Story of Civilization,* defined education as "the transmission of civilization." Is civilization being transmitted to students in the United States when only 20 percent of our children graduate from high school with reading and writing skills?

Another immorality of several powerful religions is their prohibition against birth control. Nowhere in the Bible or the Koran is birth control mentioned, much less designated as the venal sin it's considered to be by Catholics, Muslims, and Mormons. Why do these religions cling to a doctrine that causes more misery in poor families and in poor countries than all the plagues and natural disasters in the history of the world? The answer is simple. The primary growth of these religions is from the children of members—lots of children. The prohibition against birth control allows these churches to thrive and grow, because the huge majority of people accept the religion of their parents.

Population pressures caused by religious prohibitions against birth control can also cause resentments leading to war. How moral and ethical is it for wealthy religions to condemn their parishioners to lives of poverty by bearing children they cannot afford to clothe and feed? Shouldn't a question as basic and private as whether to practice birth control be left to the individual, free from interference by religions and governments? Are religious people more apt to be law-abiding than nonreligious people? The answer is no. Religion reflects society, and the religious have the same levels of crime and delinquency as the nonreligious. The intellectually religious, however, commit far fewer crimes than true believers.

Many statistical analyses and conclusions related to religion are based on relatively thin samplings, and thus only show general trends, because religious people generally will not participate in surveys and studies seeking answers to religious questions. Perhaps they feel the results would represent a personal attack on their religious beliefs, and perhaps they are correct. Religious beliefs, other than one's own, appear nonsensical.

Religious beliefs change over time. Any orthodox believer at any time in history would a mere hundred years earlier have been either burned at the stake or excommunicated for today's beliefs. Such is the connection between religion and morality.

---

*See Ellen Dempsey, "First Word," *Omni,* April 1990.

8

Traditional Morality and Ethics versus the Right Stuff

If religious beliefs are inaccurate guides to ethics and morality, what then is the proper road? Philosophers and the rest of us have been grappling with this problem forever. Empirically, morality varies by country and the religion that dominates that country. It's considered immoral to walk around an American beach naked while many European countries would take a dissimilar view. As a practical matter, much of morality is relative. The core objection against relative morality is that it's not morality at all, but only a social or individual viewpoint. The argument concludes that truth cannot be based on viewpoint and neither may morality, otherwise, any individual view of morality would be correct, and, if my view differs from yours, it would have to be incorrect, or vice versa. Religious doctrines are relative too, however, as none agree on much of anything, and on nothing completely.

Before describing a simple and arguably superior solution to questions of morality, an overview of historical theories will provide a foundation and introduction to the inherent problems of a universal theory of what one ought to do in all circumstances.

One early philosophical moral theory is hedonism, which teaches that pleasure is the primary good. The value of actions are judged by the level of pleasure produced or the happiness obtained. Probably the most widely practiced ethical system is egoistic hedonism, which is represented by the question, "What's in it for me?" The Epicureans elevated hedonism to an arguably higher level by emphasizing physical health and peace of mind as the purest pleasures.

Hedonism has been criticized as not being a moral system at all because it doesn't answer the question of what one ought to do. It simply says, "Be happy." Perhaps that's enough of a goal, but it neither erects the guideposts necessary to achieve happiness nor does it answer the core question of what actions are moral in particular situations, though it may be an accurate description of the most common goal of humans, once basic necessities are satisfied.

Another major defect of pure hedonism is that it doesn't prevent a person from bloodying your nose if that makes him happy. When combined with altruism, however, hedonism may be an acceptable moral system; i.e., the proper goal should be the happiness of others instead of merely one's own happiness. This combination is most likely unachievable and impractical because one can never (or seldom) know what will achieve happiness for others, when most (or certainly many) people don't know (particularly in a time frame greater than five minutes down the road) what will make them happy. Such a system is summed up by the admonition to love our neighbors as ourselves and has had little historical success.

A similar moral system that appears more practical, though it has at least one glaring defect, is utilitarianism, also called social hedonism: seek the greatest good for the greatest number. Democracy is a related political system and suffers from the same defect—the minority is subject to trampling. Jeremy Bentham and J. S. Mill debated the details of utilitarianism. Bentham emphasized the quantity of happiness for the most people and counted the individual as having only one vote in that calculus, which would consider the intensity of the pleasure, its duration, certainty, propinquity, future availability, purity, and number of people affected. Such a calculus is fine in theory but unworkable as a practical guide to daily living. Mill argued that quality was more important than quantity and so felt that intellectual pleasure was superior to physical pleasure, thereby excluding most people in the world. Mill was a bright guy, but he made the fatal assumption that everyone should be judged on the same intellectual basis as himself. Pleasures of the intellect may be illusory to half of the population, and Mill's theory also excludes obvious pleasures of the flesh.

Another major theory of morality was proposed by Immanuel Kant, who believed, similar to most religions, that moral absolutes can be deduced by an appeal to pure reason and cannot be based on experience or ideas of happiness. Kant's theory posits that acting in accord with one's duty is acting in accord with moral law, which is to say that one should only do those things that everyone should do: the Universal Imperative. Therefore, suicide would be unacceptable, as would be hedonism. If everyone acted only for their own pleasure there would be no progress and little morality. Kant's theory depends on the fallacious assumption that the full development of talent is the only moral course. That may be a high ideal, but it is of little solace to a populace beset by armies girded for battle with their fullest potential being the absolute destruction of the other.

My simplistic proposal for a practical and infallible system of morality is summed up in four words: harm no one else. As long as we harm no one else, we, as adults, should be allowed to do exactly as we please, including harming or risking harm to ourselves. If being an adult means anything, it means being able to do exactly as we please in this life as long as we harm no one. Although simplistic and innocent appearing, this is a radical theory of morality that flies in the face of every religion and system of government on earth, as we shall see. It avoids the defects of traditional theories of morality and also provides a specific and workable guide for morality in everyday living.

Simply harming no one else avoids the central defect of hedonism, which is that if it makes you happy you should be able to bloody someone else's nose. It also avoids the impossibility of altruism, to make everyone happy when few can know enough to make themselves happy, much less the rest of the world. Avoiding harm to others skirts the unworkability of utilitarianism, which must rely on a pleasure calculus that would stump a computer or becomes caught up in the eternal questions of whether quantity or quality of pleasure is better and whether pleasure should be restricted to intellectual pleasure. It goes Kant's Universal Imperative one better by reducing it to one concrete commandment, which is based on both experience and basic ideas of happiness. (It's a happy person who harms no one else.) It also avoids Kant's imperative that intellectual development is the only or highest good but fully allows and encourages such development. It pushes armies back from the brink of mutual destruction and negates half the purpose of the governments of the world. It should be the law, the only law: harm no one else.

This can never be the law, however, as long as there are organized religions with their artificial rules or as long as governments seek to regulate every aspect of their citizens' lives, such as those governments in the United States and China do, to identify two of the obvious offenders.

Harming no one else allows all resources to be employed in the pursuit of individual happiness, similar to the principles espoused in the Declaration of Independence, though unrealized in any country in the world. Whether happiness for the particular individual is intellectual, physical, or of any other sort should be solely up to the individual and not to any church or government.

The true test of any ethical system is equal treatment of all so that what is right for one is right for all. Justice and fairness are defined in this fashion. Immorality is that which destroys well-being or happiness. The best guide to justice and fairness appears to be intelligence, not organized religion or superstition. Only a good man is a happy man. No man is ultimately happy who is not good. Let "God" deal with the transgressors against him. He has the time and the means. Otherwise, interfere with no one that doesn't interfere with you and don't do unto others as you would like for them not to do unto you, which is to say, harm them not.

How can it be determined whether an action harms someone else? In other words, from whose viewpoint should "harm" be determined, that of the actor or the person being acted upon? The only workable solution is to prohibit only that which appears harmful from the perspective of the person threatened with harm and which is also objectively harmful. Therefore, the fact that I think my action is harming no one is not conclusive if someone else can show that he would be harmed by my proposed act and a majority would agree that the action is objectively harmful. Any action that another person says does not harm him should be allowable, even though someone else similarly situated would in the same circumstance feel harmed. Thus, adults would be allowed to engage in any activity if both solemnly agree to do so. Any adult would have the right to harm himself, or risk harm to himself, as he deems appropriate.

How does harming no one else fare when applied to everyday situations and to the major moral debates of our time? For instance, when can we justify a lie? When it harms no one else. We do it all the time; we lie to spare the feelings of another, which is to say we avoid harm to another. *The Catholic Word Book* dodges the issue in its definition of "equivocation":

> (1) The use of words, phrases, or gestures having more than one meaning in order to conceal information which a questioner has no strict right to know. It is permissible to equivocate (have a broad mental reservation) in some circumstances. (2) A lie, i.e., a statement of untruth. Lying is intrinsically wrong. A lie told in joking, evident as such, is not wrong.

The Catholic approach is nonsensical, prohibiting a lie to save another's life. Additional questions arise: Who has a "right" to elicit information from another, except in a parent-child relationship or a court proceeding? What "circumstances" allow skirting the truth? Why is lying intrinsically wrong when it harms no one else, or may benefit either or both parties (harming neither)?

When can we break a promise to another or breach a contract? When it doesn't physically or monetarily harm the other party. When can we justify taking or damaging another's property? When it harms no one else, which is likely never. When is euthanasia justified? When it harms no one else, which means it is justified when the recipient consents (and is mentally competent to consent) or is a vegetable. Harming no one else does not condemn suicide. The competent adult (would a competent adult contemplate suicide?) should be allowed to risk harm to himself as much as he pleases, no matter the danger of the activity, including alligator-wrestling and hang-gliding. Suicide would include preplanned and voluntary euthanasia, such as with a living will. Naturally, 99 percent of competent adults would never consider an act as foolish as suicide, alligator-wrestling, or driving in Los Angeles. Harming no one else is a do-it-yourself system of freedom which everyone can easily understand and follow.

Capital punishment would no longer be allowed under the prohibition against harming another. Instead, the ultimate punishment would be life in prison. Execution of murderers and the like is primarily for revenge and deterrence, but it results in dropping society to the moral level of the murderer. Can we eventually rise above "an eye for an eye and a tooth for a tooth"? Outlawing capital punishment would greatly simplify and streamline the criminal justice system. The system would save enormous sums of money by eliminating automatic death penalty appeals that keep murderers and other capital criminals in limbo for an average of ten years and treats offenders so inefficiently (and unequally by race) that the odds of execution for murderers are one in twenty-five hundred.

The balance of this chapter is a detailed analysis of the practicality of harming no one else as a system of ethics and morality and how it works in concrete situations, illustrated by the key ethical issues of our time: abortion, the "war on drugs," poverty, and the environment.

The Ethics of Abortion

The respective positions on abortion and when life begins were summed up by Tribune Media Services, Inc. columnist, Donald Kaul:

> On one hand we have those who believe it [life] begins at the moment of conception and that your average fetus will probably become Albert Einstein, given half a chance. At the other extreme there are those who believe life begins at birth and before that, an unborn fetus deserves all the consideration generally reserved for pet rocks.

Abortion is a muddied up moral issue, which without the colorful language used boils down to when the mother's right to autonomy over her body is overridden by the life of what would otherwise be a legal person in a few months. The most comprehensive poll taken by Gallup (1990, released in 1991) found nine of ten Americans cannot describe the rule of *Roe* v. *Wade;* 42 percent believed it prohibited abortion after the first trimester and 16 percent believed abortion was legal only if the mother's life was endangered. *Roe* v. *Wade* marks the point of theoretical viability prohibiting abortion at the beginning of the third trimester. However, the concept of viability is one the Supreme Court pulled out of a hat, there being no legal precedent for the concept; neither does the concept have a medical basis (though it does have a psychological basis). Even a normally delivered healthy baby is not viable. Without constant attention to bodily needs, a newborn would die in a few days. Physical development milestones such as the establishment of a heartbeat or the development of brain waves would be more logically supportable than viability. However, we routinely distinguish between a miscarriage and stillbirth, based upon the age of the "fetus." The Supreme Court in *Roe* v. *Wade* chose an expedient middle ground it thought would solve the problem.

Eighty-eight percent of American abortions in 1989 occurred in the first trimester. The first ethical question is whether the convenience of the mother, no matter her right to bodily autonomy, is a moral justification for the termination of life (whether called fetal life or human life), when balanced against the life of a soon-to-be legal person and an existent, though unborn, human being. The 1990 Gallup poll found that 66 percent of Americans disapproved of abortion for *any* financial reason, even though a teenager would otherwise have to drop out of school. Sixty-six percent opposed abortion for a woman "abandoned by her partner," 79 percent disapproved of abortion to prevent interruption of career, and 88 percent opposed it for "repeated" birth control.

It seems peculiarly illogical for "It's my body" to be seen as an acceptable argument to justify abortion when "It's my body" is no arguable defense to the use of illegal drugs, which have no implications for the life or death of a potential human being, unless the drug user is a pregnant female. In other words, based on a harm-no-one-else analysis, abortion harms "someone" else, while illegal drug use does not. The second fallacy of the "It's my body" argument for abortion is that the fetus is not the body of the "mother" but something separate and distinguishable from her body. It would be a viable argument that a women can decide whether to cut off her own finger for that is clearly her body; the fetus, however, is not, but is only a temporary parasite within her body and which she had primary responsibility in placing there.

In October 1990 a Massachusetts judge dismissed illegal drug charges filed against a mother whose son was born addicted to cocaine and with cocaine in his blood system. One critic remarked that "I'm sure no one in the country ever expected *Roe* v. *Wade* meant to protect a woman's right to inflict illegal drugs on an unborn child." When harm is inflicted on another, does it make any difference whether the harm creating mechanism may be legally bought or sold? An opponent also said, "One of the reasons this whole area of the law makes no sense is, if it is legal to kill an unborn child, how on earth can it be illegal to inflict a little harm?" Proponents argued that defeating fetal-rights cases is crucial because if a pregnant mother is ever held responsible for damage to the fetus, the door is open for regulating her every move. This "slippery slope" argument reasons that if the state can forbid drug use during pregnancy to avoid harm to the fetus, then it can as logically dictate what a pregnant woman can eat or drink, the number of hours she can work, and conditions under which sex is permitted. Most agree that imposition of criminal law sanctions against women using drugs is inappropriate and counterproductive because they will otherwise avoid prenatal care, thus compounding the harm. The question remains whether it's appropriate to regulate the privacy of those who use drugs to harm themselves and not to regulate the privacy of those who use drugs to harm others, though the other is an unborn child with no legal rights.

The perfection of a foolproof means of contraception will hopefully defuse the destructive debate surrounding abortion. Certainly if abortion could safely occur through chemical rather than physical means and in the privacy of one's own home with no physical danger to the "mother," most people would lose interest in the question.

Opponents and supporters of abortion confuse more than they fairly debate. The question whether a fetus is a human being shouldn't be confused with the question whether the fetus is a legal person. A human being is a biological entity and the question of its existence is answerable by biologists, or even by common sense. A fetus is not a cat, or a dog, or anything other than a human being, but until the third trimester the fetus is not yet a legal person with legal rights, according to *Roe* v. *Wade*. Dogs give birth to dogs, and cats to cats, and human beings to human beings. Most people, pregnant women included, wouldn't consider sticking a needle into the head of a cat and killing it, yet many pregnant women would hesitate little in doing the same to a soon-to-be-born human being. Why are we more reverent of cat life than of human life? Why is it illegal to kill a cat or destroy the egg/fetus of a bald eagle but legal to kill a fetus? If we are unsure when "human" life begins wouldn't simple ethics require that we err on the side of life? Isn't the touchstone of civilization the right of each of us to develop into the best we can be without our lives being cut short without our consent and for the convenience of others?

A person is a legal entity, which a fetus is not, or is not until the third trimester. The rights, if any, of a fetus, are determinable by asking, "rights against whom?" The fetus has a right to life as against strangers. No one has a right to step from a crowd and abort a fetus, though one person may have that right during a finite period of time: the "mother." Therefore, the fetus has a demonstrable right to life as against strangers.* The remaining question is when the fetus, if ever, has a right to life as against its "mother's" convenience.

In 1988, a Flagstaff, Arizona, man was charged with the murder of a fetus. His attorney argued that the fetus was not a human being, which is misleading. The proper question was whether the fetus was a legal person with legal rights; currently an unborn baby is not a legal person and therefore the man legally should not have been charged with murder. However, it appears inconsistent to argue that an aborted twenty-six-week-old fetus is not a human being while a baby born prematurely after twenty-six weeks in the womb is a human being. The real question is whether the twenty-six-week unborn fetus should be considered a legal person with rights like the rest of us; it's certainly a human being though unborn. We must then explore the relative moral rights of the unborn human being and its mother and whether those rights should logically differ depending on the circumstances under which the mother became pregnant.

Sex carries responsibilities. With few exceptions pregnancy is avoidable. Less than one percent of all pregnancies are unavoidable, resulting from rape or incest; rape/incest is almost a non-issue based upon its infrequency in the abortion equation. For example, of 15,684 abortions performed in Louisiana in 1988, only one person claimed to have become pregnant as a result of incest or rape, an incidence of less than one hundredth of one percent.

On February 10, 1991 the *Los Angeles Times* published a letter to the editor from a female gynecologist:

> All too frequently I have had the following conversation with my female patients: "Are you sexually active?" "Yes." "Are you using any form of birth control?" "No." "Do you want to get pregnant at this time?" "No." "Then why aren't you using anything?" "I don't know." . . . I'm angered with women who are so irresponsible with their bodies that they use abortion as a form of birth control. How hard is it to get a condom [anywhere] . . . ?

If a person, male or female, chooses to avoid the responsibility for birth control when no child is wanted from sex, the ethical answer would not appear to be abortion when that means the ending of a soon-to-be legal person and an existent unborn human life. The 1990 Gallup poll on abortion found that

---

*A fetus may sue for injuries suffered in the womb due to actions of a third party, in which case a guardian is appointed by the court. In some states the murder of an expectant mother results in two charges of murder, which means the "mother" may legally accomplish half the murderer's act. The fetus is a legal entity insofar as it may inherit property, which could present an inherent conflict with a pro-choice "mother" who can disinherit the fetus with impunity.

75 percent of Americans agreed that abortion takes a human life, a percentage shared among men and women, contrary to popular belief. The 75 percent varied little among young, old, Republicans, and Democrats. Americans overwhelmingly (88 percent) opposed abortion for "repeated" birth control. There is surface logic to taking an eye in retaliation for an eye plucked out but there is no similar logic to ending a human life because the sexual participant was too irresponsible or lazy or shy (or religious) to use birth control. The plain fact is that most of us give more thought to the purchase of a house or car than to insuring that our sexual acts do not result in pregnancy, though the costs of raising a child far exceed those of a car and are similar to those of an average house. It would seem a far more irresponsible act to engage in unprotected sex when no child is wanted than to take drugs of any kind, legal or illegal.

William F. Buckley pointed out in a March 1990 column what we all know about responsibility and abortion; the terms are mutually exclusive and illustrate the primary fallacy behind the feminist argument that only women should take part in the discussion of whether abortion is ethical. There are a finite number of possibilities why an unwanted pregnancy occurs: (1) ignorance of birth control methods or religious prohibitions; (2) reckless failure of either party to use birth control; (3) either party being carried away by passion; (4) inebriation through legal or illegal drugs; or (5) rape or other nonconsensual sex. Because the last category accounts for less than one percent of all unwanted pregnancies, over 99 percent are left to irresponsibility by both the "mother" and the "father." Before abortion was legalized/decriminalized by the United States Supreme Court, 10.7 percent of all births were to unwed mothers; by 1986 the number had doubled to 23.4 percent. Anglo illegitimacy correlatively went from 5.7 percent to 15.7 percent; black unwed mothers from 37.6 percent to 61.2 percent, which is a lot of irresponsibility. Yet these "mothers" tell us they are the only ones with the ethical responsibility to determine whether an abortion should occur. Buckley concludes:

> The point, then, is that women who go to an abortionist, or who procreate illegitimate births, are not the best judges of right and wrong. . . . Is a mortal assault on a fetus something on the order of assault and battery? Or is it no different than stuffing a tomato in a blender? These perplexities may continue to confound us. But really, one shouldn't designate the class of people who have this problem as the class of especially responsible people.

Feminists argue that women shouldn't put the considerations of others first because that's the linchpin of female oppression. Only by putting selfish needs first can a blow be struck for the freedom of women. The first question is what happens when the "others" are also female? When a teenager decides to abort a female "fetus" against the wishes of her mother she is destroying the life of a female and depriving her mother of a grandchild. The abortion of females, which presumably runs at least 50 percent of all abortions, seems antithetical to female freedom.

Feminists for Life of America, with three thousand members (small) and thirty-six chapters in 1991, says "Abortion is the result of male domination. The main problem has always been that men set the terms for sex. Women need to have the power to set those terms. . . . [Abortion] allows men to continue to be virtually free of responsibility for the results of their sexual activity." This group of feminists believes men should be made more responsible for the children, which is a point well-taken. Men have an equal responsibility to harm no one else, particularly by failing to support their children. Early feminists such as Susan B. Anthony, Elizabeth Cady Stanton, and Margaret Sanger, the founder of Planned Parenthood, were against abortion. A president elect of a National Organization for Women responded that "We don't favor abortion. We're in favor of women being able to make the choice. That's what liberating is all about." Southern slave owners in the United States didn't favor slavery; they favored Southerners having the choice whether to own slaves.

Planned Parenthood, which does a marvelous job of encouraging birth control and which is where ethical efforts should arguably be concentrated, ran a full-page ad in the *New York Times* explaining "What's Wrong With Parental Consent: Indeed, after hearing evidence of family conflict and brutal violence, an appeals judge wrote 'compelling parental notice . . . is almost always disastrous.' " Forgetting the confusion of consent with notice, the assumption is that children/non-adults should have absolute sexual license, which as a practical matter they always have had and always will have, but parents should be shielded from knowledge of their child's pregnancy because they would otherwise beat their child senseless. Anyone who beats anyone else senseless or harms another, other than to the least extent necessary for self defense, should suffer the appropriate penalty. Does gratuitous and separately punishable violence against another justify abortion?

The assumption of some feminists is that their reasoning is innately morally superior to any other possible ethical argument, including those supporting the sanctity/value of human life. Whether the result is the aborting of more female fetuses or the deprivation of other female (and even male) family members of offspring, to which they have no moral right to demand but which they may have a moral right to ask not be destroyed, the balancing of selfishness and convenience against sexual and other irresponsibility doesn't appear to weigh heavily in favor of the feminist view. Only recently have feminists opposed abortion as a method of sex selection, such as is routinely practiced in India as a means of avoiding the birth of dower-expensive females.

Abortion for any reason or no reason at all is legal in India. The dowry of an Indian girl is prohibitively expensive for most Indians, thus most families who can afford it find out early the sex of the child through amniocentesis, or other means. The result is out of every 7,000 abortions in one province sampled, 6,999 were female. The 1990 Gallup poll on abortion found 91 percent of Americans oppose abortion for the purpose of sex selection.

The common law, which is the basis for the legal system in England, the United States, and other former English colonies, has long contained the concept of "assumption of risk," which means exactly what it sounds like. Simply put, if a risk is known, yet a person decides to proceed in face of that risk, then the person is barred from recovering for injuries suffered as a result of taking the risk and is instead liable for injuries caused to others. For example, when making a left turn, it's an assumption of risk to complete the turn when on-coming traffic is so close that it is unsafe. If an "accident" results, the left-hand turner is barred from recovering damages caused by the on-coming traffic, even were the driver of an on-coming vehicle negligent; the person assuming the risk is held liable for any damage caused to on-coming traffic, including that caused to the negligent on-coming driver who could have otherwise avoided the "accident" by simply being vigilant. Similarly, there's no excuse for unprotected sex by either the male or the female when a child is not desired; the "heat of passion" argument is for children, not for supposedly responsible adults. Every male is legally responsible for providing eighteen years of support for any child he fathers; no female is similarly responsible because she is legally entitled to avoid having the child during the first two-thirds of the pregnancy. The male has no legal right to take part in this decision though his liability for support may equal the cost of a thirty-year mortgage. Does religiously inspired guilt for using birth control or engaging in sex justify a refusal to protect against unwanted pregnancy, or justify an abortion so authority figures don't find out we're sexually active?

Abortion should not be a reward for irresponsibility or for assuming the risk of pregnancy through unprotected sex. However, based on a 1989 *Los Angeles Times* poll, over 20 percent of us believed abortion should be legal under any circumstances, which is abortion as birth control. Eighty-eight percent believed abortion should be legal under circumstances when the mother's life is in danger and 84 percent when pregnancy results from rape or incest. Seventy-four percent believed abortion should be legal when there's a strong chance of a serious defect in the baby. In January 1991, the Utah legislature prohibited abortion except in these cases where 74 percent to 88 percent of us believe abortion should be legal. Also in January 1991, the voters of Corpus Christi (body of Christ), Texas, voted 64 percent to 36 percent against a city-charter amendment which would have declared that life begins at conception. The measure was defeated as "an effort to impose a personal religious belief on the citizens."

The primary pitfall with abstract questions, such as those asked in polls, is the removal of the personal factor, which is the moral factor. Would the results of the above poll have differed if it had instead asked whether our mother should have had the right to abort us for the various reasons used to justify abortion? If your mother was in financial difficulty should that have justified your abortion? What if she "believed" you might have a serious physical defect, or her health were in danger?

When deciding morally who should be first taken off a sinking ship it's traditional that the women and children are saved first. When abandoning ship, what should be the logical priority between a ten-year-old child with a seventy-year life expectancy and a fifty-year-old adult with a thirty-year life expectancy? Most of us feel that the person with the greatest life expectancy should first be saved from a sinking ship. Why do we reverse the presumption as between mother and expectant child? Why do we prefer to save the life of a mother with between forty and sixty years life expectancy, instead of the "fetus" with eighty years of life expectancy?

We justify legalized abortion on the grounds that many women died from illegal abortions. It's tragic that thirty-nine women died from illegal abortions in 1972, the last year before most abortions were made legal in the United States; through 1989 we'd aborted over 21 million, an average of 1.3 million human beings each year, in 1989 almost 1.4 million, which is beyond tragedy. In 1989, the National Centers for Disease Control reported a total of 1,396,658 abortions; 346 for every 1,000 live births.

We don't care much whether the poor abort themselves to oblivion. Only 49 percent in the 1988 *Los Angeles Times* poll (up to 66 percent in the 1990 Gallup poll) opposed abortion when the family was too poor to support more children. Is it easier for white, male-dominated state legislatures and Congress to encourage the abortion of the poor, which are our minorities, than to instead promote the elimination of poverty, or lift the onerous federal restrictions on research and development for better forms of contraception? Coincidentally, white males receive most of the profits from abortion.

A 1989 *Glamour* magazine compilation of national polls revealed other basic statistics: 57 percent of abortees had no children; 70 percent wanted more children. At twenty-five weeks, 28 percent of fetuses survive; 55 percent at twenty-six weeks and 75 percent at twenty-seven weeks. Sixty-one percent believed public funds should not be available for abortion. Twenty-six percent obtained an abortion because the father wanted it; 76 percent because of a possible adverse effect on their life, or for convenience. The overwhelming majority of abortions are for convenience. In 1972, 65,000 babies were available for adoption; in 1989, there were 51,000. In 1986, 92 percent under age nineteen kept their babies; 95 percent of these are estimated to be neither married nor financially self-sufficient. Every day 1,994 babies are born to unwed mothers in the United States; 4,352 abortions are performed every day in the United States, 181 each hour and three each minute. Thirty-nine percent of the world's population lives in countries where abortion is available on request; 24 percent where abortion is prohibited or allowed only to save the life of the mother; these are primarily Muslim or Catholic-controlled countries.

The U.S. ranks first among industrialized nations in both teen-age pregnancies and the number of abortions per capita; 29 percent of U.S. pregnancies end in abortion versus 14.7 percent in Canada.

The United States allows abortion through twenty-six weeks of pregnancy when the fetus is a recognizable human form. France allows abortion through the tenth week, Italy and Poland through the twelfth week, and Japan through the twenty-second week. China allows abortion thoughout pregnancy and, because of government policy limiting family size to one child, may require an abortion at any time.*

---

*Time, May 4, 1992, p. 32.

The legal analysis attending abortion is in a quagmire out of which the Supreme Court will need much luck to extricate the legal system. The Supreme Court ruled in two separate 5–4 decisions in 1989 that teenagers don't have the same mental and moral development as adults (obviously correct) and their diminished capacity shields them from the death penalty. Retarded teenagers over age 16 may be executed for their capital crimes. Applying this rationale to pregnant teenage girls under age 16, whether retarded or not, how can they legally consent to an abortion?

A March 1992 poll by the *Washington Post* jibed closely with the U.S. Supreme Court's June 1992 ruling affirming the legality of abortion with restrictions and regulations. The public supports abortion during the first three months of pregnancy by a 55 percent to 38 percent margin; parental notification is supported 80 percent to 18 percent.

Much of the abortion debate is perceived as a religious war, instead of an ethical debate. Catholics, Baptists, and other fundamentalist religions are against abortion for any reason. Judaism holds that a fetus is not human life because the Talmud distinguishes between actual and potential life. The Evangelical Lutheran Church in America, the Presbyterian Church-USA, the United Methodist Church, and the Episcopal Church condone abortion in certain circumstances, though each have anti-abortion factions.

In January 1990, a Catholic bishop said Governor Cuomo of New York was "in serious risk of going to hell" for supporting abortion rights. Cardinal O'Connor agreed:

> Would anyone deny that the bishop has the right and even the obligation to warn any Catholic that his soul is at risk if he should die while deliberately pursuing any gravely evil course of action, and that such would certainly include advocating publicly, as the bishop puts it, "the right of a woman to kill a child"?

The Catholic Bishop named to the Brooklyn Diocese in February 1990 reiterated that Mayor Cuomo was endangering his soul by publicly supporting a woman's "right" to an abortion while privately opposing abortion. This issue was called "a public battle for the soul of the nation," according to the head of the anti-abortion National Clergy Council. The threat of hell isn't much of a threat these days, according to recent polls previously noted and Rev. Richard McBrien, a Notre Dame professor of theology, who also asked, "Is the flag more sacred than human life?" when the (former) president supports a constitutional amendment prohibiting flag-burning but opposes an amendment prohibiting abortion.

Members of the Catholic Church more closely reflect the views of society than the views of the Church on almost all questions. Based on an October 1990 poll, 71 percent of American Catholics oppose the excommunication of a doctor who performs an abortion; 73 percent oppose such action against a legislator and 76 percent oppose such action against the "mother." Three fourths of all respondents and 70 percent of Catholics oppose Catholic bishops using political means to advance their moral opinions. If religion isn't about morality, what is it about? Should the religious arena be the place to debate moral issues, or does religion have any connection with morality?

Catholicism and other religions opposing birth control are promoting abortion, according to a February 1990 report issued by the National Academy of Sciences entitled, *Developing New Contraceptives: Obstacles and Opportunities:*

> Currently available contraceptive methods are not well-suited to the religious, social, economic and health circumstances of many Americans. The inadequacy of current contraceptive methods contributes to the problems of unintended pregnancy, unwanted children and high rates of abortions. The stronger the desire to reduce abortion, the greater should be the investment to develop new methods of contraception.

The report concluded that half the 1.4 million abortions performed yearly in the United States could be avoided if a broader range of contraceptives were available. (Ninety-eight percent of all abortions could be avoided if either or both parties practiced birth control.) A combination of legal liability, federal regulation, and religious restrictions on birth control are the reasons new contraceptive development has been completely stopped in the United States. Religion, by prohibiting birth control, is encouraging abortion.

In November 1989, clergy throughout the Phoenix area were asked by the Religious Affairs Advisory Council of Planned Parenthood to preach a pro-abortion sermon on a particular Sunday, creating controversy on exactly what the religious response should be to the request. Most ministers whose denominations supported abortion complied, confirming the lack of a single religious stance on abortion. As one minister pointed out, "Our society believes in killing." Police may shoot to kill; capital punishment is legal in most states (thirty-six of fifty); war is waged; each cut in a social program to feed the homeless or provide organ transplants may cause death. However, there's a crucial distinction between killing in these circumstances and the killing of an unborn human being by abortion. In all cases where society allows killing, there are actors involved who have a choice whether to participate in crime or war (even draftees may draft-dodge), or who have the possibility of raising money necessary for food or a transplant. The fetus has no opposition opportunity or say-so at all; to argue that a child would rather be aborted than born into poverty, without consulting the child, would appear nonsensical. Naturally the fetus cannot be consulted, yet if any fetus could respond, likely none would choose death. Of course, the entire debate over abortion is to settle the question whether the fetus is a lump of flesh without rights or a legal person with rights of due process, which would require no harm without consent or an opportunity to be heard and which would make the whole question moot. How the answer to this question can depend on the circumstances by which the mother became pregnant is unclear. The circumstances of conception make no difference to the victim of an abortion, unless we return to the years where a bastard was ostracized and required to be guilt-ridden by society. For example, the late blues singer Ethel Waters was the product of the rape of her twelve-year-old mother. She and others were grateful she was not aborted.

To those who assert the certain defective health of the child should justify abortion, there is Beethoven, the fourth child of a syphilitic father and consumptive mother, and with two tubercular sisters during a period when tuberculosis was a dread disease. How many of the 1.4 million yearly aborted fetuses in this country would fall into such categories, or is it relevant? If it is not relevant or important, why not? These questions must be answered to justify abortion, instead of evaded or ignored. The only possible answer is that we will never know; does this mean it makes no difference and is this a sufficient answer?

The language of abortion advocates is strikingly similar to the terms and logic used by slave owners in the early 1800s. Southerners weren't pro-slavery because anyone was free to own or not own slaves. Southerners were pro-choice on slavery. By this logic no one has ever been either pro-slavery or pro-abortion because no one ever proposed that Southerners be required to own slaves any more than anyone has ever advocated that all pregnant women be required to have an abortion. Southerners asked, why don't those Northerners leave us alone and mind their own business instead of imposing their druthers on us; how many Northerners would be willing to support and feed slaves if they were freed? Similarly, one main argument of pro-abortionists is that all opposed to abortion must be prepared to adopt any baby not aborted when the mother, for her personal convenience, would rather have an abortion. As Leo Tolstoy, the inspiration for the nonviolent philosophies of Gandhi and King, wrote in his diary in 1852, "It is true that slavery is an evil, but an extremely convenient evil." Abortion is similarly an evil of convenience.

Language in the abortion debate is sanitized; the killing of the fetus/child is called termination of pregnancy; a human life becomes a fetus or potential life; the man or woman doing the killing is called a doctor, or provider. Precisely what does the right to choose mean; that is to say, what is being chosen? Is there an answer other than the death of an unborn child? How can a human being choose the death of another human being without that human being's consent in a society where consent to a physical injury is illegal and tortious, giving rise to civil liability? Why do pictures of an aborted fetus enrage pro-abortionists when the pictures accurately portray exactly what occurs in an abortion? If abortion is morally neutral, what difference does it make how many abortions have been performed each year or whether abortion is routinely used for birth control? Why is a confessed murderer entitled to a jury while a truly innocent unborn child may be killed on the whim of the "mother"? Why does the father have no legally allowed interest in the question of whether to abort when the father is responsible for eighteen years of child support if the child is born? Only by denying the existence of human life can these questions be answered, and even then, any answer is unsatisfactory. We do, however, distinguish between the age of the fetus in how we feel about its death. An early death is called a miscarriage, which for many is relatively untraumatic. A later death is called stillbirth, and most feel more intensely about such a death. This distinction is logical based on fetal development. At the moment of conception the zygote consisting of a single egg and sperm is barely visible to the naked eye, about the size of the period at the end of this sentence. After one month the fetus is the size of a quarter in diameter, and by the third month the size of a large hen egg. Half the weight of the fetus is gained the last six to eight weeks. However, the fetus is reactive from the fourth month onward as shown by its movement when startled by noise or in turning away from a light shined on the mother's stomach. Most abortions occur at the end of the first trimester, perhaps justified by the arguable lack of reactivity until the beginning of the fourth month, a day later. By the sixth month the fetus responds to music as we do, soothed by ballads and agitated by hard metal rock, and grins, grimaces, and frowns. Except for weight, a third-trimester fetus is practically indistinguishable from a newborn child, and this fact is recognized by most abortion advocates who do not advocate abortion after this time. A logical difficulty for pro-abortionists is in drawing the line between the one hundred seventy-ninth day and the one hundred eightieth day, but it's also difficult to justify abortion any time after reactiveness begins in the fourth month, after which abortion is currently legal for the next three months. How can abortion be moral on one day and not on the next, when there's no significant difference in reactiveness?

Assuming a fetus is not a sentient being then is the killing of any non-sentient human life equally acceptable? For example, if my father is senile and bed-ridden and an inconvenient burden, what distinction is there between the killing of that nonsentient being and the killing of the nonsentient fetus? One clear distinction is that the fetus has a fruitful life expectancy of eighty years, while father has a maximum life expectancy of a few months and none of that will be conscious. Logically then, it should be less immoral to kill father than to kill the fetus.

The "Public Conversations Project" in suburban Boston succeeded in establishing a common ground for mid-1992 pro- and anti-abortionists; almost all of us, no matter our label, agree that abortion as birth control is wrong, that preventing pregnancy is of prime importance, and that sex education is needed for all.*

I suggest the following as a solution to the current abortion quagmire, which hopefully technology and education about birth control will primarily solve. Most of us believe abortion is immoral but most of us also believe a woman should usually be able to choose whether to have an abortion during the first months of pregnancy without outside interference. We can distinguish between legality and morality; notwithstanding the percentages who believe abortion should be legal in many circumstances, most of us also believe abortion is immoral. The same 1989 *Los Angeles Times* poll found that 61 percent of 3,583 people surveyed felt abortion to be morally wrong (the figure was up to 75 percent by 1990); 22 percent said abortion is morally correct and 24 percent were unsure. Fifty-seven percent said abortion is murder; 35 percent disagreed, but 74 percent agreed that "I personally feel that abortion is morally wrong, but I also feel that whether or not to have an abortion is a decision that has to be made by every woman

---

*Ellen Goodman, *Boston Globe, Arizona Republic,* June 3, 1992.

for herself." Accordingly, 62 percent opposed a constitutional amendment banning abortion. We appear internally confused on abortion, perhaps for the first time in our history having a majority believing an act to be immoral but opposing *criminal* sanctions. The distinction between criminal sanctions and civil remedies is crucial, but has never, to my knowledge, been made in connection with the abortion debate.

We should reject criminal justice sanctions, which is the specter that likely provides the most support for the status quo on abortion. Instead, abortion should be reserved solely as a civil law question, so that if any person is directly impacted by an abortion, then a civil suit for damages can be maintained. As in any civil case, damages would be recoverable only by an immediate relative, someone with a direct legal interest in the question. Those who have no direct personal interest would be required to avoid harassing pregnant mothers and abortion clinics, but any affected person, whether the potential father or other close relative, should be allowed to sue for damages caused to them, if any, by the aborting of their soon to be offspring or relative. The specter of the criminal justice system should be removed from the equation.

This is only a temporary solution. Because abortion harms another, whether that other is called a fetus or human being, and is thus immoral in the ultimate sense of what morality is all about, a compromise is necessary until we as a species can become more civilized and caring toward our offspring, potential and actual, who are all human beings. Birth control should be removed from the list of religious prohibitions, allowing the shy and the rest of society to practice prevention when no child is wanted from sex. The bottom line of abortion is that it harms some one else and is thus immoral and unethical. Unprotected sex is not personally responsible and does not justify harming another for the convenience of the irresponsible.

Illegal Drugs: An Example of a Proper Ethical Response—Harm No One Else

The traditional purpose of government is to protect its citizens from harm, which justifies the criminal justice system. Those harming others are incarcerated, taken off the streets, and put behind bars to punish them and to prevent the further harm of other citizens. Traditionally, and with some logic, the seriousness of a crime is judged by the harm caused to its victim. Because murder causes more harm to the victim than burglary, the sentence for murder is longer and more severe than the sentence for burglary. For a narrow class of "moral" crimes, however, the criminal justice system dispenses with this logic and punishes those who primarily harm themselves and only incidentally, if at all, harm others. These are commonly called victimless crimes.

Crimes without victims raise serious questions of ethics and the proper role of the criminal justice system. Victimless "moral" crimes include drug crimes, excluding drugs sold to minors and drugs ingested by pregnant women, and such crimes as gambling, pornography, and prostitution. To fully understand the appropriateness of criminalizing victimless behavior requires the consideration of (a) the relative harms of the most popular victimless behaviors, (b) the ethical justification for imprisoning an individual, (c) the costs of and our ability to prevent or punish victimless behavior, (d) the reasons people "commit" victimless crimes, (e) the special status of minors, (f) how valuable we consider privacy, liberty, and freedom from interference by government, (g) the source of "moral" crimes without victims, and (h) the impact if victimless crimes were legalized. These eight factors, as they relate to illegal drugs and other victimless crimes, are explored in detail in this section.

THE RELATIVE HARMS OF ILLEGAL AND LEGAL DRUGS
AND OTHER THINGS WE LIKE*

Americans are as well-educated about drugs as we are about geography, history, and most other things. Few of us know that the most dangerous drug in the world is tobacco, which killed 454,000 Americans in 1990, up substantially from 390,000 in 1985 and 188,000 in 1965. The second most dangerous drug is alcohol, killing 125,000 yearly. Our illegal drugs, including cocaine and its many derivatives, heroin, opium, and all the others, kill 6,700 each year with almost no variation on this number. The only illegal drug we hear much about, cocaine, kills 2,700 people a year in the United States. Most of the other 4,000 yearly deaths are caused by the use of amphetamines. Thus, the "war on drugs," insofar as it's aimed against cocaine and its derivatives, seeks to eradicate the use of, and imprison the users of, a drug that kills one person for every 210 killed by tobacco and alcohol.

Even proportionately, alcohol and tobacco kill far more users than illegal drugs. Alcohol kills the same percentage of alcoholics as cocaine kills of its addicts. Seven percent of alcohol users are hopelessly addicted, and 7 percent of these die yearly. Ninety percent of tobacco users are hopelessly addicted and 6 percent of these die yearly. Eighteen percent of cocaine users are addicted and .25 percent of these die yearly. No one dies from using marijuana. The question is why we spend billions of dollars to imprison people for using our less dangerous drugs, while the most dangerous and addictive drugs are legal and easily available to our children.

Camus said, "Every ambiguity, every misunderstanding, leads to death; clear language and simple words are the only salvation from this death." The drug problem in the United States is largely due to our almost complete ignorance

---

*Information in this section is based on the following sources: tobacco—Ellen Goodman, *Boston Globe, Arizona Republic,* Dec. 17, 1990; *Arizona Republic,* Nov. 21, 1991; Anastasia Tonfoxis, *Time,* Jan. 23, 1989; *alcohol*—Peter Aleshire, *Arizona Republic,* May 19, 1990; Ann Walton Sieber, *New Times,* Dec. 12–18, 1990; *drugs*—Joel Fort, M.D., *The Pleasure Seekers: The Drug Crisis, Youth and Society* (1969); Peter Aleshire, *Arizona Republic,* Sept. 1989.

about drugs and our obfuscation of their relative effects and dangers. Any drug is dangerous if too much is consumed, or if the drug is impure, whether the drug is aspirin, alcohol, or heroin. Conversely, no drug (other than a pure poison) used in moderation is dangerous to the user, with the exception of some highly addicting drugs such as tobacco, alcohol, cocaine, and, when available in relatively pure dosages, morphine, opium, and heroin. No drug is totally harmless. The potential for harm depends entirely on the dosage and purity.

One drug that has been used for decades acts directly on the brain and causes thousands of deaths and injuries every year; in lower animals it causes chromosomal breakage and birth defects. Yet Americans ingest eighty million aspirin each day. Since aspirin kills and injures about as many people as cocaine, should its possession or sale result in prison? Is a drug good if it relieves pain and bad if it creates pleasure?

Instead of distinguishing among our drugs, we lump them together and make most either illegal or obtainable by prescription only on the assumption that the government must make drug decisions for its adults. No other country in the world has anywhere near as many illegal and "prescription only" drugs as the United States. When it comes to drugs we are among the most paternalistic nations in the world.

Drugs generally fall into eight broad and unscientific categories:

1. *Narcotics.* These drugs relieve pain, reduce coughing and diarrhea when used in moderation, and are physically addictive. Most illegal drugs are labelled as narcotic, though they are not, such as cocaine and marijuana. Only opiates are properly classed as narcotics. The two primary narcotics are morphine and codeine produced from opium and the semi-synthetics used by the health profession. All produce euphoria.

When heroin was outlawed by Congress in 1914, there were a few hundred addicts. By 1968, there were 200,000. Simply put, criminalizing any activity tends to encourage it for certain people, especially the young. Although violent crime is increasing, our spending to prevent and solve violent crimes is dropping precipitously in proportion to our increased spending on victimless drug crimes. Comparing the "dope fiend" or heroin addict to the alcoholic, years of heroin use causes no permanent physical damage (unless the addict uses a dirty needle) while alcohol destroys the body. Prison harms a person more than the use of heroin or any opiate.

As described by a Harvard University psychiatrist in a November/December 1990 article in *In Health* magazine by Deborah Franklin:

> [Weekend warriors restrict] their heroin use to a Friday night pop without becoming addicted. They could walk away from heroin, and did every now and then, without undergoing the withdrawal pangs that junkies suffer. They never increased the amounts they used, and they never stole nor otherwise compromised their values to get more heroin. Most were successful, middle-class students

and businesspeople who, when they wanted to relax, happened to snort or shoot heroin instead of drinking martinis. To understand why these people didn't become addicted . . . it was necessary to look beyond biochemistry, to the motivations and environment of the drug user. The idea that "hard" drugs can be used moderately is as surprising today as it was two decades ago [when described by the Harvard psychiatrist]. The $10-billion-a-year [grossly understated in dollar amount!] federal drug war has taken wide aim, and in its wartime vernacular, every drug user is an abuser, and every drug abuser a budding addict.

2. *Central Nervous System Depressants.* These create tolerance resulting in dependence, and their withdrawal causes psychological dependence.

Marijuana is a central nervous system depressant which has never caused a single confirmed death; those who smoke marijuana to excess go to sleep. It causes calm and giddiness, prevents nausea, reduces blood pressure, stimulates appetite, kills pain, and suppresses convulsions. Marijuana is a dangerous drug only when used around dangerous machinery, such as when driving an automobile. There is recent medical evidence, however, that marijuana may cause large benign tumors of the mouth and neck in a small percentage of younger users. Surgeons at the University of California-Davis noticed this possible link to fast growing tumors that had only been seen previously in people in their sixties who had been heavy tobacco smokers and drinkers of alcohol for decades. Some of those afflicted had smoked as few as two or three marijuana cigarettes a week, though most had been heavier users.

Marijuana was targeted in the 1930s because it was used by the outcasts of society—blacks, Mexicans, jazz musicians, and a few intellectuals, and it became a partial substitute for alcohol during prohibition. It was denounced as the cause of crime, violence, assassinations, and insanity, having been linked to the 1930s crime wave of Bonnie and Clyde, Ma Barker, and petty crooks who smoked marijuana, which was in turn characterized as giving criminals a feeling of false courage and freedom from restraint.

The prohibition of marijuana drove it underground, attracting more users. Law enforcement lumped marijuana use with heroin addiction and penalties escalated. Billions are now being spent to stamp out marijuana use. The AMA is silent as to its relative lack of harmfulness, primarily because the AMA is both powerless and timid against politicians and lawyers. The AMA also prefers that most drugs be dispensed with a prescription for obvious reasons of profits.

Marijuana, however, doesn't lead to the use of harder drugs and apparently retards the use of alcohol. The higher the use of marijuana, the lower the use of alcohol or heroin. Marijuana also substantially lessens violent behavior, according to studies in Tunisia, Nigeria, South Africa, Canada, Brazil, and the United States. To stop all crime, a government could issue marijuana to its citizens, who would then sit around and do nothing all day, similar to the average American who watches hours of television each day.

Marijuana is therapeutic for glaucoma, asthma, and nausea and vomiting caused by radio/chemotherapy. The Director of the Drug Enforcement Administration, however, on December 29, 1989, rejected reclassifying it as a Schedule II drug, preventing it from being made available for medical uses, such as controlling nausea in terminal cancer patients. In 1991 the Florida Court of Appeals granted an AIDS victim legal access to marijuana to control muscle spasms, the first such ruling in the country.

In March 1992, the United States Public Health Service decided not to provide marijuana to any AIDS, cancer, glaucoma, or other patients because of fears that it could further harm the immune system. Medical advocates say it combats nausea, vomiting, and weight loss common to cancer patients undergoing chemotherapy and to some AIDS patients. It also reduces eye pressure in the treatment of glaucoma and reduces muscle spasms common to neurological conditions such as multiple sclerosis. Forty-eight percent of cancer specialists, based on a 1992 poll, said they'd prescribe marijuana for their patients if it were legal.

An estimated twenty-one million Americans smoked marijuana in 1990. A spokesman for the Office for National Drug Policy responded, "Legalizing marijuana would further complicate our effort against illicit drugs. In addition, we are not in favor of legalizing anything that causes damage to people." A physicist at the Argonne National Laboratory replied, "Everyone who wants it [now] will get it. It's kind of like outlawing gravity. It doesn't make sense."

3. *Sedatives/Hypnotics.* These drugs calm the user, induce sleep, and are physically addictive. The most used sedative is alcohol. The first sedative to be widely used, other than alcohol, was bromide, which dates to 1857. Barbiturates, introduced in 1912, were produced in the United States at the rate of 971,000 pounds in 1965, when over a million pounds of equanil/miltown were also manufactured. Sedatives account for 20 percent of our prescription drugs. The number of prescriptions for anti-depressants rose from seven million in 1965 to thirty-two million in 1989.

4. *Anti-anxiety drugs and minor tranquilizers.* These drugs cause psychological dependence.

5. *Ethanol/Alcohol.* These are the second most widely used and physically addictive drugs. Alcohol builds small tolerances, causes traumatic withdrawal symptoms, and is widely used throughout the world for recreational purposes, causing more deaths than any other class of drugs, except for tobacco. The public fails to fully recognize alcohol as addictive; only alcohol is legal among the hundreds in similar catagories. Alcohol causes great physical deterioration of the user and lowers the ability to function.

Depending on the definition used, there are between fourteen and eighteen million alcoholics in the United States; 5 percent become bums or derelicts. A similar percentage applies to the addicts of any drug. A study published in an April 1990 issue of the *Journal of the American Medical Association* concludes that susceptibility to alcoholism may be caused by a gene far more common to alcoholics than to nonalcoholics.

About 30 percent of our prison population is there for illegal drug possession, or crime associated with illegal drug use and purchase, but 50 percent of our prisoners were under the influence of alcohol when they committed their crimes. Many crimes are related to alcoholism, such as rape, murder, theft, burglary, and embezzlement. Suicides and accidental deaths are also closely linked to alcoholism. The drug most directly associated with violent behavior is alcohol. Half of all violent crimes are committed when alcohol has been used to excess. The comparative effects of alcohol, narcotics, and marijuana are illustrated by an old Persian folk story. Three chronic drug users approached locked city gates late one evening. The alcoholic insisted on breaking down the gates. The opium user went to sleep, waiting for the gates to open in the morning, and the marijuana user proposed flying through the keyhole.

6. *Anesthetics.* These are rarely used illegally, except for cocaine, which overlaps many general drug categories; anesthetics are physically addictive.

7. *Stimulants of the Central Nervous System.* These include amphetamines and cocaine (also an anesthetic), originating from plants and synthetics; they are psychologically addictive. Widespread use of cocaine began in the United States in the 1890s; by the 1930s, amphetamines (uppers or speed) were also widely used. Amphetamines were synthesized in the United States beginning in 1933 and are widely used today, causing almost twice as many deaths as cocaine. Cocaine, cocaine derivatives, and amphetamines cause 95 percent of the deaths suffered from illegal drugs.

Amphetamines are over-prescribed and have little legitimate medical use, which is limited to treatment of hyperactive children and narcoleptics or epileptics. Their original use, similar to NoDoz, was to postpone sleep for students and truck drivers, primarily with benzedrine and inhalers. Psychological dependence results rapidly. Dependency on amphetamines is similar to narcotic addiction because the user becomes primarily concerned with where to get the next dose.

Cocaine was the first form of speed used in the United States. The chewing of coca leaves had been traditionally reserved for high-ranking Incas in religious ceremonies. The Spanish encouraged the use of coca leaves because it kept the natives docile, compared to the processed and far more powerful powder/crack/ ice form available in the United States today, which portends violent behavior for many (mostly males). Cocaine and amphetamines are closely related. Cocaine has been used for thousands of years by 90 percent of Andean Indians (about ten million) in Peru, Bolivia, Columbia, and Argentina, helping them tolerate the high altitudes of the Andes, reducing fatigue and hunger. There's no record of any having died from chewing coca leaves. The Coca-Cola Company still uses the leaf for flavor after the drug is extracted. We took the leaves and refined them, concentrating the active ingredients and injecting them directly into the bloodstream, with predictable and unpredictable results. The predictable result is that people die when injecting any powerful drug excessively; the unpredictable result is that we now wish to hunt down and kill Andean Indians for growing coca leaves as they've done with no harm to themselves for thousands of years.

All drugs directly harm another when used by pregnant women, with the greatest media emphasis on cocaine use. (Do those supporting abortion have moral authority to oppose dangerous drug use by pregnant women?) The number of babies addicted to illegal drugs at birth rose from half of 1 percent at the primary indigent hospital in Phoenix, to almost 4 percent in 1990. Most of these babies suffer withdrawal but survive with little adverse health effects. No criminal cases had been filed in Arizona against these mothers through 1990, though cases were pending in other states. Prosecutors are reluctant to file charges unless the mother has been forewarned of drug use dangers, or has used cocaine in successive pregnancies. Many believe criminal prosecutions would drive "cocaine" mothers away from pre-natal care.

Arguably the most serious problem associated with the illegal cocaine trade is its destruction of the world's rain forests, particularly in the Amazon basin, and the dumping of millions of tons of toxic wastes, which result from the refining of cocaine, into the drainage areas of the Amazon highlands and headwaters. Five hundred thousand acres of tropical forests were destroyed and 1.5 million acres deforested by 1991, with coca plantations growing sevenfold since 1975 to meet U.S. demand for cocaine. No government is equipped to prevent this destruction because the area is controlled by the Mafia and the guerrillas of Peru's Maoist Shining Path movement. Until drugs are legalized and the enormous illegal profits removed from the Mafia and Shining Path control, these areas are as uncontrollable and dangerous as Vietnam or Afghanistan. In addition, the cultivation of coca strips the soil and causes widespread erosion, with large portions of the Tingo Maria, Cutervo, and Abiseo national parks and the Alexander Von Humboldt and Apurimac national forests largely destroyed. Until the drug trade can be wrested from the Mafia and other violent outlaws these areas cannot be preserved, and the lungs of the earth may disappear, along with our atmosphere. The legalization of drugs is urgent, not merely the theoretically best thing to do as a solution to a wasteful drug war.

Nicotine is another physically addictive central nervous system stimulant derived from tobacco and, together with crack and ice, the most addictive substance known. Tobacco is the deadliest drug on earth, far more dangerous than heroin, opium, crack, cocaine, or even alcohol. The number one cause of premature death in the United States and the world is from the use of tobacco. It is the deadliest known carcinogen.

American health costs from smoking reached $100 billion in 1989, or an average of $1,500 for each adult, based on higher medical and disability costs and lost work time. Tobacco is "the single most important preventable cause of death, responsible for one out of every six deaths in the U.S."* The American Heart Association also concluded in 1990 that fifty-three thousand nonsmoking Americans die yearly from second-hand smoke, making this the third-leading preventable cause of death.

Arizona Republic, April 2, 1992.

Tobacco users have a far higher incidence of illness than any other segment of the population, particularly the lung diseases of emphysema and bronchitis, but also sinusitis and peptic ulcers, with many more days of illness than the nonsmoking population. The February 1993 issue of the *Archives of Internal Medicine* found that cigarette smoking increased the risk of leukemia by 30 percent and accounts for 14 percent of adult cases. Excessive intake of nicotine causes tremors, convulsions, and vomiting and stops the production of urine. It also raises blood pressure and heart rate, impairing respiration and breathing. It's highly addictive, causing tolerance and severe withdrawal symptoms.

Congress has gradually stiffened its resolve to retard use of tobacco, doubling the excise tax to $.16 a pack in 1982, requiring warning labels in 1984, banning radio and television advertising, and prohibiting smoking on short airline flights in 1987, with the restriction extended to most flights in 1989. Still, the $36 billion a year tobacco industry remains a powerful lobby, and Congress is hesitant to move too quickly, recognizing the logrolling necessary and the number of votes wielded by tobacco states. Health and Human Services Secretary Louis Sullivan, in a report issued in February 1990, said, "It is morally wrong to promote a product which, when used as intended, causes death, trading death for corporate profits."

The United States forces its trading partners, on pain of trade sanctions, to import American cigarettes by the billions. In May 1989, trade sanctions were threatened against Thailand for refusing to import American cigarettes. Thailand finally agreed in November 1990 to import them. The United States is pressing South Korea, Taiwan, China, and other Asian countries to eliminate trade barriers against American tobacco. How could we argue with a straight face that General Manuel Noriega should have been assassinated for selling cocaine, but George Bush could properly force tobacco on other countries when tobacco kills 150 times as many people as cocaine each year? We're trying desperately to increase the number of smokers abroad, while we seek to lower the number at home. Former Surgeon General C. Everett Koop said in discussing tobacco, "It's reprehensible that this country allows exportation of disease, disability and death to the Third World, putting a burden on them they'll never be able to handle."

By 1991 smoking also was recognized as the most dangerous contributor to problematic birth outcomes, higher than use of cocaine, heroin, or alcohol, based on a study of forty thousand Montreal women by McGill University. Almost 50 percent more women who smoked miscarried compared to nonsmokers. Smoking during pregnancy causes premature births, spontaneous abortions, and infant deaths because nicotine reduces blood circulation and, thus, oxygen intake, adversely affecting the skin, hair, and eyes. By 1993, smoking was additionally recognized as causing crossed eyes and behavior problems in the child proportionate in severity to the level of smoking both during and after pregnancy.*

Coffee, tea, chocolate, and caffeine are the most widely used "soft" drugs

---

*Brenda C. Coleman, Associated Press, *Arizona Republic,* Sept. 4, 1992; *Pediatrics* (September 1992); David Connella, *Arizona Republic,* March 1993.

and constitute central nervous system stimulants. Caffeine is contained in most of our "soft" drinks. The drug is relatively mild and inexpensive. At a level of ten cups of tea or coffee each day caffeine becomes a major stimulant.

Coffee was first mentioned in an eleventh-century Arabian medical text and has always been used to keep the sleepy awake. The first coffee house was established in Constantinople in 1554; many reformers sought to ban its use. Over five billion pounds of coffee are consumed yearly in the United States, which averages twenty pounds per person per year, including children. Similar to marijuana, caffeine has caused no reported deaths, but people gain tolerance and suffer withdrawal illness, so it is also addictive.

8. *Hallucinogens.* These drugs are ill defined and ill-named. They seldom cause hallucinations unless used in high dose, which can also occur with high doses of amphetamines or cocaine. Hallucinogens cause psychological dependence.

The consequences of prolonged drug use vary according to the drug used. The real danger of drugs is excessive use, which is the Catch-22 of drugs; many people are ill equipped to restrict drug use to moderate levels. The number of people using drugs to excess, however, is minuscule in any society, except in the cases of alcohol and tobacco, which we appear to care little about. Putting people in prison won't change the percentage of those who use drugs illegally, though education may lower it, as has happened with tobacco, alcohol, and illegal drugs. (Illegal drugs are as readily available in prison as outside of prison, which makes a startling statement concerning the efficacy of a war on drugs.)

Dependence or addiction develops rapidly once a drug is used with initial regularity at any level of dosage, though the extent of dependence, addiction or craving varies according to individual physiognomy and physiology. The following chart* lists the generally accepted comparative levels of addictiveness for our favorite drugs, based on how easy it is to become addicted and how hard it is to stop using them, on a hundred-point scale, with a hundred points constituting almost immediate physical addiction:

Nicotine	100
Ice, glass (methamphetamine smoked)	100
Crack	100
Crystal Meth (injected)	92
Valium (Diazepam)	86
Quaalude (Methaqualone)	83
Seconal (Secobarbital)	82
Alcohol	82
Heroin	81
Crank (Amphetamine nasally)	80

---

*See Deborah Franklin, "Hooked, Not Hooked: Why Isn't Everyone an Addict?" *In Health,* Nov./Dec. 1990.

Cocaine	74
Caffeine	73
PCP (Phencyclidine)	60
Marijuana	24
LSD & Mescaline	20

Nine of every ten people who light a first cigarette will have trouble quitting or be unable to stop smoking nicotine. Two of every ten who snort cocaine will have trouble quitting or be unable to quit. Alcohol and tobacco are more addictive than heroin, cocaine, LSD or marijuana.

One reason we don't understand drugs is because much of our information comes from police and politicians, who know as little as the general populace, instead of from medical experts and pharmacologists. The use of alcohol and tobacco by our politicians and opinion makers has made our two most used and dangerous drugs sacred cows, which removes them from rational scrutiny and comparison with other drugs. All drugs, legal or illegal, are used in every country in the world no matter the economic system, form of government, or predominant religion. Until humans give up pleasure as a pursuit, or the drive for intoxication ceases being the fourth strongest human drive, this will never change.

Psychological dependence is not restricted to drugs; it exists for all the important and pleasurable things in our lives—coffee, tea, cola, tobacco, alcohol, sports, television, and sex. If the television burns out, the family becomes irritable and restless, the same as anyone deprived of morning coffee, cocaine, or alcohol. The key question with any dependence, physical or psychological, is the extent of interference with life-functioning and self-development.

Dangerous, bizarre, antisocial, and crazy behavior by a drug user is unrelated to the drug used (with the exception of hallucinogens, which may frighten the user, resulting in injury) and is instead dependent on the personality of the user and the social setting. In other words, no drug changes the personality of the user to the extent that the user would commit a crime that the user has no unintoxicated proclivity to commit. In this regard drugs are similar to hypnosis. When an excessive dosage of any drug is taken the result is sleep, unconsciousness, or death. No drug is either demon or innocent; all depend on the user, the dosage, and the environment of use. Compare the effects of alcohol at any social gathering, 90 percent of which feature alcohol; some people are boisterous, others passive, a few aggressive, some sleepy, several amorous, and many change little. Every other drug acts similarly; its effect depends on the personality of the individual, the amount consumed, the social setting, and the user's interaction with others.

Our drug stereotypes are based on our social ethic, which is to say religion. Drug stereotypes have no connection with reality or the physiological effect of the particular drug. As a result of stereotypes, the attitude of the public is that drug users are spineless, hedonistic criminals who should be jailed as quickly and for as long as possible. We thus describe 99 percent of society (is there even 1 percent who use no drugs?) who are drug users and who are ourselves.

Because of our diets an average American has a 50 percent chance of dying from a heart attack. Since fatty and high-in-cholesterol foods are more dangerous than illegal drugs, why don't we criminalize fatty foods and the like? The criminal justice system has been uniformly used to protect us from ourselves, preventing us from using heroin, cocaine, and opium. Because fat is more dangerous and kills many more people, why don't we criminalize that? The answer is, of course, simple. We regard eating whatever we want as a basic human right, no matter the potential harm. We've never thought of criminalizing improper and dangerous eating habits, even though the American Heart Association estimates that 25 percent of 158 million adult Americans are significantly at risk of a heart attack due to high cholesterol.

Were we to think clearly about what is dangerous about drugs, whether legal or illegal, and the improper foods we eat, the bottom line is how they affect our lives. We are concerned about illegal drugs because they are addicting, though no more addicting than alcohol and tobacco. Addiction means we spend time nonproductively instead of doing those things we should be doing with family, friends, work, and recreation. This simple fact is highly important for a clear understanding of what is bad about addictions. Addictions may shorten our lives but the most immediate problem is they make us unproductive. When we are high, intoxicated, or ill from the side effects of drugs, we can't function to work or take care of ourselves and our families. We can't fulfill our human responsibilities. This is only true, however, if the addiction is a full-blown one, which is to say that it takes more of our time than its incidental pleasure objectively should. Why should we imprison people who use any drug in moderation, harming no one, not even themselves? Why should we imprison people who use drugs to excess, harming no one directly but themselves? We don't criminalize any other behavior that harms no one else, except those few crimes commonly known as victimless. The point is that we can't afford the resources or loss of basic freedoms necessary to stop everyone from doing anything that may indirectly harm someone else. If we were to attempt that we'd have to outlaw most foods we like because they contain high percentages of fat, which will eventually kill us, thus indirectly harming our friends and relatives, parents, and children.

If we judge a drug, food, or activity based on its addictiveness and wastefulness of time, one of the worst addictions is television, which we're dependent on. It's the hearth around which we gather and no longer communicate. The average American household in 1991 watched almost fifty hours of television every week of the year, each person watching thirty hours per week. The average child watches twenty-eight hours per week and a fourth of our children watch up to forty hours per week. Most of us don't work fifty hours per week, or go to school that many hours, or do anything else that many hours; not even sleep. Unless a person is hopelessly addicted to drugs, whether alcohol, cocaine, tobacco, marijuana, or tranquilizers, dozens of hours per week aren't spent/wasted on the mindless, yet pleasurable use of drugs, yet most of us spend/waste that much time watching television.

William F. Buckley calls television our most dangerous drug because it may cause the United States to become a third world nation by the turn of the century. Both the level of illiteracy and the number of illiterates is growing in rough proportion to the number of television sets sold. We are becoming short of skilled labor, semi-skilled labor, and unskilled labor. Instead of learning to read and write our students watch television.

A thirteen-year study by two Rutgers University professors found television to be highly and classically addictive, resulting in a book published in March 1990 entitled *Television and the Quality of Life: How Viewing Shapes Everyday Experience.* One author calls the result a "passive spillover effect":

> People report feeling more passive and less able to concentrate after they view television. The passivity spills over into how they feel after viewing. A kind of inertia develops, and it becomes more and more difficult to get up and do something active. In other words, viewing leads to more viewing.

The authors compared television to addictive drugs,* finding it made people feel worse and derive less satisfaction the longer they watched. Because of our addiction to television, the authors found we spent half our free time watching it:

> More Americans now have television sets than have refrigerators or indoor plumbing, and the medium has clearly become an American institution, substantially altering and influencing every other institution and ranking with the family, the school and the church as contemporary culture's prime forces of socialization.

The more we watch, the more depressed, sadder, lonelier, hostile, and irritable we become. The 1983 edition of the psychiatric diagnostic manual, which defines addiction as compulsive and difficult-to-control behavior, conceded to include the television viewing habits of millions.

We may not realize how dangerous television is. Brandon Centerwell, professor of psychiatry at the University of Washington, found that television may be responsible for half the yearly 20,000 murders in this country, possibly doubling the murder rate since it was introduced in the 1950s. Professor Centerwell analyzed the murder rates in three countries; the United States, Canada, and South Africa. Like clockwork, ten to fifteen years after television was introduced, the country's murder rate shot up dramatically. Ten to fifteen years is the time necessary for the first generation of children weaned on television to reach adulthood and move into their more criminally susceptible years. By the early twenty-first century, Centerwell believes we'll find television as dangerous to our minds as we have found tobacco to be to our bodies.

An illustrative example of television numbing reality occurred in Redwood City, California, in November 1989, when a man forgot to pick up his girlfriend at the doctor's office. Knowing how irate she would be the man convinced a

---

TV Guide reviewed a poll in its October 10, 1992, issue finding that 46 percent "would refuse to give up television for anything under a million dollars."

"friend" to shoot him in the arm with a .25 caliber pistol so he would have a good excuse for not picking her up as scheduled. The man almost bled to death and almost died from shock; concerning the gunshot he told the investigating police officer, "It looks nothing like this on television."

Another hazard of television is it's delaying of maturation in children, protracting their immaturity.

Television also promotes obesity, particularly in children. An Auburn University study of 6,000 male viewers concluded that fatter and less fit men spend more time watching television. Those watching three or more hours a day were twice as likely to be obese as those watching an hour or less. Worse results were found for children. Children watching four or more hours of television daily are four times as likely to have high cholesterol levels as children watching two hours a day, according to research reported to the American Heart Association based on a study of 1,077 suburban Southern California children. A war against television may be more deserving than a war against drugs.

The war on drugs is a war on ourselves. An Associated Press poll in 1989 revealed that, in the United States, casual drug users, who don't use drugs to the point that would prevent them from holding a regular job, are estimated to number twenty-five million. They work with us every day without us having the slightest indication that they use illegal drugs any more than we would know whether they had drunk a beer, a glass of wine, or a mixed drink the night before.

We fail to recognize that things taking our productive time and tending to habituate us to continuous nonproductivity are drugs, no matter the name. Whether the thing occupying our time is alcohol or television, heroin or fudge, cocaine or religion, it acts as a drug and is as potentially debilitating as those things which happen to have been designated as illegal drugs because of societal traditions. Religion can be included in this category, as explored in *Breaking the Chains,* a book by Episcopal priest Leo Booth. Booth recognized, while working as a counselor at New Life Centers (treatment centers for excessive users of food, drugs, and alcohol in Los Angeles), that "People hooked on religion experience the same powerlessness in trying to control their relationship to God as other addicts do concerning any chemical." Thus, many people use God to escape from reality. A cogent argument can be made for the proposition that all the addictive things we love are an alternative to thought, that we use drugs, sex, food, and other pleasurable things to avoid doing the one thing homo sapiens, thinking man, is supposed to do.

We now believe it necessary to warn adults that anything they do may be dangerous to themselves or others, posting warnings on items that everyone knows to be dangerous such as cigarettes, alcohol, and swimming without a personal lifeguard. The human race was produced through survival of the fittest, evolving to a level where we seek to tell its members precisely what they can and cannot do though their behavior harms no one but themselves. We are expending our resources in protecting the weak against themselves, with the risk that evolutionary progress will end while our basic freedom to be left alone evaporates.

WHAT ACTS JUSTIFY INCARCERATION OR THE DEATH PENALTY?

It would take the GNP of the world to build the prisons necessary to house twenty-five million people, which is the number using illegal drugs (mostly marijuana) in the United States. In 1989 we spent sixteen billion dollars to imprison one million people, the largest proportion of any nation's citizens in the world, including the former Soviet Union, South Africa, Iran, Iraq, China, and Albania. The United States is the world's most repressive nation in imprisoning its citizens, otherwise known as "criminals." The simple reason is that most "criminal" activities are now considered felonies, carrying long mandatory sentences though involving no violent behavior. For example, recidivism statutes in most states require life in prison following a third felony conviction. Because shoplifting merchandise worth one hundred or more is a felony, the compulsive shoplifter could spend life in prison upon a third conviction. By 1990, 426 of every 100,000 Americans was in jail or prison compared to the number two nation, South Africa, with 333 per 100,000 incarcerated.* Is it rational to spend tens of thousands of dollars to send a twenty-year-old to prison for smoking a joint, or for doing a line of coke, and for harming no one, other than (possibly) himself?

We've doubled our prison population in ten years, mostly by incarcerating nonviolent criminals, while violent crime has risen by 10 percent. The U.S. murder rate in 1990 was 10.5 per 100,000, making us the "most murderous industrial nation." Congress and the state legislatures blame our highest murder rate on illegal drug turf wars, but there'd be zero drug-war related murders if our less dangerous drugs were legal.†

Why do we put people in prison? There are several given reasons but the only cogent ones are revenge and prevention of future crime. Estimates vary on how many people are currently in prison solely for the use or sale of our less dangerous illegal drugs, though federal prison statistics put the federal level at 46 percent, while the state statistics are substantially less, around 25 percent, but rising rapidly. With a nationwide prison population of a million adults, about 300,000 (federal and state) are there solely because they possessed or sold drugs.

In 1990 in Massachusetts several government officials admitted having smoked marijuana, blaming it on youthful indiscretion. U.S. Representative Joseph Kennedy said, "Like many people my age, I tried it when I was younger, but I certainly believe that there is no benefit to drug use, and there can be terrible consequences."

Democratic senator from Arizona Dennis DeConcini is a staunch supporter of illegal drug penalties and is responsible for the anti-drug smuggling radar blimps tethered on the Mexican border, but he supported Clarence Thomas for the U.S.

---

*Associated Press, *Arizona Republic*, Jan. 5, 1991.

†The 1992 meeting of the American Associates for the Advancement of Science featured a section on urban drugs, gangs, and crime, directed by David C. Lewis of Brown University. Dr. Lewis split violent crime into three categories: crime caused by drug use, by a need to buy drugs, or among competing drug sellers. The only drug that produced a higher rate of violent crime was alcohol. Almost all violent crimes associated with illegal drugs were tied to trafficking, leading Lewis to ask, "Could the war on drugs be a diversion from the war on crime?"

Supreme Court even though Thomas had admitted to casual (whatever that means) use of marijuana in college. DeConcini said if casual use of marijuana in college was a bar to U.S. service or public office, "more than half our pilots in the Air Force would not be pilots today . . . [and] that's certainly true in the executive branch and the judicial branch and in the legislative branch." Under Arizona law these pilots, judges, and congressmen would be required to spend one and a half years in prison for each instance of casual use.

Former drug czar William J. Bennett was asked by a caller to a radio talk show, "Why build prisons? Get tough, like Arabia. Behead the damned drug dealers." Bennett responded, "That's an interesting point. What the caller suggests is morally plausible. Legally, it's difficult, . . . but morally I don't have any problem with it at all."

The successful Republican candidate in the 1990 election for the Arizona governorship, Fife Symington III, called for the death penalty for drug dealers. The death penalty is usually reserved for first-degree murder, espionage, and treason. Is a drug dealer who sells a gram of cocaine to his broker, or lawyer, or any adult, the equivalent of a first-degree murderer?

In 1987 the Drug Enforcement Agency trumpeted the success of Operation Closing Bell, perhaps the largest drug investigation carried out in the financial district on Wall Street. Nineteen brokers were charged with the possession and distribution of cocaine, and thirteen were convicted with sentences ranging from probation to forty-two months in jail. Is society better off? Should the brokers instead have been executed?

During December 1990 Iran arrested 1,900 people for drug trafficking and 16,000 alleged drug addicts. Addicts are sent to hard labor camps and dealers are executed; 1,500 were hanged in 1989 and 1990. Iranian groups opposing the government and independent civil-rights organizations claimed the executions were intended to crush political opposition in Iran. In October 1991, the Irish Republican Army began a crackdown on "antisocial crimes" by shooting four suspected drug dealers in the kneecaps. (The other primary antisocial crime avenged by the IRA in Northern Ireland is joy-riding.)

James Buchanan points out that it is naive to believe that executing drug dealers will have any impact. Drug dealers sprout faster than a court can say continuance, or an attorney can file an appeal. The majority of Americans avoid illegal drugs and would continue to do so after legalization for the same reasons most of us don't show up drunk at work every morning: self-respect, common sense, peer pressure, economic need, and concern for health. If we had to depend on police action to curb legal drug use without these molders of individual action, the police would fail as miserably as in the drug war.

The American experiment with prohibition must have faded from the memories of those now alive. Federal laws forbade alcohol except for "medicinal" or religious use, but imposed no penalties for buyers, users, or possessors. Bootleggers received stiff fines for the first offense and six months in jail and a ten-thousand-dollar fine for the second offense. State laws, on the other hand, imposed brutal penalties for possession. In its eleven years of existence, the Prohibition Bureau hired 17,972 employees, fired 11,982 without stated cause, and terminated 1,604 for bribery, extortion, theft, falsification of records, forgery, and perjury. Journalist Franklin P. Adams described the Prohibition Commission under President Hoover:

> It's left a trail of filth and slime;
> It's filled the land with vice and crime;
> It don't prohibit worth a dime.*

By 1930, a third of all federal inmates were incarcerated for alcohol offenses. The only difference between alcohol and illegal drugs is public opinion. If an alien were to read about the war on drugs and learn that legal drugs kill seventy-five people hourly for each person killed by illegal drugs, what argument would prove our sanity?

As stated by Spinoza:

> All laws which can be violated without doing anyone any injury are laughed at. Nay, so far are they from doing anything to control the desires and passions of men that, on the contrary, they direct and incite men's thoughts the more toward those very objects; for we always strive toward what is forbidden and desire the things we are not allowed to have. And men of leisure are never deficient in the ingenuity needed to enable them to outwit laws aimed to regulate things which cannot be entirely forbidden. He who tries to determine everything by law will foment crime rather than lessen it.

Spinoza could have been describing the war on drugs.

Americans are quick to define a social problem as something that displeases them and to seek a remedy through the criminal justice system, which is an expensive method of achieving little. Simply because one or more religions deem victimless behavior as sinful doesn't mean the behavior deserves to be criminalized. A third of the prison population is there because of illegal drug possession or sales and mandatory sentences; the killing of another human being often requires far less time in prison than illegal drug offenses. If we are so concerned that drug users will become a burden on society, why are we not concerned in the same manner about the users of our more dangerous legal drugs and about those of us who become a burden on society when incapacitated because we eat excessive fat and end up with a debilitating heart attack? Why is the criminal justice system seen as an answer to drug usage, or are drugs criminalized because they offend religious precepts? Because alcohol and tobacco are condoned by most religions, and we learned the hard way about the impossibility of criminalizing the use of alcohol, they will never be criminalized. Why do we continue to make the same mistakes about less dangerous illegal drugs, sapping our national resources in a course doomed to failure? Will we eventually execute all those found with illegal drugs, such as is done in Iran? Still, drug use has not diminished in Iran. Even if the United States were prepared to execute drug dealers, drug use would continue.

---

*See Joel Fort, M.D., *The Pleasure Seekers: The Drug Crisis, Youth and Society* (1969).

Prohibiting anything is the surest way to get many people to try the prohibited act. Such is human nature. The only sensible course is education. Those who refuse to be educated can harm themselves all they want. That should be their privilege as adults.

It's immoral to punish victimless crimes. The victims don't see themselves as victims so there's no possible rehabilitation, only a more diligent effort to avoid being caught in the future. In all other crimes there is a prosecuting witness or victim, without whom the crime is not prosecuted. This is true of assaults, batteries, and property crimes. Why should a person be viewed as a victim when he does not so view himself? Consensual private behavior of adults should be no business of the state or the criminal justice system; what, otherwise, did the Declaration of Independence mean in venerating life, liberty, and the pursuit of happiness?

Criminalization of victimless crimes increases social harm instead of rectifying it. These crimes take more effort and money to prosecute than any other crimes because there's typically no witness, unless the witness is an undercover police officer. Police must hire witnesses, informers, and decoys, employ wiretaps and illegal searches, invade the privacy of others, spend billions of dollars, and still be ineffective. Without informers and decoys, prosecution of illegal drug crimes, prostitution, and gambling don't happen.

Victimless crimes (including drug possession for personal use, but excluding sales of drugs) are considered a joke by those in the legal system. Ask any prosecutor, judge, police officer or defense lawyer, off the record. Few believe these crimes are evil. Hookers are back on the street in an hour. If they were a little higher class or more expensive they'd never be busted in the first place; i.e., if they were the hookers who service the prosecutors, judges, and defense lawyers. Most police aren't paid well enough to afford the more expensive hookers, except for the police assigned to victimless crimes where the real money is made. The purpose of these laws is a sop to public morality, which is religious morality. A synonym is hypocrisy.

Also, the primary opportunity for police corruption is victimless crimes. The police have enormous discretion because enforcement of all laws is simply impossible. There are more laws governing our behavior than the human mind can comprehend, and the greater the number of laws, the relatively fewer that can be enforced and the more individual police have unreviewable discretion to choose which laws to enforce and who to prosecute.

The number of laws governing our every behavior approaches the magnitude of the numbers we examined when analyzing the size of the universe. I lived in Phoenix, Arizona, with a metropolitan area population of two million people. There were several thousand city ordinances and hundreds of city charter provisions governing my conduct. The adjoining cities of Mesa, Scottsdale, Tempe, Glendale, and the others had similar volumes of city ordinances and city charters governing my conduct when I strayed across their corporate boundaries. Add to that the various city building codes, the thousands of county ordinances, the state statutes (currently forty-five volumes in Arizona, with one added each year), the thousands of rules and regulations adopted by state agencies, hundreds of executive orders by the governor, the current two hundred volumes of decided case law (Arizona is a relatively small state in population and its state courts have only been in existence since statehood in 1912), plus federal statutes, plus federal rules in the Code of Federal Regulations, plus the Congressional Record in hundreds of volumes so the federal laws can be interpreted, and to that add the United States Constitution and all the cases decided by the federal courts since the country began. Seventy-seven thousand law-making jurisdictions in the United States are daily adding more laws.

Every law controls our behavior, or seeks to do so. As a result of these laws the United States has more people in prison per capita than any nation on earth. Neither the former Soviet Union nor any other country in the world can hold a candle to the United States when it comes to the control of its citizenry via sheer weight and volume of detailed restrictions. Ethically, the sole criminal sanctions should be against those that harm others. When this is not the case, the law-making majority of the particular era will find a reason to prohibit acts later realized to be innocuous, as did Plato when he wrote that music should be regulated because it provides the equivalent of an opiate to the masses.

Victimless crimes also encourage class discrimination. People with money are seldom arrested for these types of crimes. The privacy of the rich is far more secure than that of the poor. The result is disrespect for the criminal justice system and no deterrence. Is artificial religious morality worth the cost?

There are three main arguments against decriminalizing victimless crimes. The first is that there is a victim who is harmed. The answer is that society has no business telling adults what to do, whether they harm themselves doing it or not. If we were to seek avoidance of self-harm as our main goal, we would outlaw skiing, watching television to excess, eating chocolate and other foods high in fat, driving cars, and especially smoking tobacco and drinking alcohol. Criminalization of these and other dangerous activities, however, harms the self-victim far more than not criminalizing the behavior.

The second argument is that without criminalizing the behavior, society would be encouraging it. This is an argument for children and for paternalism. Is it equally true that because we don't criminalize having sex with one hundred sex partners at once that we're encouraging orgies? Adults should be allowed to make their own choices as long as they harm no one else. No one needs to tell us what is good for us. If we can't decide that for ourselves, we don't exist as adults. What others may see as a lack of will power may be our main pleasure in life. What right does society have to deny us that, if we don't hurt anyone? We don't even normally criminalize our paternalism—seat belt laws, helmets for motor-cyclists, transfusions for religious zealots, swimming without a lifeguard. We primarily criminalize those acts that are contrary to the tenets of our major religions. The criminal justice system should never be used as a means of marking social disapproval. This kind of symbolism has no deterrent effect and may instead increase criminal behavior because prohibition of anything is a mark of dominance over those whose nonharmful behavior is being criminalized.

The last argument is that morality demands criminalization. Morality, however, only demands that something not be done, not that we be thrown in jail for doing it. Only the arbitrary, man-made criminal justice system, fashioned from the collective wisdom of legislators, criminalizes behavior. The criminalization of victimless crimes is the imposition of the majority's religious beliefs on the minority and invades the privacy of adults.

Criminalizing victimless crimes trivializes violence and injury to others. Sending a possessor of marijuana to jail for a year when the penalty for killing another human being in negligent circumstances, such as when driving a car under the influence of alcohol, is also a year in jail, trivializes the killing of another human being. Sentencing a drug seller to ten years in prison for selling cocaine to his broker, or any other consenting adult, trivializes second-degree murder, which carries the same penalty. We point to capital punishment as the severest penalty, usually reserved for heinous murder or treason, though many would impose death for selling illegal drugs.

Incarceration should be limited to those who harm others or another's property, but by 1989 we had one million in prison for the first time in our history, with this number growing at the rate of 8 percent a year. The reason for this is the drug war and mandatory sentencing. California requires all persons convicted of second degree burglary to be given a four-year mandatory prison sentence, adding 2,500 inmates yearly to the California prison system. Meanwhile, we parole far fewer than we did a dozen years ago because mandatory sentencing forbids parole.

A 1991 prison study commissioned by the Arizona Legislature concluded that Arizona's severe prison crowding will worsen into the indefinite future, taking increasingly more of the state's budget, until the legislature repeals the vagaries of mandatory sentencing. The report noted that "many thousands of persons have been sentenced to extraordinarily long sentences, and many thousands of similarly situated persons have received much shorter sentences."

Who receives a prison sentence and the length of the sentence often bears no resemblance to justice, reality of comparative harm, or equity. For instance, during 1989 in Phoenix, a women was sentenced to twelve years in prison for writing bad checks, while a priest was sentenced to a year in jail for molesting two boys. The boys had previously been molested by a parishioner and then been given to the priest for further care; the priest also admitted having molested fifteen other young boys.* The charges for molesting the two boys carried up to thirty years in prison, but the Arizona bishop asked for probation, so the judge compromised and gave the priest one year in jail.† A manual laborer whose family was hungry stole stale bread from a dumpster and was charged with burglary, a class four felony, carrying up to four years in prison. The laborer was offered the chance to plead guilty to attempted burglary, which carries only one to four years in prison, but after the local newspaper wrote a scathing column the charge was reduced to criminal trespass and the man fined $200, payable at $30 a month,

---

*John Winters, *Arizona Republic,* July 15, 1989.
†Brent Whiting and John Winters, *Arizona Republic,* Nov. 21, 1990.

while his family continued to go hungry. Several men are in the Arizona penitentiary for digging up cactus in the desert. A hit-and-run driver killed a man and was sentenced to ninety nights in jail with work release in the daytime so he wouldn't lose his job. The Arizona Court of Appeals on December 12, 1989, affirmed the sentence of a black defendant to life imprisonment without chance of parole for twenty-five years. The defendant had sold a $20 rock of cocaine to an undercover police officer in a ghetto apartment building in south Phoenix while on probation from a earlier conviction for possession of cocaine. The court said the sentence was not disproportionate to the offense, because "drug offenses are considered to be an extremely serious problem in this country."*

In 1990 Arizona continued its erratic sentencing of people based on the harm they caused to others. On one day a man was sentenced to twenty years in prison for smothering his three-month-old daughter, while another was sentenced to seventy-eight years in prison for sexually attacking (but neither raping nor killing) an eight-year-old girl. Is it worse to molest a child than to kill a child?

The Arizona criminal code lists sixty-five dangerous illegal drugs, and ninety-six illegal narcotic drugs, possession of which is a class two felony, carrying a mandatory penalty of seven years in prison. Other class two felonies include rape, arson of an occupied structure, theft by extortion when causing physical injury by use of a deadly weapon, armed robbery, child molestation, enticing child prostitution, and kidnaping. Manslaughter is only a class three felony.

In March 1992, a German judge ruled laws criminalizing possession of marijuana or hashish unconstitutional on the grounds that a definitive German study concluded that smoking one or two marijuana cigarettes a day is harmless, "or at a minimum, less dangerous than the daily consumption of alcohol or 20 cigarettes." Governing coalition leaders condemned the decision but many senior opposition figures endorsed it along with several leaders from the individual German states. The health minister of Saarland said, "It is high time to take cannabis products out of the zone of illegality," while others proposed a drug policy similar to the bordering Netherlands', which offers two thousand coffee houses with marijuana and hashish for sale. Meanwhile, on June 27, 1991, the U.S. Supreme Court held (5–4) that states may impose life in prison sentences without parole for possessing large amounts of drugs. The justices held it not to be cruel and unusual punishment to sentence a possessor of one and a half pounds of cocaine to life in prison. In March 1992, the U.S. Attorney and prosecuting attorneys offices in Arizona by internal memo announced they would no longer prosecute possession of less than eleven pounds of cocaine or one thousand pounds of marijuana because the courts were too clogged to handle any "smaller" cases, which would justify seven lifetimes in prison under the U.S. Supreme Court rationale.†

Instead of beefing up our police to combat violent crimes and crimes against property, we beef them up to stop private drug pleasures and other victimless

---

*State v. Waits, Arizona Court of Appeals, Jan. 24, 1990.
†Ben Winton, Phoenix Gazette, March 22, 1992.

crimes. Meanwhile, violent crime rises every year, like clockwork. Instead of protecting our citizens against violent criminals, we spend much of our tax money protecting our citizens against themselves, when they as adults have voluntarily chosen to harm no one else. An *Arizona Republic* article on September 17, 1989, concluded:

> Parents, not police, are the key to the drug crisis. Today, drug and crime policies focus on the wrong institution of social control (the government), treat an inappropriate age category (adults), falsely assume a causal connection between drug use and criminal acts, and misperceive the motive of offenders. As long as this continues, no amount of taxpayer's money will win the war on [drug] crime.

Anything can be misused or used to excess, but interference by government or others should be confined to instances where a third person is directly harmed. Advocates of criminal penalties for drug use argue that such use results in the increased use of public medical resources, costing society more in taxes, but those costs are infinitesimal compared to the cost of police, prisons, public defenders, prosecutors, judges, and the productive time lost by drug users who must spend years in prison. Control advocates argue that drug use causes crime, but far more crime is caused by making drug use a criminal act and driving it underground so drug dealings must be made with organized criminals or other potentially violent entrepreneurs. The enforcement of drug laws takes its toll by raising the price of drugs so that users may resort to secondary crimes, which, unfortunately, are potentially violent crimes. Control advocates also argue that drug use leads to neglect of families, but the criminal justice system doesn't prevent familial neglect. It exacerbates it by putting the user in prison. The legality of alcohol doesn't cause familial neglect. The user neglects the family because alcohol is used excessively, which is the fault of the user, not the fault of the alcohol, and unrelated to whether the use of alcohol is legal or illegal.

Adults are still the best judges of their own interests. If they are not qualified to determine what is best for them, state legislators and Congress and city councils and county boards of supervisors and the United Nations will do no better. Paternalism stultifies and renders the intended beneficiary impotent and unable to care for self. What is best for the individual cannot effectively be written into unbending law. Codification equals stultification and inability to change. Experimentation and risk-taking is retarded, and progress slows. The whole basis for evolution and improvement of the species disappears when what is at a particular moment considered "right," is codified into the concrete of unchanging law (or religion).

Government paternalism is a synonym for tyranny. There is no act of an adult that harms no one else that is so dangerous that the public has a right to forbid it. Otherwise, we should uniformly, and without hypocrisy, forbid adults to harm themselves, whether the harm arises from alcohol, operating highly dangerous machinery (cars, planes, and implements used in dangerous sports), fatty foods and those high in cholesterol, or our illegal drugs. Then adults would be forbidden to do anything which is not good for them and compelled under threat of criminal sanction to do those things that are good for them. For instance, all citizens would be required to meet at the track every morning at six A.M. for their morning exercise, television would be highly restricted, only foods with high fibre content and low fat and cholesterol could be eaten, hang-gliding, rock climbing, auto racing, driving, skiing, sky diving, and any dangerous activity would be forbidden. Adults would henceforth refrain from risking harm to themselves, or they would go directly to jail.

Those who enjoy dangerous activities should assume the risk attendant to those activities, whether drug use or mountain climbing. If a person uses drugs or climbs mountains without considering the risks, the person is foolish and unworthy of protection. However, why should foolish people be punished twice, once by the consequences of their behavior and then by being imprisoned? What is the logic of punishing people for punishing themselves?

The following is an excerpt from a 1990 essay in *The Freeman* titled "Drugs and Dumbness" by Scott Matthews, a law student at my alma mater:

Perhaps the most important question of the 20th century has been a simple one: who owns the individual? Do I own myself, or do I belong to the state? Clearly if I belong to the state, then drug prohibition is a proper exercise of state power. The state, like any other owner, is justified in protecting its property and in using that property as it sees fit. On the other hand, if I belong to myself, then prohibition is a clear and unacceptable infringement of my right to dispose of my property—myself—as I see fit. In my opinion, drugs are a foolish way for you to spend your time. But since I don't own you, or have any property right in you or legal claim on you, my opinion shouldn't count for much. Your taking drugs in the privacy of your own home doesn't impinge on my property rights. After all, I think comic-book collecting is also foolish. Skydiving and mountain climbing are "dumb." . . . But those are decisions I can make only for myself. What a sad world this would be if everything the majority (or a vocal minority) thought was foolish were also illegal. Sometimes the one bright spark in a person's life is something most people think is dumb! . . . Your temptation is to say that drugs are different, but they are not. Drugs are simply one dumb way to spend your time. Working 80 hours a week while your marriage falls apart and your kids learn to hate you is also dumb. . . . Life is full of a million ways to be dumb and self-destructive. . . . And you know what—not one of them is illegal! Just drugs. . . . You must still *behave* yourself while on drugs. . . . To me, America is a *deal* we've all made together. . . . I promise to let you be a fool as long as you don't damage my property (including me), and in return you allow me the same freedom. . . . The decision on how to live a happy life is necessarily mine to make. It is true that I may fail, but life would be meaningless without that possibility. If, instead of working on improving my own life, I try to save you from being foolish, and you insist on saving me from being foolish, we will each reap nothing but frustration and failure.

Societal distaste for some act should be insufficient to justify exposing an adult to criminal sanctions, even if the majority agrees on the distastefulness. If there is no injury to another, distaste should remain the burden of the prude instead of being imposed on the imprudent. Those who do not wish to see pornography should not look at it; those who disapprove of a particular television program, book, or movie should avoid it, but their tastes (or lack thereof) should not be foisted on the majority or any minority, even if the minority consists of only one person.

THE COSTS OF THE WAR ON ILLEGAL DRUGS

How much is our drug war costing in dollars? Former President Bush lobbied a bill in 1990 that added over $10 billion to the $44 billion already spent annually on police and interdiction efforts, to which must be added billions for prisons, prosecutors, public defenders, parole officers, and probation officers. The federal court budget by 1990 exceeded $2 billion a year, drug prosecutions rose 6 percent in 1990, and on January 1, 1991, judicial salaries rose by 30 percent and eighty-five additional judgeships were created.* The growth was attributable in large part to the drug war. We spend close to $100 billion each year on the drug war, and we're not making a dent with an approach that depends on criminalization.

U.S. Senator Dennis DeConcini fathered the radar-equipped blimp program to deter illegal drug smuggling across the Mexico-U.S. border and in the Caribbean. Each blimp costs $25 million, and two have already crashed in Texas. The army docked five of the six in the Caribbean, because it prefers radar-equipped boats. The blimps are operational only 50 percent of the time due to bad weather and maintenance, and they also appear to signal smugglers to avoid the area when they are up. Fewer than five planes a month are intercepted as a result of blimp detection, and fewer than ten illegal drug interdictions have resulted in the last four years.

The *Arizona Republic* deployed three reporters to test the efficacy of the DeConcini radar blimps: one flew a plane to Mexico, landed, and flew back using a flight profile typical of drug smugglers; a second observed the performance of the radar center at March Air Force Base, California, and the third watched U.S. agents at the Lukeville, Arizona, border crossing as the plane passed overhead at 150 feet. Though the aircraft behaved suspiciously and the border area was displayed on the March AFB radar screen when the plane passed through, none of the U.S. agents noticed the flight.†

When confronted with the flight information the Customs officials said they had detected the flight but lost it; they refused to release either audiotapes or the radar operator's account of their "detection." The *Republic* concluded:

---

*Michael Gottfredson and Travis Hirschl, *Arizona Republic,* Sept. 17, 1989.
†*Arizona Republic,* May 14, 1992.

It demonstrates the futility of trying to control a drug trade driven by consumer demand through interdiction and high-tech gadgetry. The Aerostats have produced very few drug seizures; blimps that spend half their life on the ground are unlikely to bother resourceful smugglers. Unless evidence is produced that shows these high-priced balloons are anything but a bust, Congress should reconsider directing funds ($25 million) to anti-drug programs that work.*

In 1964, we spent $5.5 million on the drug war. Now we're spending 17,000 times as much money and the cost of our target drug, cocaine, decreased from $65,000 to $14,000 a kilo by 1989, spiking up to $20,000 in 1990 before dropping back to $14,000 in 1991. The price of cocaine continually fails on average to keep up with inflation. *Newsweek* magazine called the 1990 spike in price "Good news in the Drug War" because prices were up and purity was down. Higher prices mean greater profits for drug dealers, and lower purity means more physical danger to drug users from contamination. Was this good news?

Factoring in inflation, the cost of cocaine dropped by 1991 to the equivalent of $7,000 a kilogram in 1964 dollars, or 12 percent of its cost in 1964. The federal Bureau of Justice Statistics concluded that spending on the drug war is increasing four times as fast as spending on education, and twice as fast as spending on health and hospitals. Since 1980, the number of adults behind bars has tripled; one person in forty is under some form of correctional supervision. Yet there's been little change in the use of drugs or the crime rate. More police will do nothing, even if the numbers were doubled, because anyone can use drugs in privacy, almost anywhere at anytime.

Although we spend $90 billion a year to throw a few illegal drug users in prison, we spend comparatively nothing on treatment for excessive users of drugs. In New York City, the director of one drug treatment program, Project Return, pointed out:

> Even if you lock them up, someday they still have to get out of jail. . . . We keep a two-month waiting list, and then we stop keeping it. In order to stay on our waiting list you have to call every day. If you miss more than two days, we take you off the waiting list because there is somebody else already on it.†

What's the drug war money spent on? Arizona in 1990 sought money for night goggles and scopes ($30,000) for use in Nogales, a border town; narcotics-sniffing dogs (four for $28,000); video camera ($15,000); Mass Selective Detector (drug analysis machine, $70,000); and two million dollars for overtime pay so officers could buy drugs from local dealers. The county attorney in Phoenix targeted the "Asian community," requesting $70,000 for a surveillance van to intercept

---

*According to the *Houston Chronicle,* the two-billion-dollar anti-drug radar levee along the Mexican border is a total failure. Though U.S. Customs Service officials claim the system has closed the border to airborne drug traffic, they admit it was not responsible for a single arrest or drug seizure during 1991 and that it's almost impossible to catch pilots who fly over, drop bundles, and return to Mexico.

†Barbara Reynolds and Shrona Foreman, *USA Today,* Feb. 28, 1990.

beeper, fax, and cellular phone messages. The director of the Pacific Rim Council asked whether the county attorney had a "White community" task force. The county attorney called the van "crucial to the overall success of the described [Asian] task force" at a total cost of $161,539.*

A serious cost of criminalizing drug use is police corruption and brutality. During 1988, four Mesa, Arizona police officers accompanied a Tucson, Arizona narcotics squad, known as MANTIS (Metropolitan Area Narcotics Trafficking Interdiction Squads), on a desert drug bust. MANTIS officers wear black ski masks to conceal their identities and brag that they knock suspects to the ground when making arrests. They also place black hoods over the arrestees' heads to prevent identification. According to the Mesa police officers, the six-man MANTIS group punched a suspect in the face, knocking him down, then the six took turns kicking him at least fifty times during a five-minute period like "punting a football," doing "knee drops" to the suspect's back, and punching him in the back of the head. Not surprisingly, the suspect required hospitalization. The MANTIS officers were reprimanded for wearing gloves and spiked wrist bands.†

The FBI investigated MANTIS officers for a pattern of beatings and brutality against unarmed drug suspects and others. Tucson defense attorneys claimed nine incidents during a November 1989 court hearing. A MANTIS spokesman said, "There are times when force must be used. Drug dealing is a brutal business." A public defender stated, "Because of the way the public feels about drug cases, this kind of thing is tolerated. I think there's an unwritten code that says, if you make a drug bust, you can beat the daylights out of somebody." A federal undercover police officer said, "Once we define an enemy, we become more and more tolerant of any action designed to get rid of that enemy. But the minute we stoop to acting like the bad guys, we become the bad guys." One of the MANTIS officers admitted, "I kicked him, punched him . . . I can tell you I threw a bunch of punches. I don't deny that." The MANTIS spokesman said of this incident, contrary to the admission, "I can tell you this guy was not beaten."‡ Observers call it doubtful that Mesa police officers would have broken the unspoken "Blue Code" between officers unless they were certain about the use of excessive force.

The United States has lambasted Mexico's lackadaisical drug war efforts for years, with the result that Mexico in 1990 spent 60 percent of its justice department budget and used a fourth of its military to fight the drug war.

In October 1989, a Mexican federal judge, Benjamin Soto Cardona, freed a drug suspect because the man had been tortured for four days with multiple burns on his genitals, saying, "With the pretext of the war against narcotics traffickers, they [the army and Federal Judicial Police] commit a variety of abuses against the people." The majority of people accused of drug charges in Mexico have been tortured by the police or army, according to the judge. The suspect

---

*Ward Harkavy, *New Times,* Dec. 26, 1990–Jan. 1, 1991 (weekly).

†Eric Miller, *Arizona Republic,* Nov. 22, 1989; Sandy Tolan, *Arizona Republic,* March 25, 1990.

‡S. Tolan, op. cit.

freed by the judge had been arrested for trying out a new walkie-talkie in front of his home. The army tore his home apart, found no drugs, but arrested the man and his family anyway.*

In late 1990 the U.S.-based civil rights group, Americas Watch, documented Mexican Federal Judicial Police and its "elite" antinarcotics unit policies resulting in killings, torture, extortion, robbery, and other violence. The group concluded that "this pattern of excessive violence and abuse can only mean that either the Mexican government has adopted a policy of tolerating such behavior or it has lost control over its police security and prosecutorial agencies." In 1986 the Mexican government forbade torture by the police when bodies of tortured prisoners were found in the ruins of the attorney general's headquarters after the September 1985 earthquake.

A report by the U.S. State Department issued in February 1991 detailed torture and murder practices of the Mexican Federal Police, particularly in anti-drug activities and extrajudicial killing. As of September 1990, 408 officials in the Mexican Attorney General's Office and the Mexican federal judicial police had been fired and arraigned on criminal charges. During 1990 there were ninety-seven complaints filed by U.S. citizens against Mexican police abuse, including an American in Oaxaca for having chili and carbonated water forced up his nose and being subjected to electrical shocks after being arrested for suspicion of possessing drugs. The State Department called this case "characteristic of methods used by overzealous police." Mexico's antidrug activities, however, began at the urging of the U.S. government.

Police payoffs and corruption are routinely linked to major drug deals. The executive director of the Police Executive Research Forum, which represents law enforcement agencies, says, "There's no question the numbers [of corrupt police officers] are increasing." Drug dealers consider police payoffs a cost of doing business. Incidents from 1990 included: one hundred Detroit police officers under investigation for drug-related activities with twelve formally charged, nine Los Angeles County Sheriff's narcotics deputies suspended in August 1989 and investigated for stealing cash confiscated in drug busts, a former DEA headquarters staff coordinator indicted for cocaine trafficking, and dozens of others.†

Would anyone remain untempted if offered one million dollars to let a truck through a border checkpoint without inspection? One longtime Customs agent, Rick Ashby, described the frustration:

> My guys work so damn many hours that their overtime comes out to about 50 cents an hour. They're tired and sleepy most of the time. Hell, who wouldn't be if you spent about half your nights sleeping out in the desert waiting for some bastard to come along with a load of dope? Then, when they bust some-body, they walk into a house with four Mercedes-Benz cars in the driveway,

*Robert Kahn, *Arizona Republic,* Oct. 23, 1989.

†Richard L. Burke, *New York Times, Arizona Republic,* Dec. 17, 1989; *Washington Post, Arizona Republic,* March 26, 1989.

two or three 40-inch TVs in the house and dinnerware that is made out of gold, not silver. And sometimes, there's so damn much money laying around that you have to have machines to count the stuff. Now, if you're a customs agent or any other kind of cop whose house is mortgaged to the hilt, and whose kids need braces, and whose old lady is threatening to leave because you've been too busy to take her on a vacation for the past three years, the scene can be tempting, even if it's just for a minute.*

The U.S. Customs Service was so worried about drug-related corruption that it hired people to watch its employees, an undercover network of about forty spies to keep tabs on the rest. From 1987 through 1989, internal investigations resulted in the arrests of sixty-four employees, including twenty-one on theft counts, seventeen for narcotics violations, seven for bribery, three for embezzlement, and two in murder cases. In March of 1989, two Texas inspectors were arrested for accepting bribes from marijuana smugglers; on January 5, 1990, several officers were arrested for dealing drugs and stealing duty money at Kennedy International Airport in New York. The employees' union called the new spy network abhorrent and a tactic more suitable for a police state than a federal agency.

A federal audit of the State Department drug interdiction effort concluded that its Bureau of International Narcotic Matters was "doing a poor job of managing an expensive program with little to show for it." More accurately, there was nothing to show for the millions the agency spent since 1979, though President Bush at his February 15, 1990, drug summit in Columbia announced it would provide oversight for the president's new $2.2 billion Andean drug-control initiative. The Bureau's mission is to coordinate the activities of the DEA, Customs, the Coast Guard, the FBI, and other agencies when operating outside the United States. Instead, the audit found that the Bureau's 203 fixed-wing aircraft and helicopters were used primarily as air-taxis for U.S. ambassadors in other countries or were left idle. The Bureau was considered so unimportant that it had no representative in former czar Bennett's Office of National Drug Control Policy or the CIA's drug-intelligence center and no congressional liaison.

The U.S. State Department and congressional auditors concluded in 1991 that the millions of dollars of U.S. aid provided to Bolivia, Colombia, and Peru since 1990 under President Bush's antidrug strategy has purchased nothing. The Government Accounting Office (GAO) reported that the amount of coca leaf seized in Peru declined from fifty-five tons in 1988 to forty-three tons in 1990. The GAO also reported that U.S. intelligence agencies "agree that the estimated volume of drugs entering the country during 1989 and 1990 did not decline."

The Rand Corporation has demonstrated that no matter how much we spend on illegal drug interdiction and law enforcement, the economics of the drug trade will prevail. Production and refinement of coca leaves costs less than 5 percent of the street cost of cocaine, the cost of smuggling is less than 10 percent the street price, and the chances of getting caught smuggling are slim. In 1990 the

---

*Randy Collier and Paul Brinkley Rogers, *Arizona Republic*, Aug. 27, 1989.

U.S. military identified 6,729 suspicious flights; law enforcement tried to intercept 661 and caught 49. Mathea Falc, an international drug expert, concluded in her 1992 book, *Just Say Yes: Drug Programs That Work,* "Everyone who has looked at this problem agrees that the progress we've made has come from education, treatment and changes in social attitudes, and not because we've succeeded in cutting supplies." "Everyone" does not include law enforcement.

The war on drugs has perverted our government into "big brother" at a cost we have not yet begun to realize.

WHY WE USE AND ADORE DRUGS

Why is the demand for drugs so high and can it be changed? As with our drugs of tradition, alcohol and tobacco, the demand will always be high for one simple reason. In his book, *Intoxication: Life in Pursuit of Artificial Paradise,* pharmacologist Ronald Seigel concludes that the pursuit of intoxication is the fourth basic human drive, reporting his studies of animals and humans over the last twenty years: "The drive to pursue intoxication is a common biological behavior throughout the animal kingdom. It's irrepressible, it's unstoppable, it's never gone away and never will go away. We might as well make the pursuit of it safe." Seigel opposes legalization of illegal drugs and long resisted the conclusion that intoxication is natural: "But everywhere I looked, in every species of animal, they were all doing what we're doing: getting high on plant drugs. They were going out of their normal feeding range just to get high." Bighorn sheep climb the sheerest cliffs, not for food, but to reach a lichen with mind-numbing narcotic properties. African elephants search for the fermented fruit of the Borassus tree and become stumbling drunk. Primates particularly go out of their way to ingest foul-tasting plants to get a buzz. According to Ethiopian tradition, coffee was discovered by goatherds around 900 C.E. when they noticed their animals leaping around after eating coffee beans. Cows and horses eat locoweed because of its hallucinogens, which may also kill them. Countless animal species eat hallucinogenic mushrooms.

Seigel concludes that "trying to prevent drug use by outlawing it is like trying to treat AIDS by outlawing sex. Winning the war on drugs by eradicating nonmedical drug use is neither possible nor desirable."

James Schaefer, director of the Office of Alcohol and Drug Abuse Prevention at the University of Minnesota, suggests:

> If any society chose to reject alcohol, it would probably have other, more serious problems. There's the workplace, the homeplace and this third place where we talk, drink, and release ourselves from our everyday worries and troubles. A little bit of drinking goes a long way in terms of the health of the community. Without that outlet we'd have more fighting, violence and civil strife. In Minnesota we recently passed stricter drunk driving laws. . . . When the cops started busting people, domestic violence increased. The heavy drinkers were staying at home. Bar sales went down, but package sales went up, as did spouse and child

abuse. . . . In small-town America the bar is the gossip center, the center of social activity. Without the corner bar to go to, there would be more homicides
and violence.

Because of their addictive properties, there will always be a demand for drugs
such as cocaine, tobacco, and alcohol. A University of California-Irvine (UCI)
study found that addiction, learning, and intelligence involve the identical process
at the cellular level. Biologists have long thought of brain function as a unit,
but the UCI study discovered how individual cells respond to a cocaine fix:

> In a sense, the purpose of life is to activate our reward systems. Dopamine and
> the opioid peptides are transmitters in a very powerful control system based on
> a certain chemistry, and along come poppy seeds and coca leaves that have
> chemicals very similar to, or can pharmacologically interact with, these central
> systems. They go right in, do not pass go. So if you're tapping into the natural,
> positive reinforcement systems, then to say that cocaine or amphetamines—or
> heroin or morphine—should be highly appealing is an understatement.

The researchers concluded that drug addiction, from a biological and medical
standpoint, should be treated as a brain disease instead of a character flaw. Drug
researchers in 1990 identified a portion of the brain called the *nucleus accumbens,*
which orients us toward pleasure, including sex and drugs. Brain irregularities
in this area appear to make some more susceptible to drug addiction, which is
akin to self-medication. Some drugs may correct a genetically caused chemical
imbalance. The chief of the Alcohol, Drug Abuse and Mental Health Administration estimated in October 1990 that from a third to a half of those addicted
to a particular drug may have a genetic susceptibility, particularly alcoholics and
users of cocaine. The gene affected is linked to receptors of dopamine, a brain
chemical that creates the sensation of pleasure. Seventy-seven percent of alcoholics
have the identified gene. A psychologist at a Pittsburgh clinic reported that "Many
recovering drug abusers tell me, 'The moment I took my first drug, I felt normal
for the first time.' It stabilizes them physiologically, at least in the short term."
A psychiatrist at Harvard Medical School said, "We suspect that cocaine is a
way certain people medicate themselves for depression."

The head of the federal Alcohol, Drug Abuse and Mental Health Administration concluded in January 1990 that half of all alcoholics and 70 percent
of those using illegal drugs to excess suffered from depression or severe anxiety
before becoming addicted. Because society provides little help for people to deal
with mental disorders, the sufferer may resort to excessive use of drugs. Arizona
in 1990, for example, ranked last among all states in public funding for mental-
health programs and near the top among all states in the number of youths in
jail, teenage suicide, alcohol consumption, and child abuse. The latest research
shows that excessive use of any drug is rooted in faulty brain chemistry and
untreated mental disorders. Fourteen percent of Americans use alcohol to excess,
six percent use other drugs to excess, and 22 percent suffer from mental disorders

at some time in their lives. Thus, according to David Krogh, author of *Smoking: The Artificial Passion* (1991), we use the "workplace drugs" of tobacco, Valium, and caffeine not so much for pleasurable sensation as to "get normal." Nicotine is a startling drug in that it relaxes tenseness but also acts as a mild stimulant for those feeling below par. Depressed people and schizophrenics are likely to smoke tobacco because it allows subtle mood regulation through self-medication.

For others, however, our most excessively used drugs are not automatically addictive. This fact is illustrated by the millions of controlled users of legal and illegal drugs (excluding tobacco, the use of which cannot be controlled by almost 100 percent of users). Thus, the use of cocaine, alcohol, marijuana, amphetamines, and heroin is controlled by most because they are able to do so. Intake is regulated because if it weren't the user would damage his self-esteem, value system, and self-discipline. Thousands of American soldiers returned from Vietnam addicted to "hard" (illegal) drugs, but only 14 percent remained addicted.

We use alcohol and other pleasurable drugs because of the pleasure obtained from their nonexcessive use and their effectiveness as anesthetics, which momentarily shield us from parental voices, disappointments, and the enigma of the future. Country singer Willie Nelson was quoted in 1990 as saying, "The biggest killer on the planet is stress, and I still think the best medicine is and always has been cannabis." Drugs lessen inhibitions and are a traditional means used by the male to seduce the female. Drugs provide gregariousness and social charm. Alcohol is more than socially acceptable—it's borderline socially required.

The use of drugs and alcohol is most popular in those societies where gambling and games of chance are popular, where feats of war are admired, and where self-reliance is demanded and rewarded, which describes most modern societies. Drugs of any type are used to alleviate stress, which is what our modern societies are all about, whether based on the economic competition of capitalism, the scarcities of communism, or the stresses created by all the isms in between. This truism applies equally to the stress created by religion, where rules must be obeyed under a threat to the soul. As aptly stated by poet A. E. Housman, "Malt does more than Milton can/ to justify God's ways to man."

Our ambivalence toward mood altering substances is illustrated by a politician's statement made upon the 1920s repeal of the Volstead Act, which prohibited sales of alcohol:

> I'll take a stand on any issue at any time, regardless of how fraught with controversy it may be. You have asked me how I feel about whiskey; well, brother, here's how I stand.
>
> If by whiskey, you mean the Devil's brew, the Poison scourge, the bloody monster that defiles innocence, dethrones reason, creates misery and poverty, yea, literally takes the bread out of the mouth of babes; if you mean the Evil Drink that topples men and women from pinnacles of righteous, gracious living into the bottomless pit of despair, degradation, shame, helplessness and hopelessness—then certainly I am against it with all my power.
>
> But if by whiskey, you mean the oil of conversation, the philosophic wine

and ale that is consumed when good fellows get together, that puts a song in their hearts, laughter on their lips and the warm glow of contentment in their eyes; if you mean that sterling drink that puts the spring in an old man's steps on a frosty morning; if you mean that drink, the sale of which pours into our treasury untold millions of dollars which are used to provide tender care for our little crippled children, our pitifully aged and infirm and to build our highways, hospitals and schools—then, Brother, I am for it. This is my stand.

The sole difference between the two positions, of course, is whether one uses the substance in moderation.

THE SPECIAL STATUS OF MINORS

Children should be stringently protected against exposure to any drug, legal or illegal, unless medically necessary. Legal and illegal drugs delay and hinder maturation, preventing the child from learning responsible behavior. Drug use exacerbates the problems of adolescence and may keep the child from becoming a responsible adult. Teenagers using drugs are three times as likely to commit suicide as those not using drugs; suicide is the third-leading cause of death among fifteen- to twenty-four-year-old Americans.

The most popular illegal drug among teens is marijuana, which is severely debilitating in a learning situation. The most popular legal drug is alcohol, which is similarly debilitating. As central nervous system depressants, alcohol and marijuana cause depression and, thus, make the user more susceptible to suicide. Those using central nervous system stimulants, such as cocaine, become depressed after dissipation of the high. After a crack binge there's an "almost intolerable" depression, which may encourage suicide. Alcohol, tobacco, barbiturates, sedatives, narcotics, central nervous system depressants, and tranquilizers should not be available to children under other than medically indicated circumstances.

Teenagers have gotten the message about how dangerous our illegal drugs are, according to a 1989 survey showing teenage use of illegal drugs down across the board. Cocaine use dropped from 13.1 percent in 1985 to 2.8 percent in 1989. Monthly use of marijuana fell from 50.8 percent in 1979 to 29.6 percent in 1989. Use of PCP (angel dust) fell from 7 percent in 1979 to 1.2 percent in 1988. We're winning the drug-education war against illegal drugs. For the first time illegal drug use by high-school seniors dropped below 50 percent overall in 1990, though usage was up in inner-city schools. Use of our more dangerous legal drugs, however, steadily rose as a substitute for illegal drugs. Perhaps after our criminalization hysteria disappears, our resources (approaching $100 billion a year wasted on the war against illegal drugs) could be reallocated to education about the dangers of the excessive use of all drugs and the use in any quantity of recreational drugs by nonadults. We have a long way to travel when a high-school dropout in a 1990 Phoenix news story could say that he liked to drink beer every night, but he avoided drugs because they "mess with your brain."

Girls are taking up smoking cigarettes at younger ages, a fourth beginning by the sixth grade and half by the eighth grade. Many stores routinely ignore age restrictions on the purchase of cigarettes. Most adults begin smoking as children because cigarettes were easily available. Those who begin to smoke as teens are the most likely to become heavy, long-term smokers. Cigarettes are easily available to children in most states, resulting in 4,000 new smokers daily for a total in 1990 of three million new child smokers. Sales of cigarettes to those under age 18 totalled $1.3 billion in 1989, according to the *Journal of the American Medical Association.* Half of the tobacco industry's profits, $3.35 billion, comes from people who began smoking as children. An Arizona legislator admitted in 1990, "We have a real double standard. Frankly, when it comes to cigarettes, I see little real difference between nicotine, heroin, 'crack' and cocaine. No difference. Any substance of an addictive nature that causes harm needs to be controlled."

The effect of the drug war has been to increase the use of legal drugs by children, who are now more likely to drink alcohol or smoke tobacco than to use illegal drugs and who increasingly view the use of drugs with disfavor, but because of drug war propaganda have been "educated" that legal drugs are perfectly acceptable.

The National Commission of Drug-Free Schools concluded in 1990 that the drugs most dangerous to our children are our legal drugs, alcohol and tobacco. The twenty-six members of the Commission, including eight members of Congress, were pressured politically by the alcohol and tobacco lobbies to conclude otherwise. Former drug czar William Bennett said to the Commission, "If you come forward with this, it won't hold any water. You have to be realistic."

Smokeless tobacco is used by many; 22 percent of college men chew tobacco or use snuff, according to a nationwide survey conducted by Pennsylvania State University. More than a third of first grade boys in rural North Carolina have chewed tobacco, and the number rises to 70 percent by the seventh grade, according to a 1989 study by the University of North Carolina in Asheville. North Carolina law allows six year olds to buy chewing/smokeless tobacco, though the sale of cigarettes is theoretically restricted to those age 17 and older. During the survey, several first graders eagerly volunteered their cans of chew, which they kept in their back pockets.

HOW MUCH DO WE VALUE OUR PRIVACY AND LIBERTY?

The "war" on drugs produces a war mentality; anything goes on both sides. Police excesses are justified by public opinion, which in 1989 found that 64 percent of Americans felt illegal drugs were the country's worst problem, up from 20 percent in 1988.* We don't enjoy the fact that cocaine dealers can have an income of up to $150 billion annually, in this country alone. The drug war requires states to ante up $10 billion for new prisons every year. Where does this money come from? We know the answer and probably also suspect there'll never be a victory over illegal drugs, no matter how much money is thrown at the problem. The

---

*Harry F. Rosenthal, Associated Press, *Arizona Republic,* Aug. 15, 1989.

sale of illegal drugs is as American as capitalism, and that's exactly what the war on drugs is trying to stop—drug capita...m, supply and demand. One of two things must eventually happen in this war: either we'll legalize drugs a long time down the road or we'll opt for victory at any price, including the loss of all privacy and civil liberties, and adopt a police state.

Seventy-three percent of Americans polled in 1990 said the U.S. Constitution guaranteed them a right of privacy from government interference in sex, also allowing them to withdraw life-support systems from the hopelessly ill. Seventy-three percent of Americans, though, were flat wrong. Privacy is mentioned nowhere in the Constitution, though the U.S. Supreme Court has inferred a limited right of privacy from the Fourteenth Amendment's "right to liberty," limited to birth control and abortion. The conservative and liberal members of the Court continually bicker over the existence of any privacy rights. Sixty-six percent of Americans said the "right to privacy" protected private voluntary acts of homosexuals, but the U.S. Supreme Court ruled in 1986 that states can criminalize private consensual homosexual acts. Only 34 percent said the "right of privacy" protects against random involuntary drug testing of employees. It, of course, does not.

After President Bush's September 1989 drug speech, 62 percent of us said we'd give up basic civil liberties to help the war on drugs. How much freedom will we have to give up by 1995? Fifty-two percent would allow our homes to be searched without cause, and 67 percent our cars to be stopped and searched, even if most searches are mistaken.* Because the majority rules and minorities on any issue are considered un-American, the government could easily institute these invasions of privacy. We would willingly sacrifice basic freedoms, enjoyed for two hundred years, for a war against drugs that are less dangerous than our legal drugs of alcohol and tobacco. Eighty-two percent of citizens would allow the military to combat drugs in the United States, no matter the methods. Both the Pentagon and the DEA, however, are opposed to military intervention. Fifty-five percent supported drug testing for all Americans, 67 percent supported testing for high-school students, and 83 percent for all drug users and their relatives, with reports going not to treatment centers, but to the police. Once civil freedoms are abolished they are usually never regained, or are reasserted only through violence and revolution.

Although illegal drug use is dropping, drug testing has increased dramatically. A 1988 survey by the College Placement Council showed 60 percent of the country's major companies tested applicants for drug use (excluding the most dangerous drugs of alcohol and tobacco), while over 80 percent of aerodynamic and petroleum industry firms drug tested applicants; in 1980, the number of firms testing was less than 10 percent. A November 1990 poll revealed that 95 percent support "some sort of workplace" drug testing in Arizona, including 35 percent who believed it should be allowed under only limited circumstances. Fifty-six percent supported random testing of all employees. The majority differed, however, on how the results should be used. Over 80 percent supported education, counselling, and

---

*Tom Wicker, *New York Times, Arizona Republic,* Oct. 5, 1989.

assistance programs, though 42 percent said anyone testing positive should be fired on the spot. Questions raised during the poll included whether firing threats would drive drug use further underground and discourage treatment, whether random testing is a proper invasion of individual privacy, whether tests are sufficiently reliable, and how much attention illegal drugs should receive when alcohol presents a greater problem in the workplace. A study in 1985, the most recent year for which figures were available, showed alcohol costing $27.4 billion in lost productivity and illegal drugs costing $6 billion, according to researchers at the University of California at San Francisco.*

The central problems with drug testing are three: accuracy, enforced intrusion on privacy, and disclosure of use unrelated to impairment. A test that accurately shows an employee has used cocaine or marijuana cannot show whether the employee has ever been impaired on the job, and a negative test result doesn't mean the employee hasn't been impaired on the job or didn't contribute to an accident. Unless a person is impaired on the job, there's no logical justification for drug testing. Even without drug testing, however, any supervisor should be able to tell whether an employee is impaired to the point of being unable to competently perform a job. Testing should be unnecessary for this purpose. There is no justification for drug testing when the comparative harm of legal and illegal drugs is considered and we fail to test for alcohol. Why should any individual be fired from a job if the person has never created a problem in the workplace and everyone is allowed to use the two most dangerous drugs with impunity?

Fifty-three percent of Americans favored sending troops to Colombia in 1990. On February 15, 1990, Bolivia, Colombia, and Peru agreed with the United States to use "all the means available," including a full-fledged military campaign, to stop drug production and smuggling. The Colombian government refused to allow the American government to station an aircraft-carrier group off its shores to monitor smuggling. The government's answer to use of less dangerous drugs is more police, more jails and prisons, martial law, the use of military force, and stiffer penalties.

Patrick Buchanan asked whether we're ready to pay the hellish social cost of winning a "war on drugs," which would require at a minimum the suspension of all civil liberties, declaring a state of siege, suspending the writ of habeas corpus, imposing martial law, and authorizing police to take drug dealers and users (the police must act as judge, jury, and chaplain) before military tribunals to be executed at dawn on their inevitable conviction—no appeals. This course would require the execution of forty million Americans, including our friends, our professional associates, and our children. Meanwhile, more dangerous drugs will kill almost a hundred times more people than our illegal drugs.

Why should the practitioners of capitalism, the guiding star of our economic system, be penalized because there's a demand for a product that harms no one but the demander? Because we ignore this basic question, we've set ourselves up for abnegation of the Constitution and the radical expansion of a police state.

---

*See Kathleen Ingley, *Arizona Republic,* Nov. 27, 1990.

As stated by Professor Wisotsky of Florida's Nova Law Center, "the war on drugs is really a war on the American people, whose rights are being invaded. There's a mass invasion of civil liberties on the grounds it's necessary to win the war."

The war on drugs has changed the usual presumption of innocence into a presumption of guilt. Both federal and state forfeiture laws provide for the summary seizure of cars, boats, and planes from people accused of drug offenses, whether they are convicted or not and no matter the quantity of illegal drugs found. A trace (unusable amount) of any illegal drug is sufficient to require the forfeiture of the most expensive property, even if the property owner had no connection with the drug use. The Supreme Court has approved these seizures, though they may leave the accused with insufficient funds to hire counsel, with the result that the taxpayers must instead pay for an accused's attorneys. Justice Blackmun dissented, saying, "It is unseemly and unjust for the government to beggar those it prosecutes in order to disable their defense at trial." The American Bar Association said the decision "seriously weakens our criminal justice adversarial system," and it planned to ask Congress to revise the law to prevent such results.

The Supreme Court held on March 21, 1989, that the U.S. Customs Service could require mandatory urinalysis of all its employees, even though none were suspected of drug use. The Customs Service sought these powers, not because of suspected drug use, but to showcase itself as an example of a drug-free workplace. Thus, the Fourth Amendment to the United States Constitution yielded to governmental symbolism, concerning which Justice Scalia wrote in his dissent, "The impairment of individual liberty cannot be the means of making a point. . . . Symbolism, even symbolism for so worthy a cause as the abolition of unlawful drugs, cannot validate an otherwise unreasonable search."

If the government can require urinalysis of anyone without cause or reason, it can invade the privacy of any individual at its whim; the only pretext is the battle cry of a war on drugs. How long will it be before the police are allowed to search our homes without any reason to believe we use illegal drugs? Associate Justice John Paul Stevens described how far the Court has gone:

> An extraordinarily aggressive Supreme Court has reached out to announce a host of new rules narrowing the federal Constitution's protection of individual liberties. The prosecutors use of a coerced confession—no matter how vicious the police conduct might have been—may now constitute harmless error. The Court condoned the use of mandatory sentences that are manifestly and grossly disproportionate to the moral guilt of the offender. It broadened the powers of the police to invade the privacy of individual citizens and even to detain them without any finding of probable cause or reasonable suspicion.*

Former President Bush called drugs the "gravest domestic threat facing our nation today" as he held up a bag of crack seized in a bust agents had intentionally

---

*John Paul Stevens, *The Bill of Rights: A Century of Progress* (1992).

set up across the street from the White House, solely so Bush could hold up a bag of cocaine and say it was obtained across the street. A federal court jury trying the seller of the cocaine deadlocked for four days before being declared a hung jury and a mistrial; jury foreman Cheryl Adams-Huff said, "The majority of jurors felt it was a setup." The president said the crack he was holding up on national television "is turning our cities into battle zones and murdering our children." Senior administration officials speculated that martial law might be necessary. For casual users, Bush called for the revocation of driver's licenses, cancellation of professional and occupational licenses, and denial of eligibility for federal grants, loans, or contracts.

Bush obtained every sanction he sought in the war against less dangerous drugs. Beginning October 1, 1993, 5 percent of federal highway funds must be withheld from those states that fail to impose at least a six-month driver's license suspension on convicted drug possessors, increasing to 10 percent of highway funds by October 1, 1995, including those states where possession of small amounts of marijuana is a petty offense or is legal. A New York Republican legislator justified the law, saying, "Seventy-five percent of the drug purchases in America are done by casual drug users and that's white, upper-middle-class Americans that drive their Pontiac Firebirds into the ghetto and buy killer drugs."

Half the states enforce their drug laws with tax penalties, similar to those used in the prohibition era. When anyone is arrested for possession or sale of illegal drugs, fines can be imposed and collected immediately, before conviction, and are kept even if the criminal charges are later dropped or the accused is found innocent. Law enforcement spokesmen say, "The drug tax is one of the best pieces of anti-narcotics legislation to have come along in years." (Less than 5 percent of illegal drugs are narcotics.) To avoid the tax, an accused must prove unawareness of the drug; there is no presumption of innocence. The presumption is of guilt, shifting the burden of proof to the accused.

West Virginia newspapers in 1990 began printing coupons for anonymously implicating neighbors and associates as using illegal drugs. When the small-town Williamson newspaper printed a coupon, police received seven hundred responses listing names, addresses, or license-plate numbers of those suspected by their neighbors of using illegal drugs. Police arrested forty-six people during the first month. The State Police immediately announced their own coupon campaign. The ACLU responded:

> It creates a paranoid atmosphere, just the way it was in Germany in the '30s and '40s, when people were encouraged to spy on their neighbors. It's the thing going on today in Romania and Albania, where people complained to their government about the sense of always being watched. This kind of program will not make us drug-free. It will just make us unfree.

As a result of police surveillance many marijuana growers are cultivating indoors. In 1990, California DEA agents seized 199,105 plants, down 100,000 from 1989 because of the movement indoors. The California DEA, however, also doubled the number of raids on greenhouses from 1989 to 1990, stating through its marijuana coordinator, "We use power bills, water bills, informants, and we even track shipments by the United Parcel [Service] and other services from known suppliers to growers. We also do infrared imaging to check on the heat emitted from homes or warehouses we suspect." The DEA traces shipments of small greenhouses a few feet square. Don't send off for that attractive glass container to grow marigolds or you risk the splintering of your front door. Such is privacy in the 1990s.

Mother Jones and *Playboy* magazines published the DEA "scientifically tested profile" of suspected illegal drug users and dealers for interdiction at airports, bus stations, and on highways. The list may sound similar to that used during the various inquisitions: carrying an old suitcase, a new suitcase, or a gym bag; driving a rental car or a car that contains air-freshener; taking an "evasive and erratic path" through the airport or scrupulously observing traffic laws; wearing a black jump suit or gold chains; traveling to or from Miami, Los Angeles, or Detroit; being a member of "ethnic groups associated with the drug trade"; appearing nervous or overly calm; buying one-way or round-trip tickets; traveling alone or with a companion; and deplaning from the front, middle, or rear of an aircraft.

Those arrested in Phoenix for possession of an illegal drug can pay a local testing and counselling agency, TASC, and have criminal charges dropped, conditionally. The conditions include the payment of all TASC costs and admitting guilt in writing. If a defendant flunks the TASC course, is arrested again, tests positive during the three- to six-month probation, or is disrespectful to a TASC employee, charges are refiled and the admissions of guilt are used to obtain an automatic conviction.

The right of privacy should be preeminent in our hectic, disjointed world. Every person should have a sanctuary inviolate from government or other interference. Only in public should an individual's acts be restricted because of the sensibilities of others. In private, people should be allowed—without restriction— to peruse whatever writings or pictures they wish whether pornographic or religious (excluding those things that harm children such as child pornography), to drink or imbibe drugs as they wish, and to do as they please sexually, as long as they harm no one else. On this theory of privacy, the Alaska Supreme Court held that private drug use is not subject to criminal penalties, but no other U.S. court has followed this precedent.

The majority of constitutional violations and intrusions on personal privacy occur in connection with the enforcement of drug laws. Three fourths of all search warrants are issued to support drug cases, primarily for wire taps and electronic surveillance under the official designation of "organized crime." There's probably no crime less organized than drug dealing, except when run by the Mafia. Non-Mafia drug trafficking is done primarily by the minority entrepreneur who can obtain a cut of the capitalistic pie in few other ways. By searching airwaves, telephone conversations, and places of abode, basic rights of privacy are ignored for the purpose of imprisoning someone who is risking harm to no one but self, or selling to someone who is paying for the privilege of risking harm to self, and no one else. Why should the Fourth Amendment prohibition against unreasonable intrusions on personal privacy and the Fifth Amendment right against self-incrimination be routinely compromised by the police to stop someone from risking harm to self, particularly when harm seldom results? Such is the epitome of immorality.

THE SOURCE OF OUR "MORAL" CRIMES

Alcohol is the oldest and most commonly used drug. It was first associated with religious practices, then social gatherings and recreation. The growing of grain to produce beer likely changed our kind from hunters to farmers, giving thinking man time to think. Because our currently illegal drugs never obtained religious or social sanction they're considered more dangerous and taboo, even though they're less dangerous. As Horace said about alcohol, "What wonders does not wine! It discloses secrets, ratifies and confirms our hopes; thrusts the coward forth to battle; eases the anxious mind of its burden; instructs in the arts." A similar description could be applied to any drug, legal or illegal.

Religion can be one indirect cause of excessive alcohol consumption, according to James Schaefer, director of the Office of Alcohol and Drug Abuse Prevention at the University of Minnesota. The southeastern United States is a Bible-belt of sorts, "yet every third generation has serious drinking problems. There is strict adherence to the Bible, and Fundamentalists often teach that one must abstain entirely from alcohol. This is overdone in many households, and as a result, the next generation rejects the values and become alcohol abusers." The breadth of and solution to the problem are succinctly described by Schaefer: "With alcoholism we're only talking about seven percent of the population. The biggest societal cost is not from alcoholism but periodic abuse of alcohol and other drugs. . . . We can reduce the risk by building a culture with a better sense of individual responsibility about alcohol use." Individual responsibility is the key to any ethical system. We shouldn't expect government, religion, and social institutions to be responsible for ourselves; only we bear that ultimate responsibility.

Former drug czar William Bennett addressed the Southern Baptist national convention in New Orleans in June 1990, saying, "The drug problem in the end is fundamentally a moral problem, fundamentally a spiritual problem. Bring those in need to a God that heals." Bennett said the drug war was a struggle "of good and evil for the possession of the human soul."

Historically, acts that were considered criminal have included sacrilege, blasphemy, denial of the existence of God, refusal to swear an oath, and hundreds of other religion-related acts. The sole reason acts harming no one else are still criminalized is religion and the vestiges of religious "logic" that permeate our society. Heresy was subject to the death penalty because a society tolerating heresy was believed to be subject to death from the deity, which in its displeasure could destroy the community in retribution for the community's failure to execute the heretic. If a particular community's deity, however, doesn't have the capability of destroying the community, there's no justification for prohibiting acts in private that harm no one else. Drugs are criminalized because the criminalizers feel they destroy the moral fibre of the community, which is the same as saying the deity disapproves of drugs. Simply put, the war on drugs is a continuation of the various religious inquisitions that bedeviled the world for eight hundred years.

The moralistic temperance movement against drugs is in its third American reincarnation. The previous two lasted twenty to thirty years and were accompanied by a heightened health consciousness as now. The most recent health fad began in 1979 and should thus run its course between 2000 and 2010 before we tire of the exorbitant tax and prison burdens afflicting us and our unfortunate drug users. The first temperance movement began in 1820 and ended in 1850, followed by an upsurge in drinking that ended about 1890 when Americans again turned against their legal drugs. Prohibition resulted in 1920, lasting until 1933 when the government decided it needed the revenue from taxing alcohol. Tolerance peaked in 1979 and here we go again, until we end with a backlash against the "war on drugs" in the early 2000s.

If drugs are poison and should be outlawed, why aren't poisons similarly outlawed, calling for seven years in the slammer for their possession? Why is peyote illegal unless it's used in connection with a traditional religious rite? Should mountain climbing be similarly restricted, so that no one can climb mountains unless part of a religious journey? Why is dependency on drugs more reprehensible and less moral than dependency on chocolate, or the personal automobile, or television, or clothing, or parents, or religion? Any pleasurable thing creates cravings, dependency, and increased tolerance, whether fast cars, risk, sex or drugs. The primary human drive, once the basics of survival (food and water) are satisfied, is pleasure, whether sex, gourmet foods, intoxication, or the money to buy the pleasures of choice.

SHOULD ALL DRUGS BE LEGALIZED?

Legalizing drugs wouldn't mean condoning their use, any more than we condone the use of alcohol and tobacco. Nor would it mean allowing children to have access to any drug, as we theoretically prohibit children from having access to alcohol and tobacco. The multiple billions wasted on the attempted interdiction of illegal drugs could instead be used to rehabilitate and educate, with billions left over from the savings and billions more received in tax revenues. Drugs would be sold in pure, yet strength-restricted forms, from state-regulated drugstores, similar to state owned or regulated liquor stores. The violence of drug trafficking would be gone forever, just as violence disappeared after prohibition. California estimated a savings of $100 million a year from its decriminalization of the possession of marijuana. How much more would the nation save, in addition to the added revenue from taxing drugs, which according to a November 1990 *Atlantic Monthly* article would total $10 billion yearly?

A congress of politicians, lawyers, doctors, academics, and police from ten western European countries, the United States, and Latin America met in Rome in 1989, concluding that the war on drugs has failed and can never be won. The congress proposed to legalize all drugs, while taxing them. An Italian political party leader stated: "The Mafia fears anti-prohibition and not prohibition. If drugs were legalized, the Mafia would be badly hurt and Sicily would change dramat-

184 MYTHS OF THE TRIBE

ically." The congress added, "The crime that results [from criminalization] endangers ordinary citizens and threatens the stability of states. The modern version of prohibitionism has turned great cities into battle fields." None of the congress attendees favored the use of drugs, but only legalization, because of the failures they had experienced in law enforcement. A professor of psychiatry at Harvard proposed a tax on all drugs to finance their medical and social costs: "This would allow people to use the drugs they want to, but also eliminate the terror, chaos and attacks on personal freedoms."

Would the use of drugs rise if they were legalized? We obviously don't know, though most believe use would not rise sharply. In the Netherlands, where marijuana was decriminalized ten years ago, use dropped from 12 percent to 1 percent. The number of heroin addicts dropped from 12,000 to 6,500, with the age of the average heroin addict rising from 25 to 31. The decriminalization of soft drugs (marijuana and hashish) lowered the use of hard drugs (heroin and crack) in the Netherlands. Some accordingly believe that usage of formerly illegal drugs would drop upon legalization. The populations of Amsterdam and Washington, D.C., are about the same, but Amsterdam had forty-six murders in 1989 and Washington had 438. The primary identifiable difference is the war on drugs.

Why people stop using illegal drugs is an arguable guide to the effectiveness of our criminal "justice" approach. A 1985 poll quizzed those who stopped using cocaine. The biggest reason was health followed by pressure from family and friends and then expense. No one said they stopped because of its illegality or fear of being caught by the police. In 1989 a nationwide sample of adults asked, "If cocaine were legalized, would you personally consider purchasing it or not?" One percent said they would.

Thirty percent of Americans support the legalization of drugs, according to a 1990 *Los Angeles Times* national poll. Those supporting legalization ranged through diverse political spectrums, from William F. Buckley and former Secretary of State George Schultz, to columnists Joseph Sobran and Patrick Buchanan, to the mayor of Baltimore and federal court judges such as Robert Sweet in New York. The first congressman to publicly support the decriminalization of drugs was George Crockett, a Democrat from Michigan, who said, "Decriminalization is the only solution. Our courts are burdened down with these drug cases, and there is nothing they can do about it. And here we are, talking about spending additional billions to build jails and prisons to send people to." The congressman said the money would be better spent on education, job training for the poor, health care, and day care; however, he had no plans to introduce a bill because he believed it would have no chance in Congress.

A poll by the Portland newspaper, *The Oregonian,* in October 1989, found the most oft-suggested solution to the drug problem by its readers was legalization in order to remove the enormous profits and the associated violence.

Conservative columnist Joseph Sobran ridiculed Bush's 1989 drug speech and his Democratic critics, who argued that he wasn't committing enough money to the drug war. Sobran quoted the *Economist,* a respected conservative British weekly, which in its September 2, 1989, issue opined:

Drugs are dangerous. So is the illegality that surrounds them. In legitimate commerce, controlled, taxed and supervised, their dangers proclaimed on every packet, drugs would poison fewer customers, kill fewer [no] dealers, bribe fewer [no] policemen, raise more public revenue. . . . Legalizing the drugs trade would be risky. Prohibition is worse than risky. It is a proven failure, a danger in its own right. *The Economist* advocates its replacement with more effective restrictions on the spread of drugs. In summary, we want to legalize, control and strongly discourage the use of them all.

Where's the flaw in this statement?

By 1988, fewer than 2 percent of Dutch youngsters age ten to eighteen smoked marijuana regularly, and only 6 percent had tried it. Four hundred coffee shops in Amsterdam and at least one in every Dutch town sell marijuana. Hashish sold for $1.50 a gram in 1989. No one has to steal to pay for drugs in Holland because they're inexpensive. Nobody loses a job or is thrown in prison for using them. Although the police retain strong criminal sanctions against the so-called "harder" drugs of cocaine and heroin, the Dutch Ministry of Justice in 1985 ordered that the laws not be enforced. As a result, tolerated drug dealers don't bribe police or use force to maintain outlets. There are no cocaine gangs. Cocaine is available to anyone who wants it, and few do. There are few ill effects. The main complaint is that cocaine costs too much, which at eighty-five dollars a gram in 1989 was two-thirds the cost of cocaine in New York City. Yet consumption is falling. In 1987, 1.7 percent of adult Amsterdamers had used cocaine during the year, while in New York City that year, 6 percent had used cocaine in the last six months. Amsterdam had less than 6,000 heroin addicts, of which 2,000 were foreigners. Cigarettes killed 18,000 Dutch in 1987, alcohol killed 2,000, and heroin killed 64. There were no cocaine-related deaths. In 1988, 33 percent of Americans over age twelve had tried marijuana while only 24 percent in Amsterdam had used it.*

The Dutch are signators to the international conventions outlawing the sale and use of "illegal" drugs. They ignore them, but collaborate with their more intolerant neighbors and allies to stop exports. A senior Dutch policeman said, "The Americans offer us big money to fight the war on drugs their way. We do not say that our way is right for them, but we are sure it is right for us. We don't want their help. [Dutch policy is] to lessen the problems attendant upon drug use, instead of decreasing the use itself." The Dutch experiment shows that treating adults as adults works by lowering drug use; the glamour of drug use disappears with the removal of criminal penalties. A 1991 study of 150 drug addicts found that Dutch addicts committed fewer crimes against property than addicts in the United States. Dutch addicts were also healthier, using fewer needles and suffering a lower incidence of AIDS. The Dutch believe that treating addiction as a medical problem is more effective than a "do drugs, do time" approach. There is empirical support for this view.

---

*Richard Hessner, *Arizona Republic,* Jan. 1990.

Britain, where heroin is legal, had sixty-two heroin addicts per 100,000 population in 1989, whereas the United States had 209 heroin addicts per 100,000. Few British heroin addicts engage in serious crime as there is no need in order to obtain the drug. The reverse is true in the United States.

We worry that drug use would explode if legalized, though common sense should tell us that simply isn't so. Does anyone outside of law enforcement believe that most Americans refrain from using illegal drugs solely because they're illegal? How many people do we personally know who would start shooting heroin or snorting cocaine if possession were decriminalized? Where are all the people who are aching to risk harm to themselves, but will wait until they can legally do so?

In another article, Sobran explained why an arch-conservative like himself could support the legalization of drugs. The two facts that clinched it for Sobran were that drugs can't be controlled in our prisons, leading to the conclusion that turning the entire nation into a prison won't stop drug use, and a report by the Ludwig von Mises Institute that decriminalizing drugs would lower the street crime rate by 75 percent. As Sobran says, if the 75 percent figure is even close to accurate, there's no contrary legitimate argument supporting the current war on drugs. Sobran points out that any war against an inanimate object, such as drugs or poverty, is close to meaningless because there's no way of gauging success, which is sufficiently difficult in a real war where generals instead of admitting losses call for more troops, more money, more sacrifice from the public, and more authority to expand the war. This is exactly the history of the unending and apparently unendable war on drugs. We fail to recognize that the war is not so much against drug use as it is against the violence and profits associated with illegal drugs, which result from the fact of their illegality. Even during the prohibition against alcohol there was no violence threatening the daily lives of citizens, only the lives of rival gangs. We didn't remove excess alcohol use by legalizing alcohol, but we did remove the violence.

Columnist Jeff Greenfield wrote that Bush failed to tell the American people that the drug issue is a sacred cow. There's no opposition, no political action committees funded by a National Association of Drug Dealers poised to wire tons of money to Bush's opponents. Second, the drug war is against foreign influences—the bad guys are outside the United States. It is a symbolic issue that stands for the dilemmas of race and poverty, and the weaknesses of our children, and their future as adults, that we can ignore as long as we focus our attention on the bad guys somewhere "out there." The Cold War is apparently over so instead of Communists we focus on another enemy, and drugs are the easiest target. This is why the former president couldn't tell us that the drug war is lost and cannot be won. He's not telling us that the pictures of police and politicians in flak jackets standing next to piles of bags filled with white powder have nothing to do with the continued easy availability of illegal drugs. He's not telling us that arresting the casual user is a joke, because we no longer have the prison space to house rapists and murderers, much less millions of casual users. He's not telling us the American idea of individual autonomy is directly challenged by the concept of a war on drugs. He's not telling us that the real evil of drug use is not that it turns people into raving maniacs; most users of illegal drugs are the professionals who run the country. The problem with illegal drug use is that it's not healthy, similar to any drug, or fat, or cholesterol. The use of any drug, legal or illegal, isn't evil per se. We changed attitudes toward smoking, and we're gradually doing the same about drinking alcohol.

We'll never change attitudes by imposing criminal justice sanctions. Criminal prohibitions elevate that which is prohibited to a "must try" for many people, and it raises the hackles of a free people who, when told they can't do something that harms no one else, say in unison, "try to stop me." As pointed out by former U.S. Surgeon General C. Everett Koop, "Our efforts to reach teenagers have failed. Teenagers ignore any admonition that begins with the word 'don't.' Scare tactics don't work. We have to find another approach." Former drug czar William Bennett said the opposite, that children will respond only to tough criminal sanctions: "Should we have drug-education programs or should we have tough [criminal] policy? If I have the choice of only one, I will take policy every time, because I know children. And you might say this is not a very romantic view of children. And I would say, 'You're right.' " Who understands children better, Koop or Bennett? Does it make a difference that Bennett would have been out of a job if drugs were legalized?

The majority of us oppose the legalization of drugs because drug use is distasteful. We first worry that legalization would imply government approval of addictive and potentially destructive behavior and is thus immoral. Most of us would believe anyone proposing criminalization of our most dangerous drugs—alcohol and tobacco—to be antiquated or fanatically religious. Few blink at government run or authorized gambling in the form of state lotteries, or pari-mutuel wagering at dog and horse tracks, or the entire State of Nevada, or Atlantic City, though gambling and legal drugs are highly addictive and potentially destructive.

Any drug, whether aspirin, alcohol, or cocaine, is dangerous only when used to excess. Most drugs are psychologically addictive; the most physically addictive and widely used drugs, tobacco and alcohol, are legal. Our opposition to the legalization of drugs is an aesthetic one, as columnist Russell Baker has pointed out. How much will more tax money and more fire power reduce the basic demand for illegal drugs and the pleasure they bring (which is no more dangerous or fleeting than that of tobacco and alcohol)?

Those opposing legalization of drugs argue that the cause of drug use is despair and boredom and the misguided thought that a drug will improve a person's quality of life. To some extent that is why people use alcohol and many illegal drugs. Aldous Huxley argued in *The Doors of Perception* (extolling his experience with mescaline), "Most men and women lead lives at the worst so painful, at the best so monotonous, poor and limited that the urge to escape, the longing to transcend themselves if only for a few moments, is and has always been one of the principal appetites of the soul." People use any drug because it gives them immediate pleasure. Most use drugs in moderation because excessive use brings more pain than pleasure and may lead to addiction, whether physical or psychological. Accordingly, the legalization of illegal drugs would have little impact on use. Every aspect of legalization is positive, compared to the current state of affairs.

Many would argue that illegal drugs, such as marijuana, shouldn't be legalized because their use would lead to the use of more dangerous drugs; with the most dangerous drugs legal, how much sense does such an argument make? Research and experience shows the exact opposite; the availability of marijuana lessens the use of other drugs, all of which are more dangerous than marijuana.

John Lawn was interviewed by *USA Today* when he announced his retirement as head of the Drug Enforcement Administration in February 1990. Even Lawn admitted the drug war is a loser:

> We are a consuming nation, and if we were to miraculously stop the import of cocaine or the import of heroin or the import of marijuana, we still can manufacture enough illicit drugs in our country to satisfy every illicit appetite. . . . [If South American drug production were shut off today], we would have labs doubling, tripling right here in the United States. In 1982, law enforcement identified over 100 clandestine laboratories. Last year, we identified 814 labs, predominantly methamphetamine labs. There's only one step between meth and this new phenomenon called ice. . . . coca cultivation has increased by 400 percent over the past five years.

Legalization of drugs is considered out of the question for many. *New York Times* columnist A. M. Rosenthal interviewed the mayor of San Francisco on the subject and reported, "Mayor Agnos thought it flew straight in the face of all American social values and was heartless as well. It would abandon whole classes of Americans who suffer most from addiction, specifically young people and minorities." Such a statement is illogical. American social values condone the two most dangerous drugs on earth, which kill a hundred people for each person killed by illegal drugs. Legalizing drugs doesn't condone drugs if accompanied by educational efforts that confront the problem squarely and don't flinch from the reality of drugs, both the pleasurable side and the harmful side. It's far more heartless to put an addict in prison than to educate and rehabilitate him. Putting a person in prison doesn't rehabilitate, it educates the person to crime. Legalizing drugs wouldn't abandon anyone to addiction; it would keep the addict out of prison and stop the violence on our streets between drug dealers and police. The executive director of the National Association of Chiefs of Police complained in a letter to *National Geographic* that in 1988, 152 police officers died in the line of duty and most of these deaths were drug related. If drugs were legal most of these officers would have lived.

The drug problem is their illegality, which keeps the price high and the rewards higher for those willing to take risks, which is the basis of capitalism. Switzerland treats addiction as a disease instead of a crime, while Edinburgh, Scotland, takes the opposite stand, with the following mixed results. Fearing easy access to syringes promoted heroin addiction, Edinburgh banned pharmacies from selling them without a prescription. Addicts began sharing needles, and AIDS increased by 60 percent, while forty-five miles away in Glasgow, where the ban was ignored, AIDS increased by only 12 percent.

Switzerland has virtually no unemployment but does have one of the highest per capita rates of addiction to illegal drugs in the world, witness Platzspitz Park in Zurich which on most weekends is taken over by addicts. An independent commission appointed by the Swiss government recommended the legalization of the possession and use of small amounts of drugs. The Swiss also have the highest incidence of AIDS with a third of its cases attributed to intravenous drug users. Addicts flock to Platzspitz Park because the government provides needles, free AIDS tests, meals, washing facilities, and advice to those who will listen. Opponents of these services argue the government is encouraging addiction. The more appropriate debate should be whether crimalizing drugs has an impact on use, except perhaps to encourage use by youngsters.

The American public was shocked in 1989 when "60 Minutes" covered the Platzspitz Park tragedy, further fueling the war on drugs. The equivalent of Platzspitz Park can be seen in any downtown American city in the area called skidrow where alcoholics congregate.

No society in history has been destroyed by the use of drugs. All our illegal drugs were legal less than a one hundred years ago, and for thousands of years before that the human race suffered no crippling drug debilitation. When millions use a particular drug, such as tobacco, alcohol, cocaine, or marijuana, its use cannot be effectively criminalized and attempts to do so are foolishness.

If we wish to stop harmful drug use, the only means at our disposal is education. If the term "adult" has any meaning, it should include more than the blind obligation to pay taxes. It should mean an end to childhood and an ability to do exactly as the adult decides is best for self, without government interference, as long as no one else is harmed. Adults should be allowed to waste their time, energies, and lives as they deem appropriate because no one else, especially religion and government, are properly equipped to know what is best for the individual in each individual's particular circumstances. Public morality appears to be posturing as a surrogate for the dominant religions. Private sentiment and morality are generally more permissive and attentive to adult rights of privacy and decision-making. Criminal treatment of those not risking harm to others rends society, pitting the establishment against out-of-favor minorities. In these circumstances, the imposition of criminal law sanctions is barbaric and inhumane. Instead of throwing the weak among us into jail, they should be treated with tolerance and compassion, which the Clinton administration appears to recognize. By February 1993, Clinton had reduced the "drug czars" office to a skeleton crew from 146 to 24, was closing the office of International Narcotics Matters and on the National Security Councils list of priorities, dropped the drug war from the top three to number 29 on a list of 29. Clinton promises an emphasis on drug education, not prosecution.*

---

*Scripps Howard, *Arizona Republic,* Feb. 1993, and *Arizona Republic,* Jan. 1993.

The true opiate of the masses is hypocrisy. Nations and humans may never mature until hypocrisy is eradicated and adults are treated as adults. If drugs were legalized there would be instant peace in Colombia, Washington, D.C., and all across the nation. The Dutch are a strong resourceful people with a diligent citizenry not drained by a futile war on drugs. Let us join their sensible efforts and legalize all drugs. Only then can adults make their own decisions unfettered by paternalistic government and religious inquisition.

Other Ethical Issues: Poverty and the Environment

The leading cause (80 percent) of child mortality in the world is dehydration from diarrhea, resulting from ingesting contaminated drinking water, caused by poor sanitation and the failure to receive immediate, simple, and inexpensive medical care. Three million children under age six die annually in Bangladesh. These deaths are easily preventable with oral rehydration using a mixture of uncontaminated water, salt, and sugar costing ten cents. Oral hydration is seldom used because most health professionals are unaware of the simple technique, instead relying on intervenous hydration which is unavailable outside a hospital or clinic. Few poor parents in third-world countries have been educated to either prepare the mixture or to avoid contaminated water in the first place, which is difficult since most third-world drinking water is contaminated to some degree. Is it inappropriate to ask how much Buddhists, Hindus, and Christians (particularly Catholics, as the dominant religion in Western third-world countries) spend out of their billions on alleviating these tragedies, outside of Mother Teresa and a few others? The poorer a country, the more likely it is to be religious, and the more likely it is to have drinking water contaminated by human waste. Now, as in the Middle Ages, religion is in the business of preparing its flock for the next life and in hastening its passage. Sanitation and science are for pagans. The tithes of poor parishioners go first to supporting the minister, then the building, then the parent church, and its missions. Anything left over may be used to feed the poor on Thanksgiving and Christmas.

Of the fourteen million children who will die this year, next year, and the year after that, 24 percent (3.3 million) will die from preventable childhood diseases for which vaccines are readily available—measles, tetanus, whooping cough, polio, diphtheria, and tuberculosis. Again, poor uneducated parents don't know that inoculations are available and necessary. The rest of the children who suffer and die from malnutrition succumb from infections a healthy body would reject. The key seems to be education (as with excessive drug use and most of society's ills), raising the literacy rates of poor women, and teaching nutrition and hygiene in schools. Once the fight to stay alive is won, these women and children can divert their energies to income-producing activities, and the death cycle of the world's children can be broken.

Smug Americans say it doesn't happen here. Out of six major industrial world nations surveyed in 1990, however, the United States had the highest percentage of poor children, with 17.1 percent below the poverty line. Children in the United States are more likely to die before their first birthday, suffer violent death before their twenty-fifth birthday, or live in poverty than in most other industrialized nations. Yet we believe we're the most beneficent and moral country in the world.

According to the Washington, D.C., press, 5.5 million children go to bed hungry every night. In 1990 in Arizona alone, half a million people went hungry at least eight times a month, including one of four children. Out of an Arizona population of three million, 512,000 lived in poverty, which included 189,952 children. The Children's Defense Fund reported in mid-1992 that child poverty in the United States grew from 16 percent in 1979 to 18 percent in 1989. The child poverty rate in Arizona grew from 16.5 to 21.7 in the same time period. Apache County, Arizona, primarily Native American, had a 51.3 percent child poverty rate in 1989.* The cost of the Arizona drug war *or* the cost of one B-2 bomber could eradicate hunger and the poverty of all children in Arizona. The chairman of the House Select Committee on Hunger, Rep. Tony Hall noted that "Americans will buy and eat only perfect-looking food. I found out that we throw away 60 million tons of so-called imperfect food a year." Yet requests for food to feed the hungry in the United States goes unmet most of the time. In a column detailing these facts, Coleman McCarthy said, "The presence of hungry Americans refutes daily the patriotic blather that we are a great nation. Where's the greatness in letting the hungry stay hungry while an estimated 20 percent of our grown or produced food is thrown out or left to rot?" We pay farmers handsomely not to produce food. If our farmers produced as much food as they were able, it would be so inexpensive that no one would go hungry.

Besides avoiding harm to the individual and preserving our children from early death, we should also consider preserving our fragile environment if the race is to survive. Since the 1960s when the Environmental Protection Agency used the survival of an unknown fish to stop a dam being built by the Tennessee Valley Authority, environmental concerns have fought an uphill battle. We are uneducated concerning the extinction of species and the impact of their extinction on human chances of survival. How can a minuscule fish help human survival?

During the last ice age, which ended 15,000 years ago and lasted 3,000 years, North America lost 50 species of mammals and 40 species of birds. Today there are perhaps 30 million species on the planet, and a hundred times that number have come into being and become extinct since life first appeared over three billion years ago. Thus, 99 percent of all forms of life that have existed on earth are now extinct. During the last 600 million years, species have become extinct at an average rate of one a year; now the rate is two a day and accelerating. By 2030, the rate may reach several hundred a day so that our grandchildren will live on a planet with half the number of species existing today. Except for nuclear war and evaporation of the atmosphere, there is no greater threat to the species.

Why should we worry about the extinction of an unknown little fish and

---

*Russ Buettner and Randy Cordova, *Arizona Republic,* July 8, 1992.

insignificant plants and insects when we can't keep millions of the world's children alive past age five? Half the pharmaceuticals that control our diseases and lengthen our lives come from these vanishing species, so for selfish reason alone we should stop the extinction of plants and lesser animals such as worms, reptiles, insects, and fish. They have evolved systems for healing their wounds, digesting their food, attracting mates, poisoning prey, and other life-savers that use chemicals we are continually discovering as medicines necessary for curing human diseases. For example, a theoretically "useless" wild corn species in Mexico has been discovered to form blight-resistant hybrids, the value of which is estimated to be in the billions of dollars. Hodgkin's disease and childhood leukemia are treated successfully by recently discovered rare plant extracts. A rare meadow-foam subspecies yields high grade oil used to reduce pollution in Oregon's Willamette Valley. The list is lengthy and lengthening. Although new discoveries are made daily, only a small percentage of the species now alive have been investigated. Species continue to be lost daily, along with a universe of possibilities to benefit the human species.

When a species is lost, others are directly endangered as a result. For example, figs are normally prolific and nutritious and thus crucial for the survival of many species. Nine hundred species of figs grow in tropical forests and are an essential food source for many birds, fish, turtles, and mammals; some bat species eat nothing else. Without one particular species of wasps, figs wouldn't be able to reproduce because they wouldn't be pollinated. The loss of wasps would eventually destroy nine hundred species of figs, which would force the eventual extinction of bats, and many species of monkeys, which depend entirely on figs, then peccaries and jaguar, which depend on eating monkeys for survival. The wasp is a "keystone species" on which many mammals indirectly depend for their existence. Without the fruit pollinated by the wasp, 75 percent of all vertebrates in the tropical rain forests would disappear. Many ecological systems centered around rain forests are on the verge of an extinction avalanche, with hundreds of species at stake, and the primary cause is the war on drugs. Legalization of drugs would stop the destruction of the rain forests because mafia and other organized crime profits would cease and the incentive to destroy the rain forests would disappear.

Another example of a keystone species is the sea otter, hated by commercial fishermen because of its voracious appetite for abalone and crab. The sea otter was hunted almost to extinction, with only one thousand surviving in 1911. Protecting the sea otter brought back the harbor seals and the bald eagle, based on the following food chain. Sea otters eat sea urchins. Sea urchins unchecked by sea otters eat kelp and sea grass, which destroys the natural habitats for many fish, which are necessary to the survival of seals and eagles. Without sea otters to keep sea urchins under control, the chain collapses and we lose the bald eagle.

We extinguish species in four ways:

1. Polluting water, air, and land with tons of waste. For example, a 150-pound bluefin tuna caught eighty miles off the coast of New Jersey in 1990 rivaled Jonah's whale for the items in its stomach: an elastic ponytail holder, two cocaine inhalation straws, monofilament fishing line, drinking straw fragments, pieces of

balloon, Ziploc bag fragments, pen and marker pieces, and rubberbands used to bind newspapers.

2. Hunting species to extinction, including 40 percent of South American mammals and 30 percent in North America. The extinction of every species of bird since 1600 was completely or partially caused by hunting. Many mammals have been hunted to extinction, such as Stellar's sea cow. Others extinguished by hunting include eleven species of tortoise, six species of West Indian lizard, and four species of snakes. Rhinoceroses are threatened because their horns are believed to be aphrodisiacs. Whales are hunted for dog food, and leopards hunted to make fur coats.

3. Introducing new species without natural enemies. During WWII the brown tree snake was carried from the Philippines to Guam with the result that most of Guam's birds have become extinct. The number of Guam rails, a formerly prolific bird, by 1989 had dropped from 40,000 to 18. Similarly, since 1850, 85 percent of Hawaii's forest birds have become extinct or endangered by roof rats, mongoose introduced to control the rats, and avian malaria spread by imported mosquitos.

4. Direct destruction of the habitat. The simple rule is that every species must live where the climate is suitable, and the climate is not suitable everywhere or even most places. For example, when the Panama Canal was built, Gatun Lake was created, turning Barro Colorado into an island. As a result, the island could no longer support its diverse indigenous species. Fifty species of birds have disappeared along with their higher food chain, which includes the panther, jaguarondi, and ocelot. Deforestation along the Canal is threatening the economy of Panama by removing the barrier to unchecked silting of the Canal.

Rain forest is cleared yearly in Brazil equivalent to the size of Louisiana, destroying hundreds of species. The Amazon region of Brazil is larger than the forty-eight contiguous American states. If these forests can be replaced, it will take hundreds of years. The continued loss of trees in Brazil alone will eventually change the world's weather. If the Amazon is completely deforested, rainfall would decrease there by a fourth, raising temperatures and dropping atmospheric moisture by 30 percent. Once moisture content drops this far, rain forests could not be restarted, which would impact on the world's climate to an unknown degree. At the current rate of deforestation, the Amazon forest will disappear in seventy-five years. Removing trees allows sunlight to raise soil temperature, which raises the rate of evaporation, and changes the wind patterns carrying moist air over the entire continent. Half the area rainfall comes from rain forest evaporation. With the rain forest disappearing, rainfall decreases at an increasing rate.

The same destruction has already occurred in the United States. Of the original thirty-one million acres of temperate rain forest in the forty-eight contiguous states, 1.4 million acres are left. These virgin forests are not renewable without a wait of hundreds of years and then after the sacrifice of species that can survive only in virgin growth. Replanted tree farms bear the same resemblance to a virgin old-growth forest as a cornfield does to a prairie.

A further tragedy is that the cutting makes no economic sense. The cash value of old-growth trees cut from the Smith River watershed on the Olympia Peninsula in Washington State was $14 million in plywood and pulp. With the destruction of the Smith River watershed by logging authorized by the U.S. Forest Service, the loss of steelhead trout and salmonids totals $8 million *each year*. The total loss over the 140 years it will take to regrow the trees to their previous size is in excess of $1 billion, or eighty times the value of the raw wood sacrificed with the fish. The wood was shipped to Japan. Only three countries out of more than 180 nations allow the export of raw logs: the United States, Canada, and Chile. We ship 3.5 billion board feet to Japan each year. By 1995 there will be no old-growth forests left in the United States outside of national parks. Old-growth wood in national parks will be completely gone, courtesy of the U.S. Forest Service, by 2010. The United States, meanwhile, still lectures Brazil and other Amazon basin nations on their responsibilities in protecting the tropical rain forests.

Our oceans are becoming toilets, which are backing up. In 1988, a million bottom fish died in Raritan Bay, New Jersey, from lack of oxygen in the filthy polluted water, and 750 dolphins washed up for the year on Atlantic beaches, dead from human pollutants. From Long Island to New Jersey, bloody bandages, syringes, and vials of blood containing AIDS antibodies and hepatitis B washed up on beaches, together with used tampons, crack vials, and sludge. In the North Sea, 6,700 seals died of pneumonia and liver infections caused by human pollution. The Soviets closed many of their beaches because of pollution. The Mediterranean is saturated with untreated sewage. Seals are starving in the Baltic because their mouths and flippers are so deformed from human pollution that they can't catch fish. Formerly red Norwegian lobsters have turned black. Much of the bottom of the Baltic and North Seas are anoxic and without life, killed by algae blooms formed from nitrogen and phosphorus waste produced by industry. Of the 400,000 tons of fertilizer used yearly in Denmark, principally nitrogen based, 260,000 tons ends up in the Baltic basin. If no further pollutants were added, it would take thirty years for the North Sea to rinse, and the rinsing would be onto British and Norwegian coasts. Meanwhile, the world's oceans are littered with plastic that takes five hundred years to degrade, most of it floating on the surface trapping sea life. Fifty thousand northern fur seals have been killed by entanglement in plastic nets and debris.

The best way to stop the devastation is to be careful what products we use, avoiding those that deplete species and destroy ecosystems. We could stop using Amazon-grown cocaine (lab-synthesized cocaine is 100 percent pure and dirt-cheap) and avoid aerosols with chlorofluorocarbons. Man-made pollutants in the atmosphere cause the greenhouse effect, the extent of which we are properly concerned about. In announcing its goal to stabilize the emission of greenhouse gases (principally CO_2) by the year 2000, Japan stated, "Global warming is a grave concern likely to pose a serious threat to the very foundation of human life." Carl Sagan pointed out in November 1990, "Unfortunately the United States is the only major industrial nation taking no significant measures to counter greenhouse warming. While other nations act, we just shrug and appoint another committee." Considering environmental costs, solar and wind energy are cheaper than oil and nuclear energy, particularly when it's recognized that much of the U.S. military exists to protect "our" oil, as in the Persian Gulf war. Sagan concluded that to "prevent the greenhouse effect from increasing still further, the world must cut its dependence on fossil fuels by more than half. . . . With five percent of the world's population, the United States uses nearly 25% of the world's energy. The United States is the world's worst CO_2 polluter." If the greenhouse effect performs as predicted, global warming will turn the American Midwest into a desert; the Gulf Stream will shift course, diverting warmth from Europe; sea levels will rise as the ice caps melt, flooding the Eastern United States, Bangladesh, New Orleans, London, Venice, Egypt, Bangkok, and Beijing. Carl Sagan observed, "The typical temperature difference averaged over the whole world between an ice age and an interglacial [the present] is only three to six degrees Centigrade (equivalent to five to eleven degrees Fahrenheit). . . . A temperature change of only a few degrees can be serious business."

The United States is the largest producer of carbon dioxide, and it continues to block international agreements to place restrictions on emission of gases leading to the greenhouse effect, though it acknowledged for the first time in 1990 that the heating of the atmosphere is human-caused. A side effect of global warming is the destruction of the world's coral reefs, which the National Caribbean Research Center says are "in peril and disappearing at an alarming rate." Reefs starve in warming seas because algae normally ingested are instead rejected.

Thinning of the ozone layer has increased skin cancer rates from one in 1,500 a century ago to one in 120 by 1986. CFCs used in air conditioners, industrial solvents, and Styrofoam were estimated in 1985 to have thinned the ozone layer by .5 percent, and the estimate was updated to 2 percent by 1990. These estimates if even partially true portend global disaster. As Carl Sagan suggests, "The traditional military choice has been to take seriously not just the likely action of a potential adversary, but also the worst of which it is capable. . . . Why should this time honored principle be any less applicable to the looming world environmental crisis?"

Former President Bush gave his answer when he refused in April 1992 to commit his attendance to the June 1992 Earth Summit in Brazil, on the grounds that it could commit the United States "to a course of action that could dramatically impede long-term economic growth in this country." The only Earth Summit topic that would impact the U.S. is that resolved to stop the production of CFC aerosals.

A U.N. Environmental Program report issued in January 1992 concluded that skin-cancer rates will increase worldwide by 26 percent in eight years if the ozone level continues to deplete at the current rate. Also, the number of eye cataracts will rise by 1.7 million. The British scientist who discovered the ozone hole above Antarctica reported that ozone depletion over northern Europe may reach 30 percent in eight years, which would cause the number of skin cancers and cataracts to sky rocket.

The June 1992 Earth Summit in Rio de Janiero focused world attention on environmental issues, but little progress resulted. The reason for the lack of progress is relatively simple, according to a Worldwatch Institute study released the first day of the Earth Summit. As summarized by the Associated Press, the study concluded that the "richest fifth of the world [the U.S. and Europe, including the former Soviet Union] is ruining the planet by consuming too much. . . . The 'consumer class' [produces virtually all of the] ozone-depleting chemicals, [two-thirds of the] greenhouse gases and acid rain." The study, entitled, "How Much is Enough?", recommended curbs on advertising, longer vacations in lieu of higher wages, and the restriction of shopping malls. The United States has more shopping malls than high schools; two thousand new malls are added yearly.

Random statistics from the 1992 U.N. Environmental Report illustrate the magnitude of environmental destruction. Since 1945, England and Wales have lost 98 percent of old pasture, 70 percent of original peat lands, and 58 percent of ancient forests. In 1983 Poland designated areas where 35 percent of its population lived as an "ecological hazard." Half the newborns in Mexico City have lead levels in the blood high enough to impair neurological and motor physical development. A billion people live in cities exposed to excessive levels of particulates and unhealthful levels of sulphur dioxide. A fourth of the earth's species are in danger of extinction by 2020 because of human activity; one hundred to three hundred species become extinct daily.

At the Earth Summit the United States refused to sign any treaty that would set concrete limits on the production of carbon dioxide and other greenhouse gases; the treaty promised that signators would try to reduce emissions to 1990 levels, but the promise is neither binding nor tied to a schedule. The United States, the former Soviet Union, and China produce eleven times more billions of tons of carbon dioxide than any other countries in the world; the United States produces twice the sulphur dioxide and almost five times the nitrogen oxide as the next worse polluting country. However, in November 1992 the United States became a signatory to the Montreal Protocol amendments in Copenhagen designed by ninety-three nations to eliminate the use of ozone-depleting chemicals four to nine years faster than agreed to at the Earth Summit.

America is also the largest exporter of toxic industrial wastes, producing a million pounds a minute and shipping 150,000 tons a year. Because Congress hasn't ratified the 1989 Basel Convention to monitor shipments of hazardous waste (signed by fifty-three countries), it can continue shipments to developing countries where disposal costs $40 a ton versus $250 a ton in the United States. Although we've doubled our consumption of goods since 1957, the number of "very happy" Americans remains at one third.

We should drive as little as possible, or ride a bike, which adds the benefit of exercise. We should use phosphate-free detergents, shun Styrofoam, and bring our own bags to the grocery store. We should use biodegradable plastic bags instead of paper bags, which cannot be made from recycled paper, but must instead be made from virgin wood products. Plant a tree a year. Reduce gas consumption—gaining a mile a gallon for all U.S. cars would save as much energy as is produced by a year's drilling and production in Alaska. Eventually the internal combustion engine must go the way of the dinosaur. Our energy demands require drilling in fragile habitats and the damning of rivers for hydropower. Free-flowing rivers are crucial for many species of fish, plants, and mollusks. Insulating homes can also save rivers. As in all areas, education should be our top priority, not the imposition of criminal sanctions.

The Relationship between Ethics and Religion: An Argument

[The basis for religion is] the haunting fear that someone, somewhere, may be happy.

—H. L. Mencken

Morality and ethics are not dependent on punishment or reward, but exist independently without any necessary connection to organized religion. The human need to believe in something, whether rational or baseless, and to respond more to wishes, desires, hopes, and fears than to facts, results in a delusion of self. Why do many ruin the possibility of a pleasurable life on earth by relying on the unknown and unknowable for an illusive promise of immortality? The tragedy of religion is its deluding people into thinking misery on earth will buy an eternal paradise. Those living under the illogical and archaic rules of religion are under a dictator the same as those living under a communistic totalitarian regime with mind police on every corner: we must confess our "sins." Can there be a universally objective definition of "sin" other than harming another? If so, what is it and what is the moral basis for catagorizing any act, other than an action harming another, as sinful?

The meaning of life without the illusion of immortality is personal responsibility. When religion (or government, or any entity other than ourself) is the decision-maker, there can be no personal responsibility, only childish paternalism. Because of religion our schools are propagandizers occupied more with questions of creationism, religious studies, sex education, and prayer than with education. True education is not allowed in our schools. Never will the public schools teach evolution without creationism, the facts of science without the myths of religion, the facts of the inherent barbarity and close-mindedness of religion as illustrated by the various Inquisitions and the Crusades, the internal illogic of the concept of "God," or the irrationality of its origins in the fears and superstitions of primitive humans. The primary purpose of the public schools (and especially religious schools) appears to be indoctrination, not education. Where religion governs, the truth is absolutely known and thinking for oneself, which is the goal of education, is heresy.

Religion and morality are antithetical and contradictory. Not only is religion unnecessary to morality, but religion is immoral insofar as it teaches there is no other truth than within the narrow dictates of a particular faith. Morality is learned from the observation of parents, peers, and teachers, not by artificial religious rules that have no connection to reality. Religion, which instead of teaching that no one else should be harmed, teaches that those having other beliefs should be slaughtered or converted. Such teaching is the opposite of morality and is instead evil personified.

The pluralism of the United States is threatened by religion and religious thought. The purpose of the checks and balances of constitutional government is to prevent the enslavement of minorities by the majority. The idea that the United States is a Christian nation defeats this central principle, making any non-Christian, whether Jewish, Buddhist, or atheist, a nonentity. The stultification of pluralism is immoral. Which is more moral and ethical: religious absolutism teaching the slaughter or conversion of nonbelievers, or a recognition that all humans are essentially the same with similar fears, needs, and aspirations, requiring tolerance and acceptance of other viewpoints?

Life is not meaningless without religion. Without religion there is still success in work and profession, achievement, love, creativity, reason, the helping of others, and the improvement of society. Religion fosters guilt, demeans self-worth, and prohibits acts that harm no one. When the fact of death is hidden by religious dogma, human potential remains unfulfilled because there's no incentive for improving this life. We should choose life, not an unseeable and vaporous god whose concept is illogical and nonsensical.

Religion exists to compensate for lack of control and to create the illusion of control. Women, having less control over their lives, are more religious than men. Similarly, classes of society that have less control over their lives are more religious. The less individual control over our lives, the lower and poorer the social class, the higher the incidence and intensity of religion. A rich man fails to enter the kingdom of heaven because he has no need to.

The negatives of organized religion include its authoritarianism, which retards thought and makes religion an opiate of the masses, the same as any other drug or addiction. Religion is the defender of the status quo and of the government in power, no matter the morality or corruption of that government. Render unto Caesar that which is Caesar's. Religion controls government from within, which is easier than competing with government for ascendence. Consider Mexico, Guatemala, El Salvador, Panama, South America, Spain, Italy, and Greece. In its dealings with dictators and other terrorists, the Church is to Christ as China is to Marx. Neither have the slightest connection, except by label. No authoritarian regime is defensible, whether in the former Soviet Union, Argentina, the military of any country, or the Vatican. All require absolute blind obedience on the pain of death, whether physical death or death of the soul. The concept of soul and immortality are unintelligible, though. There is no evidence to support the existence of either. The argument that immortality is necessary to justify morality is an argument for children. Belief in immortality is reality-avoidance and an inability to face death. Why must the fear of damnation or the hope for immortality be the basis for ethics and morality?

Religion opposes free inquiry because free inquiry leads to contradiction of religions' central tenets. It is also the expert on censorship, whether art, movies, books, or another means of communication. It is not distinguishable from superstition, where magic and myth are considered truth. It means blind conformity, moral hypocrisy, and enslavement of the individual to the fears of primitive humans.

Many recently founded Christian sects are alive and growing, including the Seventh-day Adventists, Mormons, Christian Scientists, and the Unification Church of Reverend Moon. The Moonies are an example of a combination of New Age and Christian religions, with an emphasis on money and hoped-for wealth for its members. The Unification Church claims three million members worldwide with 37,000 missionaries and lay members in the United States. Its growth slowed after Rev. Moon served twelve months of an eighteen-month sentence for tax evasion from 1984 to 1985. Thereafter, the Church began giving free trips to South Korea to leaders of mainline United States' churches. The Unification Church believes in Jesus and the Sermon on the Mount, but also believes that other Christian denominations haven't lived up to Jesus' teachings, which has been the cry of every reformed Christian group since the beginning of Chistianity, and with good reason. Moon teaches that Jesus wasn't supposed to be crucified, but came to earth as a second Adam to take a bride. Together, Jesus and his bride would become the "true parents," returning the human race to the paradise of the Garden of Eden. According to a 1973 speech by Rev. Moon in New Orleans:

> The crucifixion of Jesus was the result of the faithlessness of the Jewish people. The major cause of their faithlessness was the betrayal of John [the Baptist]. . . . You may again want to ask me, "With what authority do you say these things?" I spoke with Jesus Christ in the spirit world. And I also spoke with John the Baptist.

All religions, new and old, require observances contrary to logic, human dignity, and basic human rights. Their leaders, from Rev. Moon to Oral Roberts to the pope, have all claimed to have personally talked with Jesus. They all require the conversion of heathens, bringing up children in the faith, prohibition of marriage outside the faith, and suppression of dissent.

The two most cited positives of religion are instead negatives: (1) *Religion gives meaning and direction to life.* If the direction and meaning are false, based on superstition, and lead to a wasted life, is religion a positive factor? (2) *Religion unifies society and imbues the culture with altruistic moral feelings and commonly shared goals.* If religious goals are based on superstition and if moral goals are commonly shared regardless of religion, what value is added by organized religion?

The first goal of humankind should be protection from each other. All other considerations should be subservient to preservation and safety of the individual as long as the individual harms no one else. Nations, states, classes of people, and religions are superficial "false karasses and grand falloons" without positive value and with dangerous hidden costs. Why is it unnatural to limit population by the voluntary practice of birth control in order to avoid starvation and poverty, to seek cures for disease, and to the transplant human organs to save lives? The contradictions of religion are solvable only by a declaration of gullibility.

A major difficulty with accurately judging the morality of another's act is that we can never know all the circumstances that led to the doing of the act. Without full knowledge, judging is unfair to the actor. For this reason alone, harming no one else appears to be the only absolute that can safely be applied to ourselves and to others. Under only one circumstance can we ethically harm another and that is in actual self-defense. We can, however, accurately judge the morality of our governments and religions because their flaws are openly displayed.

Imagine the benefits of an enforceable system that would forbid harming another and forbid nothing else. The armies of the world could be disbanded, freeing up half the gross international product, raising the world standard of living, eradicating 90 percent of childhood deaths, and protecting the environment for future generations. Neither self-interest nor the hedonistic pursuit of pleasure would carry negative connotations if preceded by the prohibition against harming another. We would achieve a morality made for humans instead of shoe-horning ourselves into a morality that doesn't fit, a morality imposed by the superstitions of our ancestors, which have been passed on to us in the form of organized and fallible religion.

9

The Proper Government and Economic System

Religion is the spirit of the clan. God and society are one. . . . All morals, beliefs, myths and religious feelings are a reflection of the social structure.
—John Lewis, *Religions of the World Made Simple*

The best form of government has been debated since our first governments, which were primarily democracies, before kings and conquerors gained and lost absolute power and democracies again came filtering into the power structure. Plato suggested governance by a philosopher-king who would know what was best for the people and govern accordingly. Through experience we have found that we should be allowed to muddle through to the best of our own individual abilities, with the least goverance as long as we don't impinge on our fellow citizens.

Monarchies and totalitarian forms of government are the closest existing models for Plato's philosopher-king and constitute equal quality in government. As the centuries have passed, we have increasingly realized that the best government is the least government. Governments are corrupt and inefficient in direct proportion to their size, no matter their theoretical form.

Classic liberalism, from which we get the word "liberty," taught us there are basic human rights on which governments should not tread. This is the basis for our Bill of Rights, the first ten amendments to the United States Constitution. J. S. Mill said, "The only purpose for which power can be rightfully exercised over any member of a civilized community, against his will, is to prevent harm to others." But we have strayed far from this concept.

Liberal government is a social contract between the government and the governed, and economic freedom is based on the right of commercial contract. This is not a bad form of government and economic system, but both are easily derailed through the growth of government, which tends to reproduce bureaucrats and the size of its own turf. Sprawling government bureaucracy was not what Thomas Jefferson envisioned in his first inaugural address:

Still one thing more, fellow citizens—a wise and frugal government, which shall restrain men from injuring one another, shall leave them otherwise free to regulate their own pursuits of industry and improvement, and shall not take from the mouth of labor the bread it has earned.

When was the last time a democratic (or other) government's budget was reduced or taxes cut for a period longer than the few months before an election? How much debt can a government incur before it sinks itself?

Democracies have glaring flaws that need correction and likely can be corrected while retaining the good. Because their citizenry regard democracy as a beacon of morality among inferior forms of government (such as dictators and totalitarian communist systems), democracies stray into adventurism and take on the cloak of moral advisers to the world. Is the avoidance of foreign entanglements an archaic concept, or might democracies be better off keeping their long noses out of the business of other countries, except in the case of self-defense? Did the United States learn anything in Vietnam, Panama, and Kuwait?

As columnist Joseph Sobran pointed out, democracy is not a synonym for virtue, it is a method of succession, a means to determine the next leaders at all levels of government based on the choice of the people who vote. Because democratic leaders are chosen by a majority, they usually represent the wishes of the majority (or an informal coalition of minorities), for good and for bad. The right and ability of the populace to have a voice in who leads the government is a right increasingly accepted by all people in the world, no matter their economic system. With the proliferation of opposition parties in communist countries and the right of the people in those countries to exercise a free choice in choosing leaders, democracy as a means of succession is sweeping the world. This fact is meaningless, however, judging from the morality and ethics of decisions made by political leaders. Only if it is assumed that the majority of people are always moral, and that their leaders are strictly accountable to the people for their actions, can it be argued that actions of democratic leaders are uniformly moral.

Government control infringes on the actions of many minorities and may infringe on the desires of the majority. It exists to control the behavior of its citizens, and it cannot act to change or control any behavior without stopping a minority from their current actions. Whether the government is democratic or totalitarian says nothing about whether the resulting government necessarily observes personal rights of the minority (whatever those rights may be, other than the right not to be harmed by others), equitably divides power, or limits its incursions into the private lives of its citizens. Through experience we've found that it's more likely the majority will be treated better under a democracy because the majority indirectly is the government.

The framers of the U.S. Constitution knew that democracy without checks and balances would be the same as mob rule. The United States has eroded the concept of checks and balances, however, to the point that many minorities exist in no better than totalitarian circumstances. This is because government has become unlimited. There is nothing federal and state governments cannot do as long as their actions fit within the elastic confines of the federal and state constitutions. Government tells us what we can and cannot do every second of our waking day and continually attempts to extend this control into the privacy of our bedrooms and homes. This is not a model form of government, though we tend to think it's the best of all possible worlds.

Millions in the United States live off the wealth produced by others. Included within these millions are employees at all levels of government (formerly including myself), many or most of whom are doing jobs that are unnecessary or could be better performed by the private sector. By October of 1987, federal, state, and local governments employed 17.3 million people, which was 7 percent of the population. Since then, government growth has exploded, though exact figures are not yet available, caused by the boom of prison and jail jobs, and more jobs for lawyers. This means government growth has paralleled the war on drugs. (Included within other millions living off the wealth of others are our religious leaders, who produce nothing, except to the extent that illusion and forums for socialization are valuable.)

The reason for the parasitic growth of government is that power requires turf. Only to the extent that government increases the number of employees does it gain power, so growth becomes a primary goal as a means to increased power. Because some identifiable interest in the citizenry will benefit from any growth, though it may injure and extend control over many others, growth continues unchecked and uncheckable. This is the inherent character of all government. The result is that ninety million people in the United States (40 percent of the population) depend on the federal, state, and local governments for all or some portion of their support.

There are two economies in the United States and in all capitalistic countries. The first is democratic, capitalistic, market-oriented, entrepreneurial, and booming. It created twenty-two million jobs and four million businesses in the U.S. between 1981 and 1990. This economy works by responding to incentives that make work pay, such as investment, savings, and productivity. The other economy is similar to those in the pre-1990 Soviet Union, Eastern Europe, and third-world socialist economies and doesn't work, or even pretend to work. It lacks economic incentives, or incentives of any kind, except those necessary to its own growth. It is based on altruistic ideas similar to those in socialist and communist countries, that the poor and downtrodden cannot help themselves but must instead depend on government and others for survival. If we tried to create a less efficient economy, it would be difficult to better the model of our government, which destroys the link between individual effort and reward, instead offering money for joblessness and the breakup of the family unit. Eastern Europe and East Harlem, East St. Louis and East Los Angeles are looking to the United States government for solutions to their stagnant economies. Will the answer come from the government or from trade-economy capitalism? Which creates wealth and which destroys it or transfers it to nonearning others? The tax-and-government economy is challenging the trade economy in size, and at some point the government will win, to the loss of all. A prime example is the tax reform act of 1986, which closed the "loopholes" allowing tax-advantaged investments in real estate. By 1990 the savings and loan industry had collapsed as a result of its suddenly worthless investments in real estate, traceable directly to the 1986 tax reform act at a cost estimated in 1991 to total $500 billion dollars. To put $500 billion in perspective, the entire cost of World War II (adjusted for inflation) was $460 billion; $500 billion is more than the budgets of all state governments and about four times the profits of the *Fortune 500* companies. The closing of the "loopholes" brought in a few billion dollars in taxes, resulting in the loss of many hundreds of billions of dollars.

How productive and internationally competitive can any country be whose population is largely dependent on the transfer of wealth from others for its support, or a government that gobbles up over a third of the national economy without producing anything of value, instead acting primarily to limit nonharmful actions and to transfer wealth? Government produces nothing and can do nothing that its citizens could not otherwise do, a self-evident proposition since the people comprise the government. The government can't grow food or create fashion or build houses and cars. It can only confiscate and transfer the wealth of those who actually perform labor. The only essential product of government is the security and safety of its citizens, a largely forgotten concept. We pay an average of 40 percent of our income in taxes, but we can't walk the city streets without fear. American government is incompetent at performing its most basic task, and until it can keep us safe, we should refuse to allow the spread of its inefficiencies into areas better performed by the market economy.*

Democracy seeks to guarantee two things: succession without bloodshed and representation of the majority (or an accidental coalition of minorities), which are relatively excellent things to guarantee, but are hardly the only important aspects of government. Democracy guarantees nothing else, certainly not good or fair government, particularly in relation to minorities, and even the majority of taxpayers. As columnist Joseph Sobran has pointed out, democracy *may* prevent a Joseph Stalin or an Adolph Hitler, but it will never prevent a Jim Wright, or a Charles Keating, or any other megacrook. In an era of instant media and television, democracy guarantees mediocrity. (On the plus side, television and instant media may be largely responsible for the meltdown of the iron curtain. Totalitarian regimes wither under the glare of worldwide public opinion, no matter the mediocrity of that opinion.)

---

*"Governments don't protect you. They can't. All they can do is promise to make the person who hurts you pay for his crime—if they can catch him. The criminal won't pay *you* back, of course, so they punish him only as a deterrent to future crime. If you think the deterrent is working, why is crime always such a public issue?

"Occasionally, a government policeman actually prevents a specific crime from taking place or from being completed. The odds against that are tremendous, however. If you want to eliminate *all* risk of violence, your only recourse is to pay for a guard to watch over you and your property day and night. And if that's what you want, you can hire a guard to do it—but the price you already pay to the government won't purchase him.

"Small wonder that the Los Angeles Chief of Police advised residents to 'bar their doors, buy a police dog, call us when we're available, and pray' as the best methods of protecting themselves from crime." (*Los Angeles Times,* June 4, 1971, from *How I Found Freedom in an Unfree World* by Harry Brown [1973]).

There appear to be only two alternative forms of government: democracies and totalitarian regimes. Other labels, such as socialism and communism, describe economic systems, not systems of government. The reason totalitarianism is an unacceptable form of government is that it operates at the whim of its leaders without accountability to the governed. The governed have no protection from the government. The reason democracy is a relatively good form of government is that the people have some say and there is no better alternative. Rights a majority agrees should be available to the people are guaranteed for the time being, i.e., for as long as the current majority continues to believe as it did during the last election and as long as those elected at the last election remain faithful to the wishes of the electorate.

The question naturally arises whether voters need representatives, such as Congress and state legislatures, in a computer age of instant polls, and whether the need to be governed may gradually diminish, if such a "need" exists. Our representatives spend about 75 percent of their time on useless activities such as public appearances, fund raisers, and other froth; most of the balance of their time is spent on political machinations, log-rolling, and deals, leaving little time for objectively investigating and analyzing substantive issues, according to the leftist weekly *Le Nouvel Observateur* of Paris. The magazine concludes:

> If politics were to disappear, nine tenths of the useless occupations that it spawns would disappear with it. . . . The real secret is that power is useless, or, more accurately, almost useless. Its capacity to do evil is almost limitless. Government can prohibit, oppress, imprison, torture, starve and kill. For that, it has soldiers, police, judges, officials and ministers. But its capacity to do good is almost nil.

Most Western democracies guarantee core rights for their citizens through a constitution, which guarantees that the whims of a current majority may not infringe on basic rights of various minorities. A constitutional system works as intended only when core rights are neither eroded by populist and religious excesses nor smothered by unwieldy bureaucracies. No current world government has escaped the inevitable twin curses of artificial controls imposed by populist/ religious forces and the stultifying inefficiencies of sprawling bureaucracies.

Democracy in the United States taxes to underwrite the risky investments of the middle and upper classes to the tune of a $500 billion savings and loan bailout, not to relieve poverty, which is the usual excuse for unlimited democratic government. The majority should admit that it doesn't care about the poor, but only about itself, the voting majority. The government has the unlimited power to redistribute wealth, and it does, to the middle and upper classes. This fact is illustrated by the rich getting richer and the poor getting poorer. Based upon a 1990 report of the Congressional Budget Office, from 1980 to 1989 the income of the poorest 20 percent of the population (average income of $7,725) dropped by 3 percent, and their federal tax rate increased by 16 percent. The richest 20 percent (average income of $105,209) enjoyed a 32 percent increase in income and a 5.5 percent cut in their federal tax rate. The income of the poorest 10 percent fell 10.5 percent between 1977 and 1987, while the income of the wealthiest 1 percent increased 74.2 percent.

The American dream has vanished for many young families with children and for most female-headed families, black families, Hispanic families, and high-school dropouts. From 1973 to 1990, real income dropped by a third for the nine million American families headed by people under age thirty, and their poverty level has risen to 40 percent. The April 1992 report by the Children's Defense Fund concluded: "The implicit message to many young Americans is frightenly clear: Bearing and raising children may no longer be compatible with active pursuit of the American dream. No society can convey this message for long if it hopes to survive and prosper." Families without children enjoyed an 11 percent rise in real income during this seventeen-year period. Poverty levels among female-headed families in 1990 was 77 percent, for black families 68 percent, for Hispanic families 51 percent, and for high-school dropouts 64 percent. The report recommended increased government benefit programs, however, which would be the worst remedy we could attempt.

These results are unavoidable where leaders exempt themselves from the operation of laws that govern the behavior of the rest of us, and the rest of us crush the minorities around us with tax burdens, barriers to entry into the economic system, and rules with which no one can comply without an advanced education or the wealth to hire highly specialized people.

What are the necessary functions of government? We must ask this question seriously because those functions which are not necessary are inefficiently performed by government and cost us far more than if we would perform them ourselves. Do the necessary functions of government go beyond protection of the populace from domestic and foreign violence and the resolution of disputes to avoid violence, thus maintaining order while protecting life and property? If so, what are the other necessary functions of government and why are they necessary?

The purpose of government is to protect us from our own gullibility, called consumer fraud; insure peace, here and around the world, at least in countries that supply us oil; manage the economy, guaranteeing prosperity, full employment, low inflation, and an ever-rising stock market, whether it works or not; abolish poverty, or prevent it from rising at a too noticeable rate; fix historial injustices; educate all, though only half graduate high school and half of those can't function at minimal job-entry levels; prevent us from harming ourselves through the ingestion of harmful drugs, except for the two most dangerous drugs; guarantee wealth for large farmers and prevent small farmers and buggy-whip manufacturers from disappearing too rapidly; assist those calling themselves artists; care for the homeless who don't care whether we care; preserve the environment, or at least the money-making environment of large campaign contributors; inspect beef and poultry, which remain among the filthiest in the world; guarantee safe working conditions and insurance settlements for those injured by unsafe working conditions; protect everyone from discrimination by anyone else; mismanage national forests and parks; subsidize scientific research, particularly as it relates to the military-industrial complex; build highways, eventually paving the earth; subsidize small, medium, and large business; keep people from gambling unless the government sponsors it and receives a cut; discourage prostitution, except those servicing government leaders and the wealthy; or simply put, anything and everything.

Because anything government does costs two to five times more than if we did it ourselves, government should only do those things we can't do ourselves. Are government health insurance programs better (or cheaper overall) than private insurance programs? Are government welfare programs better than private charities? Any program filtered through government doubles, triples, quadruples, or quintiples in cost because of the inherent inefficiency of government. Is it a proper function of government to prop up tobacco prices or sponsor art exhibits? Is there any government function that cannot be more efficiently performed by a lesser-taxed private sector, except for those narrow necessaries of preventing domestic and foreign violence by protecting life and property?

As stated by Dwight R. Lee and Richard B. McKenzie in "The Ongoing Struggle for Liberty" (*The Freeman,* July 1990):

> A persistent tendency exists for government to expand, and then undermine both freedom and responsibility. The existence of government power creates the opportunity for people to benefit legally at the expense of others in ways that are analogous to the illegal practices that it is the primary purpose of government to prevent. . . . As with the thief, those who gain advantages from preferential governmental treatment receive all the benefits while the costs (in terms of diminished freedom and productivity) are spread over the entire population. Government can become the means by which everyone is engaged in the activity of "political piracy," or in the words of Frederic Bastiat, "the State is the great fiction through which everybody endeavors to live at the expense of everybody." Obviously this situation is collectively destructive. Piracy can be a profitable activity when the pirates are few and the victims are many. But when everyone is a pirate, everyone is also a victim, making it impossible for all to gain by a reduction in piracy.

The 1991–92 presidential budget proposal brought howls of "unfair" from groups that would be affected by proposed cuts in Social Security (destitute widows), farm subsidies (poor family farmers), welfare (poor single mothers), and education (underpaid teachers). These groups paraded examples of their plights at budget hearings, making clear they would be greatly harmed by proposed cuts, but without any analysis of the programs themselves or their overall efficacy. The arguments of these recipient groups are partially correct. When government promises anything, the beneficiaries come to rely on that promise to their detriment if it is not fulfilled. For instance, people routinely compute future Social Security benefits when planning retirement. The Arizona State Retirement System prints an analysis of the members' anticipated Social Security benefits with its annual report to its members. People save less money because they plan on Social Security benefits in the future. The program can never be ended or cut back without harming people who rely on it, which includes us all.

Why does the government pander to special interests? Is it because a former president's lips lied about no new taxes, or Congress tucks pork into every bill, or is it because of our own greed, the greed of you and me, the voters? As retirees, when we've collected twice as much in Social Security benefits as we paid in, do we call up and tell Social Security to cut us off? All candidates promise a chicken in every pot, below cost, and no new taxes, or we wouldn't vote for them. The Clinton economic plan featured something free for all with few spending cuts, mostly ignoring the every-growing deficit. The Bush defense budget dropped from the $300 billion needed to fight the Soviet Union to $292 billion when there's no one left to fight except Saddam Hussien. We buy into something for nothing because we've abdicated any semblance of personal responsibility; personal responsibility could mean we'd get fewer "freebies" from government than our neighbors. Thomas Carlyle said that "every [democratic] government is the exact symbol of its people, with their wisdom and un-wisdom; we have to say: like people, like government."

The 1992–93 federal budget totalled $1.5 trillion with revenues projected at $1.173 trillion, which means we started out with a $327 billion deficit. The budget includes $292 billion for the post-Cold War military, $17 billion in counter-productive foreign aid, $16 billion to pay farmers not to produce food, $197 billion in counter-productive welfare payments, $303 billion for Social Security, and $214 billion for interest on prior deficits. The U.S. Senate turned down efforts by progressives to cut military spending and by conservatives to cap benefit programs.

Government programs also affect the price of goods produced so that to end the program would penalize recent purchasers of the means of production. For example, anticipated government subsidies affect the price of farm land. Restricted cab licenses push their price skyward, so any change in the restriction destroys the premium price paid by the recent entrant into the cab business. Allowing programs to grow without restriction, however, is unfair to all nonbeneficiaries. Thus the system is unfair to all, because we are all nonbeneficiaries of most government programs. Such is government by special interest groups, political action committees, and lobbyists. Democratic government policies result in bounteous benefits for well-informed and well-organized special interests while the cost of these benefits is spread over the uninformed and unorganized voting public. The biggest loser is the honest and diligent worker who seeks no special favors from government. When the government borrows money (daily) instead of raising taxes to support expanding programs, future taxpayers receiving no benefit are left with the burden. In order to end the unfairness of special interest programs without being unfair, no new beneficiaries should be added to or become eligible for government entitlement programs that would then die along with their current beneficiaries. Farm subsidies should be phased out over twenty to thirty years, as should every other benefit program that takes from Peter to pay Paul; otherwise, government can never stop growing and will eventually bankrupt itself.

The United States government has deteriorated into rule by a government elite, perpetuated in power by an institution approaching pure democracy, or mobocracy, with few checks and balances against excessive power. They rule who are equipped to take advantage of popular opinion. Minorities and those seeking no special benefits or tax breaks from government wither and struggle for survival under a crushing system of rules as rational as the rules of organized religion.

Without safeguarding minority rights, a democracy becomes the breeding ground for fascism such as in 1930s Germany, Italy, and Japan. Small interest groups in these countries mobilized the democratic process to overthrow the system, eradicating minorities with the excuse of purifying the racial and religious characteristics of the majority.

Democracy today suffers similar problems all over the world. The third most powerful political party in India, for instance, is dedicated to advancing a Hindu majority at the expense of Muslim and other minorities, severing the distinctions between religion and government, which is also the agenda for much of religion in the United States.

Muslims and Sikhs in India seek a final solution for non-Muslims and non-Sikhs, and Muslims may eventually cause the collapse of democracy in Pakistan. Many Middle Eastern governments are monarchies or totalitarian regimes, which many believe are less oppressive than a democratically elected government that would likely establish Muslim fundamentalism and allow no minority rights. Iran is a democracy and allows free and open voting procedures, but with little resemblance to what Westerners traditionally view as democratic, because dissent and minorities are not allowed. The United States has gradually become less the land of the free and more the land of the absolutely controlled, because certain political and free-spirited minorities are imprisoned for their views or actions. These minorities include those using drugs or opposing the slaughter of foreign nationals. A majority vote doesn't make an action ethical, correct, or the best, only locally legal.

If the best government is the least government then no government should be allowed to expand territorially, except perhaps in those situations where the overwhelming majority consents to the reuniting of ethnic groups, such as the reunification of Germany. There should be an enforceable and strict prohibition, however, against the slaughter or expulsion of minorities by majority ethnic or religious groups. It would be highly civilized to further prohibit discrimination based on race, religion, or lack of religion. National boundaries should be frozen, except to the extent that groups within a country wish to subdivide by the consent of the affected populace. Neither the former Soviet Union nor the United States should be allowed to increase in size. Should any portion of either wish to secede, however, it should be allowed upon majority vote of the affected area. This would apply equally to Latvia, Texas, Lithuania, and Massachusetts. Such a concept would have solved and can solve problems in many places, including former Yugoslavia, the former Soviet Union, China, Africa, and elsewhere. Denying autonomy to a state or area within a nation ensures an end to allegiance, but allowing autonomy leaves open the possibility of allegiance and even encourages it, witness the former French and English colonies. With the Soviet Union fractured, the Russian Republic still constitutes 76 percent of the land area and 52 percent of the population. Peaceful secession promoted favorable trade and political relationships throughout a splintered U.S.S.R., while the alternative was too bloody to seriously contemplate. An additional benefit is that the smaller the country, the less the threat to world peace. Ethnic, racial, and religious groups should be allowed to control their own national and political destinies as long as minority rights are left sacrosanct, which means there should be worldwide guaranteed rights of free speech, religion, association, and economic activity. Many countries have these lessons to learn, including all those in the Middle East, the Balkans, parts of Southeast Asia, and much of Africa.

Distinguishing Government from Economics

A frequently listed form of government is Marxism/Communism, which is not a theory of government at all, but a theory of economics that posits equal distribution of wealth. Under Marxism, government is supposed to wither away, to which we can say only, "Good luck, Comrade." We should be so lucky that all governments would mostly wither away, leaving the few functions for which government should legitimately exist.

Capitalism is the economic theory of the West and is based on competition through free market pricing (as opposed to monopoly pricing or price controls), not on equal division of wealth. An analogy of how capitalism works was described by Adam Smith in 1776 as the "invisible hand": "[The individual, when left alone, is] led . . . to promote an end which was no part of his intention. . . . By pursuing his own interest [the individual] frequently promotes that of society more effectually than when he really intends to promote it." The result was described succinctly by F. A. Hayek:

> Suppose that either a new use for tin has been discovered or . . . an important producer's ability to provide tin on the market has declined. Either way, tin is now more scarce. Some consumers of tin, because of their proximity to and knowledge of the impetus of the change, are immediately informed of the new situation. Without anyone intending to help others, the information of the new scarcity of tin is spread through the price system. Signaled by the rising price of tin, the vast majority of tin consumers, not privy to the direct knowledge of time and place, are "told" that they must somehow economize their own use of tin. The marvel is that in a case like [this] of a scarcity of one raw material, without an order being issued, without more than perhaps a handful of people knowing the cause, tens of thousands of people whose identity could not be ascertained by months of investigation, are made to use the material or its products more sparingly; that is, they move in the right direction.

Communism replaces the invisible hand with a far less efficient bureaucratic hand, as in "I'm from the government and I'm here to help you." But no government or economic system can know the constantly changing needs and wants of its citizens or the availability of resources; such knowledge can exist only in the market, which disgorges its information efficiently and continuously without the necessity of government involvement.

Western and United States capitalism does little better than Marxist theory: both rely on central planning through government intervention. As Western governments grow, there is less room for private decision-making. Many government functions exist to limit entry to the marketplace, making goods and services more expensive and less efficient. For example, all licensing functions of government limit market entry and add to costs. The justification for licensing is that the consuming public would otherwise be victimized by unskilled labor or shoddily produced goods. This justification is contrary to the central theme of capitalism, which allows free competition among goods and services based on quality and price. Consumers then choose goods and services by voting with their pocketbooks. Licensing doesn't protect the public except insofar as the public is too lazy or unintelligent to protect itself. It primarily protects the licensed industry, limiting market entry through regulation by industry representatives who serve on licensing boards, restricting competition, raising prices, protecting the inept, and fostering discrimination. The lazy deserve no protection and government does a poor job of protecting the unintelligent. Perhaps the unintelligent should rely upon family or private charity instead of the inefficient vagaries of government.

Every state has an annual budget crisis. During the 1980s average state spending increased 7 percent a year while revenues increased by only 4.5 percent. Arizona ranked number one in the 1980s with a 213 percent increase in state government spending, which was 9 percent higher than state number two, Connecticut. Traditionally big spending states like Massachusetts and New York increased spending 155 percent and 137 percent, respectively, according to the Washington-based American Legislative Council. The national average of state government spending increases during the 1980s was 122 percent. The big demand for increases came in the areas of indigent health care and welfare benefits, prisons, and education. Much of what states spend their money on includes the ludicrous. While the U.S. Department of Agriculture employs one person for every six farmers in the United States, the State of Arizona duplicates its function, costing $11 million a year in 1990, which is pocket change that mounts up. Arizona spent $4 million in 1990 to maintain a state livestock board with 108 employees, but it doesn't regulate the computer industry, or the restaurant industry, or communications, which may be unsafe to mention lest the state legislature decide the time is ripe for their regulation. Arizona has an egg inspector with numerous employees and yearly budget increases. Arizona spends millions of dollars to haphazardly regulate contractors and realtors and accountants and doctors, who also regulate themselves. Because there's no regular review of government functions for necessity (after a few years any government function is not only considered necessary but crucial to citizen security), government can only grow. Bureaucrats insist that services can't be cut, and we blithely go along with the cry because there's no organized opposition to the special interest that created the "need" in the first place.

The State of Alaska makes Arizona look like a piker among state governments' inherent ability to waste money. Alaska's per capita spending in 1986 was $7,309, over twice that of its nearest rival, Wyoming, and five times the national average. The higher cost of living in Alaska accounted for less than 10 percent of the difference. In 1978, Alaska spent $50 million to subsidize barley farming through loans to farmers, which were never repaid, by building access roads to anticipated barley fields, which were never planted; by buying railroad cars for barley, which was never transported; and by constructing grain elevators. The Alaskan farmers also collected money from the federal government for not growing barley. Alaska spent $5.8 million on a barley processing terminal in Seward before halting construction of the projected $8.2 million project, which would have processed all the barley grown in Alaska's peak production year in 4.5 hours.

By 1987, loans made by Alaska totalled $233 million in default and $1 billion delinquent. These loans had been made to encourage ventures such as dog-powered washing machines, wild berry candy, and fur farming. Alaska bought a meat plant in 1985 for $3.5 million and it lost money from then on. The state-owned dairy, from which public schools must purchase their milk at a price 7 percent above that in privately owned grocery stores, lost $887,000 in 1987. To finance this spending, Alaska exacts the highest oil tax in the country.

The Rhode Island government didn't open for business on March 8, 1991, and there were no reports that anyone missed the "essential" state services. With the worst budget deficit of any state in the nation as a percentage of total spending, Rhode Island had to shut down nine more days before June 30, 1991. The only services provided on shut-down days were police, prison guards, hospital personnel, one airport, one public TV station, and transportation construction. Were all of these "necessary" functions of government? Is the private sector incompetent to run hospitals, TV stations, and airports?

The daycare industry is an example of limited market entry. One woman's need for daycare is another woman's opportunity, until government steps in with licensing requirements. A daycare center may not operate in any jurisdiction without space, safety, and health requirements that couldn't be met by many homes from which the children come to be cared for. Any parent should be sufficiently adult and responsible to decide whether a particular daycare operation, licensed or not, is suitable for that parent's child. Government licensing doesn't guarantee safety or health, but it does guarantee that those women not meeting government standards cannot sell daycare services and must instead seek other employment or remain unemployed. Government's role is a substitute for individual responsibility on the theory that adults are unable to care for their own welfare or the welfare of their children. The result is more unemployed or underemployed women, a lower standard of living for their families, and increased costs of government. The identical situation exists for a single mother starting a business in her home as a hairdresser, computer technician, caterer, seamstress, and many other occupations.

A striking example of government limiting entry to the marketplace is the cost of entry into the New York cab-driving market. The cost of a license in 1989 was $70,000, which raises substantially the cost of cab services in New York with no resulting protection for the public. Such paternalistic regulations perpetuate discrimination against women and others seeking entry to the marketplace, raising prices for all and treating adults like children. The result is a citizenry that mirrors the regard held of it by the government. Childlike behavior is perpetuated and encouraged by government. It would be far less expensive for people to protect themselves against potentially shoddy or dangerous goods and services produced by others than hiring government to do it for them. The likelihood of successful protection when a personal stake is involved is proportionately higher and the cost proportionately lower.

The Japanese traditionally discourage market entry by women, who are left to be nurturers of Japanese children, making sure they achieve in school, with the result that Japanese children do far better academically and technically than American children. This system is arguably worse for the individual woman but better for the productivity of the country and the education of Japanese children. Adults in the United States depend almost entirely on the impersonal public school system to educate their children, with predictable results. Responsibility for anything left to government, partially or entirely, results in comparatively poor performance. Government has no personal stake in solving problems, no matter its particular role, so there is little incentive for a job well done.

An additional disincentive for the recipient of any governmental benefit is the removal of responsibility, which is the removal of freedom. Without responsibility and personal freedom, the individual becomes dependent on government services with multiple bad results: the growth of government continues as inevitable citizen reliance on government rises. As it becomes bigger, government becomes less efficient and more expensive, and the individual loses the freedom to make individual choices and the incentive to become more efficient. Government grows to the point that it becomes the controller of individual actions that harm no one else, and the individual gradually ends up with the freedom of one living in a totalitarian regime, no matter the mode of succession, whether democratic or not. The pervasive control of absolute government is precisely what Eastern Europe has rejected, while the multiple overlapping governments in the United States impose greater controls daily.

Responsibility is increasingly shirked by a majority of Americans, to the point where it's becoming our national ethic to avoid personal responsibility. Instead of taking responsibility for our mistakes, we blame any convenient other. *The Economist* analyzed our slide into irresponsibility as "decadent puritanism." A drunk sues his host for injuries sustained as a result of his drunkenness. Everyone is a victim and no one is personally responsible. Genes cause alcoholism instead of the alcoholic who could have said no but didn't. Genes may make a person more susceptible to alcoholism or other harm, but this is no justification for shirking personal responsibility. This process is fueled by greedy lawyers and by us, their greedy clients. Any burden must be shifted to another. A Nevada man shoots himself in the head while guzzling beer and listening to Judas Priest and the blame is placed on Judas Priest and its recording company. A tequila company is sued by the parents of a college freshman who drank too many shots of tequila and drowned in a swimming pool. Cigarette companies are sued for selling what most realize is the world's most dangerous drug, but if we become addicted we're not responsible. Blame society, big business, our parents, genes, and anything else we cleverly think up. Cigarette companies can blame Pocahontas or the tobacco farmer for tempting the company with pretty green leaves, and we can all blame Congress for tobacco subsidies.

With the shirking of personal responsibility comes the urge to control the actions of others. As stated by William Murchison, "Embedded in the human personality is the love of ordering others around." This is amply illustrated by governments and religions that purport to know better what is best for us than we ever can or will. The results are erosion of human freedom, growth of government, and growing puritanism. We decide that parental leave is a necessity that business must provide for all employees. The cost of goods and services rises accordingly, and business shifts to hiring the single and senior citizens. We must understand, as stated by Rep. Dick Armey of Texas, "The market is rational. Government is dumb."

This proclivity to control and shift responsibility is shared by religion and government. As pointed out by Arnold Toynbee in *An Historian's Approach to Religion:*

> Christianity appealed to the masses, and this for three reasons: it treated them, not as proletarians, but as human souls; it showed its consideration for them in a practical way by taking care of the widows and orphans, the sick and the aged, for whom neither the municipal governments of the city-states nor the ecumenical government of the Empire performed any comparable services; and it did all this disinterestedly, under the inspiration of Christian ideals, and not with the ulterior aim of recruiting supporters.

The role of early Christianity has been taken up by our governments, resulting in government becoming our religion, which is demonstrated by the term, "patriotism." The government is not altruistic in performing services for the poor and infirm, but it recognizes that its growth is uncappable when harnassed to the noble causes abdicated by religion. As Toynbee also recognized:

> [There is] a human craving to escape from the burdensome responsibility of having to make decisions for oneself. It may look as if this burden can be escaped by submitting one's own intellect and will to some authority to which one can feel it proper to submit because one has recognized its claims as being unique and final. This craving to escape responsibility can be reconciled with an unexorcised self-centeredness by the belief that, in submitting to the authority of the Church, one becomes a member of the "Chosen People." This craving for an authority that will lift the burden of responsibility from one's shoulders is, no doubt, at its strongest in social situations in which Society is in disintegration; but it is an innate and perennial craving which, in every soul everywhere and always, is on the wait for an opportunity to break out.

Toynbee's observations about religion apply equally to government.

Capitalism or Marxism could exist under any form of government. As the "communist" regimes switched to a democratic form of succession, they also altered their economic systems. The Supreme Soviet voted 350 to 3 in March 1990 to allow private citizens to own small factories and hire their own workers, which was a "main plank" in Gorbachev's economic reforms. This small change signaled an alteration in the basic economic system from communism, Marxism, and collectivism to capitalism.

Alexander Solzhenitsyn in September 1990 proposed democracy as a model for the former Soviet Union, though repeating his long-held abhorrence of materialism. He argued that efficiency in production required the breaking up of collective farms and the redistribution of land to private ownership on the grounds that "private ownership of land . . . guarantees long-term improvement rather than exhaustion of the soil, and only with it can we be sure that our agriculture will not move backwards." Solzhenitsyn also suggested that the central Russian provinces, Russia, Byelorussia, and the Ukraine allow the secession of the other twelve provinces because they differ culturally and ethnically.

Marxism is altruistic on paper but in reality works as well on the national level as a rusting hulk with no incentive to apply the oil can. The theory is that wealth should be equally distributed, which has superficial appeal similar to that of organized religion. This theory, however, is as contrary to human nature as religion with its artificial rules, because under Marxism there's no incentive to work. Work doesn't benefit the individual or accumulate wealth.

The nature of man is competitive, which the Marxist countries understood well at the Olympic games and are understanding better as time goes by. Competition is necessary for progress so we may claw ourselves upward through evolution. A government not open to new ideas and innovations will stagnate, similar to organized religions. Unfortunately, the party line of Marxism, which militates against change as surely as if it were a be-all, end-all religion, mired the communist countries deeper in the quagmire of bureaucracy than even the Western democracies. There are two primary alternative economic systems: communism and capitalism. Either everyone owns everything in common and little or nothing is owned by the individual, or everyone owns little or nothing in common and almost all ownership is by the individual. As stated by Robert J. Samuelson in his November 27, 1989, *Newsweek* column, "Capitalism is a great, though flawed, engine for progress. Communism is an economic failure, but its ideals express a widespread yearning for a fair society. In the East and the West today, there's renewed striving for an elusive utopia that combines growth with fairness."

Economics and Government: Efficiency and Ethics

Socialism is considered to be, but is not, a compromise between communism and capitalism. It is a means of transferring wealth to those who, in theory, have insufficient means of obtaining wealth, which tells us nothing about who owns the means of production or whether property is owned in common or individually.

The most successful socialist state is Sweden, which provides care for its citizens from cradle to grave. Both parents receive eighteen months of paid leave upon the birth of a child. National health insurance pays all medical costs and 90 percent of income lost while ill or while caring for an ill child. Education through college costs little. Retirement pensions contain inflation compensators and pay two-thirds of an employee's earning during the best paid fifteen years of employment. Unemployment is 1.4 percent, but the means of production is only 13 percent owned by the government. The Swedish success, which recently has been losing its lustre, is founded on a free market economy. Sweden is no more socialist than Great Britain or the United States, which is to say little of significance. To pay for this high level of cradle-to-grave services, however, the tax rate was up to 72 percent in 1990, dropping to 50 percent under 1991 reforms. Furthermore, adding all sources of taxation, Sweden takes 56 percent of its GNP after the top income tax rate drops to 50 percent.

The Swedish economy is in trouble because of burgeoning inflation approaching double digits for both wages and prices, primarily due to high worker absenteeism. The average number of sick days per worker rose from 18.5 in 1983 to 23.4 in 1988, reducing the real work week to thirty-one hours. (In 1991 Sweden limited sick days to payment of a percentage of salary and they immediately dropped 20 percent.) Growth in production is half that of Western Europe; Sweden's share of the international market dropped 4 percent between 1988 and 1990, and its GNP grew only 2 percent during the decade of the 1980s, more than eaten up by higher taxes. One third of Swedes work for the government. Sweden's buying power dropped to 14th among European countries by 1989, ahead only of Spain, Portugal, Greece, and Ireland. Socialism and communism share the same unavoidable defect: When support of all citizens is guaranteed, less is produced and the economy stagnates. We know this as a matter of common sense, needing no sophisticated economic theories or the collapse of communist economic systems to prove this truism.

To combine growth with fairness the United States and most Western democracies have adopted socialist capitalism, distinguishable from Swedish socialism only by the level of social benefits provided to its citizens. The reason we have combined the concepts is the thought that capitalism by itself is unfair to the poor, the uneducated, and other minorities. Accordingly, we believe wealth should be transferred to these minorities, no matter how badly this transfer works from a viewpoint of effectiveness.

CBS telecast a holiday movie in 1989 titled *No Place Like Home,* which depicted a couple who had been laid off work and couldn't find other employment. Their apartment burned and they moved in with the husband's brother. The brother was embarrassed when the father used food stamps at the local grocery store so the family moved on, to motels, to campsites, to a city shelter, and finally to a welfare hotel. What should be the role of government, if any, in such a circumstance? What is the proper limit of government control? Is man born to serve government or government created to serve man?

Capitalism has been criticized as a socially unjust system because it allows one person to bask in luxury resulting from luck, inheritance, or quirks of physical or mental talent, while others live in poverty. A question seldom explored is whether government should be the means to balance economic inequities. Americans and all other peoples are socially conscious, but this social consciousness is squarely contrary to the growing aversion to Marxist theory, "from each according to his ability, to each according to his needs," which 23 percent of 1988 college graduates in the United States not illogically believed was part of the United States Constitution. The essential question is whether government should be the means for our natural beneficence. The fact that government increasingly is "responsible" for the poor shifts responsibility from individual and traditional charities, relieving the individual from a sense of responsibility to the less fortunate and relieving the unfortunate of responsibility for themselves. If government were not in the business of supporting the poor, they would not go without but would instead be supported by charities receiving contributions from those who voluntarily determine the amount given and know precisely where the contribution goes. There is no similar attachment or personal involvement by those paying taxes to a sprawling impersonal government.

Most of our taxes go to administration of the government by the government and for the government, with a small percentage trickling down to the needy recipient. The Urban Affairs Center at Northwestern University studied poverty-related programs in Cook County (Chicago) for 1984, when $4.8 billion was spent. Dividing this amount by the number of poor people (781,330) averaged $6,209 per person, or $18,600 a year for a family of three (over $20,000 in 1991 dollars). However, two-thirds of this amount went to pay the bureaucrats administering the programs and only a third was received by the poor. Such is the efficiency of government.

Government is a ready vehicle for the unscrupulous to siphon off moneys meant for needy others; witness the HUD scandal, the savings and loan scandal, welfare and Medicaid fraud, and numerous others. The less government, the less opportunity for corruption, inefficiency, and fraud, which should be particularly guarded against in government, which draws its revenues from poor and rich alike.

President Franklin Pierce said in an 1854 veto message to Congress:

> I readily and, I trust, feelingly acknowledge the duty incumbent on us all, as men and citizens, and as among the highest and holiest of our duties, to provide for those who, in the mysterious order of Providence, are subject to want and to disease of body or mind; but I cannot find any authority in the Constitution for making the Federal Government the great almoner of public charity throughout the United States. . . . It would, in the end, be prejudicial rather than beneficial in the noble offices of charity.

Volunteerism is the opposite of government. Volunteering is the opposite of being forced, relying instead on education and persuasion. The distinction between whether force is used or is available to be used is crucial. Government forces action, assuming people are too selfish to help others and their communities. Government may be correct, but only to the extent that government has extinguished the helping urge by burdening its citizens with an overall tax rate taking 37 percent of their time, work, and income to support the government. How much beneficence can be left over? When government becomes involved in "volunteerism," it brings loss of independence, shattered idealism, and lowered morale. Government operates on hypocrisy because money to feed volunteerism is raised through the involuntary taxing of others.

We are generous givers, notwithstanding government. In 1988 we gave more than $106 billion to religion, human services, health, and education. This is twice the amount distributed by all U.S. corporations to their shareholders in 1988 and exceeds Federal spending on nondefense goods and services. We could be exceedingly more generous and efficient in our charitable giving if the portion of government purporting to be in the charity business were excised and our taxes proportionately reduced. The tax cut spur to the economy would create jobs for those able to earn their own way and free spendable income for further charitable giving.

The propriety of the American welfare system has been debated for years, with conservatives arguing that welfare traps people in poverty by removing incentives to work and liberals arguing that the unemployed poor must have an opportunity to get back on their feet and that welfare benefits are necessary to provide that opportunity. Studies in the 1980s found that both conservatives and liberals are correct. Welfare does trap some people in poverty, making them parasites on the system; however, welfare also saves many from hopeless unemployment and provides a breather for the unemployed to obtain future employment. The Family Support Act of 1988 codified these findings by requiring able-bodied welfare recipients to find work or lose welfare benefits; the result is to convert the welfare poor into the working poor.

Public opinion is uniformly hostile to the idea of giving money to able-bodied poor people, and rightly so. Largess removes incentives for personal responsibility, similar to a communistic economic system. The poor in the United States, however, aren't composed primarily of able-bodied, inherently lazy men. They are mostly young single mothers, usually from a minority group. Many are poor because a majority of organized religion prohibits the use of birth control and opposes sex education.

Perhaps the new welfare reforms will force the lazy to work, but many will be unqualified for most jobs while saddled with young children to raise and while belonging to socio-economic classes that are the most discriminated against in society because of sex and race. These mothers, who are also likely to be members of a religion that prohibits birth control, may be relegated to the 14 percent of the population who live in poverty forever. What would happen if government welfare programs were abolished, with resultant tax savings in the billions of dollars, and those few who both need and deserve benefits were made to depend on private charity instead? Would there be more or less corruption, poverty, wasted contributions, homeless, and hungry?

A last theory of government is libertarianism, which posits that government should be limited to only essential functions, such as protecting the citizenry from harm by its national defense and an internal police force. The purpose of government is to keep the peace. Libertarians would require government to leave the citizenry alone except to keep them from harming each other, protecting them from violence and related physical harms, and resolving disputes. With refinements, this may be the most efficient and ethical of all possible systems of government.

Solon described the perfect government in 500 B.C.E. as "where the least injury done to the meanest individual is considered an insult on the whole constitution." If our government were reformed so its primary mission was to prevent injury to all by anyone, it would lose volumes of laws, cut the budget to a tenth its current level, and end paternalism. We could become adults instead of children dependent on the beneficence of government to take from some and give to others.

Criminal laws would prohibit two levels of culpability: intentionally harmful acts and recklessly harmful acts. Recklessly harmful acts are such as firing a gun toward an occupied building, where there is no necessary intent to harm another directly, but the risk of harm is so high that criminal law sanctions should be imposed. Victimless crimes would no longer exist. No acts other than those intentionally or recklessly harmful toward others would be subject to criminal sanctions imposed by the state. The civil courts would remain available for other harms, such as those negligently caused or breaches of contract. Subject to possibilities of civil liability, adults would be allowed to do as they wished to further their own happiness, as long as they harmed no one else. Children would be restricted from doing other than as permitted by parents, schools, and government. The adult political party members in a majority would witness their tax bills cut in half and government paternalism and growth stopped short. Adults would avoid in all circumstances, excepting those of actual self-defense, harm of any other person or person's property, and this would be recognized as the core of ethics. Such an unbending rule would do more good for humankind than the rules of organized religions.

Classic libertarianism would go one step further and require government to provide for the national defense, but, undisputably, if no nation had a military, national defense would be unnecessary. We have examples of two such existing governments—Switzerland and Costa Rica—neither of which has a standing army (though the Swiss serve a two-year reserve commitment). Military might and armies are the result of national ego and should be abolished for all countries. There would be no need for disarmament if there were no armies or men to use the arms. The abolition of armies would be the ultimate disarmament, resulting in all nations unable to act violently toward any other nation. Instead of the United States spending half its budget on guns and armies, those billions could be left in the private sector for use in education, educating the poor to feed and protect themselves, renewing our infrastructure, and protecting the environment, incidentally emasculating taxes. One day of the Persian Gulf war wasted sufficient money for private industry to provide mass transit for the City of Chicago. The former Soviet Union recognized the fact of military waste in the adoption of its 1990 budget, reducing its military and capital outlay budgets by $100 billion and cutting its national deficit in half. For the United States to cut its budget deficit in half we'd have to stop government spending for two years. This appears impossible because we cherish our tax bills and the innumerable government services essential to our happiness.

A study of the rise and fall of great powers reveals that those nations paying for the defense of other nations lose power rapidly, while subsidized nations prosper. Japan's defense is provided by the United States, both because Japan's participation in war was outlawed after WWII and because Japan understands that stockpiling military weapons diverts resources from international competition. Japan is prospering and the United States is losing economic clout. The United States continues to spend more than any other country in the world on its military. The European Economic Community and former Soviet Republics are rapidly reducing military budgets as the United States continues to maintain its huge military establishment so that the world will not go unpoliced.

We tolerate increasing taxes on the promise of community improvements and greater government services, but most taxes are contrary to community betterment for four reasons: (1) Anything government does costs at least twice as much as if we did it ourselves, and often triple because government is an insatiable money-grubbing servant. (2) Taxes discourage investment, business spending, and savings, instead encouraging untouchable bureaucracy and loss of individual liberty. (3) Government programs paid for by taxes weaken the charitable generosity of taxpayers and their consideration of others. To make ends meet and also pay taxes requires hardened selfishness, looking out for number one, an unending "me" generation. (4) Government largess discourages individual responsibility because anything an individual receives "gratis" is devalued and discourages self-reliance, instead encouraging either avoidance of or lying about income. This is particularly true when the level of payment is insufficient for subsistence because of program cuts that are justified when benefits received are received by those perceived to be unworthy.

When will we say enough is enough? A 40 percent tax rate has not reached that point in the United States. Taxes averaged 40 percent of earnings, according to a Cato Institute study released in mid-1992. A family making $34,000 yearly and buying a new car costing $10,000 pays an additional $7,038, on average, in taxes; sales tax of $400, state income tax of $784, Social Security taxes of $1303 and federal income taxes of $4551. Because self-employed workers pay double the Social Security tax, the $10,000 car costs them $18,320 and those living in high tax states pay twice the sticker price. It must take a tax rate of 50 percent or 60 percent or more before we've had enough. As stated by Thomas Jefferson, "The natural progress of things is for liberty to yield and government to gain ground."

Economist Lester Thurow, Dean of MIT's Sloan School of Management, points out some inefficiencies that are caused by ever-sprawling government. In order to compete internationally, we must become more productive, producing goods more efficiently. Instead of producing more goods, however, our economy, since 1973, has expanded primarily in the service area. Much of the demand for services comes directly from the growth of government. In order to deal with the spreading government bureaucracy, services of specialists must increasingly be hired to intercede on our behalf with government. More and more people each year are unable to file their own tax returns, for instance, so more accountants are needed to deal with the government. Services, though they have made our economy grow at a positive rate, cannot be exported except in connection with the goods they have helped create. Only goods can effectively be exported. Because we are instead producing more services in order to deal with our voracious government, our production of goods suffers and we are beaten in most areas of international competition. Our reliance on a service-oriented economy relegates us to increasing and unending trade deficits. Only by bolstering our manufacturing capacity and its quality will we be able to compete internationally. Instead, we continue to concentrate on services in the health care, finance, and legal industries, much of them government related.

The inherently unproductive services necessary to cope with government bureaucracy need to be replaced by a productivity that will allow us to compete internationally, and the key to that productivity is our schools. Any country with an unskilled, undereducated work force cannot compete. IBM must teach its workers basic skills, which adds to the cost of its products. As stated by Thurow:

> If IBM has to teach Algebra I and Algebra II, then the cost of IBM semiconductors has to include the cost of teaching Algebra I and Algebra II. If Hitachi makes the same chips and they don't have to teach Algebra I and Algebra II, because the kids already learned it in high school, then Hitachi chips are cheaper than IBM chips and IBM goes out of business.

Spending on U.S. education increased by 30 percent (adjusted for inflation) from 1983 to 1991, yet school achievement remained constant. Our school system forces everyone to learn at the same rate or be declared uneducatable, and it teaches competition instead of cooperation, humiliating those who learn more slowly than the norm. A longer school day doesn't mean a better education any more than raising graduation standards prevents dropouts or the rampant cheating in public schools, according to George Leonard in the May 1992 *Atlantic Monthly*. It appears that the effectiveness of education depends on the frequency, variety, quality, and intensity of interaction between teacher and pupil. There is little in our public schools. Students learn faster and with more retention when they are placed in "table groups" with no classroom front or rows of desks lined up. Because the first responsibility for learning lies with the group, which is encouraged to constantly interact, the dropout rate for such a system in Cologne, Germany, fell to 1 percent, compared to the average German dropout rate of 14 percent. The cooperative "table group" school enjoyed a 60 percent college admission rate compared to the German average of 27 percent. Education in creative civilizations occurred historically through mentoring and tutoring, replaced by bureaucratic education similar to U.S. public schools in their final periods of stagnation and decay.

U.S. schools have a 30 percent dropout rate, and no other developed country has such a high rate. One reason is that our fifteen thousand local school boards are more concerned about religious issues of sex education, creationism, and prayer than about education. The primary burning educational issues in this country are religious issues. Why should school boards spend their time on whether to teach sex education and how much sex education is appropriate? A study by two University of Washington physicians in 1989 found that teenagers receive their sex education from television, motion pictures, music, advertising, peers, and adult role models. Because of organized religion, birth control—the only sure escape for many from instant poverty—cannot be taught in our public schools. Our teens might learn to use birth control if it were vigorously taught daily, such as in conjunction with the Pledge of Allegiance.

Another reason our schools do an abominable job and encourage dropouts is that they are boring. Students are taught as they've always been taught, sitting placidly in their chairs while a teacher exhorts them to memorize this and that with little creativity or explanation of how the subject matter relates to reality. Adults and children both tend to snooze when subjected to a static boring environment. Even top teachers can do little with such a methodology. Our children come to the schools with curiosity, imagination, and a burning desire to learn, but we erase these traits in a few short years. The inherent colorfulness of history, science, math, reading, and writing are expunged because a particular religion or vocal minority might be offended. For instance, no school in the country teaches what actually happened in the Middle Ages because Western relgion would be offended. The examples of conflict between our religions, and the ability to teach anything of interest are endless. Students are left with educational fodder as dry as sawdust, their creative juices dried by the fear of controversy embodied in our local school boards.

Government should get out of business and do nothing that can be accomplished by private industry. The Mercer Group, an Atlanta consulting firm, surveyed thirty-four states in 1991 and found that most had contracted out an average of three government services to private industry, resulting in cost savings ranging from 10 percent to 40 percent. One example of the results of privatization of most government functions began on December 3, 1986, when the Chief Wayne County Circuit Judge ordered Ecorse, Michigan, an incorporated area of downtown Detroit, into receivership because it had bankrupted itself with a perpetual $6 million deficit. The receiver discharged forty paid political employees and privatized the Department of Public Works, which handled vehicle maintenance, snow removal, sidewalk repairs, and the like, selling its equipment and building. The contract for private garbage collection was renegotiated, saving $120,000; the city boat-launching facility was privatized, as was the city's pension fund. The full-time fire department was replaced through attrition by a volunteer part-time force, and the city work force of 140 was reduced over 60 percent. The $45,000 a year dogcatcher's duties were shared with another city under private contract for a 50 percent savings. All local and state governments, and particularly the federal government, could similarly benefit by privatization to promote efficiency, carving away the deadwood of bureaucracy.

Government and labor unions argue that the safety and security functions of government can't be privatized because such is the core reason for government. An initially successful example of police service privatization occurred briefly in Oro Valley, Arizona, until shut down by the state. Rural/Metro provided fire-fighting, police services, alarm response, and paramedic operations to 1,200 residents beginning in 1975 for a yearly fee of $35,000. Control of policing was retained by the town. The company patrolled the community in four-wheel drive vehicles in areas the city had previously avoided and checked property twice daily for those residents who had given notice they'd be out of town. The burglary rate fell from fourteen a month to .7 a month. Because the Arizona Law Enforcement Officers Association Council refused to provide training and legally required accreditation for the company, however, Rural/Metro was forced to abandon its contract in 1977. By 1982 the police budget in Oro Valley was $241,000 a year, and the burglary rate was back up where it belonged. The police are more concerned with victimless crimes than crimes with victims.

Originally our personal rights as United States citizens were limited to three: life, liberty, and the pursuit of happiness. These three have been curtailed, and in their place has been substituted a laundry list of far less important rights such as a minimum wage, Social Security, health care, education, and holidays with pay. Our primary right was to be left alone and allowed to find our own way as long as we harmed no one else. Our substituted rights are material things that must be supplied by the toil and labor of others, to the detriment of their right to the pursuit of their own happiness and liberty. The pursuit of happiness is considered anti-Christian and thus antisociety. The real basic human right should be the right not to be harmed or killed, not a right to have all material things to support life. No one, not even government, owes the individual a living. To be left alone to make a living brings happiness. There is no more important right than to be left alone and unharmed. Without this central right all others pale. As stated by Immanuel Kant, each of us has the right to pursue chosen ends "as legislating members of the Kingdom of Ends." This principle is similar to the Golden Rule, yet more basic and more important because it is achievable. We can't force everyone to treat others as they would prefer to be treated, but we can prohibit harm to any other and enforce it. When Confucius was asked to sum up his philosophy in one word, he paraphrased the Golden Rule by saying, "reciprocity." True morality is simpler and purer. If you harm those who harm you, that is reciprocity and one interpretation of the Golden Rule. Instead, harm no one else and the odds are they will not harm you. If someone does harm you, then criminal law sanctions (and criminal and civil restitution/damage recoveries) should apply, and only then should criminal sanctions apply.

The distinction between our three original rights and the new shopping list of rights is that none of our original rights were parasitic of others. There was no cost to others when we exercised our right to life, liberty, and the pursuit of happiness. The cost of any right bearing a price tag must come from somewhere. The cost of Social Security, instead of having come even mostly from those benefitting by it, comes primarily from current workers. If Social Security had been properly funded or privatized, it would have worked as it should, not resulting in a burden on others. The government spends Social Security payments to support the general budget instead of building a self-sustaining fund to support present contributors. If those receiving Social Security payments today had instead been allowed to invest their contributions in a reasonable fashion, they would be better off financially today and there would be no burden on today's workers. Instead, past and present contributions were and are filtered through a government bureaucracy that exists to live off the earnings of those it purports to serve. Theoretically, workers today will benefit similarly when their time comes to draw Social Security, but only at an increasingly higher cost filtered through the inefficiency of government.*

Federal entitlement programs have flip-flopped their original purpose, which was to aid the poor and the less fortunate. By 1991, only one of every eight dollars in federal benefits reached the poor! The Congressional Budget Office found that the most affluent Americans collect more from federal entitlements than our poorest. Thus 1991 U.S. households with income over $100,000 collected an average of $5,690 for in-kind and federal cash benefits, while those making under $10,000 received $5,560. Including tax breaks, those making over $100,000 averaged $9,280 in federal benefits, almost double that received by those making under $10,000. Half of all entitlements went to households with incomes over $30,000 and a fourth to households with incomes over $50,000. A fifth of American children live in poverty, ill-housed and ill-nourished, and meanwhile, each of the 30,000 largest farmers in the country received $50,000 or more in direct cash benefits. Considering only tax breaks, those households under $10,000 received $131 yearly while those making over $100,000 fared over thirty times as well with an average yearly tax subsidy of $3,595. These federal entitlements and tax subsidies constitute two-thirds of the federal budget over which the government has any immediate control, which excluded the savings and loan bailout and interest on the national debt. Such a system is unfair to both beneficiaries and taxpayers and grossly unfair to those with the greatest need, who originally constituted the justification for the establishment of most entitlements.

The cost of the minimum wage is paid for by the higher costs of goods and services. The only beneficiary is the lower end worker at the expense of all, including other lower end workers. If an employer must pay four dollars an hour for work that under free market conditions would bring two dollars an hour, one person remains unemployed and the other overpaid. This unavoidable fact was proven after the minimum wage was increased by forty-five cents in 1989, a move that the U.S. Department of Labor estimated would result in the loss of 200,000 jobs among the young and unskilled. The number of jobs lost,

---

*In addition, the Social Security tax base has plummeted from 46 workers per recipient in 1945 to three workers per recipient in 1992, and is still shrinking (*Statistical Abstract of the U.S.,* 1992).

however, was not 200,000 or the 186,000 predicted by the U.S. Chamber of Commerce; 489,000 jobs were lost. Before the new minimum wage went into effect 624,000 black teenagers had jobs; a year later the number had fallen by 12 percent to 550,000, constituting 30 percent of the jobs lost as a result of the new minimum wage.

Universal rights are not those dependent on government-coerced transfer payments or the earnings of others. Rights are universal only if they impact identically at all times in all places and result in no cost to others. Our basic rights and freedoms are civil and economic, allowing absolute freedom of the individual to do precisely as he pleases as long as he harms no one else. Our civil freedoms from government interference include freedom of speech, religion, and association. The Constitution seeks to protect core freedoms of the individual from majority rule, which is often a fortuitous coalition of minorities. Necessary economic freedoms should include the right to own and transfer property without government and majority interference. Without property rights, there can be no civil rights. Because these rights erode over time with small but gradually increasing government interference, we tend to retain only the right to vote on how the government will further restrain formerly sacrosanct rights.

The *Lexicon of Economic Thought* (1989), published in Canada, contains definitions illustrating comparative economic concepts. Politics is defined, courtesy of H. L. Mencken, as an election determining the futures market in stolen property. Social justice is defined as nonexistent; only individuals can be just or unjust, or be treated justly or unjustly. The excuse of government expansion for social justice purposes is similarly oxymoronic. Economic justice is explained:

> While entitlements are always expressed positively, such as, "she has a right to support from the state," the truth of the relationship is quite different. In fact, the only way somebody can be delivered the right to support is if some other person is denied access to the resources they have earned. In the most prosaic terms, for every person who receives a dollar they didn't earn, somebody else earns a dollar they don't receive [less fifty or eighty percent to pay middle-man government].

Why should any taxpayer be required to contribute money to subsidize tobacco growers, or steel, or agriculture? If these industries cannot compete without taxpayer subsidy they should cease doing business and their former employees should seek employment in more efficient competitive industries. The subsidization of inefficiency causes the loss of competitive edge in international commerce. It's inefficient to buy American if the American product, though competitively priced, is of lower quality than those made elsewhere. It's similarly inefficient for people in other countries to buy domestic products when those produced here are of higher quality and competitively priced.

Government regulation doesn't protect consumers, but instead harms them by creating a producer's cartel, limiting competition and placing barriers to market entry. This stifles competition, removing pressure to lower prices or raise quality, thus harming consumers. While Eastern Europe rejects government planning and control, the West increasingly embraces government planning and control. Marx and Engels described the process in *The Communist Manifesto* (1848): "The theory of the Communists can be summed up in a single sentence: Abolition of private property." This is an inherent flaw in Communist theory because without private property there can be neither individual freedom nor political rights. For example, unless an individual is allowed to own a printing press and the building in which it is housed, there can be no freedom of the press. A press owned by the government or allowed by government sufferance on government property cannot constitute a free press. Neither can there be freedom of speech if criticism of the government is forbidden on government property and all property is owned by the government, which means there also would be no place to freely assemble. Property rights are the key to human rights and political freedom.

The ten steps to abolishing private property described by Marx and Engels include a progressive income tax (the U.S. income tax has never been progressive) and "free" public schools. Once the taxation level reaches 100 percent pure communism/socialism has been reached; there's no more private property. We're only 40 percent along the road in the United States, while Sweden is at 60 percent. Most of the entitlement portion of the U.S. budget, however, goes to transfers of wealth from one part of society (primarily the productive) to another segment of society (the relatively wealthy and the nonproductive). We've trained the nonproductive to be nonproductive by promising the benefits which we must yearly raise taxes to provide because of the inflationary effect of necessary taxes and the increasingly rewarded nonproductive members of society. Joseph Heller could write a book describing the evolution of the U.S. government, which like the U.S. military could be described as *Catch-22*. Any large bureaucracy is substantially similar.

All Western democracies share the inherent defect of encouraging irresponsibility and nonproductivity. The average government spending for the European Community rose from 36 percent of GNP in 1967 to 51 percent by 1987. Canadian government spending rose from 32 percent to 46 percent and Japanese from 18 percent to 33 percent in the same period. Ludwig von Mises described the choices in *Human Action* (1966):

> Laissez faire does not mean: Let soulless mechanical forces operate. It means: Let each individual choose how he wants to cooperate in the social division of labor; let the consumers determine what the entrepreneurs should produce. Planning means: Let the government alone choose and enforce its rulings by the apparatus of coercion and compulsion.

Free market pricing, or capitalism, works best without government interference. The alternative economic system of communism/socialism, which is more alive in the West than in the formerly communist regimes, requires substantial and continuing government control, which is why it failed, and illustrates why its Western cousin, capitalistic socialism, must eventually fail. Government bureaucracy necessarily leads to inefficiency and an inability to compete, which Lenin foresaw in a letter dated February 19, 1921: "The greatest danger is that the work of planning the state economy may be bureaucratized. . . . A complete, integrated, real plan for us at present equals 'a bureaucratic utopia.' Don't chase it." Any bureaucracy develops its own agenda (compare the Curia in the Vatican, which will survive all popes), is self-perpetuating, cannot shrink on threat of death, and exists to exert more control. Such is the nature of both government and organized religion.

Bureaucracy under a capitalistic economic system is no better than bureaucracy under communism. A 1989 General Accounting Office investigation of the Pentagon found the military had bought $30 billion worth of unneeded items. *Webster's New International Dictionary* defines bureaucracy: "a system of carrying on the business of government by means of departments or bureaus, . . . in general, such a system which has become narrow, rigid, and formal, depends on precedent, and lacks initiative and resourcefulness." George Roche in his book, *America by the Throat: The Stranglehold of the Federal Bureaucracy,* cites prime examples of the waste of government bureaucracy, such as federal mousetrap regulations 700 pages long or a $97,000 grant for a professorial study of "the social and behavorial relationships" in a Peruvian brothel. Pretty funny until we realize we paid for it, and there are numerous other examples, such as $62,000 to determine the length of the average flight attendant's nose (2.2 inches); $107,000 to explore the sex life of the Japanese quail; $84,000 to find out why people fall in love; $46,000 to find out how long it takes to cook eggs for breakfast; $100,000 to find out why people don't like liver or beets; and $219,000 to teach college students how to watch television. We tolerate these examples because they cost only fractions of a cent per taxpayer, but to quote Thomas Paine, "Public money ought to be touched with the most scrupulous conscientiousness of honor. It is not the produce of riches only, but the hard earnings of labor and poverty. It is drawn even from the bitterness of want and misery. Not a beggar passes, or perishes in the streets, whose mite is not in that mass."

The Council for Citizens against Government Waste, located in Washington, D.C., estimates that waste accounts for twenty-five cents of each tax dollar, with fifty-eight cents for the national debt and perhaps seventeen cents for "essential" services.

During the 1980s under a Republican and theoretically anti-big government president, Ronald Reagan, the size of the federal bureaucracy tripled. By 1988 the federal bureaucracy cost $4,000 for each child and adult in the United States. The reason was not the disdain of ordinary Americans for individual liberty and responsibility, but our sheer laziness and refusal to accept personal responsibility for much of anything.

Farm subsidies in 1980 cost $3 billion; when Reagan left office they'd increased to $26 billion a year, far above the percent increases in defense and health care benefits. Today's farmer is not the farmer my father was, a sole practitioner farming a few hundred acres. Farming today is big business, with most of our billions of dollars in subsidies going to corporate farming interests. The average 1989 income of the full-time American farmer was $168,000, and he was a millionaire; the average American income was $38,742. Our farm subsidies are the equivalent of giving each farmer two new Mercedes-Benz automobiles yearly. We pay farmers to kill 1.6 million cows a year and to leave 61 million acres unplanted, almost doubling our food prices while millions are hungry here and around the world. The annual subsidy for *each* dairy cow exceeds the per capita income for half the world's population. As noted by James Bovard, author of *The Farm Fiasco* (1990), "With the $260 billion that government and consumers have spent on farm subsidies since 1980, Uncle Sam could have bought every farm, barn and tractor in 33 states. The average American head of household worked almost a week a year in 1986 and 1987 simply to pay for welfare for fewer than a million farmers." The goal is artificial scarcity to maintain high prices. If we planted our farmland and raised our cattle to capacity, the United States would dominate the world agricultural markets. The prices of wheat and corn would tumble, which doesn't seem a radical result in a hungry world. To survive, farmers would switch to more lucrative crops, and some would leave farming. The correct number of farmers, and the correct numbers in any business or profession, is the number who can make a living under free market conditions. The alternative is waste, paternalism, protectionism, and hunger. The House of Representatives in 1990 voted 327–91 to further increase farm subsidies. The Senate refused by a 66–30 vote to limit subsidies to those farmers with gross sales of less than $500,000 yearly. The resulting bill cost $53 billion over five years. The majority argued that without subsidies production would double or triple and prices would drop, hurting the family farmer, and subsidies would then have to go up, hurting the taxpayer. This is true. If subsidies stopped, the family farmer would go out of business because the small operation cannot compete with the large corporate farming enterprise. We must choose between efficiency and waste; low food prices and hunger for millions; logic and sentiment.

Many western farmers double-dip their subsidies, according to an Interior Department audit in 1990, collecting for both crop and irrigation subsidies. Irrigation subsidies in 1986 included $66 million to irrigate lands producing surplus crops, while the same farmers received $379 million to limit surplus crop production. The Department of Agriculture refused to support a bill to eliminate the dual subsidies.

The way farm subsidies work also encourages depletion of the soil and waste. If a farmer reduces a subsidized crop to plant another crop, such as alfalfa to replenish the soil's nutrients, the subsidy is cut. Subsidies insulate farmers from the true cost of farming, resulting in soil erosion, loss of nutrients, and increased use of chemicals. Federal disaster insurance discourages the prudence of diversification, placing the entire risk of loss on the government, which is us, the taxpayers. The most insidious aspect of subsidies, however, is the resulting absolute loss of wealth. Crop restrictions enrich farmers at the expense of consumers and, by discouraging production, cause a net decrease in wealth.

The Department of Agriculture is an anachronism created under Abraham Lincoln to serve a nation of farmers. The USDA in 1992 received a budget larger than that of 160 countries and smaller than only 17 countries. Fewer than 2 percent of Americans live on farms. In 1960 the USDA spent less than $6 billion; thirty years later USDA spending exceeded $62 billion. Have the needs of farms increased over tenfold in thirty years? The USDA budget adopted in August 1992 included $175 million for market promotion of U.S. companies overseas; $500,000 for McDonald's Corp. to promote Chicken McNuggets, $450,000 for Campbell Soup Co. to advertise V-8 Juice in Latin America, $150,000 for Canada's Seagram & Sons to market whisky in Europe. The U.S. Senate continued a $23 million subsidy to 3,000 honey producers, averaging over $7500 each, a program started to meet sugar shortages in World War II, fifty years ago.

The USDA subsidizes 363,000 farms with the top 1 percent receiving 30 percent of the money, as much as the bottom 80 percent. The USDA exists primarily to benefit millionaires in agribusiness, suporting 108,000 USDA bureaucrats, one for every three recipients.

Thousands of small businesses file bankruptcy weekly, which does not include those simply closing their doors, yet no one proposes a massive bailout of this source of jobs. Why must small or large farmers benefit from the public dole? If certain crops cannot be raised economically, the business should fail. This is the way the market is supposed to work.

The 105 nation-members of the General Agreement on Tariffs and Trade (GATT) met in Geneva in 1990 after four years of talks resulting in a tentative agreement to reduce tariffs and gradually open free trade worldwide. The talks collapsed after the European Community (twelve members) refused to eliminate most farm subsidies over a ten-year period. Amazingly, the United States had been willing to do so. The Europeans would agree only to reduce farm subsidies by 30 percent over ten years, continuing its $100 billion yearly subsidies to its ten million wealthy farmers.

Another example of popular, yet illogical government giveaways is disaster relief. If I prefer to spend my money on a VCR instead of homeowner's insurance and my house burns down when struck by lightning, should the taxpayers pay for my new house? The answer seems obvious. I took a risk and lost. If I were wealthier than my neighbors, the answer is even clearer. Those living in San Francisco are somewhat wealthier than the average American, yet taxpayers paid to rebuild their houses when struck by an earthquake, though earthquake insurance was available and San Francisco homeowners may have preferred instead to buy a second BMW. Should investors have been compensated when the stock market dropped 500 points in October 1987, a disaster that made both the San Francisco earthquake and hurricane Hugo look puny? Is a hurricane victim simply more photogenic than a stock market victim? When risk-takers are responsible for their miscalculations they take only rational risks. When all taxpayers are jointly responsible, recklessness is encouraged. We've become so dependent on government that we expect it to do everything for us. Because most people in a democracy desire some government benefits for themselves, government obligingly increases its functions, incidentally benefitting the bureaucracy.

Government works equally badly where it seeks to repeal the laws of supply and demand, such as with rent control. New York City established rent control during WWII in order to prevent wartime profiteering. The result was accurately predicted by Swedish socialist economist Assar Lindbeck, who wrote, "rent control appears to be the most efficient technique presently known to destroy a city— except for bombing." Attempts to take advantage of shortages by price gouging are futile in a free market, except over the short term. Excess profits attract additional investors who increase supplies and drive prices down. Eastern Europe has learned this lesson. Perhaps the Western democracies will learn it too. When prices are kept low by rent control, investors refuse to build more units or improve existing units because there's no incentive.

Similar to communism or socialism, the impetus behind rent control is altruistic, to keep rents fair and affordable. As with communism or socialism, the opposite effect results. Affluent tenants reap the benefits, while poor and potential renters wait in a static and depressed rental market, there being no incentive to build further apartments. Landlords are able to pick their tenants, which encourages under-the-table bribes and discrimination against minorities and those with children. With no incentive to maintain less expensive apartments, landlords have simply walked away. Five hundred thousand apartments were abandoned in New York City by 1990, destroying neighborhoods and depleting apartments that would otherwise be available to the poor. The only beneficiaries are existing tenants, who receive a windfall when rents are artificially kept lower than the value of the space.

There is but one place on earth where capitalism operates without fetters, without subsidies, without minimum wages, without barriers to market entry, without rent controls, without licensing, and without a government bureaucracy overseeing every aspect of private and business life, and that one place may disappear from the face of the earth in 1997. The shining example of capitalism is Hong Kong, which has avoided the socialistic and bureaucratic approach to capitalism practiced by the Western democracies. Hong Kong has no tariffs or other restraints on international trade. (The United States imposes more tariffs than any other country in the world, including Japan.) Hong Kong owes its success to limited government and absolutely free markets. Eliminating tariffs eliminates inefficient industries so that no buggy whip factory remains in Hong Kong, though the equivalent is found throughout the Western democracies. Only the market determines what is best produced, not central planners or Congressmen intent on protecting their largest campaign contributors and the military-industrial complex. The money saved by not paying a tariff allows people to buy commodities and raw materials as cheaply as possible, giving them an unbeatable competitive edge. French economist Frederic Bastiat described the savings in this way: "When a product—coal, iron, wheat or textiles—comes to us from abroad, and when we can acquire it for less labor than if we produced it ourselves, the difference is a gratuitous gift that is conferred on us." The economy of Hong Kong exists and prospers on these gifts, while the United States rejects most similar gifts out of hand.

Because Hong Kong has no barriers to market entry, no licensing, no government-regulated boards or other bureaucratic devices stifling the economy, it expanded from 1,050 separate industries in 1947, employing 64,000 people, to 17,239 industries in 1970, employing 589,505 people. Notwithstanding its tiny size it easily outproduces countries as large as New Zealand. *Fodor's Hong Kong and Macau* in its "Doing Business" section describes the reason for Hong Kong's success:

> Hong Kong is one of those rare places on earth that plays the free-trade game according to the classical rule. . . . A national of any nation may do business or set up business (so long as it is legal). . . . The rules of business in Hong Kong are few. Whether you are a visiting businessperson or a potential entrepreneur, you will not go far wrong if you remember this: You are in a "free country." If you succeed, you can take all the credit; if you fail, you must take all the blame. The authorities give some help (but no subsidies, tax reliefs, or featherbeds); what is more important, they don't hinder you. . . . There is no capital gains tax . . . income arisen from abroad goes tax free. . . . The Hong Kong salaries tax return is one simple sheet. . . . There is no income tax withholding. . . . The government intervention in business affairs is minimal.

Compare the situation in the Western democracies, which are actually socialist regimes with heavy-handed bureaucracies existing to transfer wealth and stifle the economy at every turn. Hong Kong will revert to the Chinese in 1997. The Chinese promise business as usual, according to the accords signed between Margaret Thatcher and Deng Xiaoping, who ordered the Chinese army to fire on Chinese students in June 1989. The present form of Hong Kong may disappear forever in 1997 because the Chinese may not allow the last jewel of capitalism to sit next to one of the few remaining examples of communist economic failure. Meanwhile, the United States acts more like China than like Hong Kong in erecting trade barriers.

Civilization began with self-sufficient villages, then developed self-sufficient city-states, which traded little among themselves. For the last few centuries we've developed nation-states, also largely self-sufficient and only recently beginning extensive trade. Each nation was and is geared toward self-sufficiency, with inefficiency resulting when tasks are divided primarily within a discrete geographical area. Finally we're moving toward a global economy with economic tasks divided among nations and the entire world growing toward economic interdependence. Because economic considerations eclipse political and religious considerations, this global community is the world's best chance at peace. A regressive alternative is seen in Eastern Europe. For one marketplace to work to everyone's advantage, all trade barriers between countries must disappear. The evolution has begun. In 1988 the United States and Canada agreed to gradually drop all trade barriers; a similar agreement by the United States and Canada with Mexico will eventually be reached, making most of North America a free-trade zone, likely to be joined by Costa Rica, Belize, Honduras, and Panama. Perhaps Guatamala, Nicaragua, and El Salvador will also join. The twelve nations of the European Economic Community will likely be joined by the other countries in Europe, both East and West. A free-trade agreement between Australia and New Zealand went into effect in December 1988. Brazil and Argentina are negotiating a free-trade agreement that may eventually lead to a South American Economic Community. When these "continental" groups coalesce and all trade barriers evaporate, involuntary poverty will mostly disappear and the world (eventually including Africa) will share more equally in a relatively high level of wealth.

Abolishing trade barriers and allowing free market entry are analogous to my proposed system of ethics: do as you please with your money and your business, as long as you harm no one else. This provides freedom of choice, encourages cooperation and individual development of abilities, provides automatic account-ability and wealth for large numbers of people by their own efforts without government giveaways, and limits the exercise of power and control by others, including government. An opposite type of economic system, whether government-controlled communism or socialism, seeks and exercises control over others for reasons of paternalism or other rationalizations such as religion, which harms others by removing self-reliance and the ability to improve individual circum-stances without taking from others. The United States is moving away from capitalism and toward socialism, notwithstanding the axiom that economic freedom breeds political freedom, as illustrated by Milton Friedman in recent decades. As U.S. citizens lose their freedoms to the crushing weight of laws controlling their every action and to excessive taxation based on the excuse of punishing victimless crimes and transferring wealth to the nonproductive, the economy moves closer to socialism. The pre-eminence of the United States in world politics and economics did not come from a government controlling all aspects of its citizens' lives, but from the central idea of individual sovereignty. We have lost the will to follow that guiding star.

The reason the West has uniformly rejected capitalism is the same reason many embraced the communist and socialist vision. We could theoretically achieve a social utopia by eliminating unemployment, bankruptcies, economic failure, and the personal embarrassment of having to rely upon charity when devastated by personal problems. Unfortunately, a healthy economy depends on information generated by individual economic failures to continue to be healthy. An analogy is survival of the fittest as necessary to biological progress and health. Unless the weak and unhealthy are allowed to fail, evolution halts as surely as economic health falters when resources are diverted into nonproductivity, inefficiency, or the avoidance of economic failure, even though the diversion is based on an altruistic notion of protecting the weak and the bankrupt. Undeniably, when a sufficient portion of resources are diverted to nonproductive uses, an economy must neces-sarily collapse. The government cannot protect all citizens against failure. At most, a privileged few obtain protection at the expense of everyone else. Seeking to protect individuals from failure encourages many failures, because individuals are no longer responsible for their actions. The marketplace, however, is the epitomy of fairness, because each individual is held responsible for individual choices.

Capitalism through the automatic mechanism of the market never dictates the best way to do anything. Taking opposite examples, cooperatives and labor unions, neither are mandated or prohibited under a capitalistic economy. If individuals freely agree to form a cooperative or a labor union, they may do so. If they do not wish to form a cooperative or a labor union, they are not required to do so.

How do morality and ethics fit into a capitalistic economy, or a political system that is limited in its powers, so that it may control only those who harm others? A capitalistic economic system is ethically neutral, being descriptive instead of prescriptive. Capitalism is not necessarily materialistic. Adam Smith, for instance, was more attuned to Henry David Thoreau than to Cornelius Vanderbilt or John D. Rockefeller. (See Adam Smith's *Theory of Moral Sentiments,* published seventeen years before *The Wealth of Nations.*) Smith recognized that capitalism can supply us with an array of gadgets, which is precisely what it does. It's up to us to decide whether any of these gadgets are worth owning. One can be both a capitalist and antimaterialistic. Capitalism can as easily satisfy our choices for less commercial things, such as education, books, ideas, and new methods of communication, as satisfy our desires for the gadgets filling our shopping malls. Goodness, humanity, and benevolence are the mainsprings of capitalism, arising from the opposite impulse, self-interest. Paradoxically, the marketplace looks after the welfare of people through the mechanism of their own self-interest. The profit motive spurs people to produce those items needed for pleasant living. Direct benevolence from government is self-defeating, creating a dependent nonproductive class with no incentive to provide for itself or others.

Neither is communism necessarily equatable to antimaterialism. The reason it crumbled in the East is that it failed to meet its material goals. Thus, capitalism represents an economic system that works well, nothing more and nothing less, with no inherently positive or negative moral aspects.

Government, organized religion, and cultural values, on the other hand, are prescriptive, imposing value judgments on their citizens and flock. Government, organized religion, and cultures operate under artificial rules, while capitalism operates under natural rules dictated by the market and human preferences. A communistic economy operates similarly to government and organized religion. Consider Zbigniew Brzezinski's description of communism (and how equally well it applies to organized religion) in his book *The Grand Failure* (1989):

> The Communist phenomenon represents a historical tragedy. Born out of an impatient idealism that rejected the injustice of the status quo, it sought a better and more humane society—but produced mass oppression. It optimistically reflected faith in the power of reason to construct a perfect community. It mobilized the most powerful emotions of love for humanity and of hatred for oppression on behalf of morally motivated social engineering. It thus captivated some of the brightest minds and some of the most idealistic hearts—yet it prompted some of the worst crimes of this or any century. . . . Communism's grand failure has thus involved, in summary form, the wasteful destruction of much social talent and the suppression of society's creative political life.

Compare the Soviet pogroms with the religious inquisitions and the current religious wars. The common intolerance of all stifles the individual. None are institutions of morality, though all were born from the highest of moral intentions.

How do morality and ethics relate to a free market system of economics? This question must be simplified before it may be logically analyzed and answered. First, is there a moral obligation for the wealthy, or the affluent middle class, to share their wealth with those having less? *If* the only moral exhortation is to harm no one else, then selfishly keeping wealth unnecessary for survival is not morally improper. Most people would likely prefer a system that reduces their taxes, increases the opportunities to acquire wealth, and allows them to personally direct their charitable giving, instead of a system that requires highly inefficient charitable giving through government welfare and similar transfer programs. Only if wealth has been obtained by harming others should it be mandatorily redistributed to those who have been harmed as a result.

A free market economy, though not protecting the individual against economic miscalculation and bankruptcy, has numerous other positive attributes that appear to overbalance the risk of failure. As pointed out by Adam Smith and David Hume, a free market economy provides an unending opportunity for obtaining not only basic necessities but also a comfortable standard of living through one's own efforts without depending on the charity of government, religion, or others. Lessening dependency on government strengthens individual initiative, character, and feelings of self-worth. A free market economy, especially global, brings together people of diverse cultural, religious, and philosophical creeds, which illustrates better than abstract religions that we are all more alike than different, thus encouraging trade and interdependence and discouraging petty religious, ethnic, and nationalistic antagonisms. Free market entry tends to blur class resentments because the poorest retain the opportunity to climb the class ladder as far as talent and political skills will allow. The intermixing of classes, cultures, religions, and ethnic groups necessitated by free trade causes each and all to obtain knowledge and understanding of each other, thus adding to the general level of world social knowledge, skills, specialization, and mutual understanding. A free market requires civility among its actors. One may not profitably do business on a long-term basis without a willingness to serve the customer, to compromise, to explain, and to display civil manners. Thus, free markets are the antithesis of isolation, parochialism, and war. One refrains naturally from bombing one's trading partners—a prime reason for the abolition of all national trade (and other) barriers between peoples. These are the tangible and enviable results of free market economics without trade barriers.

The opposite is illustrated by those institutions founded upon the highest of motives, but which in reality are contrary to individual freedom, achievement, and ethics. Thus have nationalism (worship of government) and organized religion perverted their ideals to set us one against another. The good guys (based on religion, ethnic group, or nationality) versus the bad guys (also based on religion, ethnicity, or nationality). Such divisions are inimical to the well-being and prosperity of both the species and the earth itself.

Two moral questions, racism and protection of the environment, illustrate how unfettered capitalism works. Racism is costly from an economic viewpoint. If an apartment must remain vacant because the landlord will not rent to a particular race, the landlord pays a cost the same as an employer who refuses to hire a particular minority. In a free market, the nondiscriminating businessman has the economic advantage. These facts were explored in *South Africa's War Against Capitalism* by Walter E. Williams (1989):

> The mere existence of South Africa's extensive [racial] regulatory laws is evidence enough that racial privilege is difficult through free market forces. Consider South Africa's job reservation laws, which mandate that certain jobs be performed by whites only. . . . The presence of job reservation laws suggests that at least some employers *would* hire blacks in the "white jobs." The fact that they would hire blacks to do white jobs neither requires nor suggests that these employers be necessarily any less white supremacist than anyone else. It does suggest that those employers who would hire blacks considered such a course of action to be an attractive alternative because blacks were willing to work for lower wages— "uncivilized wages"—than white workers. The business pursuit of profits—which caused employers to be less ardent supporters of the white supremacist doctrine— has always been the enemy of white privilege. This is why South Africa white workers resorted to government.

Williams concludes that "the whole ugly history of apartheid has been an attack on free markets and the rights of individuals, and a glorification of centralized government power . . . [Only when the people of South Africa, white, black, and others,] declare war against centralized government power" will there be progress toward freedom, economic and political.

This analysis of racism illustrates the fallacy of affirmative action. Under free market conditions, if one business discriminates for or against blacks, women, or Catholics in other than menial jobs, then its products will be or should be shunned by discriminated-against groups. The racially or otherwise discriminating business will not only be less efficient and competent, having excluded an entire group of talented workers or hiring a particular group to the exclusion of better qualified workers, but it will be less competitive if its products are avoided by consumers from the discriminated-against groups. A competing firm that hires women, blacks, or Catholics in positions of responsibility based on merit will attract business from those sectors and enjoy the talents of a diverse group of employees. Thus are racism, sexism, and other forms of discrimination contrary to the tenets of a free market system. If a firm fails to hire the best available talent for a job, no matter whether the pretext is altruistic (affirmative action) or discriminatory, that firm will hobble its competitive ability.* Although free markets may allow racism and other discriminatory behaviors to survive in the

---

*Barry Becker, 1992 recipient of the Nobel Prize for economics, concludes that social discrimination can exist only where markets are not fully competitive, because discrimination is economically inefficient and costly to its practitioner. (*University of Chicago Magazine,* December 1992, p. 13.)

short term, competitive advantage eventually will render these behaviors impotent. Efforts to end the historical effects of discrimination through affirmative action, however, are anticompetitive because they (1) discriminate against some other race, sex, or class; (2) fuel racial and other tensions among those passed over for the less qualified; (3) mandate a present harm to cure a past harm suffered by other individuals, constituting equally insidious discrimination; and (4) increase government power in order to insure enforcement. Every increase in government power reduces individual freedom. Vigorous education of our young that we are all the same, distinguished only by ability, no matter our race, religion, sex, or nationality, is a better solution to discrimination than affirmative or discriminatory action.

Prof. Richard Epstein of the University of Chicago Law School suggests, in *Forbidden Grounds: The Case Against Employment Discrimination Laws* (1992), that the laws banning discrimination by nongovernment employers should be repealed, though at the time of its passage he felt the 1964 Civil rights Act "was long overdue, that patterns and practices of discrimination that existed . . . were apt targets of legislative correction." Epstein concludes that laws prohibiting discrimination by private employers "are an unjustified limitation on the principle of freedom of contract," undermining traditional hiring based on merit, encouraging evasive and inefficient employment practices. Antidiscrimination laws impose enormous costs and actually mandate discrimination in favor of various races and other categories of discrimination. Business avoids neighborhoods with protected minorities to avoid the mandates of proportional hiring, thus harming the supposedly protected class. Epstein suggests the best way to discourage discrimination is to encourage a free and open marketplace allowing business to easily locate in areas of efficient and inexpensive labor, instead of being driven, for example, across the Mexican border or to developing countries.

Our environmental problems would also be better handled through the free market mechanism, according to Tibor Machan's book, *Private Rights, Public Illusions* (1990). Pollution remaining within the boundaries of an owner's property is not a problem because without dispersion no one else is harmed. The property owner bears all damages, which are confined to him alone and reflected in the resale value of the property. As in any moral system, pollution straying across property boundaries and thus harming others would be absolutely prohibited. If such pollution cannot be contained, its creation would be prohibited or full compensation would be paid to those harmed. If the condition cannot be avoided, then either production would be prohibited or compensation would be paid. The fact that a majority in society would vote to allow a pollution source because it provides an item desired by the majority would be irrelevant without full recompense to those injured. The rights of individuals become the touchstone of societal and governmental action, thus assuring that neither the majority nor a populist leader threatens individual rights to be left alone and to do as the individual pleases as long as he harms no one else.

Most wealth is not created by taking from others. Most is created by consensual transactions benefitting both parties. People voluntarily enter only into transactions that provide personal advantage, which does not necessarily imply advantage over another party. Some would argue that both parties to a contract or transaction don't necessarily benefit, that paying the lowest salary the market will permit exploits workers, for instance. The acceptance of a low wage offer always means there is no better salary available, however; otherwise the worker would hold out for a higher salary.

The only way government can provide assistance to the poor is by *less than* a zero-sum system, taking wealth from one and giving what's left over, after the expenses of government are taken out, to the poor and other needy. For every ten dollars collected, bureaucratic government transfers far less to the recipient (between one and five dollars). Honest charities and beneficent individuals are more efficient, screen deservedness better, and don't force giving. Because the creation of wealth through a free market is not zero-sum, the other parties to transactions with wealthy-becoming individuals are similarly benefitted, adding proportionately to all wealth. Wealth should be created only by pleasing others in mutually beneficial transactions: Great wealth is created only by pleasing the masses.

Government-forced transfers of wealth to the poor destroy accountability, while voluntary giving strengthens accountability. In addition to government waste, special interest groups squander resources lobbying government for the transfer of wealth to themselves, whether they are poor or wealthy. Democratic government always responds to powerful people who make large campaign contributions. This fact was vividly illustrated by an investigative reporter series on the Phoenix City Council. Firms affiliated with major campaign contributors received over $10 million in unbid city contracts after the October 1991 election. Special interest money constituted 82 percent of the $500,000 contributed to council members; campaigns and council members distributed millions of dollars in aid to developers who made large contributions. (David Rosmiller and Brad Patten, *Phoenix Gazette,* January 1993.) Voluntary charitable giving occurs only when the giver is convinced (rightly or wrongly) of the efficiency of the transferring agency and certain the intended recipient will receive most of the gift. If taxes were lowered, more money would be available for charitable giving. No one knows precisely who gets what from the money commandeered by government, except that much of it is wasted.

There are sufficient numbers of us who are naturally altruistic that it shouldn't be necessary for government taxes to subsidize the poor, the rich, and the special interests, for multiple reasons. First, it appears immoral to take tax money from the poor or middle class for transfer to wealthy farmers, steelmakers, and such, at least as immoral as taking anything from anyone without their express consent, which is why it is equally immoral to tax the wealthy and middle class to transfer money to those poor who could earn their own way if not disincentived to do so by the structure of our governments. The cause of poverty should be a consideration in determining whether the particular poor person merits assistance, but that decision has never been competently made by government. If a person is poor because of laziness, should anyone be compelled to shift their wealth to the undeserving? If not, should people who are only temporarily between jobs be assisted by all taxpayers, or should both society and government at least attempt to first allow charities, families, and beneficent individuals to provide assistance instead of controlling the legally obtained wealth of others and mandating its transfer to the temporarily needy? It is human nature that one does what one must.

Government is a bad Good Samaritan because it must make eligibility rules for charitable assistance based on income and asset levels. Any potential assistees know they must have little or no income or assets to qualify and magically, as is wont with human nature, income is reduced or assets hidden. Thus, any charitable assistance program administered by government contains an unavoidable incentive for the recipient to remain or become poor, or to lie, succumbing to the built-in moral hazard. Programs to aid the poor thus encourage poverty, helping to expand government programs, which also works to the benefit of government employees, whose salary and influence is dependent on the size of the program administered.

Private charity is a far better Good Samaritan because aid is granted based on individual need and not on general and easily manipulated income and asset criteria. Private aid is more closely monitored for true need because funding comes from uncoerced and limited sources as opposed to an almost unlimited supply of taxpayers. Private donors scrutinize the efficiency of the charity to make sure little of the money is spent on administration and most reaches the intended recipients. Government harbors the opposite incentive, to skim as much as possible for administration, leaving proportionately less for the originally intended beneficiary.

In summary, government aid causes both the number of the poor and the number of government employees to grow, resulting in advancement of government employees while retarding advancement of the poor. The increase in government employees reduces the tax base and burdens the economy. Success of a government program is marked by its expansion, not by its disappearance. Massive government programs cannot become personally acquainted with aid recipients and determine their true needs. No one spends money as carefully when the money is someone else's or comes in avalanches from hordes of unknown taxpayers.

Examples of how government naturally works exist in our major programs. When the income tax was passed in 1913 our Congressmen promised that no one making *under* $200,000 a year would ever have to pay income tax. The actual income tax imposed in 1913 amounted to 1 percent on income over $3,000 ($4,000 for married couples), equivalent to over $50,000 now. Until WWII only 3 percent of the population paid any income tax. During WWII Congress, however, adopted the temporary Victory Tax withholding system, and by 1950 the average U.S. family of four paid 2 percent as income tax. Now the vast majority pay federal income taxes at a higher rate than those making over $200,000 a year, averaging 24 percent for a family of four in 1990.* Americans with incomes between $50,000 and $200,000 pay taxes at the marginal rate of 33 percent, and less than 1 percent of taxpayers making over $200,000 a year pay as high as 28 percent.

If the federal government could be sufficiently reduced (or an alternative point of tax found) to allow abolition of the nonprogressive income tax, individual savings would be encouraged, which would provide capital for economic expansion and vitality, and better jobs for most. Corporations could compete nationally, putting income tax savings into research, development, production, and marketing. U.S. goods would compete more favorably in foreign markets because their price would not include a 34 percent income tax. The Internal Revenue Service and most other government employees would be released to the private sector for productive labor. We'd take home all we earned and foreign capital would flow into the economy. We'd have little use for accountants, CPAs, and attorneys.

When President Reagan moved into the White House the national debt approached $1 trillion. With horror, Reagan told Congress that $1 trillion in $1,000 bills would stack sixty-seven miles high. It grew 56 percent in the Reagan years, and when Ronnie left office, the $1,000 bills cleared 200 miles. By 1993, even with reading the lips of Mr. Clinton, the stack cleared 268 miles, or $4 trillion. The uncuttable part of the debt is the $200 billion a year for interest, which is 15 percent of the budget. The cost of interest is more than the entire federal budget was in 1968. The interest on the national debt means that everyone living west of the Missippissi River buys exactly nothing with their federal income tax dollars, not one soldier, bullet, missile, food stamp, or the latest Congressional pay raise. Instead, every cent of federal income tax paid by those living west of the Mississippi goes to pay the interest on the national debt, according to Lee Iacocca's April 16, 1990, article in *Newsweek,* titled "Let's End the 'Poltroonery.' " Iacocca concluded that we have no hope of reducing the national debt. Our only hope is to avoid raising it further so that with inflation it will disappear, relatively, over time. The impact of the national debt on the United States economy is devastating. Iacocca summarized what that means:

> For the American businessman, this burden of debt is heavy indeed. It means higher capital costs that he has to carry like a piano on his back while he's trying to compete with companies from Japan and other places around the world.

---

*The cost of federal regulation is more than that of federal taxes, according to the conservative Heritage Foundation, which estimates a burden of between $8,338 and $17,134 per household; federal taxes average $11,000 per household. For example, 95 percent of the cost of children's vaccines and a third the cost of single-engine aircraft are for complying with federal regulations. During the first three years the Bush administration, over 14,000 pages of new federal regulations were added to the Federal Register, totalling 67,716 pages in mid-1992. The number of federal employees administering federal regulations rose 20 percent, from 105,000 in the last year of the Reagan administration to 125,000, beating the rate of inflation by 18 percent. The total cost of federal regulations was estimated between $881 billion and $1.65 trillion compared to $1.05 trillion for taxes in 1992.

As long as the federal government swallows up two thirds of all American savings every year, American companies will be paying through the nose for the investment capital they need for new plants and the development of new products. For example, the real cost of capital in this country right now is roughly 7 percent. In Japan, it's about 3 percent. That four-point spread means that if both Chrysler and Toyota decide to develop a new engine and spread the cost over five years, it will cost Chrysler about $500 million, compared to $408 million for Toyota. Who's going to produce that engine at the most competitive cost?

What are the odds of government spending ever dropping so the national debt can be maintained at its current level? President Bush's sole pledge was that he wouldn't raise taxes (and he couldn't even keep that one promise), not that he wouldn't raise the national debt, which is raised daily by borrowing to pay on past debt. If all other factors were held constant, every $50 billion reduction in the national debt would reduce interest rates by 1 percent, lower the trade deficit by $25 to $30 billion, and increase investment by $15 to $20 billion, which would fuel economic growth, lowering the costs of unemployment insurance and welfare. When Ronald Reagen announced fiscal conservatism in 1980, the debt service on the national debt took 8.5 percent of the budget; the debt took 15 percent of the budget in 1990.

As suggested by Scott Burns in a November 1990 column, "If any publicy held business reported its affairs in the same way that our government does, it would have a qualified opinion from its auditors, and the officers of the company would be under investigation by the Securities and Exchange Commission and destined for jail cells. This is not hyperbole." Examples given by Burns include the accounting documents issued by the Treasury, which calculate the percentage of tax burden without including the deficit debt service, which is one-seventh of the budget. How would auditors or the SEC react if a company excluded one-seventh of its liabilities and debt?

The 1986 tax reform act closed a several-billion-dollar loophole, allowing the accelerated deduction of depreciation on real estate and related limited partnerships. The result was a nationwide tailspin in the real estate industry, resulting in a $500 billion savings-and-loan debacle that worked out to $2,000 for every man, woman, and child in the country. Thus the government collected a few billion more in taxes at a hundred times the cost. The real estate slump (and tight money) formed the basis for the 1990 recession. The only thing known for certain about government is that when it tinkers with free markets, everyone suffers. Real estate and limited partnership tax loopholes fueled overbuilding in commercial and residential real estate markets, leading to their collapse when the loopholes were closed. If there'd been no tax break (or taxes) in the first place, the overvaluation and resulting recession would not have occurred. If there'd been no S&L deposit insurance protecting those relatively wealthy people able to save money, the S&L directors would have been more careful with their investments and depositors would have been more careful where they put their deposits, another illustration of government moral hazard.

Most of our waste and debt was incurred in connection with the sacred cow of defense; not solely the defense of the United States, but also of Japan and Europe, and now of the world as its policeman. Military spending grew 50 percent in the 1980s, though the United States was involved in no major wars, only little wars in El Salvador, Nicaragua, Columbia, Panama, and the Middle East. We spent three times as much on the military in 1990, including military might on behalf of Japan and Europe, as on all domestic entitlement programs ($300 billion versus $100 billion). Japan and West Germany spent about 2 percent of their GNP on defense, shifting their allocable budget into research and development to benefit their economies. We spent our government research and development money on exotic new weapons, which when inevitably discovered by the other side resulted in more expensive counterweapons, reducing security at an ever-increasing cost. The United States has been on a crash Star Wars program to create an umbrella to repel ICBMs. For the 1991 budget Bush proposed increasing Star Wars funding to $4.8 billion, which was $1 billion more than approved for 1990. If we have the bad luck to perfect Star Wars, we'll have created a weapon deadlier than ICBMs.

The Apache helicopter, manufactured by McDonnell Douglas Helicopter Co. in Mesa, Arizona, cost $14 million each in 1990, but could not be flown in the rain because their electronics were too sensitive. In Panama the electronics had to be dried out in kitchen ovens. Almost half have problems before they run, and once they are running, something goes wrong an average of every fifty-four minutes. After one day of combat in Panama, four of the six assigned helicopters were grounded by locally irreparable breakdowns, despite twenty-four-hour maintainence by army mechanics. Its rotors cost $65,000 in 1990 and lasted 164 hours, instead of the expected 1,500 hours. Its 30mm cannon was designed to fire 4,000 rounds before failure, but failed after 1,000 firings.

It fared no better in the Persian Gulf "War," suffering severe communications system problems, allegedly caused by company fraud in falsifying data to meet army requirements, according to an engineer retired from the company. The engineer's attorney said, "The Apache [helicopter] was regarded by the troops in the Persian Gulf War as the most unreliable piece of crap they've ever come in contact with." It was manufactured by graduates of the American public school system and purchased through appropriations passed by congressmen elected through campaign contributions from McDonnell Douglas and other military-industrial PAC committees.

The military seems to exaggerate its weapons expertise. After the Persian Gulf War we were finally told that only 7 percent of our bombs were smart bombs, the other 93 percent being indiscriminate killers. The Pentagon admitted in March 1992 that the ballyhooed Patriot missile destroyed only 10 of 86 SCUD missiles instead of the 80 percent success rate claimed in Saudi Arabia and the 50 percent claimed in Israel. Nine Patriot missiles crashed and exploded in populated areas, but the death count is unavailable.

Now that the Eastern Communist bloc has crumbled and the Soviet Union appears to be no threat to United States security, it would seem logical that the government would rush to cut military spending in order to cut taxes, spur the economy, and relieve the taxpayer. Instead, Congress called the situation a "peace dividend" to be spread among its favorite programs, which did not include reducing the national debt or putting Social Security on a self-perpetuating basis. President Bush called for the United States to take on the role of global policeman. Leaders in other countries have asked when their citizens will be able to vote in our elections, since we are acting as their policemen without their representation.

There must be a use for all our military hardware or our top-ranking generals and other officers would be jobless, so we found a use. We needed the hardware to kill 120,000 Iraqis because one Iraqi, whom we hated and couldn't legally kill, threatened "our" oil. Do we comprehend what it means to slaughter 150,000 people in a "contest" so lopsided that the allies suffered 343 casualties in combat, accidents, and "friendly fire" while five million Iraquis lost their homes or jobs?

The 1990 budget required $1.2 trillion, giving lip-service to cutting the federal deficit by transferring an "excess" $63.1 billion in FICA payments from Social Security to the deficit. Military spending increased to $303 billion, up $7 billion from 1989, which our cost-conscious president pointed out was 2 percent below the level necessary to compensate for inflation. The savings was a phantom, acting initially only to slow growth; spending increased 11.7 percent across the board, except for defense. A Congressman speaking for the White House said:

> The mission of the United States is to remain an important player in Europe, Asia and this hemisphere and the purpose of our Armed Forces is not simply to contain the Soviet Union, [but] rather . . . to extend our influence, to be the glue factor, the peacemaker, the honest broker, the keeper of the sea lanes everywhere all over the world.

The Chairman of the Joint Chiefs of Staff said, "We've got to keep our shingle out: 'Superpower, leader of our way of life, prepared to defend our interest and the interest of our friends' [whether our friends agree or not]." As pointed out by Joseph Sobran, "The Soviet threat is gone. The danger of a nuclear war is nil. We can forget about an invasion of Western Europe. The Soviets are incapable of recapturing even their Eastern European empire—and they show no signs of wanting to."

Two weeks before the United States declared war on Iraq the Comptroller General estimated that it would cost $130 billion to keep U.S. troops in the Middle East *without war*. After the war began it was estimated to cost almost a billion dollars daily. To induce Egypt to support the U.S. position, we forgave its $10 billion debt. The three-year deficit-reduction cuts in the 1990 budget disappeared in one month from the beginning of the Persian Gulf war. We went to war to kick some butt and we did; the butt of the American taxpayer, fortunately harming no one else except tens of thousands of faceless foreigners. We continued trade sanctions after the "war," according to the Iraqi health minister, killing 98,669 people from August 1990 to the end of 1991 because of shortages of medicine, malnutrition, and lack of sanitation.

The "peace dividend," long since spent, engendered a "feeding frenzy" among Congressmen, according to the *National Journal.* Some Congressional leaders called for national health insurance at a first-year cost of $86.2 billion. President Clinton made the concept a centerpiece for his administration. The central problem with any universal citizen benefit, such as health care, is that carte blanche availability equals carte blanche use, which increases costs proportionately over time, particularly because of governmental inefficiencies. For example, Germans average fourteen doctor's visits a year, the French seven a year and Americans 4.5. West Germany and France have national health insurance. National health insurance in Canada has driven up demand, according to the Fraser Institute in Vancouver, "prompting a steady tightening of government regulations to control costs. These controls have created long waiting lists and chronic shortages of equipment and services in many regions, since costs are controlled not by improving efficiency but by rationing the health care delivered." Almost 25 percent of Americans delay seeking medical attention, according to an 1989 *Los Angeles Times* poll, because they can't afford it. About thirty-seven million Americans have no health insurance, yet we seldom hear of anyone dying from a lack of medical care, except in those situations requiring an expensive organ transplant. In other words, the present system is not killing people. Assuredly, if the government takes over health care, it will decrease efficiency, raise costs further and likely kill more people than the current health care system does now.

Assume shoes are a necessity like medical care and thus all Americans have a right to free government-provided shoes. The first effect is that shoe sales will explode because when they can be obtained "free" everyone will want a new pair, or maybe three pairs. After all, we're paying taxes and deserve our money's worth. Next the price of shoes will skyrocket because they're in such demand, and government costs will increase proportionately, especially for those expensive shoes not everyone could previously afford. The government, to contain costs, must either ration shoes or place a lid on the prices charged by shoe manufacturers.* With price controls the makers of expensive shoes go bankrupt, but demand for shoes remains high because they are "free." The government must then ration shoes and require endless paperwork for those still manufacturing shoes, causing more manufacturers to cease business and produce fewer shoes.† Prices keep increasing, so the government must start making shoes itself, which will limit the choice of styles and lower the quality, even though the new inferior shoes will cost several times the price for shoes before the "free" program began.

These basic economic rules cannot be avoided by any government giveaway. When government does something, it's done poorly, inefficiently, with ever-increasing cost, and in limited numbers. What the government pays for, it must

---

*In December 1992 the German Parliament forced doctors, dentists, hospitals, and drug companies to cut prices in order to curb the exploding costs of Germany's "free" health care (*New York Times, Arizona Republic,* Dec. 20, 1992).

†By early 1993 new Medicaid patients had difficulty finding doctors willing to treat them at the prices mandated by Medicaid; seventy-two of ninety-six doctors refused to make an appointment for a patient who had a severe bladder infection in Milwaukee (*Arizona Republic,* January 1993).

244 MYTHS OF THE TRIBE

control in order to assure accountability and theorectically prevent waste that would otherwise be controlled in a free market.

This is the exact history of Medicare and will become the history of any national medical plan paid for and administered by the government. Medical expenditures were 4.3 percent of the GNP in 1952, and by 1982 they were over 10 percent and rising, while the government's share of medical expenses rose from 22 percent to 40 percent. Medicare created a surge in demand for "free" services and prices soared. By 1983 Medicare threatened to bankrupt the Social Security system so taxes were hiked to no avail. The government passed more regulations, limited the charge for each medical service, and required reams of paperwork. Medical costs continue to rise without control, which is the justification for a national health care plan to be paid for by the government. When national health care passes Congress, bypass surgery and hip replacements will have to be rationed.

By declaring that everyone has a right to medical care or shoes we're actually saying that the government has the right to control the providers of medical care or the manufacturers of shoes, and they must provide their product at a fixed price. The traditional doctor or shoe manufacturer will disappear to be replaced by those willing to be dictated to by government, which means government would be telling us what goods and services we may have and forcing us to pay for shoddy goods through taxes. If competition were reintroduced, prices would fall and quality would rise. Those who must have services and cannot afford to pay can be served through private charitable organizations which receive ample support when the taxes of their donors are lowered by the excising of unnecessary government programs.

Joseph Sobran summed up the effect of the "peace dividend," which is analogous to natural government actions:

> All government institutions follow this pattern: created to meet an urgent need, they outlast both success and failure. What we were assured was a temporary measure turns out to be intractably permanent. What is true of the welfare programs liberals love is true of the military establishment the conservatives love. There are many lessons to be drawn from recent events. . . . All governments, regardless of their formal purpose of serving the people, tend to become the people's masters. They develop interests of their own and pursue them at the expense of the common good. . . . The end of the Cold War should bring enormous tax relief to the American people. It won't. . . . This means that Washington will continue to spend more than $4,000 per American per year. How many of us are receiving $4,000 worth of government services? The sad fact is that the modern state, whatever its label, effectively owns a limitless share of its subjects' earnings. It has no effective obligation to give them their money's worth. It can spend their money at its discretion.

For a hypothetical family of four making a total of $45,000 a year in 1989, eighty-three cents of every tax dollar went to four federal budget catagories: thirty-three cents for income security (federal retirement, Social Security, unemployment insurance, and the like); twenty-four cents to the Pentagon; thirteen cents to the national debt, and thirteen cents to Medicare and Medicaid, totalling $10,701 for the family of four. The seventeen cents left over went to law enforcement and the drug war, transportation, and the miscellaneous rest. The federal tax bill in 1990 for the family of four was $12,939, which is almost 29 percent of their income, and did not include state, property, and sales taxes. The average taxpayer in the United States must work from January 1 to May 20 each year to pay all federal, state, and local tax obligations. In 1984, tax obligations were satisfied by April 28. Measured differently, two hours and forty-five minutes of each eight-hour working day is spent paying taxes. Is it possible to argue that the United States is not a socialist state in the tradition of Sweden and the other Western democracies? Are we free when we are indentured to the government for 40 percent of our lives?

Notwithstanding the relatively small $16 billion spent on foreign aid in 1993, it has resulted in the destruction of national economies, established gangling bureaucracies in third-world countries, and retarded economic development. The primary purpose of foreign aid, from the viewpoint of the government, is to bribe friendly governments into staying friendly. We also bribe countries with foreign aid in case they might become friendly in the future, as Bush did in March 1991 when he refused to cut foreign aid to Jordan although it sided with Iraq in the Persian Gulf War. Little, if any, foreign aid filters down to the citizenry: instead, most goes to third world dictators, as in El Salvador, which with the full knowledge of the United States diverts the aid into Swiss bank accounts, making foreign aid the world's most expensive social security system for the privileged few.

Sixty percent of foreign aid is targeted to contain communism, as it has been for a decade, while most Americans, according to a March 1990 Gallup poll, want the money shifted to Eastern Europe and Latin America. When the State Department proposed cutting Morocco's aid for 1990, Morocco hired a Washington, D.C., lobbyist to assure restoration of the cut, and it worked. Moroccan aid was restored to its former level. Like taxes, aid can't be cut.

Foreign aid levels are the result of Congressional log-rolling, such as the three-way deal between Senator Kasten, Senator Inouye, and the White House in 1990. Kasten wanted Moroccan aid restored, so he agreed to support Inouye's aid package for Tunisia, which Inouye assured by agreeing to back the White House extra aid package for Jordan. When Tip O'Neill retired from the House of Representatives, Congress voted $20 million in aid to Ireland as a tribute to him. The allocation continues. Luxembourg, which has a higher per capita income than the United States, receives token aid to help support its eight-hundred-man army, which is "crucial" to NATO. When Senator Dole proposed cutting the $5 billion in aid for Israel by 5 percent to divert aid to the Eastern bloc, Israel gathered seventy-three senators to oppose the suggestion. Eighty percent of our foreign aid is earmarked for precisely how it must be spent, no matter actual need.

What are the results of U.S. foreign aid? The described purpose is to stimulate economic development and to raise the living standards of the poor, according to the terms of the U.S. Foreign Assistance Act of 1973 and the New International

Order of the United Nations General Assembly. Instead, foreign aid makes recipient countries more dependent and fails to help the poor. The amount of aid transferred to other countries between 1950 and 1985 totalled over $2 trillion in 1985 dollars. This amount would purchase all the companies on the New York Stock Exchange and the entire American farm system. The result has been the pauperization of several countries. The influx of aid in many countries results in the emergence of massive government bureaucracies in those countries, ostensibly to distribute the aid. The bureaucracies then become a permanent citizen burden, costing far more than the benefits of the aid itself. The World Bank in a 1983 report noted that aid totalled about 5 percent of the gross domestic investment in South Asia, while it totalled 40 percent of the gross domestic investment in Africa. South Asia's low-income countries increased their income five times faster than Africa during the same period. Meanwhile Europe, the United States, and Japan led world economic development without any aid, followed by Hong Kong and Singapore, which received almost no aid. Taiwan and South Korea are pointed to as examples of U.S. foreign aid successes; however, their economic growth began only after U.S. aid stopped.

The government admits foreign aid hasn't achieved the intended goal but argues that reform by closer grant scrutiny and more efficient foreign bureaucracies is all that's needed. Certainly reforms would help prevent waste, mismanagement, and corruption routine in foreign aid. The major problem is that foreign aid, as any other entitlement or giveaway program, retards economic growth and the development of self-reliance. The reason is simple. When the benefit received from leisure exceeds the benefit received from work, most rational people choose leisure. Assuring individuals of a certain level of income reduces the value of work in comparison to the value of leisure. The higher the level of free benefits, the less incentive to work. Thus the War on Poverty led to a higher percentage of poor, as did aid to Micronesia. When the United States acquired Micronesia as a trust territory in 1945, we discouraged foreign investment on the ground that it would "reduce the people to cheap labor." Instead, we gave the Micronesians free food, clothes, and other necessities, which bankrupted local stores and removed the incentive for production. As with most human beings, the Micronesians preferred "to accept free and usually gratuitous welfare, thus avoiding work and sacrifice required for real economic progress." As productivity dropped, the economy deteriorated and more aid was necessary. As aid increased, the economy deteriorated further, so that between 1947 and 1985 the 150,000 Micronesians received $2.4 billion. Over 60 percent of Micronesians are now employed by the local government, which is paid for by American taxpayers. Between 1963 and 1973 the acreage for coconuts fell 50 percent, for vegetables 70 percent and for citrus almost 60 percent. Imports of these same foods rose 400 percent, and the import of other items, formerly produced locally, doubled. Now Micronesia has no technicians, no plumbers, no electricians, and no economic base. As a result, U.S. aid to Micronesia has "necessarily" doubled in the last fifteen years.*

---

*David Osterfeld, "The Failures and Fallacies of Foreign Aid," *The Freeman* (Feb. 1990).

Our "Food for Peace" program began in 1940 to distribute surplus U.S. produced food to countries such as Bangladesh, India, Haiti, and Guatemala. The result is the feeding of the same people for years, "permanently decreasing the demand for locally produced food and creating an entrenched welfare class." There is no reason to work to pay for goods that can be obtained free; thus food aid has bankrupted local food producers, caused the deterioration of basic skills among the local population, and destroyed the values necessary for economic development: thrift, industry, and self-reliance.

There's no world shortage of food, only local shortages in production of food. Allowing local prices for food to rise instead of sending free food stimulates the production of food instead of removing incentives to produce food and bankrupting local producers. Once market levels of production are reached, prices fall and local producers remain self-sufficient while expensive foreign imports become unnecessary, removing one of the main causes of famines in the modern world.

Free food and foreign aid relieves government officials and prevents free markets from responding to citizen needs. The government instead uses scarce resources for its own pet projects without any relationship to need or demand. Much foreign aid is spent for industrialization projects having no connection to needs or demand. Instead of encouraging agriculture to feed its people, foreign governments use aid to build unneeded modern airports, double-deck suspension bridges for nonexistent railroads, oil refineries in countries where oil is neither produced nor known to exist, and crop storage depots inaccessible to local farmers.

The receipt of foreign aid encourages the centralization of government, politically and economically, lessening personal freedoms and diverting political activities to the distribution of aid instead of production. That which is not produced cannot be consumed, so that the diversion of talent into nonproductive government administration of aid reduces overall economic production and transfers further wealth from the have-nots to the haves. Expansion of government control over the economy also discourages private enterprise, private investment and available capital. Thus, private investment in lesser developed countries has fallen from 40 percent to under 16 percent of capital transfers to them. More domestic capital leaves these countries each year than is invested in them because foreign aid destroys the environment for private investment. As stated by economist James Henry, "More than half the money borrowed by Mexico, Venezuela and Argentina during the last decade [1975-85] has effectively flowed right back out the door, often the same year or even month it flowed in."

The net transfer of $80 billion each year from the Western democracies to less developed countries has created large foreign bureaucracies with vested interests in continuing and increasing aid programs. Much of this aid goes into the pockets of its administrators and the pockets of their friends. The wealthiest rulers in the world rule the world's poorest countries: the Marcos, Duvalier, and Mobutu fortunes are only the publicized tip of the iceberg. Foreign aid doesn't go to the pathetic children pictured on CARE literature, but instead goes to rulers and bureaucrats, providing further incentives for dictators to perpetuate the poverty of their citizens.

An egregious effect of foreign aid is the transfer of wealth from the poor in rich nations to the rich in poor nations. Most of the taxpayers in rich nations are the relatively poor or middle-income wage-earners, while the recipients of aid are the economic elite in poor nations.

As a result of the above cumulative effects of foreign aid, it should more accurately be renamed "foreign harm." The public sector can only transfer wealth, not the means to create wealth (except for the relatively minor Peace Corps). Wealth is created only by the private sector. Prosperity cannot be transferred. The key to the transfer of wealth is the transfer of skills and incentives, not the transfer of disincentives in the form of free aid.

A more effective form of aid is the Trickle Up Program (TUP), privately directed from New York City and achieving remarkable successes in Africa, Asia, South America, and the Caribbean. TUP makes grants to individuals instead of to governments. A recipient must be a group of five or more people pledging to reinvest at least 20 percent of the profits in a proposed business reviewed by unpaid TUP project coordinators. The maximum grant is one hundred dollars. In its ten years of existence, 90,000 individuals have participated in 86 countries by starting 15,000 businesses and generating over $7.5 million in profits without any government involvement, gangling bureaucracies, or social researchers. Grants go directly to street entrepreneurs. For example, in Jakarta, Indonesia:

> Of the 81 women [in the project funded by TUP], Salima was definitely the worst off in all aspects of life. She and her husband Tukiman and three children lived in the smallest packing crate in the slum. Every week . . . Salima would greet us by begging for money. . . . Finally, I [a TUP coordinator] said, there is a program where you can get money if you get five people together and produce something and sell it. Well, Tukiman was already making some money by finding old sandals and repairing them to sell. They found six other people who could either make or sell sandals and, with my help, they filled out the TUP business plan form and decided how they would spend the $50 conditional grant. . . . The TUP business report showed that eight people worked. . . . A total of 19 people benefitted from the business. They produced 180 pairs of shoes and sandals. Their income from sales in 15 months was $176. They saved and reinvested 65 percent of their profit in their business. . . . They were very enthusiastic when we met to fill out the final report. When I asked them if the business would continue they said, "It will continue until we die."

The 1989 TUP newsletter noted:

> *The World Development Report* of 1988 published by the World Bank concluded: "Poverty in the developing countries is on the rise. Between 1970 and 1980, the number of people without adequate diets in developing countries increased from 650 million to 750 million people. Since 1980, matters have turned from bad to worse: Economic growth rates have slowed, real wages have dropped and growth in employment has faltered in most developing countries." If an amount

equal to 10 percent of the $320 billion [development aid spent by the 19 donor countries that are members of the Organization for Economic Cooperation and Development] was used with the Trickle Up process it would give an opportunity for 1.5 billion of the poorest of the poor to start 206.5 million businesses in which they would invest 770.5 billion hours of their underemployed time. This would end involuntary unemployment, which is the major cause of poverty on this globe.

Banco Soliderian SA opened in the 1980s in La Paz, Bolivia, as the first bank for the poor. The bank had 600 clients by 1992, making loans valued from $25 to $300 in local currency for buying material or hiring employees. Though the bank charges 42 percent annual interest, borrowers prefer it to other banks making loans in dollars because inflation multiplies their interest rates, or local loan sharks charging 10 percent a day. Women constitute 70 percent of the bank's clients, most of whom are divided into solidarity groups to individually guarantee and make loan payments.

The New York–based Ms. Foundation, founded by Gloria Steinem, makes small loans to U.S. women seeking to expand or start small businesses. The loans depend on the solidarity system, whereby several people are responsible for re-payment, thus spreading the risk, a method commonly used in developing countries. The Foundation and a similar Collaborative Fund for Women's Economic Development obtained seed-money from corporate and foundation sponsors. A successful borrower is Uvalda Alvarado, who began selling Mexican food to neighborhood Latino factory workers when her husband was unable to support their family. Alvarado has repaid three of four loans and opened two restaurants. She told her husband she'd choose the business when presented with his ultimatum, "The business or me." He refuses to work in the business, instead chopping vegetables in a competing restaurant.

As stated by a welfare mother/housing advocate from Washington, D.C., "Poverty has been very profitable for everyone but poor people [and taxpayers]." One of the few more profitable schemes of government for special interests is the military-industrial complex.

Why can't the federal government balance a budget? The reasons are hinted at above and are numerous. Bureaucracies cannot be shrunk without being stepped on. For example, the Health and Human Services budget request for 1992, which accounts for 35 percent of the federal budget (welfare, Social Security, and the like), cannot be cut by a dime without "endangering" fifty million senior citizens and poor people. Entitlements are carved into stone and, comprising a third of the federal budget, mean no tax reductions are possible except by cutting military expenditures.

Knight-Ridder reported in November 1991 on the dozens of $80,000-a-year senior labor managers in Washington, D.C., who haven't had anyone to supervise since 1983. Their job ratings continue to be "highly effective" though they spend their time reading and playing with their computers. One stated, "I get full pay; I do what I want. There's no one really watching. As long as you don't rock the boat, no one cares." As stated by a bureaucracy specialist at the Heritage Foundation in Washington, D.C., "There are now a number of agencies in Washington where the administration doesn't take their mission seriously; the Congress doesn't take their oversight seriously, and the bureaucrats don't take their jobs seriously."

Another reason the federal and other government budgets can't be reduced is smoke and mirrors. If individual taxpayers cut spending the way the federal government did in the 1990 Deficit Reduction Act, we'd use reasoning as follows, according to Walter Williams:

> After spending $2,000 last year on entertainment, my wife and I decided to cut our entertainment budget. . . . [My wife says,] "I've met with all the party suppliers and revelers and we've agreed to a 25 percent cut in the 1991 entertainment budget." I say, "Great, let me see the budget." Lo and behold the 1991 entertainment budget is $2,625, an increase of more than 30 percent over last year's. I say, "Honey, we're supposed to cut, not increase, the budget." My wife says, "Look fool, we did. My planned 1991 entertainment expenses were $3,500. Since we're facing hard times, we decided to cut the budget by 25 percent. Can't you count? Twenty-five percent of 3,500 is $875 and $3,500 minus $875 equals $2,625. That's our 1991 budget with massive cuts.

Another reason government budgets can't be cut is that voting for cuts is political suicide. Fiscally conservative legislators who decline to participate in budgetary log-rolling succeed only in preventing spending in their own districts instead of helping to lower overall spending. By leaving more money for others less shy about siphoning off the common pool, they assure their own unemployment. Thus voters decry the actions of other congressmen and routinely return their own to Washington at a rate of 98 percent. Only the president can restrain spending, but at the risk of a single term.

Both major political parties are for increased government spending, though in different areas. Neither has a plan for tax and spending cuts. Neither favors cuts in foreign aid, the deficit, entitlements, farm subsidies, or the number of cabinet departments.

Barring catastrophe (revolution or unmarketable government bonds), budget deficits appear to be unstoppable. The November 1990 deficit increased 62 percent over November 1989 because of the Persian Gulf crisis, and a weakening economy lowered tax revenues, creating an imbalance of $80 billion in two months. Receipts were up two percent and spending up 20 percent. There are no plans to end or phase out our perennial deficits.

We believe budget myths. We believe the government is starved for revenue, though it collected $53 billion more in 1990 than in 1989. We believe federal spending is inadequate, though it rose by one third in real dollars during the 1980s. We believe Ronald Reagan's tax cuts created the deficit, though taxes under Reagan increased by 23 percent after factoring in inflation. Real spending increased every year, including that for social welfare programs. We believe

Republicans are fiscal conservatives. Spending under Nixon and Reagan increased more in real dollars than under Carter. We could blame the Democratic Congress, but Republican presidents haven't the courage to veto engorged budgets. Unfunded liabilities of the federal government for the debt, Social Security, Medicare, loans, guarantees, deposit insurance, and pensions totalled $27.3 trillion at the end of 1990, which was $109,200 for each of us. We don't have to worry about this because we'll never live long enough to pay it off. That's our children's problem.

We believe government is sacred, omnipotent, and infallible. We allow government to give or take away anything of value it wishes from anyone at any time for any reason or lack thereof. The only caveat is that the decision-maker must have been elected before he can accomplish this magic thievery. We view government as unlimited and we're absolutely correct. The right of the individual is subordinate to any publicly declared policy. This occurs because we demand there "oughta be a law" and the government must do something about whatever. To avoid an accounting for costs, both in terms of freedom and money, our policies obscure costs as much as possible, which is almost completely. By training citizens to remain children and never take responsibility for their own welfare, government becomes self-perpetuating and expansive. Thus the true costs of farm subsidies are spread among all consumers, so the impact on each individual is small and difficult to calculate. By 1987 the federal government was conducting 963 separate social programs, the bulk of which were called "entitlements." We trust government to be better able to provide security than ourselves. This is illusion of the most Freudian sort. It represents the "Pleasure Principle" as contrasted with the "Reality Principle."

The only year in which the federal government shrank was 1946, when Congress overrode wartime price controls, concerning which President Truman said, "The whole world, including the United States, has for years been driving to the left on the totalitarian road of 'planned economy.' America is by this [1946] election the first country to repudiate this road." The road remained repudiated the entire year but has become inviolate and permanent government policy in the half century since.

What tragedies would have overtaken the American people if the president and Congress hadn't reached a 1990 budget agreement and, as termed by former President Bush, "we face[d] an immediate shutdown of the federal government"? The debilitating 7.5 percent budget cut that would have been mandated by Gramm-Rudman would have required the laying off of air-traffic controllers. That's what we heard about most often; the airways would have been crippled. Ignore other countries who struggle along with private air-traffic control and fewer accidents, such as Switzerland. Can the art of air-traffic control be performed only by the government?

What if we had a 90 percent budget cut, reducing government services to the bare-bones necessary to keep the peace? Most of the following scenario was suggested by Llewellyn H. Rockwell, Jr., president of the Ludwig von Mises Institute at Auburn University. What if Commerce and HUD and Labor were abolished? We wouldn't notice, except in a shockingly reduced tax bill and greatly increased income. April 15 would be just another day. Prices would fall as government-imposed ineffeciencies disappeared. American soldiers would return from all over the world, and we could become friends with the Philippines and most other countries. Germany and Japan would have to defend themselves against nonexistent enemies. The deposed dictator of Kuwait would have to support himself and his forty wives. The dollar would increase in value, and in ten years the United States would be the dominant economy in the world. There would be no more recessions or Federal Reserve manipulation of interest rates in favor of the government or big banks. Food prices would collapse and the poor would eat, but then rich farmers would lose their welfare. Foreign dictators would have to steal their own money instead of receiving gifts from American taxpayers. Without the FDA, new drugs to treat cancer and AIDS wouldn't take twelve years to come on the market. We could buy the best goods in the world without government price tariffs and controls, reducing prices on such as Japanese cars by 25 percent. Congressmen would have to buy their own stamps and get a real job. Mail service would be cheap and efficient; postal clerks would be glad to see us. The present federal postal service would disappear in favor of UPS, fax, and the telephone. Junk mailers would pay the actual cost of mailing carloads of junk and there would be little if any junk mail. Post offices would be open twenty-four hours. There'd be no more privacy intrusions by such as a census, Social Security, drug police, and the FBI. Mr Rockwell concludes, "Well, let's not go too far, even in a dream. Maybe there are some legitimate government services. Of course, the only way to discover if any government 'services' are legitimate is by seeing if they would be provided in the market."

We can't cut the budget because government has come to be our god. Government delivers the goods to all of us at a cost we fail to recognize is grossly inflated for goods and services that could be delivered at a half to a fifth the price if we'd only do it ourselves. Because government has become our cargo god, however, we can't bear the blasphemy of suggesting cuts that would necessarily implicate our individual pet benefits. If Sam stole money from John we'd recognize the action as criminal, but when it's Uncle Sam taking money from us to redistribute to us, we accept the action as legitimized by the "democratic process." How can we delegate the right to government to rob our neighbor when we don't have the right to rob our neighbor in the first place? As stated by Joseph Sobran:

> Robbery doesn't cease to be robbery merely because the beneficiary uses a vote instead of a gun. The means is still force. . . . So most people have obeyed the state with equal servility whether it was communist, fascist or democratic. . . . The modern state has to its credit two world wars, mass murder on a scale never imagined, enslavement, terror, oppression and, even at its mildest, a steady level of confiscation, corruption and fraud that ought to enrage us. . . . Ages to come will marvel that we thought we were free.

When contemplating the spendthrift nature and bottomless debt of our government, it is nostalgic to pull out the Declaration of Independence and see exactly what caused our rage against King George III. The king had suspended the operation of laws duly enacted "till his Assent should be obtained"; every law passed in Washington, D.C., takes precedence over state constitutions and no state may hold an election without permission of the Justice Department. The king "kept among us, in Times of Peace, Standing Armies," which totalled 8,500 troops, with many of those in Canada. Today we permanently keep 2.1 million troops. The king had deprived the colonists "of the benefits of trial by jury"; a jury trial is unavailable to those whose property has been confiscated upon the discovery of a trace of any illegal drug and in connection with many other criminal matters. The king "has erected a Multitude of new Offices and sent hither Swarms of Officers to harass our People and eat out their Substance," which would accurately though understatedly describe the federal, state, city, county, and special district bureaucracies occupying every square mile of the country, whose employees total 14 percent of the population. Compare the tea tax and Stamp Act to the level of taxation today, and try not to yearn for the good old days of King George III.

10

Ethics, Goverment, Religion, and War:
Us versus Them

No president has heeded Eisenhower's warning, given over thirty years ago, that we must "guard against the acquisition of unwarranted influence by the military-industrial complex. The potential for the disastrous rise of misplaced power exists. . . ." The arms race proceeded unimpeded for thirty years until the first INF Treaty was signed by Reagan and Gorbachev in December 1987. During the six months between the signing of the agreement and its ratification by Congress, both the United States and the Soviet Union manufactured more nuclear weapons than would be destroyed in the three years covered by the treaty.

When the START treaty was signed in August 1991 after nine years of negotiations, weapons were reduced by the amount they'd increased during the nine years. Bush and Gorbachev toasted each other and called relations between the U.S. and the former Soviet Union "nearly normalized," which left 16,000 nuclear warheads aimed at each other.

The nuclear weapons race continues, and the fault is completely that of the United States, which refuses, despite repeated offers by the Soviet Union from 1985 to 1990, to stop producing nuclear weapons. How does it serve U.S. interests to continue the stockpiling of nuclear weapons which are already sufficient to destroy every city in the world twenty-five times (see *A Path Where No Man Thought,* Carl Sagan and Richard Turco, 1990), when the sole target of our stockpiling has repeatedly offered to stop production and has essentially disappeared? The United States continues to produce an average of four strategic nuclear weapons each week, though the Strategic Arms Reduction Talks (START) treaty requires that our 19,000 nuclear weapons be reduced to 17,315 by 1998. The government tries to help the economy by subsidizing the military-industrial complex. The government could better spur the economy by reducing the size of government.

During the 1990s, sixty countries will have the technical ability to build nuclear weapons. Only five countries admit to having nuclear weapons: the U.S., former Soviet Union (10 or 12 countries), China, France, and Britian. Experts conclude that Israel (100–200 warheads), India (60–80 warheads), Pakistan, and South Africa have built "small" nuclear arsenals. Does this make anyone a little nervous? Iran, Iraq, Brazil, Argentina, Algeria, and Libya are expected to produce weapons by 1995, along with North and South Korea. The breakup of the Soviet Union and the Eastern Bloc has made tens of thousands of high-level nuclear arms engineers available to the highest bidder.

We know that if nuclear war occurs, hundreds of millions will be killed and possibly all life on the planet will be destroyed. The nuclear weapons on board just one of our Trident submarines contain eight times the firepower expended in all of World War II.* Need it be said that the stockpiling of such weapons is abject irresponsiblity? In addition to the danger, the cost of weapons systems depletes resources crucial to the health of any nation—education, health, and housing (privately provided)—and bankrupted the former Soviet Union. Eisenhower said, "every ship launched and every missile fired is a theft from every child who is cold and not clothed, hungry and not fed."

For decades it has been considered unpatriotic to discuss the effects of nuclear war, or the consequences of nuclear winter, because that might diminish the will of the American people to oppose Soviet aggression.

Former Soviet President Gorbachev said, however, on August 18, 1986, and February 16, 1987:

> The explosion of even a small part of the existing nuclear arsenal would be a catastrophe, an irreversible catastrophe, and if someone still dares to make a first nuclear strike, he will doom himself to agonizing death, not even from a retaliatory strike but from the consequences of the explosion of his own warheads. We reject the right for the leaders of a country—be it the USSR, the U.S. or another—to pass a death sentence on mankind. We are not judges, and the billions of people are not criminals to be punished.

The touted Intermediate-Range Nuclear Forces (INF) Treaty affected 3 percent of the world's nuclear weapons. No nuclear warheads were destroyed; all were instead recycled into new nuclear weapons by both sides. START created an agreement in 1991 to reduce the number of nuclear weapons from over 60,000 to slightly over 50,000 in seven years. START, however, also allowed both sides to replace older weapons with more "modern" ones and to increase stockpiling.

The United States and Russia agreed in June 1992 to eventually eliminate all land-based ballistic missiles, limiting nuclear warheads to 3,500 each by 2003. This leaves enough nuclear weapons to destroy the industrialized world ten times. Russia and the U.S. had 10,000 warheads each in 1992; the new treaty limited the U.S. to 8,556 and Russia to 6,449, with the U.S. agreeing to cut submarine-launchable ballistic missiles from 3,840 to 1,750.

In 1990, eighteen nations had ballistic missiles and sixteen had nuclear weapons, likely to increase up to sixty nations in the decade of the 1990s. The odds

*John Paul Paulos, *Omni,* April 1993.

of nuclear war double with every new nuclear power, yet the Big Powers—the United States, Great Britain, France, and Germany—for political advantage have supplied long-range missiles to Argentina, Brazil, Pakistan, Iran, and Iraq. Many customers lack control systems to properly safeguard their new weapons, and many sell them at a profit to traditional enemies of the West. For instance, Argentina deployed Exocet missiles obtained from France against Great Britain during the Falklands crisis, sinking a British cruiser, and Iraq almost sank a U.S. destroyer with the French Exocet missile in 1987. China supplied ballistic missiles with a 2200-mile range to Saudi Arabia. Israel shipped missiles to China after the Tiananmen Square massacre. Libya purchased missiles from Brazil, which originally bought them from China. Other fully missiled nations include India, Pakistan, Taiwan, South Africa, and Syria. The reason for this proliferation is simple: weaponry is a symbol of a country's sovereignty, machoism, testosterone level, and worth.

The United States intends to retain its ranking in these catagories, according to a March 1992 leak from the U.S. State Department reported by the *New York Times*. The mission of the U.S. after the Cold War is "to ensure that no rival superpower is allowed to emerge in Western Europe, Asia or territory of the former Soviet Union." The policy justifies the Bush administration's "base force" proposal to maintain a 1.6 million-member military over the next five years at a cost of $1.2 trillion, pre-empting Germany and Japan (who aren't interested) from rearmament, including modern nuclear weapons. The policy is called "Defense Planning Guidance" and contains no reference to collective action through the United Nations.

Both the Soviets Republics and the U.S. supply weapons to many other countries, including those in the tinderbox Middle East where organized religion acts as the sword of Damocles over an area where prophesies since the beginning of civilization have accurately predicted continuing and major wars. The Persian Gulf War found that the weapons used against United Nations forces by Iraq were obtained from U.S. allies and from the United States itself. During the Iraq-Iran war, twenty-six nations, including the U.S., France, and the Soviet Union, provided weapons to both sides. Everyone hoped both sides would lose, and they both did lose with an estimated one million casualties. The defense budget of the United Arab Emirates increased fifty-six-fold during the 1980s. Oman devoted up to 40 percent of its budget to defense, and Egypt had more men in uniform in 1991 than in 1979 when it signed a peace treaty with Israel.

By 1990 the United States surpassed the Soviet Union as the largest supplier of arms to the Third World and the Middle East, according to the Congressional Research Service, a nonpartisan research arm of the Library of Congress. Global spending on arms totals about $2 million a minute.*

The Defense Department in 1992 began spending federal funds to spur the sale of American-made weapons at foreign trade shows. U.S. jets and arms were exhibited during the first half of 1992 in France, Canada, Dubai, Paraguay, and Chile, courtesy of our tax dollars.

World Press Review, September 1992.

Similarly to members of any religion, the citizens of any country cannot objectively judge the actions of their own country. As admitted by a Soviet spokesman Georgi Arbatov, in March, 1988, when responding to criticisms by Carl Sagan leveled at the cold war posturings of both the Soviet Union and the United States:

> As an historian, I object to Professor Sagan's approach to the arms race in the post-war period. His view can be characterized as "a plague on both your houses"—that is, equal blame is assigned to the USSR and the U.S.A. But that is unfair. . . .
>
> I caught myself thinking that perhaps my reaction was a reflection of the very thing that had so seriously worried the American scientist: a tendency to apply different standards to one's own country than to another, a desire to avoid "inconvenient" facts, a readiness to savor the details of any false step if it was made by "them" and to strike a pose, as Sagan writes, of wounded pride and professed moral rectitude when "they" say something bad about "us."

The reaction of "us" versus "them" is universal, whether it's one religion posturing against another, one nation verbally skewering another or, from my own personal experience as a trial lawyer for over twenty years, one litigant suing another. Both sides posture and blow smoke and justify most anything by rationalized principle. We do this on every level of our existence. The lowest posturing level is that of sibling rivalry, then family feuds, community rivalries and juvenile gangs, with the less savory examples including state rivalries, religious hatreds, national hatreds, cultural hatreds, and ethnic hatreds. As stated by Arnold Toynbee in *An Historian's Approach to Religion*:

> Since self-centeredness is innate in Human Nature, we are all inclined, to some extent, to assume that our own religion is the only true and right religion; that our own vision of Absolute Reality is the only authentic vision; that we alone have received a revelation; that the truth which has been revealed to us is the whole truth; and that, in consequence, we are "the Chosen People" and "the Children of Light," while the rest of the Human Race are gentiles sitting in darkness. Such pride and prejudice are symptoms of Original Sin, and they will therefore be rife in some measure in any human being or community; but the measure varies, and it seems to be a matter of historical fact that, hitherto, the Judaic relgions have been considerably more exclusive-minded than the Indian religions have.

For all of humankind there's an inherent desire to be superior and immortal, to be better than other people, races, countries and religions. This competition for racial, national, ethnic, and religious superiority where none exists, leads to hatreds resulting in arms races and religious wars, us versus them. As concluded by Gordon W. Allport, "Many studies have discovered a close link between prejudice and 'patriotism.' . . . Extreme bigots are almost always super-patriots." Loyalty and insecure self-interest obscure objective facts (as opposed to cultural "values") about any class, nation or religion, naturally generating hatred. We all appear to have someone or something to hate.

The biggest hatreds are between groups identified as nations, tribes, and religions. Joseph Sobran, in a January 1990 column, explored the absurdity of hatreds between individuals and between ethnic groups, concluding that the origins lie in closed-mindedness, refusing to see anything positive about the object of hatred:

> We recognize it sometimes in divorcing people who are absurdly eager to have us believe that they have somehow fallen in love, lived and slept continuously with Absolute Evil. Or at least an Absolute Jerk. It wouldn't say much for them if it were true. We pardon the lover a lot of absurdity. It's harder to pardon the hater, who really needs pardon, as well as pity. Dislike may be justified. Anger, even very deep anger, may be justified. But hate is so self-consuming that it can never be worth justifying. If the hatred of an individual is so irrational, the hatred of a whole group—most of them total strangers—is madness.

The roots of hatred were explored at a three-day seminar organized by Elie Wiesel, Nobel Prize-winning humanitarian, at Boston University in August 1989, which brought together philosophers, writers, and political psychologists. In preparation for the conference the Elie Wiesel Foundation issued the following statement:

> To ask why hate continues in the face of humanitarian cooperation and political understanding is neither naive nor utopian. It is a necessity. In a world where global annihilation lies seconds away and the technology of destruction, whether plastic explosives or nerve gas, is readily available to a handful of extremists, the costs of hatred are too high for the subject of hate not to be a topic of highest concern.

Examples of hatred explored at the conference included the ethnic violence in Soviet Armenia and Azerbaijan and the continuing strife between Catholics and Protestants in Northern Ireland, both primarily religious issues. A participant from the Harvard Divinity School said the religious aspect of hatred is particularly delicate:

> Religion is a very dangerous thing. These are enormous powers we are dealing with. My tasks are to ask why there has been this dark side . . . [People who see the world] in a strongly adverse, antagonistic form [can] easily play into the hands of the patrons of hatred.

For example, though U.S. whites oppose racial discrimination, when asked they retain their stereotypes of minorities so that 75 percent believe blacks and Hispanics are more likely than anglos to prefer living on welfare, based on a January 1991 survey by the National Opinion Center. Most anglos believe these minorities are more likely to be lazy, prone to violence, less intelligent, and less patriotic.

The executive director of the Chicago chapter of the NAACP responded that "Racism is as American as apple pie and mother."

Racism is the basis for nationalism, and the flag of every country in the world. Human organizations from the beginning of time have been based entirely on an identity of their members, protective associations organized against the outsider, to exclude the "them" and preserve the "us." Thus the entire basis of nationalism is, in the broadest sense, racist. Racial, ethnic, and religious discrimination are institutionalized by the "nation," which creates an identity of language, culture, and belief, and becomes the mechanism for realizing hatred against others.

Americans are unsettled at no longer having the Soviets as their chief object of dislike, so we've shifted our dislikes to foreign drug dealers, those who would take "our" oil, and restrictive trade policies by Japan. But dislike of "them" is little more than intense competition with the "them." Thus the roots of hatred are simple; they are innate in competitive man, in the genes at the core of evolution and survival of the fittest. Without the impetus for this intense competition or dislike, there would be no evolution and no progress over the long haul. Nothing adds to the cohesiveness of any group, whether ethnic, national, or religious, than a common object of dislike, whether that pits Greek against Turk, American against Russian, or Iraqi against Iranian. Hatred and war bolster the identity and cohesiveness of the group. Without a "them," there can be no "us." There must always be bad guys to typify the stuff of which we are ashamed—greed, anger, avarice, and our innate insecurity and lack of control over others and our own destinies.

How the process begins in children was described in *Newsweek* magazine on August 28, 1989:

> When a child observed at play stumbles and hurts herself, she immediately accuses her teddy bear, as if it were the bear who tripped her. If she is scolded for misbehaving, she turns and scolds her doll. In infancy we are just beginning to develop a sense of where we end and others begin. Unable to tolerate the "unpleasurable" parts of ourselves, we "externalize" them onto others. Although our attitudes mature as we age, we never quite outgrow this self-versus-other mind-set. . . . The very idea of ethnic and national groups is an extension of the same impulse, a way of distinguishing the good "us" from the bad "them."

"Us" is distinguished from "them" on Cyprus by the Turks wearing red sashes and the Greeks wearing black; in Northern Ireland, the Catholics paint their doors green and the Protestants paint theirs blue. The purpose of such group-oriented behavior is twofold: (1) it helps individuals avoid personal responsibility for their actions, and (2) it attempts to impose control over "them," such as organized religion and seeks to impose control over the unknown and death.

The plain fact is that those who believe and act differently from ourselves, though causing us no harm, are the objects of our dislike. Until we assume personal responsibility for our actions and relinquish our attempts to control the nonharmful actions of others, our hatred and dislikes will continue through organized religion, nationalism, and our inherent fear of the unknown.

Many Americans dislike the Japanese, 20 percent of us because of World War II. Others are resentful of Japan's economic success, which was fueled by U.S. aid after WWII, and Japan's restrictive import policies (which are less restrictive than those imposed by the United States on most other countries). By February 1990, 30 percent of Americans polled saw Japan as a threat to U.S. economic interests. Forty-two percent said Japanese products are superior to ours, and 48 percent thought our high wages limited our competition with Japan. These negative feelings have led many to decry the purchase of U.S. real estate by foreigners, particularly the Japanese. During 1988, Japanese citizens spent $5.2 billion to buy real estate in California and $2.8 billion in New York, with other large purchases in Illinois, Hawaii, Georgia, Texas, Massachusetts, Washington, and Arizona. In few other places can the Japanese spend their excess dollars resulting from our trade imbalance. Why do we feel our sovereignty and security are compromised or that foreign ownership is harmful to our economy?

United States citizens bought $307 billion in foreign realty during 1987. The total foreign realty investment in the U.S. was only $250 billion at the end of 1987, with the British holding the biggest share at 26 percent, the Dutch with 21 percent, and the Japanese with 12 percent. "Foreigners" own less than 5 percent of U.S. assets, while the U.S. owns well over 5 percent of foreign assets. The United States produces a fourth of the world's GNP, which is more than the next two countries combined, Japan and the Soviet Union. Our real per capita output is 70 percent higher than Japan's, partially due to the rich ethnic diversity of the United States. Neither Japan nor any other country could buy enough real estate in the U.S. to have any impact on the production of basic commodities.

The sale of anything requires two willing parties. By definition the sale is beneficial to the seller, or he wouldn't have sold, and to the buyer, or he wouldn't have bought. The proceeds from those sales don't disappear into thin air, but become part of the economy through reinvestment. Forbidding the sale of real estate to foreigners would prevent creation of other assets in this country. In addition and more importantly, no country is going to engage in hostilities with a country where it has a substantial economic stake. Investments in American real estate should be encouraged for our worst enemies, who may then become our business partners and friends.

Lest we feel our resentments toward the Japanese are one-sided, they don't much like us either. A November 1989 poll in Japan revealed that 54 percent had no admiration for the United States as a nation, 56 percent no admiration for our economic success, and 63 percent didn't like us as people. James Fallows, writing in an 1989 *Best of Business Quarterly,* points to one reason for Japanese economic success:

> . . . The Asian development model . . . divides the world quite sharply into "us" and "them" spheres. The basic goal is to make sure that important industries

remain in territory controlled by "us." Japanese industrialists still quite typically explain their market expansion as a victory for *ware-ware Nihonjin,* "we Japanese."

Bumper stickers in the United States demand, "Buy American," or declare, "Made in America by Americans," the idea being that to buy a foreign product is un-American, similar to Japanese attitudes. Is Japanese dislike of us, and their urge to dominate key world industries, any more rational than our dislike of them and our desire to dominate key world industries? Japan continues, as does the U.S., to unfairly restrict imports from international trade.

Religion and government, based primarily on ethnocentrism and economic motives, have caused or been used to justify every war fought in the history of the world. The religion of government adulation is nationalism, the belief that every other country is an inferior and threatening "them." People who love their own nation (or race or religion or other group) must necessarily love other nations less; many of us are contemptuous of other nationalities and nations. The nationalistic state finds its expression most clearly in standing armies and weaponry, particularly nuclear weapons. Naturally no nation will voluntarily dismantle its nuclear talisman of sovereignty. The question whether peace will ever reign on the planet is answerable (ignoring hatreds among organized religions) by asking whether nations will ever be primarily motivated by trade and the prosperity that follows from economic interdependence.

Unfortunately, nations are motivated not primarily by economic considerations, but rather by political considerations of power. The best examples are the United States and, until recently, the Soviet Union. Instead of arming to the teeth, Germany and Japan became economic dynamos, allowing the United States to sink deeper in debt and relative trade disadvantage.

Religious justification, however, is likely the greatest catalyst for war. Compared to religion, nationalism pales. From the viewpoint of fundamentalist Muslims, for instance, Western capitalism and materialism pose a profound threat to Islam, and they are surely correct. Neither fundamentalist Muslims nor fundamentalist Christians (or fundamentalist anything else) are prepared to accord equality to "them," though Islam was more tolerant than Christianity until the advent of the fundamentalist Islam nations in Iraq and Iran. Fundamentalist Islam, recently tempered in Iran after the 1992 elections, blames Western secularism, the Jews, and the United States for most of its problems, and it is indirectly correct in this clash of civilizations and religious dogma and oil.

The inherent tendencies of the human race to divide itself into artificial segments of "us" against "them" depending on race, nationality, and religion is racism at its most primitive and savage. Although we are far more alike than different, humans are highly competitive, which is to say we have high testosterone levels, both men and women. This fact may be illustrated by observing any freeway or crowded city street in the world. Dave Barry accurately described the scene:

In the left lane, one behind the other, were two well-dressed, middle-age men, both driving luxury telephone-equipped German automobiles. They looked like responsible business executives, probably named Roger, with good jobs and nice families and male pattern baldness, the kind of guys whose most violent physical activity, on an average day, is stapling. They were driving normally, except that the guy in front, Roger One, was thoughtlessly going only about 65 miles an hour, which in Miami is the speed limit normally observed inside car washes. So Roger Two pulled up behind until the two cars were approximately one electron apart, and honked his horn. Of course, Roger One was not about to stand for *that*. You let a guy honk his horn at you, and you are basically admitting that he has a bigger stapler. So Roger One stomped on his brakes, forcing Roger Two to swerve onto the shoulder, where, showing amazing presence of mind in an emergency, he was able to make obscene gestures *with both hands*. At this point both Rogers accelerated to approximately 147 miles an hour and began weaving violently from lane to lane through dense, rush-hour traffic, each risking numerous lives in an effort to get in front of the other, screaming and getting spit all over their walnut dashboards.

Similar behavior is observable immediately prior to any war, conflict, or confrontation between nations or religions, such as in the Persian Gulf conflict. Kuwait was part of Iraq for eight hundred years until it was sectioned off by the British in 1913 out of three former provinces of the Ottoman Empire, Basra, Baghdad, and Mosul, under a treaty never ratified because of World War I. In 1914 Britain declared Kuwait "an independent government under British protection." In 1920,Saudi Arabia attacked Kuwait City but was repulsed by British troops. Under a 1922 treaty, Kuwait lost two thirds of its territory to Saudi Arabia and thus before the August 2, 1990, invasion by Iraq, was smaller than Maricopa County, Arizona, in which Phoenix is located. Kuwait was basically worthless (to everyone but Iraq) until 1946, when it began to produce oil. In 1961 Iraq declared Kuwait's northern border void and reasserted its claim to all of Kuwait. Seventy-six percent of Kuwait's population were Iraqis or people of Iraqi descent; less than half of its residents were Kuwaiti citizens.

The week before the Iraqi invasion of Kuwait, the U.S. ambassador to Iraq told Saddam Hussein that "we have no opinion on . . . your border disagreement with Kuwait," later claiming this statement, though admittedly accurate, was taken out of context. Four days before war was declared, the Center for Defense Information estimated that a six- to twelve-week war would leave up to 10,000 Americans and Allies dead and kill between 6,000 and 35,000 Iraqi troops and tens of thousands civilians. The war actually killed 148 Americans (35 by "friendly fire") and approximately 120,000 Iraqis, which is several times the 58,000 Americans killed during eight years in Vietnam. Until Saddam Hussein invaded Kuwait, the United States kept him supplied with bank credits, technology, and weapons.

The husband of the first woman pilot killed in the Persian Gulf War said at her funeral, "The Lord has given this country a hero. I know someday I will see her big brown eyes again." Thus does the superstition of religion encourage war. Would our attitude toward the slaughter of our fellow human beings and loved ones differ if we realized we wouldn't see their "big brown eyes again"? Former President Bush said the Gulf War kindled an overdue respect for Vietnam veterans that was "good for the nation's soul" and pledged that the U.S. would "always be a force for peace in the world."

The United States has engaged in over two hundred separate military actions in its over two hundred-year history, but with only five declarations of war. Many of these military actions were relatively limited, but they include twenty invasions of Nicaragua and the occupation of Mexico City. We've averaged one military action for every year of our existence, though we've never been attacked, except for Pearl Harbor. We see ourselves as peace-loving, but other countries see us as we are, continuously throwing our weight around and killing others indiscriminately.

While Americans were preoccupied with Iraq, fifteen other wars were being fought all over the world, and the United States was involved in over half of these: Angola, Guatamala, El Salvador, Peru, the Philippines, Cambodia, Columbia, and Afghanistan. But no one wins in a war, not even the evident winner. The loser harbors a grudge until it can gain the strength to attempt revenge, and the cycle continues. The most horrifying fact is that an average 91 percent of modern war casualties are civilians.

The United States supports a coalition dominated by one of the bloodiest war machines in history, the Khymer Rouge, former star of the killing fields, seeking to oust the Vietnam-backed Hun Sen government. In Angola the U.S. backs the violent National Union for the Total Independence of Angola. In Afghanistan the U.S. supports a continuing rebellion by seven *mujahideen* groups against the Najibullah government. In El Salvador the U.S. backs the right-wing government against Marxist insurgents.

When we ship our guns to any country we wish on the theory that we're promoting democracy, human rights, and our own security by preserving a global balance of power, are we promoting any power other than our own? Does killing people promote human rights and democracy?

Primary reasons for the United States to become the world's policeman are to sustain the growth of government and to exert control over any country that disagrees with us. What national security interest was served by intervention in Guatemala, Vietnam, Panama, or other small countries we decided to "protect" or "liberate" in the last forty years? No U.S. intervention has ever spawned a lasting democracy and in many cases has instead installed or solidified a dictatorship, such as in Kuwait. The Sandinista regime in Nicaragua educated the populace, redistributed land to form a new middle class, and disbanded Somoza's terrorist National Guard, thus laying the foundation for democracy. As in many human relationships, the self-interest of government prevails over idealism, such as the fifteen occasions during the Reagan and Bush administrations when they refused to condemn Saddam Hussein for using poison gas to murder twenty thousand Kurds. Similar to other nations, we care little about how many are killed in war as long as they aren't ours.

Joseph Sobran asked how much Americans really cared about the Persian Gulf war beyond vocal support, comparing student supporters of Japanese officers (tried in the 1930s for conspiring to start a war with the U.S.) who chopped off their pinky fingers and sent them to the arrested officers as a gesture of support. Would the 93 percent of Americans who supported the Persian Gulf War consider it sufficiently important to sacrifice their little fingers in support of American soldiers exposed to violent death? Did George Bush mean it when he told David Frost that "No price is too great to stop Iraqi aggression"? Would Bush have sent his pinky to Saudi Arabia? How about an ear? Is it presumptuous to ask others to die or become paraplegics if it's not worth an ear? Was the Persian Gulf War worth anyone's life?

We were told that the Persian Gulf War wasn't about oil, that it was about preventing "naked aggression" because Iraq had invaded Kuwait, which was apparently dissimilar from the Soviet Union invading Afghanistan, China invading Tibet, Libya invading Chad, Cuba invading Angola, South Africa invading Namibia, or Turkey invading Cyprus, but similar to the U.S. invading Panama. If the war had been about oil, then the government would have demanded that the oil companies contribute to the war effort or purchase life insurance for the troops.

According to President Bush, the war was about good and evil. Ayatollah Khomeini was evil but he died, and our former ally, Saddam Hussien, caught the virus. If the war had been about oil, we would have tried to cut consumption by raising taxes or preaching conservation. Instead we put yellow ribbons on our cars, let everyone drive alone, demanded our cars be fuel inefficient, cooled our homes to sixty-six degrees in the summer and heated them to seventy-six degrees in the winter, generated electricity by oil-burning plants, and consumed volumes of cheap oil.

Control is what government is all about: control internally over its citizens and control outside its borders over "them." To combat the domestic unrest resulting from the economic woes of the old Soviet Union, Mikhail Gorbachev promoted nationalism by allowing freedom of religion. Religion and nationalism are closely intertwined, especially in Eastern Europe. The legalization of religion diverted the people from concentrating on their economic problems, giving the Soviet people a new direction. This is the role of organized religion in any society, to keep the majority of the people within the establishment as active allies of the government.

U.S. televangelists have also expanded into the Soviet Republics. By February 1990 new ministries to the Republics were announced by Robert Schuller, whose *Hour of Power* was then at the top of U.S. religious broadcasting charts, and Pat Robertson, whose *700 Club* opened a Ministry Center in Moscow "for the express purpose of distributing Bibles, tracts, Christian literature and Christian videos." National Religious Broadcasters president Jerry Rose said, "The challenge of the '90s is to . . . reach the world with the Gospel, using the technology God had put at our disposal. By the year 2000, there may be more Christians behind the Iron Curtain than anywhere else."

Lawyer-evangelist W. Ralph Mann said, "If the church fails to evangelize now, the world will be taken over by the New Age movement and the forces of the Antichrists." Before the Persian Gulf War, American evangelists were calling Saddam Hussein the Antichrist. (See Pat Robertson's *The New Millennium* and John Walvoord's *Armageddon, Oil and the Middle East.*) Religious "experts" have pinned the Antichrist label on Ronald Reagan, Jimmy Carter, Henry Kissinger, Kurt Waldheim, Pope John Paul II, and Mikhail Gorbechev, to name a recent few.

The inevitable result of hatred, organized religion, and governmental sabre-rattling seeking to impose control on others are violence and war. Religious and ethnic hatred is the main reason people die every day in all parts of the globe, in the Middle East, Northern Ireland, India, Soviet Armenia, Kashmir, and Sudan. Fifty years after WWII broke out an Associated Press poll found that 60 percent of those polled believed "that kind of thing could happen again, that is, the killing of millions of people because of their religion or ethnic background." It's happening this instant and will continue for the foreseeable future until we relinquish hatred of "them" and stop seeking to impose control on others.

Americans' conception of war is formed by television and the movies and is similarly unreal. The American people enjoyed watching the sanitized Persian Gulf War spectacular. A record number signed up for cable television within two weeks after war was declared in January 1991. War movies filled the non-war coverage channels. Though there was collateral damage and tanks were destroyed, not one person died in the televised Persian Gulf War.

Most haven't the vaguest conception of what war means. The American vision of war doesn't include mutilation and dismemberment; it includes pictures from *Life* Magazine, or its picture collection *Life Goes to War* (1977), and other popular collections of war pictures. These do not accurately depict war. War is more accurately described by the combatants, such as that by a British artillery forward observer in North Africa during a night attack:

> I was following about twenty paces behind when there was a blinding flash a few yards in front of me. I had no idea what it was and fell flat on my face. I found out soon enough: a number of infantry were carrying mines strapped to the small of their backs, and either a rifle or machine gun bullet had struck one, which had exploded, blowing the man into three pieces—two legs and head and chest. His inside was strewn on the hillside and I crawled into it in the darkness.

The 1943 U.S. *Officer's Guide* sanitized war:

> Physical courage is little more than the ability to control the physical fear which all normal men have, and cowardice does not consist in being afraid but in giving away to fear. What, then, keeps the soldier from giving away to fear? The answer is simply—his desire to retain the good opinion of his friends and associates . . . his pride smothers his fear.

As stated by Paul Fassell in an *Atlantic Monthly* magazine article in August 1989, titled "What War Is Really Like": "In the face of such horror, the distinction between friend and enemy vanishes, and the violent dismemberment of any human being becomes traumatic. . . . You can't take much of this sort of thing without going mad. . . .

Persian Gulf War correspondents were not allowed to report anything that would adversely affect the morale of the people back home, though Bill Mauldin said, "One of the startling things you learn in war is how much blood can come from a human body." CNN commentators covering the Persian Gulf war were accused of treason against the United States for describing civilian and other casualties. Secretary of Defense Cheney refused to discuss Iraqi casualties in March 1991: "In this business [war], the whole idea of body counts was given a very bad name a long time ago [20 years ago]. We've tried *religiously* to stay away from that sort of thing, and we will continue to do that." [Emphasis added] The reality of war is always hidden by government from its citizens.

The principal cause of war is the rationalizations proffered by government and organized religion. The primary cause of peace is war weariness. War is more normal than peace. For example, since 901 Russia has been at war 46 out of every 100 years. Since 1066 England has been at war somewhere for 56 out of every 100 years. Most wars naturally are fought by adjoining countries. Most wars begin with high optimism on both sides; initial optimism ups the odds of war. Religion gives a feeling that the country is right in going to war, such as the Israelites against their Old Testament enemies. The word of the Lord was worth ten thousand men. The United States has mystical faith in its ethical superiority as a Christian nation. The British Empire was great because God made it so. The Turks' faith in Allah assured Turkey's success against the heathen Christian hordes.

In the two hundred years between 1678 and 1878, Russia and the Turks fought ten wars, which were largely based on religious differences, Muslims against Christians. These wars resembled the Crusades; the Russians were led by priests. Before the 1877 war, the Russian Czar attended a sermon which preached, "Yours is the great destiny to raise the Cross of Christ above the Crescent in the lands of the Danube," while the Turkish Army was declared "beloved of Mohammed, . . . waiting to kill in the name of the True Prophet."

The Persian Gulf War was preceded by religious fist-shaking. Each side denounced the other as godless. The day before President Bush declared war on Iraq, the Rev. Billy Graham led the President, his cabinet, and military chiefs in prayer and declared, "There comes a time when we have to fight for peace." The altar was dominated by six flags; the U.S. flag and the flag of each of the five military branches. President Hussein later responded, "This is a showdown between the infidel and the believers, between good and evil." In August 1990, Hussein said, "God is on our side and Satan is on the side of the United States." Bush replied that the conflict "has nothing to do with religion per se. It has, on the other hand, everything to do with what religion embodies: good versus evil, right versus wrong." This is precisely what religion does not embody.

The National Religious Broadcasters treated President Bush as inspired in declaring the invasion of Iraq a "just war." As Coleman McCarthy described it, some were rallying "around the flag, others around the cross and a few [most] seeing no difference." President Bush quoted Saints Thomas Acquinas, Augustine and Ambrose on "just war," which means killing people is pleasing to God as long as there's soul-searching and two "moral" principles involved. The first principle must be that the war is one of last resort. The second principle is that the war must be for a "just cause." As stated by Robert Seeley in *The Handbook of Non-violence,* "The just war theory has allowed the church to sanction virtually every war in Western history, giving its blessing in many of them to both sides." Mr. McCarthy concluded that war has become so romanticized that the only way out of our complacency is to replace the word "war" with one more accurate. Substitute the word "slaughter" wherever the word "war" has previously been used.

The "just slaughter" theories of Christianity and Islam ask the same question. When is the incineration of thousands and the mass destruction of property necessary to prevent greater evil? The Christian answer in the Persian Gulf was to paint Saddam Hussein as evil personified, a 1990s Hitler, though in the 1980s the United States was allied with him against Iran. The director of interreligious affairs for the National Jewish Committee declared that Saddam Hussein "is evil and has to be eliminated." No religious leader in the United States made a similar declaration against the Chinese leadership after the Tiananmen Square massacre, against Qaddafi in Libya, or Castro in Cuba. Some religious leaders argued that nonviolent means had not been tested long enough before war was declared in the Persian Gulf and they were branded traitors. The religious director of the Federation of Islamic Associations in the United States said the United States "would be labeled in the eyes of Islam as the aggressor," but the secretary general of the Islamic Society of North America said Hussein was "sloganeering in the name of Islam." Jehan Sadat, widow of the slain Egyptian president, said "What is happening in the Middle East is very, very frightening to the whole world. This killing and revenge is not Islam at all. Islam is love and peace." A week before the Persian Gulf War was declared, the Society of Christian Ethics voted 97–20 that the use of force in the Persian Gulf did not meet the requirements of a just war.

Almost no one is or can be objective about the justness of any particular war. The conclusion that any war is a just war depends on whether the declarer supports the war, in which case "war" is interpreted as "peace." The following is a verbatim Associated Press description of the United States confusing the two terms on Sunday, February 25, 1991, in the middle of the Persian Gulf war (or the Persian Gulf peace).

President Bush, surrounded by family and members of his cabinet, heard prayers for peace Sunday at a specially arranged church service. As Bush stepped from his armored limousine at St. John's Episcopal Church, just across Lafayette Square from the White House, a handful of anti-war demonstraters banged on drums and a woman shouted, "Stop the War!" Bush quickly walked inside with his wife, Barbara, and two of their children, Marvin Bush and Dorothy LeBlong. They joined Vice President Dan Quayle; his wife, Marilyn; and their three children in a front-row pew. Behind them sat more than 100 top administration officials and their families. Secretary of State James Baker joined Defense Secretary Dick Cheney in the second row. Bush often attends an 8 P.M. Sunday communion service at St. John's, the 176-year-old 'church of the presidents,' where every chief executive since James Madison has worshiped. This specially arranged service began at 7 A.M. The Rev. John Harper, the rector, read from a 19th-century hymn by Henry William Baker, *Christian Responsibility*: "O God of love, O King of Peace / Make wars throughout the world to cease; / The wrath of nations now restrain, / Give peace, O God, give peace again." Harper then prayed "for our president" and "for all those serving in the Persian Gulf, the men and women of our armed forces." He added, "I ask your prayers for our enemies; for all the people of the world who seek for peace . . . (and) those who lay down their lives (for) a just and lasting peace." The organist played the melody of *Christian Responsibility* and members of the congregation exchanged handshakes in a gesture of peace before taking communion. The anti-war drums could be heard at the start of the 35-minute service and near its end.; Police arrested one man, accusing him of violating a noise ordinance. Harper took exception when told that some reporters had described his sermon as "pacifistic." "I've been very supportive of the president from the very beginning," he said.

Wars are prolonged by religious fervor. Wars are never civilized affairs deserving of religious veneration, though we romanticize them as such, which further encourages war and, because of religious support, has caused each century to describe the wars of its era as saving the world for the "us."

World War I was far from the first world war. Five wars covering most of the world were fought in the eighteenth century. The United States fought seven major wars in the hundred years between 1798 and 1898, against France, Tripoli, Britain, Algiers, Mexico, the Confederacy, and Spain. In the past fifty years the United States fought four major wars and invaded Panama, Grenada, and the Dominican Republic; bombed Libya; supported Iraq against Iran in the Persian Gulf; opposed Iraq two years later; supported rebel groups in El Salvador, Nicaragua, and other Central and South American countries; conspired to assassinate three foreign heads of state; stopped a coup in the Philippines; and assaulted Cuba. Only one of the above involved the defense of U.S. soil, WWII after Pearl Harbor. No other country in the world can match this twentieth-century record for armed conflict. American Presidents are never more popular than when they go to war.

The history of religion in war goes to the beginnings of recorded history. The holy war provides a motive for combat, the proper attitude toward military violence (approval) and rules on how to engage the enemy. The purpose is to save the world from evil by doing evil. Holy wars become necessary when faith lags, such as antecedent to the Crusades, to re-energize the church. Describing the First Crusade taking Jerusalem, Raymond du Aguilers wrote:

Wonderful things were to be seen . . . numbers of Saracens were beheaded
. . . others were shot with arrows, or forced to jump from the towers; others
were tortured for several days and then burned in flames. In the streets were
seen piles of heads and hands and feet. [The horses walked in blood up to their
bridles.] It was a just and wonderful judgment of God that the same should
receive the blood of those whose blasphemies it had so long carried up to God.

The history of organized religions, save a few pacifist sects, is a history of
wars. The Greeks and Romans (and primitive tribes today) had gods of war
and regarded war as religious activity, as we do today. The idea of conflict and
battle was central to Zoroastrian thought, which became the basis for Persian
nationalism, Islam, Judiasm, and Christianity. Hinduism places soldiers second
only to the priesthood of Brahmans, similar to Plato's caste system in *The Republic*. Those slain in battle are automatically passed to the next life. For a warrior
or soldier it's a sin not to kill in battle. As Gandhi said, "Argument follows
conviction. Man often finds reasons in support of whatever he does or wants
to do."

Buddhists are traditionally pacifist, prohibiting the killing of anything ever:
"Some do not think that all of us here one day will die; if they did, their dissen-
sion would cease at once" (Dhammapada 3). There are notable Buddhist exceptions to pacifism, however, with Buddhist monks leading armies in China,
Japan, Ceylon, and Korea, on the theory that the enemy was not human and,
therefore, the prohibition against killing did not apply. The Japanese shoguns
were Buddhist, though most of the military Buddhist monks were slaughtered
beginning in 1571. Zen Buddhism in Japan was headed by a soldier aristocracy.
The Bushidi ideal was the militant knight or samurai of the Shinto cult, which
is not really Buddhist but was formed by Buddhist influence. Buddhism accepts
killing only to protect the doctrine, which, similar to most religions, allows and
encourages the killing of heretics. Under Buddhist doctrine it's justifiable to kill
one to save two. Thus Mao as a Buddhist could justify killing to preserve the
revolution and its idealogy. Contrast Buddha, who in a former life was reputed
to have fed himself to a lioness so she wouldn't devour her cubs, out of compassion
for them. On the other hand, Vietnamese Buddhists said, "Men cannot be our
enemies—even men called 'Vietcong!' If we kill men, what brothers will we have
left? With whom shall we live then?" (*Condemnation*, Thich Nhat Hanh.)

Taoists and Confuscianists are pragmatic about war, fighting if they believe
the struggle is right, in which case they have the strength of thousands. Pacifism
is a central concept, however, similar to originally pacifist Christians. Yen Fu
brought Western thought to China in the early 1900s, but finally rejected it saying, "It seems to me that in three centuries of progress the peoples of the West
have achieved four principles: to be selfish, to kill others, to have little integrity,
and to feel little shame." Shinto is highly militaristic with weapons as symbols
of deities. Its focal point is militant nationalism. All wars are holy wars, fought
under the motto, "The whole world under one roof."

For their first 250 years Christians were conscientious objectors; then they came to power and that ended. In the fourth century, when Christianity was declared the official religion of Rome, pagans were culled from the army and replaced with an all-Christian army. The concept of a just war emerged to justify this action, the goal of any war being justifiable peace. Priests were excluded from battle as in today's armies. The Crusades began at the impetus of the pope as a righteous war against the infidels. Not even Islam engaged in such broad-ranging holy wars; their jihads were relatively limited. Thomas Aquinas exempted the state from Christian pacifism, emphasizing that any war is against sin. All European wars (except in Spain and Austria against Muslims) have been fought by Christians against Christians. Any general can appreciate the motivational value of religion in inducing otherwise sane individuals to expose their bodies to bullets and bombs (we are told there are no atheists in foxholes).

Although Christians pay lip-service to pacifism, they are second to no other religion with their participation in and starting of wars. Gandhi said, "The only people on earth who do not see Christ and his teachings as non-violent are the Christians."

Much of Christian support for American imperialism was support for Christian expansion into "heathen" countries. When the United States contemplated the annexation of Cuba, Puerto Rico, the Philippines, and Hawaii in 1898, religious leaders lent enthusiastic support. The Congregational magazine, *Advance,* for May 19, 1898, illustrated the common sentiment:

> The churchmen of our land should be prepared to invade Cuba as soon as the army and navy open the way, to invade Cuba in a friendly, loving Christian spirit, with bread in one hand and the Bible in the other, and win the people to Christ by Christ-like service. Here is a new mission field right at our doors which will soon be open. Shall we not enter it?

Within months after troops withdrew from the Spanish-American war, missionaries entered Cuba, Puerto Rico, the Philippines and Hawaii.

The foregoing should not be taken to mean that Americans are any more savage or bloodthirsty than any other nation; only that those who have the means are more likely to wage war. Neither does the foregoing mean that the United States has been responsible for all the world's evil for the last several decades, but having the capability we have taken numerous opportunities, as have all other nations with the capability to wage war and violence against others. Nor are the Christian religion and Western governments all to blame. The blame is shared by us all because we're all the same. We are all one people in a violent, competitive world, who would do far better if the single rule of harming no one else were universally enforced against our governments, our religions, and ourselves. Violence should be outlawed and this single law enforced globally.

The World Council of Churches, an exclusively Christian organization, published its official document, *Violence, Nonviolence and the Struggle for Social Justice* (1973) with three main assertions: (1) Nonviolence is the only Christian method; (2) Violence is permitted in extreme circumstances, which means circumstances with just cause (somewhat eroding the "only" in rule number one), exhaustion of other possibilities, reasonable expectation of attaining the desired end, a just method (of violence?), and a positive concept of the ensuing order; (3) In situations where violence begets more violence, Christian participation requires humanizing the means of conflict [is this a joke?] and building structures for peace. Violence ruled out altogether includes conquest, oppression of a class or race, torture, taking hostages, and killing noncombatants. The methods of Gandhi, Martin Luther King, Jr., and Christ appear somewhat more civilized than official Christian doctrine, which encourages war.

War works because there's no individual responsibility or control over the violence. If war required individual responsibility, there would be no war. Instead, war is waged by governments deemed to know omnisciently the needs and desires of all their citizens and what's best for the country. Governments are and have been abominable failures at knowing what is best for either the country or the citizenry. What are the legitimate interests of any country outside its own borders? What is vital to the interests of the United States beyond a good relationship with its neighbors? The true answer in the Persian Gulf was oil. Does the United States have any business inside El Salvador or Nicaragua or Panama or Colombia? Do they have any business inside our borders? Do we have so little confidence in our economic and political systems that we feel compelled to force them on other countries? Could the events in Eastern Europe mean that the basic principles of capitalism, that is competition without coercion, are sufficient to allow other countries to form their own destinies? What right do we have to force democracy on Nicaragua or Panama or the Philippines or any other country? With time, television, and instant media on our side, we found there was little reason to fund contras to kill noncombatants and priests. With the political climate of the late twentieth century, what people want, they eventually get, whether it's monarchy, democracy, communism, capitalism, socialism, or some combination thereof. It's not vital to the interests of the United States or worth the life of one civilian or soldier to force our way of life on anyone else. Imposing an idea on anyone by force is counterproductive. By advertising our insecurity in Central America we devalue our way of life and earn the enmity of our neighbors.

Will we ever be able to give up war and preserve spaceship earth? As stated by Buckminster Fuller:

> We are going to have to find ways of organizing ourselves cooperatively, sanely, scientifically, harmonically and in regenerative spontaneity with the rest of humanity around earth. . . . We are not gong to be able to operate our spaceship earth successfully nor for much longer unless we see it as a whole spaceship and our fate as common. It has to be everybody or nobody.

Lest we believe the reference to spaceship earth is hyperbole, consider the effect of the Apollo space program, which was not about science or space, but about ideological confrontation and the Cold War. Representatives from several countries flew on the Discovery shuttle in 1985 and later recalled: "The first day or so, we all pointed to our countries. The third or fourth day, we were pointing to our continents. By the fifth day, we were aware of only one Earth." Global cooperation and recognition of our kind as one people is a precondition for our survival as a species. Nations (and organized religions) are artificial entities whose existence provides the vehicle to threaten world peace.

The manner in which world powers operate is on the kindergarten level. One example was the United States Justice Department move to allow American F.B.I. agents to arrest accused criminals anywhere in the world, whether permission had been obtained from the criminal's country of residence or not. The policy was adopted with express recognition by the United States government that it violated international law. This conclusion was based on a June 21, 1989, opinion by Assistant Attorney General William Barr, citing numerous court cases holding that the United States could violate international law to protect Americans from terrorists or drug traffickers. In February 1990, the U.S. Supreme Court by a 6–3 decision allowed American agents to seize evidence abroad without constitutional restriction; the U.S. Constitution is operative only within U.S. borders. Thus U.S. drug agents may now search homes and offices owned by anyone anywhere outside the U.S. without a search warrant. Evidence so obtained is not subject to suppression in U.S. courts, whether sought to enforce U.S. antitrust laws, securities laws, or drug laws, removing Noriega's defense of illegal seizure. The State Department's chief legal adviser cautioned: "We need to consider the fact that our legal position may be seized upon by other nations to engage in irresponsible conduct against our interests."

Iran reacted by passing a bill allowing its government to arrest any American who offends it in any country where the American may be found. The Iranian Chief Justice said the bill was passed in response to the "bullying nature" of the United States. Several Iranians are wanted for hijacking a TWA jet in 1985 and killing a U.S. Navy diver. The first Iranian target was announced to be Capt. Will Rogers III, commander of the missile cruiser Vincennes when (on behalf of Iraq and Saddam Hussein) it shot down a civilian airliner over the Persian Gulf in July 1988, killing the 290 people aboard.

The United States announced in November 1989 that its new policies allowed it to seek the removal of Panamanian President Noriega, including the use of "high risk" tactics that could lead to his injury or death. The reason justifying this action was Noriega's dealing in illegal drugs, while the President of the United States had announced trade sanctions against those countries refusing to import American tobacco, a drug that kills hundreds more people each year than those killed yearly by illegal drugs.

What would have been our reaction be if another country had announced plans to take "high risk" measures, including injury or death, against former President Bush because of his pushing tobacco? The CIA was appropriated $3 million to recruit Panamanian military officers or other dissidents to topple Noriega. The United States used military force to effect the final coup in Panama, largely to placate the President of the United States, who had been called a wimp by *Newsweek* magazine. We provided support to four previous coup attempts in Panama. If the Soviet Union had crushed the independence moves of Latvia and Lithuania, pointing to the United States actions in Panama, exactly what could we logically have said in defense?

Both the United States and the Soviet Union have interfered in the internal affairs of countries all over the world. We did it because we thought we were right, and that's why the Soviets said they did it, too. Similar logic is used by organized religions that send missionaries to convert those of other religious faiths and nonbelievers. Our smugness as a nation is grounded in a Christian democratic moralism positing that we know better about every moral issue and are more civilized than any other country in the world.

Fundamentalist religions, superpatriots, and many governments have in common their reliance on theories of conspiracy to explain the world around them. If something occurs that is not written in the Bible, or the Koran, or the constitution of the particular country, Satan must be behind it. For example, when a mark similar to a cross appeared on veils of Muslim women in Upper Egypt, a Cairo newspaper reported the two most common explanations:

> Some people said that Christians had sprayed a chemical on the veiled women's clothes and this material assumed the form of a small cross no larger than an ant; as soon as the clothing was moistened, the size of the cross would increase to about three centimeters. Some people offered another interpretation, which held that the cloth of the head covering had been imported from Israel and that it was scientifically treated to form crosses with the purpose of stirring up dissension between Muslims and Christians.

When the intellectual foundation of most of the world's people is belief without evidence, conspiracy theories sprout easily. Other examples of conspiracy-driven thinking were recounted in the *Atlantic Monthly* magazine for May 1989:

> Muammar Qaddafi is deemed by Baghdad radio to be "subservient" to the United States and Israel . . . ; a Saudi Arabian king holds that Zionists are behind the Palestinian terrorists . . . ; Turkey's Mustafa Kemal Ataturk is denounced by an Egyptian newspaper as a crypto-Jew . . . , the argument being that he imposed secularism on his Muslim country to punish the Turks for not ceding Palestine to the Jews. . . . In 1986 a newspaper in Bahrain called the recent incident in which a TWA airliner was blown up by hijackers "the clearest example of the West's enmity to the Arabs."

The *Atlantic Monthly* article argued that much of this sensationalism is an attempt to explain Arab inability to defeat Israel. However, the constitution of the Islamic Republic of Iran is possibly unique in formally referencing two conspiracies, calling the late Shah's land-reform program an "American plot . . . a ploy to stabilize the foundations of the colonialist government [of the Shah] and strengthen Iran's . . . ties with world imperialism." A *New York Times* dispatch illustrated the depth to which this conspiracy-seeking attitude goes: "A Teheran taxi driver explained that he thought the city's notorious traffic jams were the handiwork of American agents. 'They get people to do unnecessary things and make the drivers frustrated and lose their temper,' he said."

The campaign against Salman Rushdie's book, *The Satanic Verses,* was based on allegations of an American conspiracy, though Rushdie has no connection with the United States, is a Muslim and a Briton, and was educated in India. The controversy began in February 1989 when fundamentalist Muslims charged that the book failed to recognize Islam as the world's one true religion and Mohammed as the holy Prophet of the one true religion, for satirizing Mohammed as fallible, portraying his wives as prostitutes, and suggesting that Mohammed wrote the Koran instead of receiving it from God. The offensive part of the book was a dream sequence of a character going mad, which would appear to have little connection with historical or religious "truth." The book caused riots resulting in six deaths and many injuries in Pakistan, though it had been banned there and no one had read it. Although it became a bestseller because of the controversy, few still have read it. The U.S. government stated that it "in no way supports or associates itself with any activity that is in any way offensive or insulting to Islam or any other religion" and that it has "full respect for the religious beliefs of the Pakistani people . . . based on constitutionally protected rights to freedom of worship and to freedom of speech, which also guarantee the expression or publication of a wide range of works, not all of which will be acceptable in every society."

Iran reacted more harshly than expected, the Ayatollah Khomieni ordering Muslims to kill Rushdie: "All those involved in its publication who [were] aware of its contents are sentenced to death. I request brave Moslems to quickly kill them wherever they find them so that no one ever again would dare to insult the sanctities of Moslems. Anyone killed while trying to execute Rushdie would, God willing, be a martyr." A foreigner carrying out the order of execution was promised $1 million; an Iranian would receive $2.6 million. A former Pakistani senator and minister of religious affairs said: "The teams have been dispatched from various Moslem countries, including Pakistan, to murder the author and the publisher. I predict that the man will be murdered in a couple of months. . . . I don't know what will be their mechanism." The reward was matched by Mohammed Hashemian, religious leader in the southwestern Iranian city of Kerman, bringing the total for an Iranian executioner to $5.2 million. The European Economic Community Parliament voted to sanction Iran if an attempt were made to kill Rushdie. U.S. Secretary of State James Baker called the bounty "regrettable." Britain severed diplomatic relations with Iran and spent large sums of money hiding Rushdie.

Because of the Iranian threats, publishers in France, West Germany (Iran's principle trading partner), Greece, and Turkey declined to publish the book. The British singer, Yussuf Islam, formerly known as Cat Stevens before his conversion to Islam, created great controversy by saying Rushdie must die: "The Koran makes it clear: If someone defames the prophet, then he must die." Stevens/ Islam later explained that he didn't personally wish Rushdie to be killed but was pointing out the requirements of the Koran.

There was no media coverage of the fact that the Bible contains similar requirements. As stated by the columnist Smith Hempstone: "In Christendom down through the ages, more crimes than deeds of compassion have been committed in the name of God." However, Hempstone correctly pointed out:

> In America, we like to think of the First Amendment right of free speech as an absolute one, that prior restraint of the published word is unacceptable and everyone has a right to say and write—short of the laws of slander and libel—exactly what he pleases. But one wonders if that is really so. One wonders, for instance, whether it would be acceptable in 1989 America to write a novel glorifying Adolf Hitler's destruction of European Jewry, or portraying blacks as genetically inferior. One rather thinks not, and most people would say rightly so. Which is only to say that the Islamic world has one set of shibboleths, and the secular world has another. And they are, to a degree, mutually incomprehensible.

Government and laws, religion and catechisms, are a search for security and certainty, protection against "them." The result of this innately human search for certainty is closed-mindedness, explored by Ellen J. Langer, a professor of psychology at Harvard University, in an *American Health* article in March 1990:

> A cow is a steak to a rancher, a sacred object of worship to a Hindu, and a collection of genes and proteins to a molecular biologist. Like the cow, every idea, person or object has the potential to be many things, depending on the viewer's perspective. Unless you're mindful of your perspective on a certain type of behavior and its meaning, you're unlikely to change it.

Thus, any person, behavior, government action, or ethnic group can be seen in a negative or positive light. Compare rigidity with consistency, gullibility with trustingness, and firmness with being a pig-headed fool. The difference between a positive and negative attitude, between seeking to maintain the status quo at all costs and being open to new ideas and change, is crucial for health.

Controlling one's own environment and self in relationships is the opposite of having them controlled by government or religion. We, our religions, and our governments all have a

> tendency to seek "hypothesis-confirming" information, whether it's about ourselves or other people. If we seek evidence to prove that blacks are aggressive, Jews are obsessed with money, Wasps are unemotional, and the Irish are passive-aggressive, for instance, we probably will find some. If however, we look for ways in which these groups are *not* like their stereotypes, that evidence is likely to be just as forthcoming.

We should relinquish our controls over one another, allowing individuals to freely develop to the limit of their powers, as long as we harm no one else. Any other control exercised over an adult diminishes the individual to a child and is harmful to the individual. For example, many religions prohibit birth control, with the result that millions of people are relegated to poverty for their entire lives; the only life they will likely ever live.

We become used to control by others beginning with our infancy, and many never shake these controls to become adults. The result is that many chronological adults are actually children subject to the control of parents, government, religion, job, relationship, family, children, and addictions. We are controlled first by our parents. Under our parents we become used to being controlled and comfortable to the extent that many can't function without the control of someone else. The adverse female reaction to the feminist movement was likely based on a fear that paternalistic control by men would be sacrificed, creating a void most women had no idea how to fill. How long does it take most people to shake the control exercised by their parents? The answer for many is until the death of their parents. Few fail to alter their behavior in the presence of their parents. Our children feel the same about us, their parents.

The second pervasive institution of control is our work. Our jobs rule more hours of our lives than any other force (second and third are sleep and television). Workaholics outnumber alcoholics. The job becomes an excuse for avoiding personal responsibilities to others, particularly family. As the bumper sticker says, "I owe, I owe; so off to work I go." Such is absolute control, exacerbated by the inability of many to control credit, allowing debt to control us. Debt is an onerous form of control. Every advertisement in every medium is an attempt to assert control over the individual, and many of us succumb. Therefore, we must work excessively because our lives are under the control of someone or something else: our creditors and our ambition. (An illustration is contained in my favorite lawyer joke. The devil promises the lawyer a partnership in the most prestigious firm in New York at age twenty-eight, a U.S. Senate seat by age thirty-five, and a seat on the U.S. Supreme Court by age forty, in return for the souls of the lawyer, his wife, and children. The lawyer asks, "What's the catch?")

Adults should be allowed to watch as much television, buy as many assault rifles, refuse to wear seatbelts or motorcycle helmets, take as many drugs, spend as much money, shop until we drop, and do as little as we please, all at our own risk, as long as we harm no one else. Only individual adults are competent to judge what is best for them; neither religion nor government nor any other exterior control can fairly judge individual interest. The individual adult is infinitely more qualified to judge harm to self than government, religion, or any other person or entity.

Similarly, the adult individual should not attempt to exercise control over any other adult. Taking individual and absolute responsibility for self prevents the seeking of control over others. Those who abdicate personal responsibility allow others the opportunity to exercise control, filling the vacuum not filled by the irresponsible individual, whereas those exercising personal responsibility leave no niche for others to impose control and also keep themselves sufficiently occupied so that they normally don't seek to exercise control over others. Accepting sole and personal responsibility for one's actions avoids control of or by others. Refusing to blame others for personal errors also avoids the accumulation of enemies, which further allows the individual to function autonomously and responsibly. Unfortunately, religion and government seek to impose control over the nonharmful actions of the individual, eroding the individual's incentive to exercise personal responsibility and allowing blame for whatever goes wrong to be shifted to others in the form of impersonal institutions. This process sets up artificial enemies on whom blame for institutional and personal shortcomings can be placed, such as other religions, races, and countries. Such a process is the epitome of irresponsibility and immorality. Succinctly, immorality is the attempt to exercise control over others and the abdication of personal responsibility, resulting in the blame for our own shortcomings being imposed on others, causing them harm

I've criticized the United States, but it's neither among the most repressive countries in the world nor irremediable. It can be improved easily by prohibiting governmental control over any action that harms no one else.

It might help to form the "Adult Party" in opposition to the control-oriented Republicans, Democrats, and Independents. The founding fathers, and particularly James Madison in the *Federalist Papers,* feared the excesses of the majority imposed on the minority, directly resulting in the Bill of Rights; these fears have been realized. The majority has plenty of material things but insufficient tolerance of minorities and others. There is no other, other than the human race. We are all more alike than different, no matter our race, religion, or national origin. All races, religions, and countries have beautiful people and plain people and evil people and every other kind of people. We are one people. Nothing matters except the spirit of the human race. All else is petty bickering. Consider in this context nuclear arsenals and massed armies, which could destroy the species. Perhaps rewatch the movie *On the Beach.* We should dilute and forget our petty nationalisms. Patriotism is a synonym for "justifiable hatred of others," which is racist. When we next listen to the *Star Spangled Banner,* we should remember the other 173 countries in the world that are populated with people who are identical to us in hopes and needs. We are one world, and each of us should have equal opportunity without discrimination based on race, religion, or national origin, and without blundering government enforcement of the concept.

Our religions and governments obscure knowledge and truth, to which all else should be secondary. Truth filtered through religion and government is propaganda or superstition, which are without substance and are the opposite of truth. The truth is that we should stop wasting our resources and time on superstitions, victimless crimes, and the control of adults who harm no one else. If we can put away our false moralism, which is rooted in the fear of the unknown and the attempt to control the uncontrollable, we will have the resources to explore the universe, or at least to commandeer control of ourselves to become personally responsible adults.

Millions die while religion slowly catches up to science. Religion cares little about physical misery or the easily avoidable deaths of children; religion cares about buildings and supporting priests and ministers. Religion cares about preventing birth control and keeping people in poverty, as long as they believe.

Religion cares about destroying the believers in other religions and slaughtering those who refuse to believe without evidence. Religion is the militaristic Old Testament, the Koran, the Inquisitions, the Crusades, and the censorship of books and movies and art. Religion is Northern Ireland, the Middle East, Beirut, and, with few exceptions, the basis for all wars raging on the religious fault lines of the earth. One major religion bordering another major religion equals war, which may result in the destruction of the human race.

Mankind should learn to cooperate, but it may never be able to do so as long as organized religion has influence. The abolition of wars, famine, and child malnutrition is within our grasp if we relinquish our armies and the regulation of every aspect of the lives of our citizens, rejecting the fantasies of religion that have been drummed into our heads by our parents, who had the same drummed into their heads. Is the giving up of our armies and religions too big a price to pay? We can achieve abolition of the means to war if we can sterilize religious conflicts, such as those in Ireland, the Middle East, and India. Defusing these conflicts would relieve much of the world's misery, which has been going on long enough. The ignorant and superstitious have caused too much misery for too many thousands of years, throughout the history of mankind, as we've fought the gods and spirits and demons of imagination. They don't exist. We are creatures who must, if we are to survive, free ourselves from our ancient superstitions.

Conclusion

In the introduction to this book I promised to explain what I perceived as the three essential elements that connect the institutions governing our lives: religion, ethics, government, and economics. The book's ten chapters constructed a factual skeleton for determining who should and who does control the adults of the world. The three concepts that should and do connect our governing institutions and determine our adulthood are: (1) Harming no one else, (2) Imposition of control, and (3) Shifting of personal responsibility.

1. First and foremost—HARM NO ONE ELSE—unless in actual self-defense. This is the central core of ethics and morality. All else is secondary. Until we stop harming other people, no other ethical concept matters and there is no morality.

For organized religion this means no killing of or supporting the killing of others, even with the excuse that the opposing religion's god supports killing, war, and the slaughter of humans. Religion may claim no connection to ethics and morality as long as it fails to obey this central ethical commandment, to harm no one else. Organized religion is based on the superstitions we inherited from our primitive forbears and largely devoid of the motives of its original founders who represented the purest of human ethics and morality.

Instead of observing the ethical admonitions of its founders, such as Thou shalt not kill, organized religion has been and continues to be the vehicle for causing more harm to others and killing more people than any other force on earth. The justification for killing others is "us" against "them," based on the superstitions of our ancestors who saw spirits everywhere and naturally feared death. The purpose of religion is to control unseen spirits and, in the West, to avoid death. Instead, religion requires that we avoid the only life we *know* exists and seek the death of "them." There is no evidence of religious "truth." All religious dogmas cannot be true. How can we know whether any religious dogma is true and which one is true, if any? Religion is anti-education and anti-progress because both education and progress challenge the foundation of organized religion. The Tree of Knowledge is the Christian basis for the downfall of the species. Religion has relegated women to second-class status and teaches delusion, existing as a shill for government policies and to collect money to maintain its buildings and ministers, not for the physical and material benefit of the species or the individual. Not only is religion without logical foundation, but it breeds intolerance.

For government, harming no one else means restricting government to its proper function, which is to enforce this law. Any additional function of government is inefficient and wasteful, which means we're better off protecting ourselves from the unethical purveyors of goods and services instead of depending on government. When anyone is harmed by another person then government, unlike our current governments, should obtain restitution for the harm, which includes the cost of conviction, inprisonment, and paying back the victim. Restitution during imprisonment should be the sole determinant of the criminal sentence imposed on those who harm others. Murderers should be forced to support the dependents of those murdered while imprisoned for life without parole.

Thou shalt not harm another person or their property no matter their race, religion, sexual preference, or nationality. Government should exist for the primary purpose of enforcing this precept. All adults should be allowed to do precisely as they please when they harm no one else. Anything one or more persons wish to do they should be allowed to do as long as no one else is harmed. Government would no longer have to perform 90 percent of its current functions. There would be few taxes, so almost everyone could retire comfortably without the robbery of government transfer payments from the poor and middle classes to the rich and lazy. Religion and charity would care for the insane and unemployable poor. We are an altruistic people when government leaves us alone. The lazy and dishonest would work because they would have no choice. Unemployable single mothers would rely on religion, relatives, and charity, instead of government.

Helping those who can help themselves is immoral because "free" help cripples the individual, making him dependent on largess instead of his own resources. It's obviously ethical to help those who cannot help themselves, but for reasons of efficiency and fairness, welfare should not be a function of government. Government cannot distinguish between those who can help themselves and are feigning need, and those who cannot help themselves. Only charities and individual helpers have the incentive to make this distinction.

A government responsive to special minority interests harms the majority by draining their resources without their individual consent. We have lost sight of protecting our minorities and the vast majority from the excesses and special favors demanded by other minorities called special interests. Such government is unfair to both the vast majority and those who fail to seek or receive benefits commensurate with the taxes they pay, which is almost everyone because of government waste and inefficiency.

Except for peace-keeping functions, government is unnecessary. Because our governments, to be moral, must also harm no one else (except to protect us), armies and armaments should be abolished. If no nation could harm another nation or a single person, we would all be safe. Our lives, which is to say our freedom, are cheap in the eyes of our current governments. Until all governments disarm, our lives and freedom remain cheap. All armies and armaments should be dismantled, enforced by the United Nations in perpetuity.

For economics, harming no one else means government evaporates. The sole rule in business would be free and open market entry and competition. There would be no trade barriers among countries and everyone would be allowed to contract with anyone anywhere anytime for anything. There'd be no foreign aid to pad the Swiss bank accounts of foreign dictators and to discourage the populace from productive labor. There'd be no subsidies for anyone. We'd all be free agents economically and most of us would be relatively wealthy, not only economically, but by achieving true freedom for the individual. There would be few poor, who would primarily consist of the mentally and physically ill, for whom we would beneficently care, voluntarily, without the coercion of government. Thousands of our children would not die of dehydration and hunger hourly. Work would be attractive because much of it would be stimulating and relatively more lucrative without the voracious bite of greedy government taxes. We should call our governments' bluff and allow them to mostly shut down; few of us would miss most of their many functions. Thus would socialism give way to free market capitalism, which would bow only to the single admonition, harm no one else.

2. The second principle mandates NO CONTROL OVER THE ADULT INDIVIDUAL as long as he harms no one else. This second principle is the second law of ethics.

For organized religion this principle, relinquishment of control over the individual, would mean the end. Religion and superstition will neither soon nor perhaps ever disappear, however, because humans are particularly susceptible to self-delusion. Religions and the religious should be treated with the utmost tolerance, as should all of our kind, as long as they harm no one else. Whether adults wish to be controlled by religion is their business, as it should be equally the personal business of any adult whether to use legal or illegal drugs, enjoy sex of whatever consensual nature, watch TV ten hours a day, work weekends and nights, or retire to the couch with pizza and french fries.

Seeking no control over adults is contrary to basic religious principles because the aim of religion is to control its members, their finances, and their sex lives. Religion solicits money in exchange for immortality or nirvana. The first purpose of religion for our ancestors was to control the spirits and the unknown surrounding us, to control the uncontrollable and the nonexistent. Members of religion are now controlled in return for the safety of their souls, though there is no evidence or logic supporting the existence of a soul.

Religions seek control over education, science, sex, women, gays, government, and "them." "Them" are controlled by conversion, missionaries, war, Crusades, and Inquisitions. This sought-after religious control pits the religious "us" against the other religious or nonreligious "them." The purpose of this control has no connection with ethics or morality and in fact is unethical and immoral. Organized religion has served as the conduit for more evil, misery, and horrible death for our kind than any other cause in our history, though government is a close second.

Not harming or asserting control over another adult, no matter their race, religion, or government, means not supporting those who seek to harm or seek control over others. Thus religion, to be ethical and moral, should refrain from supporting the killing of, harm to, or control over *any* other person, no matter their religion, race, or government. Religion would ideally allow birth control, freeing its members from economic and familial slavery. Only the individual should determine family size. Those who fail to limit family size must fight the battle for survival of the fittest (which is precisely what capitalism is all about) with the others who accept personal responsibility for their sex lives, overpopulation, and an earth overcrowded in many areas with species dying daily. Those who do not practice birth control, whether because of religion, shyness, or whatever reason, must survive on their own or through the limited beneficence of charity or organized religion. They will not learn personal responsiblity through government welfare.

A government's sole function should be to prevent harm to others, otherwise it has no legitimate function. We should candidly recognize that government exists to assert control over adults through laws and taxes. Although a particular law may appear altruistic in requiring or prohibiting a particular action, billions of laws not only result in gridlock but in the sapping of individual initiative and self-reliance. Laws beget bureaucracy and the gross inefficiency of ever-expanding government. We worship this controlling government because it removes our personal responsibility. When a law or bureaucracy controls our actions, we relinquish personal responsibility for our actions and become indentured to government. Our formerly pre-eminent values were freedom, liberty, and privacy. To recapture these values, government should assert control over no adult unless the adult harms another.

Economics works best when there are free markets and free market entry. Control over markets and government transfers of wealth should be prohibited. Without government interference most of us would become wealthy in freedom and material things. Only the physically and mentally handicapped would fail to share in our resulting prosperity, but they would be amply sheltered by our natural altruism. The fittest would prosper and our kind would continue to scale the ladder of biological and social evolution.

Religion and government act ethically only when they assert no control over adult behavior that harm no one else. Any controlling function of government (or religion) imposed on adults is unethical, paternalistic, and stultifying, as exemplified by socialism and communism. Economic systems may be evaluated by comparing Hong Kong (free markets) with China and Cuba (Communism) and with Sweden and the United States (combination of socialism and free markets). The world is tending away from economic controls and toward capitalism, except in the United States and Europe. Relinquishing economic control means, among other things, abolishing trade barriers as accomplished by the EC, between the United States and Canada with Mexico soon to join, areas of South America, and increasingly the Eastern bloc. Capitalism is efficient, while other economic systems and all forms of government are inefficient. Controlling others economically or through religion or government is both unethical and inefficient. An achievable ethical system is to neither control nor harm others. Control without the express consent of the controlled adult is the equivalent of harm because it diminishes the adult, encouraging dependence and discouraging self-sufficiency.

Gore Vidal, interviewed in *Elle* magazine in April 1990, summed up the dilemma of the 1990s, which is realistically the dilemma of all adults confronted by the ever-expanding paternalism of government and religion:

> It is now assumed by the government of the United States, and by the governors, and by the governed, for that matter, that the government has every right to regulate your private life, every right to say whether you take drugs or smoke or drink or have sex. That's going to be the big battle of the next 30 or 40 years, this question of whether you have any rights at all. (But there is a lot of support for, say, preventing people from smoking on the grounds that it's better for them.) To which you have to answer, "Well, you can't say that to an American." The Declaration of Independence, the most radical political document that I know of, guarantees you that if you want to drink two bottles of vodka each day and die of cirrhosis of the liver you have every right to do so. The state has no position in this whatsoever. Many people, of certain religious faiths, feel that the state has every right, because they feel that religion has every right. This has been my all-out war all my life against monotheism. Monotheism is totalitarianism; it creates Hitlers and Stalins. Pluralism was a much better notion.

3. The third principle mandates PERSONAL RESPONSIBILITY OF ALL ADULTS. Only adults who accept full and unswerving responsibility for the consequences of their actions are entitled to do as they please. We should all aceept personal responsibility, bearing the consequences of our acts or failure to act. Adults who harm others deserve incarceration and forced labor to repay the harm caused to others. Only those adults who harm no one else are ethical and exercise personal responsibility. Both organized religion and government encourage adult irresponsibility by shifting personal responsibility to religion and government. Any adult able to support himself who allows government to support him, or any adult who religiously confesses harm to others and feels thereby absolved, has abdicated personal responsibility. Adult irresponsibility fuels growth of government and religion. Western religions suggest that belief in ancient superstitions is preferable to good works of personal responsibility. Although all religions support missions to the poor, this constitutes perhaps 1 percent of their budgets. The other 99 percent promotes belief, buildings, and bureaucracy over good works. Instead of encouraging personal responsibility, religion allows adults to live their lives as Hitler, Caligula, or Attila the Hun and welcomes these villians into its bosom if they "confess and believe" a second before death. Religious rules promote irresponsibility because they instruct us to avoid education, except as reflected in the particular religious book, and to believe without proof or logic. Knowledge, including sex education, is the forbidden fruit causing the downfall of man and the eternal downfall of religion. Acquiring knowledge is related in a relatively direct proportion to acquiring personal responsibility, while religion encourages

personal irresponsibility. Self-reliance is personal responsibility; reliance on a god or incorporeal spirit is personal irresponsibility. Children are irresponsible and believe without proof or logic; adults should be personally responsible and believe only with proof or logic.

For religion the quality of life on earth is unimportant compared to belief in myth. The single act Western religion views as most positive is the giving of money to support religious buildings and ministers, instead of supporting beneficent charities and our own families. The solicitation of money in return for unverifiable promises is the definition of fraud and the opposite of personal responsibility.

It's the opposite of personal responsibility to depend on talking to air and spirits no one has ever seen and which do not logically or otherwise exist except on tortillas, screen doors, and white-washed churches as symbols from the seer's religion and from no other religion, ever. Religion is the most ancient of self-fulfilling prophecies, our first and longest-lasting self-fulfilling prophesy. If we believe, we see; if we do not believe, we do not see. The worst sin of organized religion is its teaching of enmity toward other religions, which is the majority of our kind, no matter our religion. All of "them" are heathens, even those within the same religion when the religion is Christian and the place is Northern Ireland. This does not mean, however, that religion is always contrary to common sense. Religion (which is congruent with society and government) is perfectly correct that we shouldn't use health-threatening drugs because it is our personal responsibility to safeguard our own health. It makes no difference whether the drug is alcohol or other drugs. Some drugs, such as tobacco and cocaine derivatives, *should* never be used because they're too dangerous. Almost all other drugs can be used by most people in moderation and are relatively harmless to those adults who can control their use by exerting personal responsibility. A minority of us will never be personally responsible, whether tempted by drugs, sex, or risk of any kind. Only if an activity harms someone else is it anyone else's business, whether that anyone else represents religion, government, or our parents. Without personal responsibility, which is simply control over ourselves by ourselves and not by others, there is no ethics. Personal responsibility and ethical behavior are synonymous. Because religion, government, and race define "us" against "them," any distinction based on religious affiliation, nationality, or race is racism per se.

Government is no better than religion at encouraging adult responsibility. Government institutionalizes personal irresponsibility by setting up programs that make adults dependent on government. When we become dependent on government, government can only grow in response to the demand for further dependency, which is irresponsibility. Thus we pay wealthy corporate farming operations millions of dollars to lower food production while millions are hungry. We subsidize the most dangerous drugs while throwing adults in jail for using less dangerous drugs. These actions of government cause widespread irresponsibility of adults. There is nothing which government is prohibited from taxing to finance an articulate well-organized minority. Government programs appear to be a free lunch, but they are not. The money for these programs comes from taxpayers who must forego two to five lunches to provide a single lunch for the eventual beneficiary of government programs. (The other one to four lunches are gobbled up by voracious government, completing a process that is the opposite of personal responsibility.)

Government teaches us to depend on tax payments by our children and their children, instead of saving our own money for our old age, and calls it Social Security, yet we're unable to save our own money because the government takes too much of it in taxes. Government tells the unemployed there's no need to hurry to find a job because the government will force the employed to pay for the leisure of the unemployed. The government tells special interests to build coalitions to soak the vast taxpaying public for the idleness of the few, such as rich farmers and foreign dictators. We nevertheless worship the government and venerate its flag with the knowledge that personal responsibility is no longer necessary because government is always there, growing, to keep us from the specter of personal responsibility.

For economics, personal responsibility means the opposite of socialism, collectivism, central planning, and communism. Personal responsibility is encouraged by free trade, and the free and unhampered right to contract with anyone, anywhere, any time, for anything. The only restriction should be to harm no one else. With this single restriction, we and our capitalist economic systems would prosper at a level unheard of outside of Hong Kong.

Ethics consists of three principles: harming no one else, exercising personal responsibility, and relinquishing control over other adults. Without all three, there can be no ethics. An ethical person keeps promises and performs contracts. Personal responsibility is the basis for progress within ethical bounds. Although it is not personally responsible to harm ourselves by whatever means (legal or illegal drugs, fast cars, fatty foods, unlimited television, or unprotected sex), the choice whether to risk harm should repose solely in the adult and not in organized religion or government. Only those acts that harm others can legitimately be prohibited by government. The exercise of personal responsibility defines the adult, while the prohibition against decision-making defines childhood. Adult freedom to make unrestricted decisions promotes our evolution and the survival of the fittest of our kind.

The inseparable flip-side to unlimited license for the individual to do as the individual deems appropriate without government fetters, as long as no one else is harmed, was succinctly summed up by the president of Czechoslovakia, Vaclav Havel, in his 1990 address to the United States Congress:

> Without a global revolution in the sphere of human consciousness, nothing will change for the better in the sphere of our being. . . . We still don't know how to put morality ahead of politics, science and economy. We are still incapable of understanding that the only genuine backbone of all our actions, if they are to be moral, is responsibility . . . responsibility to something higher than my family, my country, my company, my success.

This higher calling is to a sense of our kind, unswerving loyalty to the human race, above any lesser allegiances, such as those demanded by nations, religions, and race.

Only a child is unafraid to ask questions that adults are afraid to think about. Instead of thinking, adults rely on religion and various philosophical and economic ideas which we've accepted uncritically. Most organized religion exists to relieve human anxiety about death. Organized religion lends hope that we will prevail over our fears by accepting the resolution to those fears formulated by our illiterate ancestors. Religion seeks to elevate us above the other animals and make us feel superior because immortals are superior to all, having no ultimate fears. In return for the promise of immortality, Western religion demands our only asset—control over our life on earth. Because the average person can't stand the thought of being damned forever, whether the damnation is substantiated or based on old superstitions, we settle for being damned with guilt on earth and hedging our bets in a socially acceptable fashion.

Religion and government encourage and institutionalize the idea of us against them, which is unethical and immoral. We should gradually reject the institutions that set us against ourselves, humans against humans. Nations and religions would do well to fade away, so that only the necessary function of government, to prevent actual direct physical harm to its citizens and their property, remains. To accomplish this end, the pursuit of objective knowledge, as opposed to primitive superstition, should be available to and encouraged for all citizens.

The positive siren of religion is man's search for goodness and ethics. When the concept of religion is separated from that of ethics, religion consists of a vapid set of artificial dos and don'ts. An ethical system better than that of organized religion is to harm no one else and otherwise do as we please. Governments should do the same and disband their armies so we can make progress toward civility, which is necessary before we can unite to explore our origins and environment, the stars. Our kind has always had ambitious goals, but they can be both ambitious and ethical.

Our civilization likely can continue to grow and prosper for the millions of years left to our star only if we expand into and beyond the solar system. There are finite resources on earth.

If we are to have a voice in the universe, we should understand the three concepts that can guarantee our destiny: harming no one else, control, and personal responsibility as they relate to religion, ethics, government, and economics. I suggest that a maximum of individual freedom, constrained only by self-responsibility and the ethical principle of harming no one else, is the primary condition that will allow our kind to achieve its highest rational aspirations. But government, economic systems, and organized religion have been used by special interests to thwart this goal through the crippling of both individual freedom and responsibility. Indeed, the institutions which should be most strictly guided by ethics have, in fact, been its greatest detractors. Accordingly, society would be better served by considerably less government, a wholly free-market economy and, ideally, no organized religion at all.

Bibliography

Abdul-Rauf, Muhammad. "Pilgrimage to Mecca." *National Geographic* (November 1978).

Ahlstrom, Gosta W. *Who Were the Israelites.* 1986.

Aho, James A. *Religious Mythology and the Art of War.* 1981.

Anne Frank Foundation. *Antisemitism: A History Portrayed.* 1989.

Asimov, Isaac. *Extraterrestrial Civilizations.* 1979.

Bakalar and Grimspoon. *Drug Control in a Free Society.* 1984.

Ballou, Robert O. *The Nature of Religion.* 1968.

Barrett, Michael. "The Case for More School Days." *The Atlantic Monthly* (November 1990).

Barrow and Tipler. *The Anthropic Cosmological Principle.* 1986.

Bayles, Martha. "Feminism and Abortion." *The Atlantic* (April 1990).

Beers, David. "Social Consciousness and Individual Freedom." *The Freeman* (September 1989).

Beissner, Calvin E. *Prosperity and Poverty: The Compassionate Use of Resources in a World of Scarcity.* 1988.

Berger, Peter L., ed. *The Capitalistic Spirit: Toward a Religious Ethic of Wealth Creation.* 1990.

Blainey, Geoffrey. *The Causes of War.* 1973.

Bock and Walker. *Lexicon of Economic Thought.* 1989.

"Born or Bred?" *Newsweek* (February 22, 1992).

Bovard, James. *The Farm Fiasco.* 1990.

Brown, Harry. *How I Found Freedom in an Unfree World.* 1973.

Burke, J. Ashleigh. *The X-Rated Book: Sex and Obscenity in the Bible.* 1983.

Burman, Edward. *The Inquisition: The Hammer of Heresy.* 1984.

Candy, Julien. *The Huguenot Wars.* 1969.

Catholic Word Book, reprinted from the *1973 Catholic Almanac.* 1973.

Christiano, Donna. "Abortions: Just the Facts, Not the Hype." *Glamour* (1989).

Colton, G. G. *Inquisition and Liberty.* 1938.

Cooke, Kramer, and Rowland-Entwhistle. *History's Timeline.* 1981.

Cottingham and Ellwood. *Warfare Policy for the 1990s.* 1989.

Cousins, Norman. "Hope Can Make You Well." *Parade* (October 29, 1989).

"The Crack Children." *Newsweek* (February 12, 1990).

Criminal Justice Institute, Inc. *The Corrections Yearbook.* 1989.

Crocker, C. Brandon. "Should We Stop Selling Real Estate to Foreigners?" *The Freeman* (August 1989).

Croteau and Morgan. "Combating Homophobia in AIDS Education." *Journal of Counseling & Development* (Sept./Oct. 1989).

Dennis, Richard J. "The Economics of Legalizing Drugs." *The Atlantic Monthly* (November 1990).

Duggan, Alfred. *The Story of the Crusades.* 1963.

Durante, Dianne L. and Salvatore J. "Medicare: Prescription for a Fool's Paradise." *The Freeman* (April 1991).

Durant, Will. *The Story of Philosophy.* 1926.

Elliot, Nicholas. "The Growth of Privatized Policing." *The Freeman* (February 1991).

Fassell, Paul. "What War is Really Like." *The Atlantic Monthly* (August 1989).

Feliz, Antonio. *Out of the Bishop's Closet.* 1988.

Ferguson, John. *War and Peace in the World's Religions.* 1977.

Fielding, William J. *Shackles of the Supernatural.* 1969.

Flew, Antony. "The Artificial Inflation of Natural Rights." *The Freeman* (December 1989).

Fort, Joel, M.D. *The Pleasure Seekers: The Drug Crisis, Youth and Society.* 1969.

Foster, R. F. *Modern Ireland.* 1989.

Franklin, Deborah. "Hooked; Not Hooked: Why Isn't Everyone an Addict?" *In Health* (November/December 1990).

Fulghum, Robert. *It was on Fire When I Lay Down on It.* 1989.

Gastil, Raymond D. "What Kind of Democracy?" *The Atlantic Monthly* (June 1990).

Gelman, David. "Why We All Love to Hate." *Newsweek* (August 28, 1989).

Goldsmith and Owen. *The Search for Life in the Universe.* 1980.

Goodenough, Erwin. *The Psychology of Religious Experience.* 1986.

Gordon, Mary. "A Moral Choice." *The Atlantic* (April 1990).

Graham, Philip. "A Writer in a World of Spirits." *Writer's Digest* (December 1989).

Greenleaf, Richard E. *The Mexican Inquisition of the Sixteenth Century.* 1969.

Hawking, Stephen W. *A Brief History of Time.* 1988.

Higgs, Robert. "The Growth of Government in the United States." *The Freeman* (August 1990).

Hill, Peter J. "Markets and Morality." *The Freeman* (February 1989).

Hofmann, Frederick B. *A Handbook on Drug and Alcohol Abuse: The Biomedical Aspects.* 1983.

Howe, Neil, and Longman, Phillip. "The Next New Deal." *The Atlantic Monthly* (April 1992).

Information Please Almanac 1989.

Ingersoll, Robert. *Ingersoll's Greatest Lectures.* 1944.

"Interview of James Schaefer." *Omni* (1989).

"Interview of Richard Dawkins." *Omni* (1989).

Irvine, William B. "The Other Side of Adam Smith." *The Freeman* (February 1990).

Kaza, Greg. "Ecorse's Grand Experiment." *The Freeman* (December 1989).

Kibbe, Matthew B. "The Unspoken Dialogue of the Market." *The Freeman* (November 1989).

Kotz and Stroup, *Educated Guessing.* 1983.

Kurtz, Paul. *In Defense of Secular Humanism.* 1983.

Lang, Susan S. "When Women Drink." *Parade* (January 20, 1991).

Lea, Henry. *The Inquisition of the Middle Ages.* 3 vols. 1921.

Lee, Dwight R., and Richard B. McKenzie. "The Ongoing Struggle for Liberty: Reasons for Optimism." *The Freeman* (July 1990).

———. "The Only Failure We Have to Fear Is the Fear of Failure." *The Freeman* (May 1991).

Leff and Simmons. *The Dame in the Kimono.* 1989.

Lewis, Bernard. "The Roots of Muslim Rage." *The Atlantic Monthly* (September 1990).

Lewis, C. S. *Mere Christianity.* 1952.

Lewis, John. *Religions of the World Made Simple.* 1968.

Maccaro, James A. "The Folly of Rent Control." *The Freeman* (January 1990).

MacEoin, Gary. *What Happened at Rome?* 1966.

Machan, Tibor R. "Capitalism and the Environment." *The Freeman* (July 1990).

Marrus, Michael R. *The Holocaust in History.* 1987.

Mataconis, Douglas. "The Flag and Freedom: Which Should We Protect?" *The Freeman* (January 1990).

Matthew, Scott C. "The First Civil Right is Safety." *The Freeman* (September 1990).

McCool, Gerald A., ed. *A Rahner Reader* (writings of Karl Rahner). 1975.

McCutcheon, Marc. *The Compass in Your Nose and Other Astonishing Facts about Humans.* 1989.

Michener, James. *Caribbean.* 1989.

Nielsen, Kai. *An Introduction to the Philosophy of Religion.* 1982.

Osterfeld, David. "The Failures and Fallacies of Foreign Aid." *The Freeman* (February 1990).

Paine, Thomas. *Age of Reason.* 1794.

Panati, Charles. *Extraordinary Origins of Everyday Things.* 1987.

Payne, James L. "The Real Case Against Taxes." *The Freeman* (May 1990).

Pedersen, Daniel. "The Swedish Model: Lessons for the Left." *Newsweek* (March 5, 1990).

Perl, William R. *The Holocaust Conspiracy: An International Policy of Genocide.* 1989.

Peters, Edward. *Inquisition.* 1988.

Peterson, Robert A. "Lessons in Liberty: Hong Kong, 'Crown Jewel' of Capitalism." *The Freeman* (January 1990).

———. "The Message from Eastern Europe." *The Freeman* (May 1990).

———. "Mises: The Impact of Ideas." *The Freeman* (January 1991).

Pipes, Daniel. "Whodunit?" *The Atlantic Monthly* (May 1989).

Pirsig, Robert M. *Zen and the Art of Motorcycle Maintenance.* 1974.

Pullan, Brian. *The Jews of Europe and the Inquisition of Venice.* 1983.

Rand McNally. *Illustrated Atlas of the World.* 1988.

Reagan, Nancy. *My Turn.* 1989.

Reich, Robert B. "The Real Economy." *The Atlantic Monthly* (February 1991).

Ritter and O'Neill, "Moving Through Loss: The Spiritual Journey of Gay Men and Lesbian Women." *Journal of Counseling & Development* (Sept./Oct. 1989).

Rogers, Ann Weiss. "Making Dough in the Heartland." *The Freeman* (November 1989).

Roush, G. Jon. "The Disintegrating Web: The Causes and Consequences of Extinction." *The Nature Conservancy* (1989).

Russell, Bertrand. *Why I am not a Christian.* 1957.

Sagan, Carl. "Tomorrow's Energy." *Parade* (November 25, 1990).

Samuelson, Robert J. "Economics Made Easy." *Newsweek* (November 27, 1989).

Shirer, William L. *The Rise and Fall of the Third Reich.* 1950.

Shulman, Gail B., ed. *View from the Back of the Synagogue: Sexist Religion and Women in the Church.* 1974.

Sipes, Richard. *A Secret World: Sexuality and the Search for Celibacy.* 1990.

Smith, Donald G. "Pigeons and Property Rights." *The Freeman* (April 1991).

Tannahill, Reay. *Sex in History.* 1980.

Thompson, Frank. *The New Chain Reference Bible.* 1964.

Toynbee, Arnold J. *East to West: A Journey Round the World.* 1958.

———. *An Historian's Approach to Religion.*

Turberville, A. S. *Medieval Heresy and the Inquisition.* 1964.

Van Evera, Stephen. "The Case Against Intervention." *The Atlantic Monthly* (July 1990).

Vergilius Farm. *Encyclopedia of Religion.* 1945.

Viner, Jacob. *Religious Thought and Economic Society.* 1989.

Waller, Douglas. "Foreign-Aid Follies." *Newsweek* (April 16, 1990).

Weiss, Daniel Evan. *The Great Divide: How Females and Males Really Differ.* 1991.

———. *100% American.* 1990.

Wilkes, Paul. "The Hands That Would Shape Our Souls." *The Atlantic Monthly* (December 1990).

Williams, Walter E. *South Africa's War Against Capitalism.* 1989.

Woodward, Kenneth L. "Heaven." *Newsweek* (March 27, 1989).

The World Almanac and Book of Facts. 1990.

Youden, W. J. *Risk. Choice and Prediction.* 1974.

Zebrowski, George. "Life in Godel's Universe: Maps All the Way." *Omni* (April 1992).

Index

Friedman, Milton, 232
Frost, David, 264
Fulghum, Robert, 119, 288
Fuller, Buckminster, 271
fundamentalists (Christian, religious),
    16–18, 50, 59, 65–66, 77–78, 87,
    90, 141, 182, 209, 261, 264–65,
    273–74

Galapagos, 15
galaxies, number, 14
Galileo, 17, 46
Gallup Polls, 36, 44, 65, 74, 116, 134,
    136, 138, 245
Gandhi, 16, 143, 269–71
Garden of Eden, 21, 66
God, god, gods, 11–12, 14–17, 21–23,
    28–29, 33–34, 39–42, 44, 47, 51–
    54, 59–61, 76–77, 83–88, 91, 99,
    106, 110–11, 114–16, 118–20, 122,
    126, 128, 132, 157, 182, 264, 266–
    69, 274, 278–79, 284
Golden Rule, 122, 223
Goode, William J., 69
Gorbachev, Pres. Mikhail, 215, 254–
    55, 264–65
Gornick, Vivian, 53
Graham, Rev. Billy, 266
Graham, Philip 117–18, 288
Greek(s), 10, 21, 26, 54, 90, 122, 269
Greeley, Rev. Andrew, 74, 79
Greenfield, Jeff, 186
Griese, Rev. Roger E., 70
Gui, Bernard, 105

Hammurabi, 53
Havel, Vaclav, 285
Hawking, Stephen, 29, 44, 288
Hayek, F. A., 210
Hebrews, 27, 44, 70, 115
Heller, Joseph, 226
Hempstone, Smith, 275
Henry VIII, 109
Henry, James, 247
heretic, heretical, 17, 89, 103–104, 107,

109, 182, 197, 269
Hinchcliffe, David J., 35
Hindu(s), Hinduism, 10, 21–25, 29, 35,
    39, 41, 66, 71–72, 112, 127, 190,
    209, 269, 275
Hinkley, Gordon B., 81
Hirohito, Emperor, 22, 39
Hitler, Adolph, 15, 95, 204, 267, 275,
    283
Hoffer, Eric, 20
Holy Ghost, 21, 106, 119
homosexuality, 59–66
Hong Kong, 230–31, 282, 285
Hooker, Evelyn, 62
Horace, 182
Hosain, K. T., 72
Housman, A. E., 174
Hugh of Vienne, 105
Hume, David, 234
Hussein, Pres. Saddam, 77, 208, 242,
    262–67, 272
Huxley, Aldous, 187

Iacocca, Lee, 239–40
income tax, history, 238–39
India, 11–12, 21, 72, 112, 122, 127, 138,
    209, 265, 274, 278
Ingersoll, Robert, 6–7, 20–21, 49, 288
Inquisition(s), 30, 46, 68, 81–82, 89, 98,
    101–109, 181, 183, 190, 234, 278,
    281
Ireland, Northern, 11, 126–27, 258,
    265, 278, 284
Islam (*see also,* Muslims), 10, 15, 22,
    26, 29, 32–34, 46, 66, 71, 90, 92,
    101, 104, 112, 123–24, 267, 270,
    274–75
Israel, 27, 91, 125, 245, 266, 273

Jataka, 25
Jefferson, Thomas, 201–202, 220
Jehovah, 22, 27
Jehovah's Witnesses, 48–49, 110–11
Jerusalem, 10, 27, 98–100, 104, 111,
    125